Richard Heath

Historic Landmarks in the Christian Centuries

Richard Heath

Historic Landmarks in the Christian Centuries

ISBN/EAN: 9783743349230

Manufactured in Europe, USA, Canada, Australia, Japa

Cover: Foto ©ninafisch / pixelio.de

Manufactured and distributed by brebook publishing software (www.brebook.com)

Richard Heath

Historic Landmarks in the Christian Centuries

HISTORIC LANDMARKS

IN

THE CHRISTIAN CENTURIES.

BY

RICHARD HEATH,

AUTHOR OF "EDGAR QUINET: HIS EARLY LIFE AND WRITINGS."

With Eighty-four Illustrations by John Jackson, etc.

THE RELIGIOUS TRACT SOCIETY,
56, PATERNOSTER ROW; 65, ST. PAUL'S CHURCHYARD; AND 164, PICCADILLY.
LONDON, E.C.

and that wherever he went he spoke the language of the country. "Many people of quality," Dudalæus goes on to say, "have seen this Jew, in England, in France, in Italy, in Hungary, in Persia, in Poland, in Sweden, in Denmark, in Scotland, and in other countries, as also in Germany, at Rostock, at Weimer, at Danzic, at Königsberg. In the year 1575, two ambassadors of Holstein, and particularly the *secretarius* Christophe Krauss, have met him at Madrid, always the same figure, of the same age, manners, and costume. In the year 1599 he was found at Vienna, and in 1601 at Lubeck. He has been met in the year 1616 in Livonia, at Cracow and at Moscow, by persons who have even talked with him."

The following pages will place the reader somewhat in the track of the imaginary wanderer described in this weird fable. Imagine the light a man would be able to throw on the second century, who had followed the Emperor Hadrian from Rome through Gaul into Britain; and again from Rome to Athens, Alexandria, Antioch, and Jerusalem; who had seen the ploughshare passed over the ruins of the latter, and the Roman wall begun at the extreme limit of the former. Or on the seventh century, if he had listened to the Nestorians preaching Christianity in China, and Paulinus addressing the pagans in Northumbria, and, while hurrying across the two continents which the Gospel was thus striving to embrace, had heard rumours of the rival claims for universal obedience made by the Prophet of Mecca and the Pope of Rome. What opportunities for comparing the tendency of the opposing religions represented by Rome and Arabia would the man have had who, in the eighth century, had passed through the dominions of Haroun al Raschid into those of Charlemagne. How staunch a Christian would he become, who, in the tenth century, had seen Christendom a dark world, surrounded, as with a shining band of light, by Mohammedanism, and, in the next age, not only driving its rival back at both ends of Europe, but also giving birth to forms of society which endure to the present day.

It is only a man who has had an experience somewhat similar to this venerable Jew who is likely to remind us that the first great struggle for civil liberty in England was contemporary with the first great struggle for religious liberty in France—that Magna Charta and the Albigensian massacres had a common origin. Our wanderer could not have related the story of Wallace and of Bruce without remarking that the same struggle for independence was going on in Switzerland—that in the fourteenth century the spirit of liberty was abroad everywhere, daring even to lay hands on the sacred majesty of popes and Plantagenet kings. And as he came to the opening of the new era, he would make us notice that its two great seers, Savonarola and Columbus, were exactly contemporaneous; that the Reformation no sooner found its prophet than the kingdom of darkness produced his opponent; that the most despairing period in the history of continental Protestantism was exactly that in which the Puritan navigators of England were claiming the world as the only area worthy its religion; that the efforts after constitutional liberty in the seventeenth century were contemporaneous in England and France, but with widely different results—ending in the one with the extirpation of Protestantism, in the other with its triumph as the basis of English liberty and law. Finally, what a flood of light would our Jew be able to throw on the revolution in which we are ourselves living—familiar, as he would be, with all its sources: religious, scientific, political.

Our thought, it will be seen, is great; the realisation, like every human endeavour, very inadequate. All we have done is, as it were, to pick up some stray leaves of the tablets of the Wandering Jew. But anything written by an observer of such experience must be animated by large and simple views. Slight, then, as is our work, it would be quite unworthy of the method we have chosen if it proved confusing and contradictory.

One who was gifted with the true historic vision, a seer of the full scope of universal history, tells us, as almost the last secret he has to reveal, that he saw "a river of water of life, bright as crystal, proceeding out of the throne of God and of the Lamb. And on this side of the river and on that was the tree of life, bearing twelve manner of fruits, yielding its fruit every month, and the leaves of the tree were for the healing of the nations."

To keep sight of this river has been the chief aim of the writer of this book. Often obscured by the reeds that grow on its banks, and by the weeds that continually cover its surface, he has seen it appear, again and again, like a silver thread running through the ages, bringing life, and joy, and progress wherever it flowed.

Careful not to confound the forms of things with the things themselves, he has not imagined this river to be any church, or even any religion, but that kingdom of heaven which Jesus Christ came to reveal, and which was the chief subject of His teaching. Its sources, opened up with a new and regenerative force on the Day of Pentecost, have flowed on ever since, giving birth to successive societies, which have produced not only the highest forms of literature and art, but unprecedented efforts after liberty, philanthropy, and equal laws.

The doctrine of the kingdom of heaven, as set forth in the Gospels, explains better than any historical philosophy the history of the Christian centuries, for, while it assures us of the certain triumph of that kingdom, and encourages us to continued efforts to bring that triumph about, it renders the student of history tolerant of all the forms under which it has appeared. He sees them all to be human, and is not, therefore, staggered to find them, one after the other, liable to many kinds of corruption and decay.

If, then, this book tends to increase the faith of its readers in this glorious and blessed kingdom, and, while helping in any degree to deliver them from slavery to its bygone forms, it makes them more thoroughly sympathetic with the efforts made by their predecessors for the establishment and extension of that kingdom, it will have done a good work, even if the details be not always accurate or the generalisations sound.

CONTENTS.

FIRST CENTURY.

PAGE

Rome and the Subject Nations—Rome and Britain—Caractacus—Roman Education—Julius Agricola—The Senate—Slavery—Buddhism in China—The Dream of Ming-Ti—The Desire of all Nations—Antioch—Barnabas—The Gospel and the Gentile World—Paul and the Jewish Christians—The Council at Jerusalem—The Gospel and Liberty 3

SECOND CENTURY.

Roman Civilisation—A Model Emperor—Hadrian's Travels—The Road to Lyons—Britain—The Roman Wall—Athens—The Christian Apologists—Alexandria—Ptolemy and Early Science—The Ploughshare passed over Jerusalem . . 17

THIRD CENTURY.

The Irruption of the Barbarians—The Franks in Gaul—Aurelian—Fall of Palmyra—Zenobia—Trade with China—Aurelian's Protest against Luxury—Persecution of the Church—Cyprian, Bishop and Martyr 29

FOURTH CENTURY.

Christianity and Imperialism—Arius and Athanasius—The Thebaid—Julian's Effort to Revive Paganism—Attempt to Rebuild the Temple at Jerusalem—The Saxons in France 41

FIFTH CENTURY.

The Dying Roman World—The Vandals in Africa—Augustine of Hippo—Attila and the Huns—Pope Leo saves Rome—Rome sacked by Genseric—Saxons land in England—Patrick, the Apostle of Ireland—Corruption of Eastern Christianity—Simon Stylites 55

SIXTH CENTURY.

A New Europe—The Teutons—The Merovingians—Their Crimes—Punishment of a Merovingian Prince—The Lombards—Alboin's Victories and Cruelty—Gregory's Desire to convert the Anglo-Saxons—Columba, the Apostle of Scotland . . 71

SEVENTH CENTURY.

The Eastern Church—Nestorian Mission in China—Corruption of Christianity—Asceticism—Image Worship—Veneration of Relics and of the Clergy—Pope of Rome Recognised as Universal Bishop—Mohammed—His Recognition as Prophet of God—Mohammedanism—Triumphs of Christianity in England—Paulinus and Northumbria 87

EIGHTH CENTURY.

Faith in Christ the foundation of the English State—Guthlac and Crowland Abbey—English Missionaries—Boniface—He Destroys Thor's Oak—Mohammedanism in Western Europe—Charles Martel—Leo the Iconoclast 103

NINTH CENTURY.

Divisions of Mohammedanism—The Ommiades in Spain—Abder Rahman—The Mosque of Cordova—The Abbassides in Bagdad—Story of Haroun al Raschid—Charlemagne—His Coronation as Emperor of Rome—Ecgberht, First King of the English . 119

TENTH CENTURY.

Christian Europe harried by the Northmen, the Slaves, and the Magyars—Degradation of the Papacy—Pope Gerbert—Dunstan—Murder of King Eadward—Sufferings of the Peasants in France—Horrors and Calamities all over Christendom—Expected End of the World—The Truce of God—Robert of France—Prosperity of Mohammedan Spain—Mohammedanism in India—Conversion of Russia to Christianity 135

ELEVENTH CENTURY.

The Age of Construction—The Norman Genius for Building—The Abbey of Bec—Lanfranc—Anselm—William the Conqueror—Hildebrand, founder of the Mediæval Papacy—The Cid—Peter the Hermit and the first Crusades . . . 147

TWELFTH CENTURY.

Baronial Oppression, especially in England—Bernard and the Monastic Life—Abelard and the new passion for Learning—The Council of Sens—Arnold of Brescia and the Roman Republic—The Guelphs and Ghibelines 163

THIRTEENTH CENTURY.

Feudal Europe—Effort to Found a Feudal Theocracy—Innocent III.—His Struggle with John of England—Magna Charta—Persecution of the Albigenses—Constantinople taken by the Venetians—Enrico Dandolo—Dominic and Francis . 177

FOURTEENTH CENTURY.

Dante—Comparison between the Gothic Cathedral and the *Divina Commedia*—Rise of the Spirit of Independence—The Temporal Power defies the Spiritual—Philippe le Bel and Pope Boniface—Struggle of the Swiss Cantons against Austria—William Tell—The Battle of Mortgarten—Struggle of the Scotch against England—Robert Bruce—The Battle of Bannockburn 197

FIFTEENTH CENTURY.

Invention of Printing—Caxton's Press at Westminster—Revival of Classic Literature—Lorenzo de Medici—Savonarola, the Prophet of Italy—Great Navigators—Prince Henry of Portugal—Vasco de Gama—India reached by Sea—Columbus—Discovery of the New World 213

SIXTEENTH CENTURY.

The Bible Reopened—A Galaxy of Genius—Appeal from the Church to the Bible—William Tyndale—His New Testament Burnt at St. Paul's Cross—Martin Luther—The Diet at Worms—Spanish Catholicism—Hernan Cortes—His Exploits in Mexico—Ignatius Loyola—His Conversion and Work—The Sack of Rome—Calvin and Calvinism—The Massacre of St. Bartholomew—Death of John Knox—Philip II. and Alva—William the Silent—War of Dutch Independence—The Relief of Leyden—England's Great Seamen—Drake's Voyage Round the World—Akbur, Emperor of India 233

SEVENTEENTH CENTURY.

Section I.

The Catholic Reaction—The Jesuits—Urban VIII.—Galileo's Recantation—The Thirty Years' War—Richelieu—Gustavus Adolphus—The Solemn League and Covenant—Attempt to create an English Despotism—Struggle between Charles I. and the House of Commons 269

SEVENTEENTH CENTURY.

Section II.

Political Results of the Reformation and Catholic Reaction in France and England—The French Autocracy—Protestantism to be Exterminated—The Dragonnades—Gallicanism—Revocation of the Edict of Nantes—The Restoration in England—James II.—William of Orange—The Revolution—The Turks besiege Vienna—John Sobieski—William Penn—His Treaty with the Indians—Founding of Pennsylvania 289

EIGHTEENTH CENTURY.

Section I.

Earthquake at Lisbon—Progress of Science in Europe—Franklin's Discoveries in Electricity—Influence of French Literature—The Philosophy of Enlightened Self-interest—Frederick the Great—The Wesleys—Whitefield—Methodism—The Spirit of Philanthropy 307

EIGHTEENTH CENTURY.

Section II.

Causes of the French Revolution—American Revolution—Taking of the Bastille—Inauguration of Washington—German Poets and Philosophers—England's Colonial Progress—Australia—India—William Carey—Mission of the Anglo-Saxon Race . 325

FIRST CENTURY.

CONTEMPORARY EVENTS IN THE FIRST CENTURY.

Jerusalem.—*Liberty proclaimed to the Gentiles.*
Marseilles.—*Education of a young Roman.*
Rome.—*British captives led in triumph.*
China.—*Introduction of the worship of Buddha.*

First Century.

ABOUT A.D. 50.

Rome and the Subject Nations—Rome and Britain—Caractacus—Roman Education—Julius Agricola—The Senate—Slavery—Buddhism in China—The Dream of Ming-Ti—The Desire of all Nations—Antioch—Barnabas—The Gospel and the Gentile World—Paul and the Jewish Christians—The Council at Jerusalem—The Gospel and Liberty.

CIPIO ÆMILIANUS, when attempting to rescind a portion of the agrarian law of Tiberius Gracchus, was asked what he thought of the death of that great tribune. "It was just," replied the inflexible patrician. "Down with the tyrant!" shouted the populace. Turning round upon his assailants, the destroyer of Carthage and of Numantia exclaimed: "Let not those whom I led here chained imagine that they can frighten me now that they are sovereigns in Rome."

In this haughty sarcasm we have the secret, not only of the power and beneficence, but of the weakness and corruption of the Roman Empire. Rome subdued the world, but with the strange result that the conqueror submitted to the conquered: those who were dragged in chains to Rome became its masters.

Remorseless in war, crushing nation after nation, Rome beheld the conquered crowding into the imperial city, forming its public opinion, filling the offices of the State, taking their places in its Senate, and seizing at last on the imperial throne.

———•———

THE relations of Rome with Britain and with its hero, Caractacus, afford some illustration of what has been said. Notwithstanding great and sanguinary defeats, the British people were not crushed; they rose again, they gave their conquerors ceaseless trouble, and were finally subdued only to increase, flourish, and enter into the Roman world with the air of equals and allies.

The second invasion of Britain took place in the year 43 of our era. For seven years the Romans made little way, although Claudius Cæsar himself spent six months in the country. On his return Ostorius Scapula was sent to Britain invested with supreme civil and military command. He found Roman affairs in a very bad condition; the troops were isolated and the natives insolent. He determined to recover prestige by a great blow. Rapidly marching on the enemy, who, as it was winter, little expected an attack, Ostorius routed them with great slaughter. This done, he began a chain of forts from east to west, from the Nen to the Severn, and disarmed all suspected Britons within the lines. Proud and passionate, the Britons raged like a lion caught in a snare. The Iceni rose, fought desperately, but were soon compelled to submit. Ostorius pursued their allies almost to the Irish Sea, dealing a parting blow to the Brigantes, a northern tribe, outside the lines.

He next concentrated all his attention on the Silures, who inhabited South Wales, and were the most determined tribe in the island. Their courage was animated by the presence of Caractacus. To the standard of this brave and able chief rallied every Briton who cared for liberty. At first Caractacus fell back on the mountainous district of North Wales, but ere long, with the impetuous courage of his race, he risked everything on one great battle. Tacitus, who makes all his characters speak as if they had been educated by Roman rhetoricians, represents the patriotic chief as addressing his army in this strain: "This day, my fellow warriors, this very day decides the fate of Britain. The era of liberty or eternal bondage begins from this very hour."

Whether Caractacus used these words or not, the Britons fought in this spirit. In a pitched battle, disciplined, well-armed troops must conquer an undisciplined, ill-armed host. Although Caractacus had chosen his ground well, and fortified his camp with skill, his defeat was inevitable. The carnage was great, the chief's wife and children were among the captives, and he himself was shortly afterwards a prisoner loaded with chains and on his way to Rome.

What news for the vain and idle crowds in the capital, who took a thousand times more interest in the suppression of the liberties of some distant people than in the maintenance of their own! The story of the courage, the ability, the patriotism of the captive found a thousand sympathetic hearts and voices to send it from province to province until it reached Italy and became the talk of Rome.

With Celtic tact, Caractacus caught the feeling in his favour and posed accordingly. A field-day was held in Rome, the Prætorian bands were drawn up under arms, and the Emperor took his seat on a tribune. Then, preceded by all his military trophies, by his followers, by his wife and children, Caractacus came, more like a conqueror than a captive, until he reached the presence of Claudius. Here he stopped, and comprehending his part as chief actor, made a speech in which the sentiments are so lofty that they seem not only fitted for the occasion, but also exactly in accord with the career of the hero:

"If to the nobility of my birth and the splendour of exalted station I had united the virtues of moderation, Rome had beheld me, not in captivity, but a royal visitor and a friend. A reverse of fortune is now the lot of Caractacus. The event to you is glorious, and to me humiliating. I had arms and men and horses; I had wealth in abundance: can you wonder that I was unwilling to lose them? The ambition of Rome aspires to universal dominion. I stood at bay for years; had I acted otherwise, where on your part, had been the glory of conquest, and where, on mine, the honour of a brave resistance? I am now in your power. If you are bent on vengeance, execute your purpose; the bloody scene will soon be over, and the name of Caractacus will sink into oblivion. Preserve my life, and I shall be, to a late posterity, a monument of Roman clemency."

If Caractacus in these words simply expressed the feelings of his heart, his triumph was of the purest kind; if, as is more probable, he added the tact and shrewdness of a Celt, his speech, though less ingenuous, produced exactly the right effect on the Romans: Claudius granted him and his wife a free pardon.

That Caractacus delivered himself in the oratorical manner indicated by Tacitus is more than doubtful; but a Roman could not imagine fine thoughts conveyed in any other form. Under the Empire a flashy rhetoric, in which brilliancy was chiefly sought, was supposed to be the prime requirement in education. Success had wrought its usual results, and the sons of the men who had conquered the world and destroyed its national liberties were every year becoming more and more corrupt.

ONE sign of this was the way in which they neglected their children. A Roman infant in the higher classes was placed under the care of foreign slaves, mostly Greeks or Syrians—supple, unprincipled, vicious. When the child came into his parents' society, he heard of little but horses and players and gladiatorial shows; the games were the one absorbing topic in Roman society, and everybody, from the Cæsar to the schoolboy, adopted one or the other of the colours of the amphitheatre—green or blue. "The most illustrious Roman youth," says Seneca, "are no better than slaves to the pantomimic performers."

This corruption of society in the bud had not yet become universal through the Roman Empire. There were still well-ordered families where modest reserve and purity of manners lingered. Such a household was existing at Marseilles when Claudius landed there on his expedition to Britain. Its head was a widow, whose husband, Julius Græcinus, had fallen a victim to Caligula's cruelty because he would not undertake to prosecute a virtuous man. Julia Procilla had a son, Cneius Julius Agricola, whom she trained in every liberal accomplishment.

Marseilles was then one of the most famous seats of learning in the Empire, and here the future ruler of Britain was carrying on his studies at the time Caractacus was brought a prisoner to Rome. It is probable that the British captive embarked from Marseilles for Rome, so that Agricola might have been among the crowd that watched the procession as it passed down the main street of Marseilles to the great harbour. Such sights were frequent all over the Empire, and stimulated that thirst for domination which was the ruling passion in Rome. For everything but visible power the true Roman had boundless contempt. Even Agricola's mother counselled her son to refrain from philosophical speculation, and devote himself to studies becoming a Roman senator.

But what were the senators of this particular epoch? A more cruel, mean, and selfish aristocracy never existed. They believed mainly in the gods Pallor and Terror. To protect themselves from their slaves, they had passed a law by which, if a man was murdered, every slave in his household was to be put to death, innocent or guilty. In the very year that Paul arrived in Rome, the Prefect of the city, Pedanius Secundus, was murdered by one of his slaves. The murderer and his victim were both immoral men, and the cause was well known; yet the Senate, moved by Caius Cassius, refused to listen to the popular cry for mercy, and ordered the whole of the Prefect's slaves, four hundred persons, to be executed, which was done, the soldiers lining the streets to keep down the popular fury. One senator thought the sacrifice to the god Terror still insufficient, and proposed to banish all the Prefect's freedmen; but even Nero protested against adding to the severity of the law. Not so the Senate, for when the demon of cruelty took possession of the Emperor himself, and he committed the foulest and most unwarrantable of his many crimes—the brutal murder of his wife, Octavia—the senators had the incredible meanness to offer oblations to the gods. "In fact," says Tacitus, "as often as a banishment or a bloody execution was ordered the Senate never failed to thank the gods for their bounty."

Several of these Roman patricians led such disreputable lives that they betook themselves to the voluptuous atmosphere of Southern Italy, where, in the neighbourhood of the Lake Avernus, the fabled entrance to the pagan hell, they built their villas and indulged in wild debauchery. All around —throughout Italy, throughout the provinces—groaned millions of slaves. Gibbon reckons that at this time there were sixty millions of these unhappy beings in the Roman Empire. How profound was their misery, how intense their abhorrence of the whole order of things, may be inferred from the fear and hatred of their masters.

But pagan Rome had one virtue—it did not understand the art of enslaving men's souls. Of the inner life, of the relation of the soul to God, of the authority of conscience, it knew little and cared less. Yet it was to the last degree superstitious, and even its philosophers rarely aimed at anything higher than to discover the pleasantest way of spending life.

THE home of religious speculation was the far-distant East, and the thought of India is summed up in the words, "God is all and in all." Incarnated in every object, the Divine Being suffers degradation. The highest object therefore of the Indian sage was to find out the best means of liberating the soul from material existence, so that it might be reunited to its source, as a river to the ocean. The essence of Buddhism is the misery of existence, and how to get rid of it. This was the idea the Indian thinker pondered until he declared that extinction was the highest good. Gautama, afterwards known as Buddha, the enlightened one, first preached this doctrine in the fifth century before Christ. It spread rapidly, and took such firm hold of Eastern Asia that it has continued the prevailing religion in that region for more than twenty centuries. How is this? Is existence indeed so bad a thing that a large proportion of the human race are willing to believe in a religion that promises a hope of its cessation?

Buddhism was a protest against the crushing weight of an old creed that oppressed the conscience, separated men into classes, and refused man as man any place in the universe. Self-conquest and universal charity are its fundamental ideas. It abolishes priestcraft and caste and all forms of spiritual tyranny, and exists alike for all, learned and ignorant, rich and poor, male and female, bond and free. The same path to Nirvana was open to all. Yet the weary round in human religions is nowhere more strikingly manifested than in these two great forms, Brahminism and Buddhism; this great evolution simply ends in priestcraft giving place to monkery. As existence is the great evil, no man seeking a higher life can be the author of it in others.

For 2,000 years China has been the principal land adhering to Buddhism, its introduction into that country being contemporaneous with the birth of Jesus Christ. Towards 122 B.C. a Chinese general, during a campaign beyond the mountains of Yarkand, found in a stream near a great monastery the statue of a man, made of wood, and gilt or painted the colour of gold. Although the statue was a hundred feet high, the general had it transported to China, and the Emperor, supposing it a sacred object, set it up in a place called the Palace of Sweet Springs, and burned incense in its honour. Finally the Chinese learnt something about its worship, and they understood the doctrine, but believed it not.

This state of things continued more than a century, until 2 B.C., when Ming-ti, an emperor of the Han dynasty, had a dream. He beheld soaring above his palace a man of the colour of gold and of a lofty stature, and having his head surrounded by a luminous halo. He consulted his courtiers on the subject of the dream. They replied that in the western countries there was a spirit named Foe. The Emperor therefore appointed a high officer named Thsai-yn and a scholar named Thsing-king to proceed with sundry others to Hindostan and "gather information touching the doctrine of Foe; to draw, paint, or depict the temples and idols, and to collect the precepts."

Thsai-yn brought back two Samaneans. A prince named Yng was the first to embrace the new religion. He procured the book of Foe, which the Emperor deposited in a great stone building called the monastery of the White Horse, because the book of Foe had been brought to China on the back of a white horse.

Thus Buddhism was actually establishing itself as the religion of China during the life of our Saviour, and its final recognition took place in the year A.D. 61.

Nothing can be more interesting than the thought that in lands so remote, so unlike each other as Italy, Persia, and China, a belief should almost simultaneously be awakened in the coming of some great one. The Italian poet, the Persian magi, the Chinese monarch, all saw a similar vision, but its form took the shape of the mental image which to them conveyed the highest idea of Divine beneficence under visible forms. Virgil sang the coming of a pacific prince; the wise men from the East saw his star; and Ming-ti dreamt that he beheld the form of a great Teacher soaring above his palace.

But the Light had appeared. The spiritual dawn which the world had dreamt of and waited for, and about which it sang its songs in the night, had arisen, and already some of the darkest places in the earth were being illumined by its rays.

No writer in these days dares to do more than hint at the shameful wickedness of the Roman world at the time when the Sun of Righteousness arose. Tacitus and St. Paul felt such reticence unnecessary and impossible, seeing that it was known to all the world. Vice seemed to intensify as it was traced eastward: Rome was bad; Corinth was worse; Antioch, perhaps, vilest of all. It contained a Syrian element that brought corruption to an extreme development.

Antioch had extraordinary natural beauties: the Orontes flowed at its feet, and behind it rose a lofty hill. The fortifications of the city were carried to the very summit of Mount Silpius, and thus within the walls of Antioch were to be found the most picturesque scenes—precipitous rocks hung with pinks, hyacinths, and cyclamens; ravines, cascades, caverns, and delightful gardens filled with aromatic evergreens, and adorned with the most perfect specimens of Greek art. In this civic paradise a population of half-a-million inhabitants were gathered—a population composed of all races, but mainly Greek and Syrian, trifling, light-headed, witty, insubordinate, caring for nothing but pleasure and gain. Races, games, dances, revels, wild and wicked fanaticisms of all sorts, were the ever-returning pastimes of Antioch. At two hours' distance was Daphne, the fairy-land of pleasure, the very temple of Vice. But the light had broken, and one of the very first cities upon which it shone was this wicked, beautiful Antioch.

Certain disciples flying from the persecution that arose about Stephen, came to the Syrian metropolis, and speaking to the Jews who dwelt there, began to tell them of the wonderful things that had taken place in Jerusalem. Ere long this restricted preaching proved impossible. Not only Jewish proselytes, but their pagan friends listened, and many believed the good news that God had sent His Son to bless them in turning them away from their iniquities. Little as the preachers expected it, or even desired it, they could not resist such evidence that the Gospel was really for all; and the interest once awakened in such a city spread far and wide, so that the tidings of it soon reached Jerusalem.

The Church there, with a wisdom that was clearly from above, sent the best of all possible messengers to Antioch. Barnabas, a noble and important character, was the first at Jerusalem to recognise the reality of the conversion of Saul of Tarsus. It was he who first gave the repentant persecutor the right hand of fellowship, and became his surety to the timid little flock at Jerusalem. And now it was Barnabas who was the first to recognise the grace of God to the Gentile world, and to see that this new light could not be confined to Jews and proselytes, but must extend to the whole world. No paraphrase can ever equal the force of the words of Scripture. What an unapproachable touch of character we have in these two verses :—

> When Barnabas came, and had seen the grace of God, he was glad, and exhorted them all, that with purpose of heart they would cleave unto the Lord.
> For he was a good man, and full of the Holy Ghost and of faith: and much people was added unto the Lord.

Barnabas had not only a great heart, but a large mind. He realised at once the infinite possibilities of the work, and saw that here was the field for that strong and passionate soul which had just been given to the Church, and of whose genius no one but he had any comprehension. So he went to Tarsus, that he might find Saul and bring him to Antioch. What a meeting! They return to this gay and populous city, first type of thousands who through the ages shall go on a similar errand, ready messengers of the Gospel of Peace. Then what scenes, what days of blessedness during the whole year, in which these apostles laboured and taught much people! We are told nothing of the joy of those first days at Antioch, but such scenes have been too often repeated for imagination to go far wrong. The light-hearted city felt that a new power had sprung up amongst them. With its usual frivolity, it gave the new movement a nickname: "The disciples were first called Christians at Antioch."

But the sun was rising fast, and having gilded with its rays this great city, it suddenly burst forth, illuminating all the shores of the Mediterranean.

> Now there were in the Church that was at Antioch certain prophets and teachers; as Barnabas, and Simeon that was called Niger, and Lucius of Cyrene, and Manaen, which had been brought up with Herod the tetrarch, and Saul. As they ministered to the Lord, and fasted, the Holy Ghost said, Separate me Barnabas and Saul for the work whereunto I have called them. And when they had fasted and prayed, and laid their hands on them, they sent them away. So they, being sent forth by the Holy Ghost, departed unto Seleucia; and from thence they sailed to Cyprus.

Passing through the island, they cross the north-east corner of the Mediterranean, land in Pamphylia, and, making their way to Antioch in Pisidia, go into the very heart of Asia Minor. Wonderful and most interesting of all the journeys made by mortal man! Paul and Barnabas go forth like the angel of the Apocalypse, having the everlasting Gospel to preach to every nation, and kindred, and tongue, and people. Heralds of the dawn, they have to struggle with darkness wherever they go. This first missionary journey is a type of all that will follow. Everywhere do they meet with welcome and rejection, friend and foe. They come in contact with the principal representatives of the life of the age, with Roman governor and Jewish thaumaturgist; with bigot Jews and truculent Gentiles ; with the fanatic heathen, who would worship them one day and stone them the next. But the spirit of the apostles is the spirit of the dawn : fresh, vigorous, joyous, they bring life and animation everywhere. A great multitude believed, both of the Jews and also of the Greeks ; and the disciples were filled with joy and with the Holy Ghost. Yet is there no illusion as to the real character of the course on which they have entered, for as they pass back through the cities they had visited, the apostles confirm the souls of the disciples, exhorting to continue in the faith ; telling them that it was only through much tribulation that they could enter the kingdom of God.

Returned to their brethren in Antioch, they relate the history of their journey, dwelling specially on the great fact that God had opened the door of faith to the Gentiles. Strange that in spiritual blessing there should be jealousy! Many of the Jerusalem Christians heard the tidings much in the spirit of him who said, "as soon as this thy son was come, which hath devoured thy living with harlots, thou hast killed for him the fatted calf." Mingled with this jealousy on behalf of their national privileges was a true devotion to the law of Moses, a sincere belief that this innovation might open the door to all kinds of corruption, and destroy the Kingdom of God in its very bud. With all the intense ardour that had once possessed Saul himself, these men came down to Antioch, and withstood Paul and Barnabas in the very midst of their success.

A battle had then and there to be fought, the battle which has raged a thousand times since, and will have to be fought again and again, as long as human nature endures—the struggle for liberty. Truth is great, says the proverb, and will prevail; but truth can be gagged, bound in fetters, put to death and buried. That truth will inevitably rise again is certain, for it is immortal and eternal; but while it lies in the grave whole generations sit in darkness and in the shadow of death. Liberty alone can free truth, can give it full scope, and open the world to its life-giving word.

Inspired by the Holy Spirit, Paul saw more clearly than any man of his time the connection between truth and liberty. The Council was the first step in the enfranchisement of the world, and in that glorious and progressive struggle for liberty and truth which henceforth becomes the central fact in the history of humanity. In this contention between Paul and the Jerusalem Judaisers we are at the very fountain-head of that condition of freedom of thought and action which the greater part of Christendom has now reached, and which Athens in the height of its philosophical glories understood as little as papal Rome.

When Jesus Christ said, "Go ye into all the world, and preach the gospel to every creature," He claimed rights on behalf of the human conscience which lie at the foundation of all our modern ideas of liberty. If Jesus Christ is the author of the true idea of human liberty, Paul is its first defender. Faith in Jesus Christ having set the conscience free, it shall not be bound again, even if he has to resist the apostles themselves. He will not surrender "our liberty which we have in Christ Jesus," "no, not for an hour." The liberty of the conscience, of the individual, of the Church, and of the world, were all involved in this first struggle in the new-born Christendom. To secure this great victory, the "no small dissension and disputation" which raged for a time at Antioch, the journey to Jerusalem, the efforts Paul and Barnabas made to convince the apostles and elders and the whole Church, were not too great a price to pay.

At Jerusalem Paul and Barnabas and their companions found themselves surrounded by men full of faith, but with minds still tightly bound in the fetters of tradition, custom, and education. Peter sympathised with Paul and Barnabas; he had been assured by Divine revelation that they were right. The rest of the apostles probably suspended judgment, hoping, fearing, sometimes doubting. But Paul's ardour and Paul's facts were convincing; the grace of God had been given to the Gentiles, and they could not withstand it. Not only Peter, but even James, who of all the apostles was the one most thoroughly imbued with Hebrew tradition, gave his opinion in favour of the great innovation. The unanimity was extraordinary, and the apostles might well attribute it to the Holy Spirit, by whom they could not doubt that they were led.

How natural in the whole narrative is the blending of the human with the Divine! The concession to the Spirit of righteousness, the one valuable point in the Judaisers' position; the veiling of the real victory; the tender consideration for the prejudices of the defeated party: all so characteristic of the triumphs of the Gospel! Paul might truly say, as he returned with the message of the Church at Jerusalem: "The Spirit of the Lord is upon me, because the Lord hath anointed me to preach good tidings unto the meek; He hath sent me to proclaim liberty to the captives, and the opening of the prison to them that are bound."

Thus at the time that the rulers of this world were suppressing the liberties of the ancient inhabitants of our own country, and bringing their bravest defender in chains to Rome, Paul won the Magna Charta of Christendom, and came bearing the order for release to a world that had been crushed beneath the heavy yoke of religious legalism.

Again, at the time that this great spiritual hero was led in chains to Rome, there to proclaim, in the centre of the Western world, the Gospel that brought life and immortality to light; the sad religion born of human thought, the gospel of annihilation, was established in China, and became the faith of a larger number of the human race than was contained in the whole Roman Empire.

ANTIOCH.

SECOND CENTURY.

CONTEMPORARY EVENTS IN THE SECOND CENTURY.

Britain. Defending the Roman wall.
Jerusalem. The plough passed over its site.
Athens. Hadrian receiving Quadratus.
Alexandria. Ptolemy making astronomical observations.

Second Century.

A.D. 132.

Roman Civilisation—A Model Emperor—Hadrian's Travels—The Road to Lyons—Britain—The Roman Wall—Athens—The Christian Apologists—Alexandria—Ptolemy and Early Science—The Ploughshare passed over Jerusalem.

THE Roman Empire was the strongest and yet the weakest the world has ever seen. A kingdom of iron in authority, laws, legions and roads, it was a kingdom of clay in the variety of its nationalities, customs, liberties, and religions. But the iron and clay could not mingle; there was nothing to weld them into one homogeneous mass, for this mighty Empire wanted the uniting force of a common religion which should connect it as a whole with the Eternal.

This weighty power had subdued the Western world, and had brought under its sway all kingdoms and peoples, from Britain to Egypt, from Spain to Armenia. The most beautiful of seas was its centre. Upon the shores of the Mediterranean arose magnificent cities, teeming with human beings, and adorned with stately structures, temples, palaces, amphitheatres, harbours. Across its deep blue waters vessels of many kinds were ever passing, rowed sometimes by galley-slaves, sometimes driven by light breezes from one bay to another. Let the traveller land at any point, the scene was ever the same. The same officials, the same accommodation, the same great quays, the same noble roads going straight to one centre, and that centre the city Rome, to which all things tended.

Civilisation, understood by its corresponding Greek terms, polish, policy, never attained higher finish than in the second century. The Good Emperors, as they are rightly styled, are amongst the best models the world has ever seen of the perfect monarch. The two Antonines have passed into a proverb. Still we must not forget that their immediate predecessor had set them a bright example, and was only their inferior as a private man.

Hadrian had a truly great policy, nobly carried out. Handsome in form, gracious in manner, artistic in taste, philosophic in temperament, his universal acquirements, indefatigable energy, and strong sense of duty made him a fine specimen of the higher forms of Roman civilisation. Trained by the Emperor Trajan and Greek preceptors, he was at once manly and polite, and came as near to the ideal of the modern English nobleman as was possible under circumstances so different. His accomplishments earned him the title of *Græculus* among old-fashioned Romans, who detected a foreign accent when, as Quæstor, he delivered to the Senate the imperial messages. Such, then, was the man who was called to rule the Western world during the middle of the second century; and the contemporary events find their meaning and unity in the light of his character and policy.

It was Hadrian's axiom that he would so govern the commonwealth that it should know that it belonged to the people, and not to himself. A noble resolve, and very nobly did he carry it out. Trajan, with all his virtues, had been misled by the vulgar bait of military glory to go on adding to the Roman possessions in the East. Hadrian determined to give them all up, and to withdraw into the old lines marked out by Augustus as the proper limits of the Roman Empire. That Empire Hadrian determined to make peaceful, prosperous, and happy. To study its condition, he took upon himself the stupendous task of constantly travelling all over his vast dominions. "A ruler," he said, "should be like the sun, which illuminates not only one place, but all the corners and regions of the earth."

He was the greatest of crowned travellers. He did not merely make a progress now and then, in order to stimulate the flagging loyalty of the people by the sight of imperial magnificence, but during the whole twenty years of his reign he was continually on the move, marching at the head of his legions from station to station, from city to city, often on foot and bareheaded; stopping at every camp to review his troops, to inquire minutely into their appointments, even tasting their black bread and their wine or vinegar, and restraining the luxury of the officers. He made halts, long or short, at the various cities, learning the character and temper of the officials, holding assemblies, to make the people acquainted with his wishes, improving or adding to the public buildings, and generally doing all that a thoughtful and highly-civilised ruler could do to perfect the public service.

One of his earliest visits was to our own shores. To reach Britain he passed through Gaul; and if his landing-place in the latter country was Marseilles, he took the road running parallel with the Rhone to Lyons. Solid as a sea-wall, and elevated above the surrounding country, it was traversed by an innumerable throng of passengers, on foot or in chariots; slaves in simple tunics, bare-armed, bare-legged; citizens wearing the toga, and sometimes the chlamys; senators in their rich purple laticlaves, studded with gold or precious stones; Iberians, Rhodians, Massiliotes, Egyptians, Greeks in their varied costumes. The Emperor marched at the head of his column among spectators who well represented the world he governed. Hadrian's interest in everything Greek might have led him to single out from among the throng some humble group of traders from Ephesus, bearing the tidings of God's peace and goodwill to the great city of Lugdunum.

If Hadrian saw, in the luxuriant valley through which he was passing, with its vine-clad hills and rich orchards, its river studded with many islands and alive with light craft, and, above all, in the densely populated Gallic metropolis, every sign of the glory and power of the great Roman Empire, these humble representatives of the kingdom of heaven beheld nothing to strengthen, but much to depress, their faith. As they approached Lugdunum, they passed through signs of human mortality, a series of tombstones lining the way. At the gates Roman luxury began to display its magnificence. They saw temples of different forms, triumphal arches, well-trimmed gardens, handsome pleasure-houses, at times woods and shady copses surrounding palaces whose halls and galleries were full of statues and mosaics.

Two rivers flowed through the city, and at their confluence was an altar dedicated to Augustus. On the heights rising above the Saone stood a semicircular amphitheatre, from which the spectators, during the interludes, could refresh their eyes by looking across the two rivers over a vast and beautiful landscape. In the centre of the city stood the Forum, lately built by Trajan, and here, in the ample space enclosed by a stage of porticoes, surmounted by a gallery adorned with statues and bas-reliefs, the public fairs were held, and justice dispensed by the magistrates.

Lugdunum was the Birmingham of the Roman Empire, the centre where the greater part of the arms borne by the legions were manufactured. The sword-makers were quite a peculiar corporation, and any member who deserted was punished on his capture by a brand on the arm. It was also a centre for the corn trade, the grain of Central France coming to Lyons for distribution to other parts of the Empire. Besides these industries, tanning, currying, weaving, were probably staples, and in addition to all these sources of wealth, in Lyons was the treasury which received the tributes paid by the various tribes of the North.

Coming like the first rays of the morning sun into a land of darkness and the shadow of death, with what different feelings from those experienced by the Emperor must these simple unknown foreigners have entered this rich and prosperous city. The first marched, amid the applause of myriads of spectators, into the noble Forum, there to sit on the highest seat and to hear from the assembled hosts the cry of *Ave Cæsar nos te salutamus;* the others to be lost in the alleys of the poorer quarters, and to be found again at eventide in the deep recesses of the woods that crowned the neighbouring heights, in their cavernous hollows, singing hymns of praise and celebrating simple rites.

From Gaul Hadrian passed into Britain. What a change since his great predecessor had first planted the Roman standard on British ground! The wild tribes of tattooed savages had become Roman ladies and gentlemen! They no longer lived in mud hovels, in towns hidden in the midst of woods, ten or a dozen families in one dwelling, and after a fashion little superior to the brutes. They could scarcely be distinguished from their conquerors, and lived in miniature Romes, adorned with arches, temples, amphitheatres, and baths. The natural resources of the country had been discovered and brought into use. In the south-west, the tin, copper and silver; in the midland and south-east, the iron; and in the north, the lead ore had all been worked, the coal-beds had been discovered, and pottery and glass were manufactured; while corn and cattle were raised in such abundance that they were exported, together with British slaves, to foreign markets.

In adopting the toga these Britons had lost the courage of the free man fighting for liberty, and, with their warm baths and perfumes, now offered a rich prey to the painted savages (Picti) of Caledonia. It was Hadrian's chief care therefore to see to the protection of this outpost of Roman civilisation. The Emperor accordingly advanced northward, and after making a survey of the country determined to withdraw the limits of the Empire in Britain to the inner line of forts, where the land between the Solway and the Tyne was narrowest and most inaccessible. The point chosen was only sixty miles wide, and was evidently marked out for the purpose by nature, since towards Caledonia the land fell abruptly, with a base protected by swamps and marshes, and every break in the cliff was obstructed by dense forests. The camps that Agricola had formed in this locality, Hadrian connected by a deep ditch and palisaded ramparts of earth, strengthening the whole line by subsidiary entrenchments at every third or fourth mile. Thus was begun the great wall, of which the remains are to be seen on the Border even to the present day.

Hadrian's stay in Britain lasted during the winter of 119–120. He gave his name to a bridge that spanned the Tyne, and organised a fleet for the protection of the island and the transport of soldiers.

After passing through Gaul and Spain this ubiquitous Emperor appears on the borders of Parthia; from Syria he returns homeward through Asia Minor, perhaps winters at Athens, and with indefatigable curiosity lands, on his way to Rome, in Sicily, that he may see the sun rise from Etna.

During his second progress he makes a long stay at Athens, his favourite city; for Hadrian was heart and soul an Athenian. There was nothing he would have liked better than to wander from hall to hall, from lecturer to lecturer, spending his time in nothing else than either to tell or to hear some new thing.

But the glory of Athens had departed, and the philosophers who represented Socrates and Plato were little better than babblers—men who cared more for the rhetoric with which they adorned their doctrine than any truth that they had to defend. Every one of the recognised philosophies had its professors, who were amply paid to defend their peculiar doctrines. The most contradictory doctrines, provided they had a footing in old time, were thus taught, the result being absolute indifference to truth and a common hatred to all that was new. Athens had reached that intolerant latitudinarianism which is the last stage of decrepit religions and philosophies; and it was philosophy in this condition that seized on Christianity, now fast becoming a power throughout the Empire, and began its corruption.

Certain philosophers at Athens who had adopted the Christian religion begged Hadrian to listen to a thesis in its defence. The Emperor was of too Athenian a spirit to deny himself the pleasure of listening to something fresh, especially if it wore the air of mystery; and it is very likely that he not only consented but listened with interest to what Quadratus had to say on its behalf. The "Apologia" as a whole is lost, but Eusebius has preserved a remarkable sentence: "The works of our Saviour were always to be seen, for they were real; those that were healed, and those that were raised from the dead, were seen, not only when they were healed or raised, but they were always there; not only whilst He dwelt on earth, but also after His departure, which they long survived; so that some of them have lived even to our own times." There was nothing extraordinary in this, since, if Quadratus were a man in years, his memory might easily go back half a century, when there would have been living some who had been cured by our Lord.

Hadrian was a ruler to whom Quadratus might have very properly addressed the magnificent words of the orator Tertullus: "Seeing that by thee we enjoy much peace, and that by thy providence evils are corrected for this nation, we accept it in all ways and in all places, most noble Hadrian, with all thankfulness." For this Emperor, receiving complaints from Serrenus Granianus, pro-consul of Asia Minor, of the way the populace treated the Christians, forbade all accusations against them except in legal form, or that they should be arrested at the instance of popular clamour. All this was done in the cause of justice. In Christianity itself Hadrian had no more interest than he had in the Eleusinian mysteries or the worship of Serapis. What really touched him while at Athens was the wretched state of the city. The glorious Acropolis with its beautiful temples still existed, but around them were congeries of squalid hovels, with here and there a better dwelling, marking the residence of some wealthy man; but, save that the hovels were of stone, they were more unwholesome, more utterly wanting in every comfort than the lairs in which the Roman proletariat hid themselves.

Rome and Athens were in outward appearance widely different. In the former the houses were very high and all crowded together. There were splendid quarters, in which everything was wide, open, and magnificent; there were narrow thoroughfares, choked by traffic, in the neighbourhood of which it was impossible to sleep for the noise of the waggons and the swearing of the drivers; there were ugly lanes, in which it was very easy for a belated passer-by to meet a fate similar to that which befell respectable Londoners who encountered late at night the Mohocks of one hundred and fifty years ago. According to Juvenal, young patricians, returning from their midnight revels swollen with drink, and meeting some poor wayfarer, would thus accost him: "Where have you been? Whose beans and vinegar have swelled you thus? Speak! what cobbler has been regaling you on leeks and garbage? What! not answer me? Tell, or be kicked." Whatever the victim did or said, his fate was the same: he was soundly beaten, and if he complained, was told he would be cited in the morning before the magistrate for an assault.

Athenians, we may suppose, knew nothing of such brutal customs; but their squalor and filthiness must have troubled the energetic Hadrian, who set about rebuilding the city, and that on such a magnificent scale that the new quarter was called Hadrianopolis. Temples rose at his command, and he earned the demonstrative gratitude of the people by completing the Olympicum, a great temple to Zeus, that had been building for centuries, but which, on account of the costliness of the design, had never been finished.

FROM Athens, Hadrian went to Alexandria, where a very different scene and an utterly different mental atmosphere awaited him. Alexandria was the university of progress, as Athens was that of conservatism. It stood in the very focus of the new life; allied in some measure with three continents, it sympathised with them all. From Asia it welcomed many deep and mystic thoughts; from Africa came a certain sensuousness and gaiety of heart; from Europe a looking to the future, a restless desire for better things. It was a strange place: fickle, energetic, pleasure-loving; full of earnest thinkers and scholars. The greatest of these scholars was the learned Claudius Ptolemais, whose name is attached to the astronomical system accepted by the ancients, and even by the moderns up to the fifteenth century. Although this system has now been entirely superseded, Ptolemy made real contributions to astronomical science. He was not only an astronomer, but a mathematician and a geographer. As he was a native of Egypt, and made most of his discoveries between the years 125 and 140 A.D., and is known to have been living there in 139 A.D., it is not improbable that he may have seen Hadrian when the Emperor was there in 131 A.D.

The Alexandrians were far from reverent to the Emperor, and especially gibed at his favourites, Antinous and Verus. Hadrian, however, found much to amuse him; but he never liked them. Years after, in a letter to a friend, he accuses the Alexandrians of being a vain and fickle people, ready to run after any new doctrine. Hadrian, moreover, was not a man to penetrate much beneath the surface; a universal genius, dabbling in all the arts, a dilettante philosopher, he had much of the spirit of the Roman prefect who asked so contemptuously, What is truth? His curiosity was insatiable, and before he left Egypt he paid a visit to Thebes, and in all probability tried to hear the music said to issue at sunrise from the broken statue of Memnon.

HADRIAN next visited Syria, where he found a state of things still more disagreeable. Antioch, with its frivolity and ribaldry, utterly disgusted him, but none of his subject nations gave him so much trouble as the Jews. Although Jerusalem had been so completely destroyed by Titus, the Jews cherished the hope of its restoration. Scattered all over the civilised world, often badly treated, and at Rome especially ill-used, the Jewish nationality was indestructible. Wherever they came to live they formed themselves into a community. This was organised under a synagogue, and the synagogue was in communication with those in Judæa, so that without any hierarchy there was in these communities an indestructible unity. The source of that unity was a common religious faith; a common belief in their relation to God as a nation. They were the only people at that period preserving this faith, and they were the only people therefore who could still claim to have a national life of their own, and courage to pit themselves single-handed against the matchless power of Imperial Rome. What it cost Hadrian to put them down may be judged from the fact that the insurrection was maintained for three years, and only terminated after more than half-a-million of Jews had been killed. Hadrian had to summon Julius Severus, the greatest general of the time, all the way from Britain to carry on the war; and from his letter to the Senate announcing its conclusion it is evident that he felt there was nothing to boast of, for he omits the congratulatory phrase.

Although the Romans had no other national religion than the worship of their own power, they were by no means an irreligious people; perhaps from some points of view they were too religious. They had a firm belief in spiritual influence, and feared even the gods of their enemies, to propitiate them always bringing their statues to Rome and placing them in the Pantheon. But the Jews worshipped a God whose graven image was to be found nowhere—a God before whom these idolatrous Romans knew not how to bow the knee, for there was no visible form to tell them where He was or what He was like. As long as the Jews did not awaken their fears, this was only subject for contempt, but when the Romans really felt themselves in danger from the obstinate and courageous resistance of the Jews, then they became cruel, and their anger was especially directed against what they felt to be the seat of this irreconcilable obstinacy—Jerusalem—and they sought to blot out its very memory from the face of the earth. When Titus had finally concluded his great siege, he utterly destroyed the city and the Temple, so that no one would believe that the place had ever been inhabited. But in sixty years after its destruction Jerusalem was again capable of being the centre of an insurrection, and it was only after two years or more that it was again taken and again destroyed. Then Hadrian, as if to force on the Jews the conviction that the power of Rome had finally conquered the God of Zion, so completely removed every vestige of the city that he ran his ploughshare over its site. A colony of Roman citizens was brought to inhabit the new city he determined to build in its place, and which he called after himself and the Jupiter of the capital, *Ælia Capitolina*. He erected the usual theatres and arches, and a temple was dedicated to Jupiter on the site of the House of the Lord, Hadrian's own statue being placed where the Holy of Holies had once stood. It seemed the final doom of the Hebrew nation; but they exist to-day as strong, as able, as irrepressible as ever, while the Roman Empire has for ages ceased to be.

ARCH OF TITUS, ROME.

THIRD CENTURY.

CONTEMPORARY EVENTS IN THE THIRD CENTURY.

Rome.—*Aurelian's protest against luxury.*
Gaul.—*Invasion of the Franks.*
Syria.—*Capture of Zenobia.*
Carthage.—*Martyrdom of Cyprian.*

Third Century.

ABOUT A.D. 250-275.

The Irruption of the Barbarians—The Franks in Gaul—Aurelian—Fall of Palmyra—Zenobia—Trade with China—Aurelian's Protest against Luxury—Persecution of the Church—Cyprian, Bishop and Martyr.

N the early part of the third century the Goths are found settled on the shores of the Black Sea about the mouth of the Danube. Three centuries before the Christian era they were believed to be living on the shores of the Baltic; all agree that they were a German tribe. When did their migration take place? and what was the attraction that drew those fierce Teutons from the Baltic to the Black Sea? Was there, about the middle of those five centuries, during which their history seems lost, some magnet in Jerusalem attracting men from the north and from the west, as well as from the land of Sinim? It was the same with the Vandals, who, coming from the gloomy northern shores, are in the second century heard of in the south of Germany, and in the third appear with Goths and Getæ in the Roman province of Dacia.

ALL around this dying Roman Empire, along every frontier, hover, like flocks of vultures, countless tribes, eager for the moment when the old Roman charger shall stagger and fall, and they may pounce on their prey. The whole Empire recognises the danger, the very children rejoice at the slaughter of these fierce tribes. Just as the women of Israel met King Saul after the slaughter of Goliath of Gath with the refrain :—

> Saul hath slain his thousands,
> And David his tens of thousands;

so when the story flew over the Empire that the tribune, Lucius Domitius Aurelian, had killed forty-two Sarmatians in one day with his own hand, and in a single campaign no less than nine hundred and fifty, the children came dancing in military step, singing,—

> Mille, mille, mille, mille, mille, mille decollavimus,
> Mille, mille, mille, mille, mille, mille decollavimus,
> Mille, mille, mille, vivat, mille, mille occidet,
> Tantum vini habet nemo quantum fudit sanguinis.

The soldiers themselves recognised the immense circle of the peril when, after this same Aurelian had prevented a band of Franks from passing the Rhine and scattering themselves over Gaul, they marched singing,—

> Mille Francos, mille Sarmatas semel et semel occidimus
> Mille, mille, mille, mille, mille Persas quærimus.

This is the first time that name, which was to become one of the most famous in the world, appears in history. In A.D. 242, *Franci* was a name for certain German hordes on the banks of the Rhine; in the fifth century a large portion of Gaul had become the kingdom of the Salian Franks, and for centuries the whole of that country has had no other name. But from this time the terror of the Franks was upon the land. From A.D. 260 to 268 they scoured Gaul from north-east to south-west, plundering and devastating until they reached Spain, burnt Tarragona, got possession of certain ships, and passed over to Mauritania, where for about twelve years they did as they pleased.

As one Teuton tribe thus swept through the west, another swept through the east. In the early part of this century the Goths entered Dacia; in the reign of Philip the Arabian they besieged Marcianopolis in Mœsia; in A.D. 250 they took Philippopolis by storm, massacred a hundred thousand of its inhabitants, and then in a tremendous battle utterly defeated the Romans, killing both the Emperor and his son. In A.D. 253 they obtained a fleet, and ravaged the south-western coast of the Black Sea and the Propontis, taking several great cities. In A.D. 262 they sailed with a fleet of five hundred vessels into the Ægean, ravaged Attica, and anchored in the Piræus, plundering not only Athens but many other important places in Greece. In A.D. 269 they appeared in larger bodies than ever on the coasts both of Europe and Asia, but at last their immense hosts, said to have numbered three hundred and twenty thousand men, suffered a great defeat from the Emperor Claudius, who drove them into the passes of Mount Hæmus, where they perished from famine. However, other hosts soon appeared, and in such force that Aurelian, who by this time knew their power, thought it best in A.D. 272 to cede to them the province of Dacia, by which means the Romans for half a century secured peace in that quarter.

Thus, during the years A.D. 242-272 these Teutonic tribes swept like a great cyclone almost round the Roman Empire. No wonder that great soldiers like Aurelian rose from obscurity to wear the purple. But Aurelian was much more than a mere soldier, he was an able commander, a severe disciplinarian, and a shrewd politician. He had been one of the best generals during the reign of Claudius, and had been recommended by that Emperor as most worthy to be his successor. Notwithstanding the great defeat of the Goths, the Empire was in dire distress. At the moment Aurelian began to reign the two wings of the Empire were in open revolt: Britain, Gaul and Spain in the west; Egypt, Syria and Asia Minor in the east; while Italy was ravaged by one of these German tribes—the Alemanni. Aurelian chased the barbarians out of Italy, and began a great wall round Rome—proof of the decline of the proud mistress of the world, since for many generations the streets had pierced her ancient walls, and the city had spread far into the suburbs.

When Aurelian had thus secured his centre, he turned against the rebellious provinces in the east and west. Strange to say, those who in each part were trying to found rival empires to that of Rome were women—Victoria in Gaul, Zenobia in Spain.

In these days of anarchy, Emperors rose and fell with such astonishing rapidity that every daring pretender was encouraged to aim at the imperial purple. The provinces of Gaul had thus had several ephemeral monarchs, when at last the government fell into the hands of one named Victorinus. He was assassinated, and his mother, Victoria, a woman of energy, took upon herself the supreme control. She appointed rulers, coined money, and assumed the title of Augusta and Mother of the Camps. Her success was probably due to the reverence felt for great women among the Frankish peoples, and to the miseries now experienced under the bad fiscal arrangements of old Rome. "So enormous," in the latter part of this century, "had the imposts become, that the tiller's strength was exhausted, fields became deserts, and farms were changed into forests. The fiscal agents measured the land by the clod; trees, vine-stalks, were all counted; the cattle were marked, the people registered. Old age or sickness was no excuse: the sick and the infirm were brought up, every one's age was put down, and a few years were added on to the children's and taken off the men's. Meanwhile the cattle decreased, the people died, and there was no deduction made for the dead." The system was intolerable, but inseparable from a government now mainly dependent on military authority. The people might rise, but there was little hope of better government; so, after the death of Victoria, her successor, Tetrius, was glad to surrender his authority into the hands of Aurelian.

The Roman arms were at once turned against a more real enemy, Zenobia, the celebrated Queen of Palmyra. Sapor, King of Persia, had in A.D. 260 defeated the Emperor Valerian, and had taken him prisoner. He treated his captive with every insult, compelling him to act as a footstool whenever he mounted on horseback. Sapor wished to appoint a successor to Valerian, and to this end led an army to Antioch, destroyed and pillaged the city, killing or taking captive its principal inhabitants. Odenatus, a senator of Palmyra, was the only person who dared oppose him. He collected a small army, and so harassed the Persians that Sapor was obliged to recross the Euphrates. This conduct gave Odenatus a great position in the East, so that he was acknowledged by Gallienus as his colleague in the Empire. At his death Zenobia, his beautiful and accomplished widow, assumed the imperial authority, and styled herself Queen of the East.

Palmyra, the Tadmor of Solomon, appeared in the wilderness as some fairy creation. In this Paris of the desert, in the midst of art, learning, and commerce, Zenobia pursued a noble and enlightened existence. Her prime minister was the philosopher Longimanus, a pupil of Origen, and almost the only true follower then existing of Plato. Neither Zenobia nor Longimanus professed Christianity, but they nearly approached its more intellectual forms, and Zenobia herself is said to have been attached to the Jewish faith. Her position had, at least tacitly, been acknowledged by Claudius; but Aurelius not only refused it, but determined that she should acknowledge his supremacy. Zenobia prepared to resist to the utmost, and the siege of Palmyra followed. The Roman army suffered frightfully from the ingenious methods of defence adopted by the inhabitants; but the city fell at last (A.D. 273), but not before Zenobia and her daughters had taken flight. Mounted on swift dromedaries, they made their way to the Euphrates; but as they were about to embark they were overtaken by Roman horsemen, and brought prisoners into the camp of Aurelian. The Emperor spared their lives, Zenobia's prime minister, Longimanus, alone being executed.

Aurelian having thus for a time secured the peace and unity of Rome, returned thither to enjoy his triumph (A.D. 274). It was a grand day for the Emperor when his captives and his trophies were led in procession to the Capitol. First came the prisoners of the various tribes against whom he had warred: Ethiopians, Gauls, Arabs, Indians, Persians, Iberians, Saracens, each carrying productions of their country; Goths and Vandals, Alani, Roxalani, and Sarmatians, tribes dwelling in what is now Russia and Poland; Franks, Suevians, and Germanic tribes, all with their hands tied behind them. Then came the Amazons, who had been taken fighting among the Goths. Tetricus, the Gaul, next appeared, arrayed in a purple robe with a green tunic, and wearing the Gallic breeches. Last of all was seen Zenobia, her hands bound with a chain of gold.

———

THE Emperor had promised every Roman a largess of two crowns if he returned in triumph from the East, and the populace hoped that they would be gold. But Aurelian ordered them to be of bread, making it a standing order that they and their descendants should henceforth receive this as a continual dole. To this donation he subsequently added pork, and to pork, oil. Finally, he added an ounce more to the bread, and planted a number of vines, seriously thinking of placing wine and chickens on the table of every Roman.

Although it was one of his favourite amusements to see a prodigious eater of the day gorge himself by consuming a whole pig at a sitting, Aurelian was himself austere and frugal in his own habits. He would allow no luxurious dresses in his court. His wife begged him to permit her to have a dress of silk. "No," he said; "I like not the thread which is worth its weight in gold;" a pound of silk costing in Rome twelve ounces of gold. China, from whence the raw material came, was utterly unknown to the Romans, and the great risks and heavy expense incurred by the merchants of Samarcand and Bokhara, who alone knew how to procure it, rendered the price so costly. Those who ventured to make the journey were three parts of a year before they returned, and were in constant peril of being robbed and murdered.

Aurelian carried his private austerity so far, that, excepting drinking-vessels, he would have no gold in his apartments, nor would he allow gold or silver wire to be woven into the imperial dress. The glorious robes he had brought from Palmyra, whose hue and texture made the finest dresses of the imperial wardrobe look dim, he hung up in the Temple of the Sun. The sun, as it shines in Southern Europe and in the East, is at once beneficent and terrible, the source of life and death. This was the deity Aurelian followed, and to whose shrines he was always faithful.

Thus in Palmyra the Temple of the Sun was the only object that escaped the general destruction. All else was pitilessly destroyed. "We have," he writes to the Senate, "not even spared the women; we have killed the children, cut the old men's throats, and murdered the country people." He was very careful not to take the credit of his victories to himself, but attributed them to the favour of the gods, especially to the Sun, who, on one most important occasion in his life, he declared before the Emperor and his brother generals to be a faithful god. He had a far greater opinion of the benefit of consulting the oracles than of the wisdom of the Senate, and once rated them for deliberating like an assembly of Christians rather than acting like true worshippers in the temple of the gods. "Let inquiry," he said, "be made of the sacred books, and let celebration take place of the ceremonies that ought to be fulfilled. Far from refusing, I offer, with zeal, to satisfy all expenditure required with captives of every nationality—victims of every rank. It is no shame to conquer with the aid of the gods; it is thus that our ancestors begun and ended many a war."

This religious tendency on the part of Aurelian would be a striking fact, were it not generally true of the Emperors of the Decline; and in Aurelian it appears with unusual sincerity and consistency. The rulers of Rome no longer affect the indifference of Gallio, or even the philosophic interest of Hadrian. The Spirit of God has convinced them that there is no stability on earth for any power unless it has its roots in a Divine soil. This is a great step in the awakening of the human conscience; and though at present that conscience, working in darkness, often acts madly and barbarously, Aurelian is nearer the kingdom of heaven than Gallio or Hadrian.

MEANWHILE a power has arisen in the world which will help to educate the human conscience—a power which, having its roots fixed in God, will advance, and, clothing itself in the forms of the Roman Empire, will succeed that Empire, conquering the enemies who are now hemming it in on all sides. That power is Latin Christianity, which may be said to take definite form about the middle of this century.

The antagonism Christianity aroused resulted in persecution : persecution developed organisation and helped to turn purely spiritual aims into earthly ones. Persecution tended to produce unity, secrecy, obedience, and authority. As when a country is threatened by invasion, individual liberty must be curtailed, and loyalty to the governing power increased, so was it in those days. The power of the bishops grew rapidly in times of persecution. They were not only the nucleus round which the Churches gathered, but being their leaders, in the eyes of the world, they were marked out specially for the severest forms of persecution. It was for them that the capital penalty was principally reserved. In days of trial, strength of character, wisdom, learning, and ability came to be thought of even more importance than piety. Distinguished men who became Christians were chosen bishops ; in one case—that of the great Ambrose—before they were even baptised.

Cyprian is an instance. A rhetorician and a man of culture, he had been only three years converted when he was chosen Bishop of Carthage (A.D. 248). He was bishop only ten years, yet he influenced the character of Latin Christianity more than any man of his age. His episcopate was one long fiery trial. The persecution under Decius broke out within a year after he assumed the post. It grew in intensity. First the Christians were only summoned to renounce their religion by sacrificing at a pagan altar. If they failed to appear, they were at once arrested, torture applied, and if that did not extort recantation they were hurried to execution. The Church at Carthage was scattered, Cyprian fled (A.D. 250), and while a few were martyred, many abjured the name of Christ.

During the absence of Cyprian, a presbyter who was opposed to him, named Novatus, took the lead, and, to strengthen his party in the Church, received back the lapsed. This was a hotly-debated question. A large party in the Church, the Montanists, refused place for repentance to those who denied Christ in the moment of trial, and Cyprian took the milder view. We next hear of Novatus at Rome, where he had completely gone over to the sterner party, and was a supporter of Novatian, the Montanist, who had become Bishop of Rome. Novatian, however, had to give place to Cornelius, and is now regarded as an anti-pope. Cyprian sympathised with Cornelius, not only because of the affair with Novatus, but because he was himself in a similar difficulty, Fortunatus having been elected bishop by Montanist influence. These troubles led him to take a very formal and distinct view of the organisation of the Church, and being a man of strong will, and finally a martyr, he impressed the whole of the Western Church with his ideas. "Whosoever," he said, "is not in the Church, let him be who or what he may, he is not a Christian." Thus the schismatic and heretic, even if he lived the purest life, was in a more hopeless condition than the grossest liver, if the latter only kept in unity with the visible Church. The visible Church was to Cyprian an ark floating in the midst of a lost world; out of its pale there was no salvation. It was needful to know, therefore, what was, and what was not, the true Church. Every idea, till then in its germ, concerning the authority of the apostles and their successors, received a sudden impetus. Peter was, in Cyprian's idea, the head of a college of co-equal apostles; all bishops were equal in authority, though they acknowledged Peter's successor as their primate. The legend that Peter was Bishop of Rome being accepted as a fact, gave religious sanction to what was otherwise a natural development of Cyprian's doctrine, that the metropolitan bishop should have supremacy over the rest.

War was the great business of the Roman Empire, and even the Christian Tertullian looked upon war as one of the legitimate professions. The new society became military in form and militant in spirit. The old stood merely on the defensive; the new was at once defensive and aggressive. But the weapons of its warfare were not carnal: it might not use the sword, it might not wound, nor do anything but meekly receive every blow; it was bound to struggle simply by sacrifice, by suffering, by love. Nevertheless, it had to carry on an enormous warfare, and to be ready at every moment for actual contest. Every man and woman and child was bound to feel as truly a soldier as any warrior who followed Aurelian against savage Goth or infuriated Syrian. The Church was in the strictest sense militant and actually in the field; it naturally followed that it had to submit to military organisation and military discipline. Each province was an army under a general, and when war broke out in that quarter discipline became rigid, deserters were dealt with severely, unusual daring was promoted on the field, the strong men rose everywhere to supreme command.

Thus the age of martyrdom is the age of Christian victory, of Christian triumph, and, as its correlative in the more mundane sphere, the age in which the liberties of the Church were destroyed, and spiritual despotism established. The glowing exhortation to the individual Christian to array himself in the whole armour of God received a further development, and the commanders in the Christian army added to the virtue of steadfastness the virtue of implicit obedience. The most brilliant achievements, the most daring courage, were not to exempt Christian soldiers from obedience to their officers. Cyprian admonished martyrs and confessors that it behoved all Christ's soldiers to keep the precepts of their commander. Martyrs and confessors were admitted to a right of intercession on behalf of those who in the moment of battle had submitted to the enemy, and, animated by that flow of enthusiastic love which made them so brave, they used their right without discrimination and with injury to the cause.

Nothing can give a better idea of the sternness of the warfare, of the fortitude required in those leading the Christian army, than the refusal to listen to petitions on behalf of mercy to the fallen, signed by the trembling hands of the racked and wounded soldiers of Jesus Christ. Novatian and the Montanist party were the representatives of the sterner view, Pope Stephen and the Roman bishops generally inclined to the milder, while Cyprian of Carthage took the truest and wisest position — unswerving severity during war, the utmost charity during peace.

Cyprian had the true genius of a commander, even to the point of knowing when to spare and when to expose himself. On the first great persecution after his accession to the episcopate he withdrew from Carthage, but from his place of concealment kept a continual watch over his army, exhorting and encouraging his soldiers, quelling mutinies, rewarding distinguished conduct by promotion and praise, and keeping up correspondence with what he considered the very centre of the war and the headquarters of the contending armies — the see of Rome. In this spirit Cyprian ruled the Church, ever conscious that his own hour was at hand. "At last," (A.D. 258) as his deacon, Pontus, writes, "that day dawned—that destined, that promised, that divine day"—the particular facts of which had been revealed, according to the same authority, a year before.

Beneath a deep blue sky, while the sun is pouring down scorching rays on the low white buildings of Carthage, a band of Roman soldiers are escorting through the streets Cyprian, who, with clear eye and serene countenance, walks as one going gladly to a triumph. A great army of followers accompany him, silent, but hardly sad, for beneath a serious mien a well of joy and hope, as of coming victory, is springing up in every heart. Passing the racecourse, the procession arrives at the Prætorium. The Proconsul is not ready, and as Cyprian waits he, as all else, is sweltering in the blazing sun. An officer, who had been a Christian, offers to change clothes with him, thinking that Cyprian would feel more at ease in his dry garments, while he himself would possess relics full of "the blood-stained sweat of the martyr going to God." But Cyprian is indifferent to an annoyance which is so soon to cease. Suddenly the Proconsul is announced, and the Bishop is placed before him and interrogated. He answers to his name, and nothing more. Then the judge reads from a tablet a sentence which his followers regard as worthy of such a Bishop and such a witness; for he is called, as indeed he was, a standard-bearer of the sect and an enemy of the gods. He is told that he is to be made an example to the people, and that with his blood discipline will begin to be established.

He is immediately taken to the place of execution, honourably guarded by centurions and tribunes. It is a large level place, surrounded on all sides by trees, up which his followers climb, that they may behold the moment of his death. They felt as a congregation engaged in a great liturgic act. A sacrifice and a victory were about to be consummated, and they believed the Lord to be present in their midst. If Cyprian spoke, it would be the Lord's words. In all his sufferings, as in all theirs, the Lord shared; and in this sense of fellowship with the Divine there was a triumphant consciousness of victory over the world. With fixed and tearful eyes and intensely sympathetic hearts, they watched the arm of the executioner as it inflicted a triumphant death upon the martyr. From the blood of one Cyprian hundreds of thousands rose ready to follow him to death and victory: "He that overcometh, to him will I give power over the nations."

FOURTH CENTURY.

CONTEMPORARY EVENTS IN THE FOURTH CENTURY.

Rome.—*Revival of Paganism. Julian the Apostate.*
Egypt.—*Athanasius in the Thebaid.*
Jerusalem.—*Attempt to Rebuild the Temple.*
France.—*Invasion of the Saxons.*

Fourth Century.

A.D. 361-363.

Christianity and Imperialism—Arius and Athanasius—The Thebaid—Julian's Effort to Revive Paganism—Attempt to Rebuild the Temple at Jerusalem—The Saxons in France.

ALILEAN, Thou hast conquered!" is the cry that resounds through the fourth century, as the pagan gods silently vanish from the Roman Empire, and leave their empty fanes. But one great effort was needed to prove this, to show to all time that paganism under its highest form, Hellenism, was dead for ever.

Christianity, as the fourth century advanced, was seen by all who had eyes to be not only the greatest fact of the age, but the only living, advancing power. A clever, shrewd man of the world, Constantine, son of Constantius Chlorus, governor of Britain, became Emperor. Possessing the faculty of making all things useful for his own advancement, Constantine has secured immortal renown by being the first Roman Emperor to recognise the new religious force, and to make it the foundation of his empire: a true inspiration, and one which, notwithstanding his selfishness, must argue some moral power in the son of Helena.

No doubt the organisation of the Christian Church won his respect, but it might at the same time have excited his jealousy, had he not possessed the wisdom to see that there was a Divine power at its basis; that so much love, gentleness, self-sacrifice, courage, and faith could not arise out of mere organisation, and for the sake of the honour and aggrandisement of its leaders.

Yet Constantine was the most dangerous ruler that Christianity had ever had to encounter, for there is nothing more antagonistic to spiritual life than the smiles and the patronage of the great. The result was soon manifest. The bishops were turned into courtiers, and lost their virtue; the Church, vastly increased by venal accessions, was in danger of becoming more and more careless and worldly.

While the decay of strength was shown in the enervation of the moral tone of the Church, it was equally evident in the rapid falling away from apostolic doctrine. The essential doctrine of Christianity, that God had manifested Himself in the flesh, and had Himself borne the sins of the world, and made a sacrifice and atonement in His own person, was more and more lost sight of, until a form of Christianity, which in course of time would have become nothing more than Christian Hellenism, had taken possession of a large section of the Church, and, from the very strictness of the new principles of visible unity and military discipline, threatened a rapid conquest of all the rest.

It was a terrible crisis for Christianity when, thus emasculated, it gave itself up to the dominating rule of emperors who were only veneered with its outward form and language.

What marks the fall, and shows how rapidly evil communications corrupt good manners, is the persecuting spirit that Christianity began to evince. Instead of letting the old faiths die away, instead of trusting to the force of that Spirit who had led them from victory to victory, the courtly bishops who surrounded the emperors urged them on to edicts, cruel and unchristian. Doubtless this determination to suppress paganism, just as paganism had tried to suppress Christianity, sprang to some extent from the despotic temperament of Constantine himself; but it was not until the reign of his son that anything like real persecution began, showing that it took years to transform the successors of the gentle martyrs, Lucius, Sextus, and many other of the early Roman bishops, and of the brave and noble Ambrose and Cyprian, into persecutors and inquisitors.

Pagan priests, and all who sincerely held to the old religions, must have indeed felt their faith shaken when such terrible edicts as those of Constantius appeared, for in the public places, where within the previous half-century had been posted up the Diocletian edicts, forbidding all Christian assemblies, and ordering the destruction of the Christian churches, and the burning of their Bibles, now were seen such words as these:

"Let superstition cease. . . We will that all renounce the exercise of the pagan religion. If anyone disobeys, let him be struck down with the avenging sword.

"Penalty of death against whosoever visits the temples, lights fires under an altar, burns incense, pours out libations, adorns with flowers the hinge of the doors.

"Civil death to all who relapse into the old religion; their goods to devolve upon their nearest relatives.

"Priests to be exiled outside the metropolis, and submitted to due coercion.

"The temples to be closed, destroyed, and razed to the ground.

"The stipends of the priests to be applied to the support of the troops."

These laws were promulgated in the years A.D. 353 and A.D. 356, and during the next eighteen months three other decrees appeared, ordering the infliction of the horrible tortures of the rack and the hot iron on all persons connected with the court who took part in magical rites.

Meanwhile, Christianity showed many signs of deterioration in the splendid churches, the swarms of priests, hermits, anchorites, monks, and virgins, and in its internal dissensions. Judged by the magnificent basilicas, and the scandals of every kind which they covered, Christianity was fast becoming a whited sepulchre. The bishops did little else than fulminate anathemas at each other, and accuse each other of all kinds of outrageous crimes.

A great question had sprung up in that city of subtleties, Alexandria. A learned and eloquent presbyter, named Arius, accused the Bishop, Alexander, of heresy, in that speaking of the Trinity he had said that it contained one single essence or indivisible unity of substance, a conception which, according to Arius, led to a denial of the distinctness of the Persons. In the dispute arising, it turned out that Arius was himself the greater heretic, for he maintained that the Son was not co-equal or co-eternal with the Father, but only the first of finite beings. Large numbers of the clergy and the laity of Egypt, Syria, and Asia Minor were of the opinion of Arius, and in A.D. 321 a synod of bishops, held at Alexandria, deposed Alexander. Constantine, who was much chagrined to find the power which he had thought to make the nucleus of the unity of the Empire thus splitting into fractions, assured the combatants that the point in dispute was a trifling one, and ought not to provoke a serious quarrel. But, finding his exhortations of no avail, he convoked a General Council at Nicæa to settle the question (A.D. 325). Three hundred and eighteen bishops, besides a greater number of priests and deacons, were present, and Arius fully expounded his views. However, he met there a greater doctor than himself, the deacon Athanasius, who had accompanied the venerable Alexander to the Council. Although so young, he convinced the assembly that Arius was wrong, and persuaded the bishops to adopt the view since held to be orthodox—the unity of the Divine essence, and the equality of the Three Persons. Arius was anathematised, and, refusing to submit, was banished by Constantine. Through the influence of Eusebius of Nicomedia, who was a kind of court chaplain, the Emperor recalled Arius, and ordered his great opponent, now become Bishop of Alexandria, to receive him back into the Church. Athanasius refused, whereupon he was cited before the Council of Tyre, where he was accused of the most monstrous crimes. His enemies being his judges, he was, in the face of the clearest evidence, found guilty and deposed (A.D. 335).

It is a striking fact that some of the very greatest and strongest of our race have risen from among the most frivolous populations, and in the most frivolous times. Alexandria was noted for its levity, and the age was rapidly sinking to the last degree of folly. The Roman world was not so madly wicked as in the days of Tacitus, but it had fallen into a kind of dotage. The last style in phaetons, or the newest fashion in gossamers, was the subject that most interested a society on the very brink of destruction. Ostentation and foolish parade were so much the order of the day, that when rich men went out for a drive they took with them a whole posse of servants, grooms and lacqueys leading the way, while a troop of cooks, scullion-boys, and sallow-faced eunuchs followed in the wake. As to the lower classes, alternately pampered and kicked, they grew more and more turbulent. Poetry and art had fallen so low that when Constantine wanted to build a triumphal arch he had to pilfer from those of his predecessors.

— ♦ —

IN such a world, Athanasius was a moral colossus. When he was recalled to Alexandria, the people welcomed his return as if he had been an emperor. However, the struggle went on, and in A.D. 341 he was again deposed, and another bishop, Gregory of Cappadocia, forced on his see. The decrees of the Council of Antioch were rescinded by those of Sardis, Gregory was murdered by the mob, and Athanasius was once more Bishop of Alexandria.

Constantius seems to have been quite fascinated with these ecclesiastical pursuits, and very proud of his position as moderator of the various and contending Councils of the Church. He let the bishops have all kinds of privileges, reserving to himself the pleasure of browbeating them, somewhat in the same fashion as "that bright occidental star, Elizabeth, of most happy memory." As a matter of fact, he was entirely under the influence of Eusebius and a tool of the Arian party, so the condemnations of the unmovable Athanasius came thick as autumn leaves. Not content with procuring his condemnation, Constantius banished those who befriended him. Thus, Liberius, Bishop of Rome, was driven into exile, and such influence brought to bear on him that he gave way, and subscribed the condemnation of the great opponent of Arianism. Athanasius continued, however, to exercise his office until suddenly, as he was holding a midnight service, the church was surrounded, and he just managed to escape alive.

The Thebaid, to which Athanasius fled, had not yet become the fashion, and it was still a real retreat for men, who, sick of the world, fled to a spot where nature shut out all external sources of vanity and corruption. Here, in the sheltered clefts of the rocks, they had hewn out their cells, and gave their lives to prayer, to daily toil, to brotherly intercourse. Their lauras were verdant retreats amid the blinding dust and scorching sunlight of the desert — glens green with millet, maize, and beans, the reward of many days of happy toil, in which brother after brother had climbed the Nile banks, bringing with him his palm leaf of mud, to form a soil for future harvests. No sound came from these peaceful homes, save when at sunrise and sunset a Christian hymn rose sweetly in the still air, ascending straight to heaven, as the smoke of a patriarchal sacrifice. It was to such a retreat that Athanasius now fled (A.D. 356).

CONSTANTINE had divided the Empire into three parts, so that each son might be a Cæsar. To make their position secure, they commenced by murdering all their father's brothers and nephews, destroying the whole Flavian race, with the exception of their two young cousins—Gallus and Julian. The latter, six years of age, was old enough to remember the horror of the days when, hidden by the good Mark of Arethusa in the recesses of a church, he had been told in fearful whispers of the tragedy enacting (A.D. 337).

For long years he lived a prisoner of state, the pupil of the family eunuch, Mardonius, a precise, old-fashioned pedagogue. A loving, eager, wistful boy, this poor orphan was compelled to walk to school with his eyes fixed to the ground, to refrain from all child-like sports, the dull monotony of his life being only relieved by church-going, and at very rare intervals by a visit to the theatre, as part of his educational training. At thirteen he was removed to the country, where he and his brother Gallus lived, moved, and had their being among spies, all of whom called themselves Christians. There, under the direction of the very godly Eusebius of Nicomedia, he had a careful ecclesiastical training; he not only was instructed in the Holy Scriptures, but was made to observe fasts, to build shrines, and to perform subordinate clerical functions. Christianity was taught him as an accomplishment, and the very air he breathed compelled him to be a dissembler. Add to all this that the Christianity taught him was after all a distorted form of the gospel, and the unhappy bias with which Julian started is more than explained. With such a preparatory education, Constantius sent him to study philosophy at Nicomedia. A man of literature by nature, Julian for the first time felt a sensation of real joy as he sat in the lecture rooms of the philosophers at Nicomedia, Pergamos, Ephesus, and finally Athens. Neoplatonism was the form of philosophy in vogue. It was wonderfully attractive, for it seemed as elevated as the purest Christianity, and broad and catholic as the universe. Its teachers seemed to be men in love with the truth and with mankind; while those who had surrounded his childhood he knew were false, and the instruments of cruelty. Julian now consciously ceased to be a Christian, though for years he was obliged to conform outwardly.

What a world surrounded the young student! A self-sufficient defender of the faith, really the tool of a sect in the Church; bishops quarrelling, or striving for individual advancement; a people immoral and frivolous, pretending to be Christian, but with hardly any true faith; a few circles where the learned and the cultured debated lofty questions in philosophy and metaphysics, while some dreamed of a grand revival of Hellenism, such as it was in the old Homeric days. The ardent youth—pure, earnest, devoted—drank in the great thought, and, mindful of his high destiny, felt that it was he who was called to build the old waste places, to raise up again the foundations of many generations. With the piety of a sincere Christian, he offered his life to the gods, and especially to the sun, who, in the new theosophy, seemed to be the active form of the one God whom, behind their polytheistic talk, these philosophers held to be the source of all things: gods, dæmons, and men.

Constantius died, and Julian, by universal consent, attained the imperial throne, A.D. 361. He walked a little warily at first, but ere long threw off every mask, and made it clear to the world that he considered the restoration of 'paganism the great mission of his life. But this work was to be done in a very different spirit to the cruel despotism of his Christian predecessors. Julian would show the better way: he proclaimed universal toleration.

His sincerity ere long received a great trial, for there, like another Elijah, stood in his path the great champion of the faith, Athanasius. Although his reappearance did not take place immediately upon the edict of toleration, it was one of its direct results. George of Cappadocia, who had taken possession of his see, had been murdered by the populace. Athanasius, at once, with characteristic energy, appeared in Alexandria, and was welcomed with every honour. Julian received the news in much the same spirit as the King of Israel: scoundrel, knave, adventurer, intriguer, accursed, such were the terms in which he vented his spleen against the man he instinctively felt would be his conqueror. He declared that his edict did not contemplate the reinstatement of exiled bishops to their sees, all he meant being permission to return home. To Edikius the Prefect he wrote: "Persecute him! Drive Athanasius not only out of Alexandria, but out of Egypt;" and to stimulate the Prefect he threatened in default to lay a fine of one hundred pounds weight of gold on his division.

Athanasius was once more a fugitive. Ascending the Nile in a boat, he was pursued; suddenly he ordered the head of the boat to be turned. "Let us show," he said, "that our Protector is more powerful than our persecutor." Ere long they met the pursuers. "Where is Athanasius?" "Not far off," was the reply. "If you make haste you will quickly come up with him." The Bishop had taken the measure of his foe. There was more contempt than enmity in his prophetic word, when, on going this time into exile, he exclaimed, "It is a little cloud that will soon blow over."

Never was reformer more in earnest than Julian; never was reformer purer in intention, better furnished with mental and material power. He possessed real enthusiasm, an elevated sense of duty, a cultivated philosophy, literary genius, æsthetic tastes, a prayerful spirit, and constant devotion to all celestial influences. Yet, though the pagan philosophers and priests were delighted to avail themselves of his powerful patronage, hardly one among them had a like faith, and few really believed in his ultimate success. As Pontifex Maximus, everything was in his hands, and he could do what he would. He restored pagan shrines that had gone to ruin, he set up the statues of the gods, he revised the liturgies, he cultivated music, training in every town choir boys, whom he arrayed in white surplices, richly ornamented; he drew up rules for the growth in holiness of the priesthood, and, not resting simply in splendid ritual, he erected pulpits in the temples, from whence addresses might be delivered by trained expositors of Hellenic dogma. For sacrificial purposes such hecatombs of oxen and sheep were consumed, that the supply of animals threatened to run short; and on great festivals his soldiers, particularly some of the more barbaric, gorged themselves to such an extent with the meat and drink thus offered that they had to be carried home on the backs of the bystanders. In one of his writings Julian thus satirically describes his own conduct: "The Emperor, to be sure, offered sacrifice once in the temple of Zeus, again in that of Fortune, and then marched off thrice running to Demeter. For I have lost count of the number of times I resorted to the shrine of Daphne, that august fabric which the negligence of its warders betrayed, and the presumption of the atheists abolished. The Syrian Kalends are here, and the

Emperor is off again to Zeus Philios; then comes the state festival, and with it the Emperor on his way to Fortune's precincts: and no sooner is one fast day over than he is once more paying his vows to Zeus Philios."

Had Julian been a man in whom the religious sentiment was developed, to the exclusion of all practical ability for his office, his failure as the restorer of paganism might have been expected; but when it is considered that he was one of the ablest of the Roman Emperors, there can be no reason, except in the direction of his reform, why he should have succeeded less easily than Constantine.

If purity of intention, a great moral purpose, and indefatigable industry can insure success, Julian had more reason to expect it than Constantine and Constantius. When he ascended the throne, he cleared the palace of a whole army of cooks, butlers, serving men, spies and eunuchs. His own habits were most simple, his diet spare; he was active as a bird, applying himself with the utmost assiduity to business, and despatching it with ease. His writings were done at night, when everyone was asleep; yet he was up at dawn, ready to receive complimentary callers or petitions, or to give audience to his ministers. As a financier he was admirable. He strove to reduce the burdens of the over-taxed officials, and to reinvigorate industry. He withdrew immunities from favoured classes, looked severely after the tax-gatherers, and improved the judiciary laws. Of course, in doing this, a man with his power and religious proclivities could not fail to be a little hard on the party he detested and wished to crush. The Christians had been subsidised to the extent of pauperisation by Constantius; they had got possession of pagan temples and pagan religious property, and it was not strange that a Pagan Emperor should take away what a Christian Emperor had given. It cannot, therefore, be denied that Julian was, on the whole, a just and able ruler, and that to this he added military genius, always a necessity in the Roman Cæsar. No one could speak contemptuously of the Student Emperor, however much they might think him a servant of Satan, or deride his religious enthusiasm.

And yet there was never a man more to be pitied. All his efforts led to nothing. His vexations were continual, and would have driven a less philosophic mind into some passionate excess. Many Christians resisted him to his face, sometimes in a very insulting manner. Thus Valentinianus, captain of the Jovians, whose duty it was to follow the Emperor on festival occasions, ostentatiously shook off the lustral water with which he had been sprinkled on entering the temple of Fortune. Leading officers resigned their commissions in the army rather than take part in heathen ceremonies ; Christian soldiers in their cups grew mutinous, and talked of Julian as the Ironsides might of Charles I.; nuns loudly sung hymns as he passed under their windows ; town councils treated his edicts of toleration as a farce, and instead of restoring the pagan temples commenced anew the havoc.

In Antioch the whole population seemed in league to make him ridiculous. There was an oracular fountain in a neighbouring village, which he desired to visit and consult. He found it blocked up with stones. The stones were removed, sacrifices and libations were offered; nothing could be heard but a muffled voice reiterating, "The dead! the dead!" Julian thought the place polluted by the bones of a certain martyr who had been buried there, and he ordered the bones to be removed. Little did he expect the demonstration that would follow. All the Christians in Antioch turned out, and walking in long procession behind the bier, men, women, and children sang in chorus, "Confounded be all they that worship graven images, and delight in vain gods!" While the vexed monarch was wondering what he should do, striving probably to preserve his philosophic calm, he was informed that the splendid shrine of Apollo, which stood in the beautiful gardens of Daphne, and which had lately been restored, was in flames. At daybreak nothing remained of the magnificent temple but charred walls and columns and a heap of ashes. Julian was sure that it was the work of the atheists. A suspected Christian was racked, but he hung for a whole day bearing the cruel tortures of tearing-hooks and branding-iron, singing again and again the triumphant refrain, " Confounded be all they that worship graven images!" What could be done in a city like this, where the master of the world was bearded to his face, and where he found only one pagan priest and one sacred goose?

———⧫———

ANOTHER of Julian's failures was the attempt to rebuild the Temple at Jerusalem (A.D. 363). He caused a vast quantity of material to be collected together, put the matter in the hands of Alypius of Antioch, a man on whose loyalty he could thoroughly rely, and the work was heartily supported by the enthusiasm of the Jews. Their very women took a part in it, carrying off the earth which covered the ruins of the Temple in the laps of their garments. But the building was stopped by circumstances not unlike those at Daphne: an unaccountable fire broke out. Everybody seems to have been possessed with the idea that it was supernatural; and among the Christians it was believed to be a direct manifestation from heaven. A sudden whirlwind and earthquake had, it was said, broken up the former foundations, and the workmen had fled to a neighbouring church, which was closed against them by an invisible hand, and from the Temple mount a fire had issued, raging for a whole day. Many perished, some who escaped from the fire being crushed to death under a portico that fell in the night.

WHILE the heart of the Empire was thus torn by religious dissension, the great Teutonic invasion continued. Besides those who, like the Saxons, are for the first time heard of on the shores of Gaul, and who finally establish themselves in Normandy, on a tract of land named after them, *Limes Saxonicus*, numbers of the German barbarians enter as volunteers into the Roman armies, and obtain lands, held by military tenure, as the reward of their services. Men of Teutonic race rise to every honour and dignity short of the imperial throne.

But Julian, who in religious matters was so woefully deceived, was equally blind to the tendency of things in politics. He seems to have imagined that Persia, rather than Germany, was the foe to be dreaded. We find him, accordingly, the spring after the effort in Jerusalem, marching eastward, at the head of one of the largest armies ever led by a Roman emperor, against Persia. He had 65,000 effective troops, and 1,100 ships on the Euphrates. The course of the invading army was marked by the usual line of destruction and death. At last its leader fell into a trap. A Persian nobleman, who professed himself a traitor to his own country, offered his services as guide. With what seems to ordinary eyes almost madness, Julian determined to destroy his own fleet. Reserving only a supply of twenty days' provisions, he, in the midst of an enemy's country, abandoned to the flames his magazines and his 1,100 ships. He soon found himself in the most alarming position. At his appearance the inhabitants fled, and set fire to the grass and ripe corn. His provisions nearly exhausted, his artful guide was no longer to be found, and Julian had no other resource than to make his way back, surrounded by the whole force of the Persian army. The retreat bore some faint comparison to that of Moscow; only, instead of dying of cold, the Roman veterans sank beneath the sultry heat of an Assyrian summer. Julian's courage and skill were ever maintained; but one hot day, riding without his cuirass, he was struck by a Persian javelin, which pierced his ribs and entered his liver. He fainted, and was carried to a tent. Ere long it was apparent that he was dying, and the philosophic Emperor passed away after the manner of one of his ideals, moralising on death and the future state (A.D. 363). Thus died the last champion of expiring polytheism. His character has had fierce assailants and brave defenders. "In his childhood he had seen his nearest kinsmen massacred by the heads of the new Christian state; till the age of twenty-five he held his life on sufferance. The only sympathetic friends he met were among the heathen rhetoricians and philosophers; and he found a suitable outlet for his restless and inquiring mind only in the studies of ancient Greece. In this way he was attracted to the old paganism; but it was a paganism idealised by the philosophy of the time, and still further purified by the moral influence of the Christianity which he rejected." A Christian emperor succeeded him; Athanasius came back to Alexandria, and the tide of Christian progress recommenced. Popular legend took up Julian's story, and it was related how, some time before the fatal wound, Christ had appeared to Julian in a dream, and warned him of his approaching fate; and that Julian, overcome with remorse, bowing his head, had exclaimed, "O Galilean! Thou hast conquered."

Perhaps, indeed, in an hour of deep depression, caused by the failure of his campaign, some such thought arose in his heart; but Julian would appear to have been of a more superficial nature than the magnitude of his effort and the tragedy of life would suggest. At any rate, the words were prophetically true, and the whole story sums up the great fact of the age. What was that fact? That religion, separated from its true source, is powerless, and that a Christianity without Christ is equally so. The Arians had their day under Constantine and Constantius; the Neoplatonists under Julian. They could not say that their systems were tried under unfavourable conditions. They had power pretty much in their own hands. Their failure was complete; and now the truer thought preserved by Athanasius came forth to nourish and shield the world through long ages of ignorance and fraud.

FIFTH CENTURY.

CONTEMPORARY EVENTS IN THE FIFTH CENTURY.

Britain.—The Landing of Hengist.
Ireland.—The Preaching of Patrick.

Rome.—Leo mediates with Attila.
Syria.—Simon Stylites.

Fifth Century.

A.D. 432-460.

The Dying Roman World—Augustine of Hippo—The Vandals in Africa—Attila and the Huns—Pope Leo saves Rome—Rome sacked by Genseric—Saxons land in England—Patrick, the Apostle of Ireland—Corruption of Eastern Christianity—Simon Stylites.

HAT could more accurately describe the progress of the kingdom of heaven than that simple word, "The kingdom of heaven is like unto leaven, which a woman took and hid in three measures of meal, until the whole was leavened"? The kingdom of heaven has no outward form of its own; its mission is to permeate and adapt the forms and institutions of this world. Hiding itself in them, it chiefly reveals its presence by a new and extraordinary working, which cannot cease until it has leavened them all with its own nature. Thus from age to age we find it taking many forms, and giving them all a heavenward direction. If it meets forms or institutions congenial to its own spirit, it animates them with fresh energy and a Divine glow. If it meets forms or institutions repugnant to its nature, the struggle is fierce and the battle long.

All this is fully seen in the fifth century. The kingdom of heaven, to all appearance, is absolutely hidden. Who in that Christendom of the fifth century, with its effete, corrupt society, its dissoluteness, its Manicheeism, its turbulent monkery, and its domineering episcopate, could believe that the kingdom of heaven was in active operation, working through the length and breadth of this apparent anarchy?

With what sorrow have some of the truest servants of this kingdom always spoken of the alliance consummated between the Church and the Roman Empire in the days of Constantine! Their regret rests on a misconception. The kingdom of heaven is essentially spiritual, and in no wise to be confounded with any ecclesiastical organisation. It is the leaven that has come to leaven the whole lump, and could no more avoid taking the forms of the Roman world than a human spirit can the body prepared for it.

Fully to understand the fifth century, and all the ages between the break-up of the Roman Empire and the Reformation, we ought to comprehend the meaning of the life and thoughts of the great man whose name towers high above all his contemporaries, and whose doctrine and influence overshadow the whole of the Middle Ages.

When this century opened, Augustine was already in middle life, and had been Bishop of Hippo for five years. But into the previous forty-six years of his existence he had crowded a wide and varied experience. The ardour of his passions resembled his own Africa—to love and to be loved was his greatest joy; the profundity and lucidity of his intellect might have sprung from the soil of Greece; in his practical earnestness he vied with any Teuton. While his abilities combined all the varied powers of the society in which his lot was cast, his soul passed through all its sufferings.

Augustine died in his seventy-sixth year. His great works were written during the last thirty-three years of his life; but it is as a young man that art has given us his portrait, and that he will ever interest men. It is Augustine in youth and early manhood who is the type of this age; it is this which constitutes him its greatest man, its most perfect representative.

Full of physical and mental disorder, this age is the scene of every kind of conflict, but most of all of a conflict between light and darkness, between the "kingdom of heaven and the kingdoms of this world." The Christian society has passed through all the earlier stages of its existence— its infancy in Judæa, its school-days between the pedagogues of Athens and

Alexandria—and has now begun to choose for itself, and to follow its own tastes theologically and philosophically. But it has not reached the virile age; it is still a dependent beneath the old roof, and submits to the rules laid down by its progenitors. But it feels that the paternal protection is slipping away, and that it will have to shift for itself.

But having fallen before the lusts of the flesh, the lust of the eyes, and the pride of life, the Christian society is tormented as much inwardly as outwardly. In its anguish it hears a voice calling it back to God; and it would obey that voice. But it is too material, too much affected by the traditions of imperialism, too much horrified at its own spiritual and moral anarchy, and the fearful disorganisation of the old society, to seek any form for itself other than that which is strictly systematic and sternly organised. The Catholic Church, as developed in the militant ages, presents the sole refuge it can understand; and if Augustine could feel safe only in submitting his conscience to its doctrine and practice, what more could be expected of his less enlightened and less spiritual brethren? If Augustine made the Scriptures and the Gospel itself to depend on the authority of the Catholic Church, how could his contemporaries do otherwise?

If we look beyond the circle of the Roman world to Asia, we see that the misery of Europe is shared by the East; but whereas Christendom is torn by the turbulence of youthful energy, the unhappy pagan world is sinking more and more into the hopelessness of a worn-out old age, this period being especially signalised in India by the triumphs of Buddhism. Méghavâhâna, King of Kashmere, and the restorer of the dynasty of the Gonardhás, who were at once Buddhists and snake-worshippers, carried his arms apparently through India, for he invaded Ceylon, and made himself its ruler.

But in Europe the final stages in that revolution from the Old Order to the New now began rapidly to be accomplished. The masses which for centuries had been surging all around its coasts poured over and inundated the Empire.

First came the Goths, the old enemies of Rome, already Christianised, but in the Arian form—sons of Anak, rough, coarse men, with globular heads, and red beards, and yellow hair knotted fantastically. Eager for battle, these terrible foes had, at the very end of the fourth century, swept over the Eastern Empire, totally defeated Theodosius, and threatened Constantinople. At the beginning of the fifth century they appeared in Italy. Rome was saved by the skill of Stilicho, who, three years later, rendered similar service against a tremendous host of Vandals, led by Radegast from the plains of the Vistula.

These Vandal hordes, which, when defeated, still numbered a hundred thousand men, did not return to their native plains, but crossed the Rhine and entered Gaul, overrunning the country, destroying its cities, and driving before them a promiscuous multitude. The Goths, Vandals, and Burgundians now made permanent settlements in Gaul and Spain, forming kingdoms, so that henceforth these two great provinces are lost to the Empire.

In Britain, the Roman troops being withdrawn, the Romanised Celts formed an independent republic. If to all this we note that the Franks had established themselves on the Lower Rhine, we shall see that the Western Empire had lost more than half its provinces.

On the other hand, the Eastern Empire was strangely increased by the addition of Armenia, orientalising the old Roman Empire more and more, and making its material as well as nominal centre Byzantium, or New Rome.

The history of the imperial family is itself typical of the revolutionary condition of affairs. The dominion of the great Theodosius, divided into two parts, is governed by women. From the very beginning of the century feminine influence had been paramount in Byzantium. Arcadius, the son of Theodosius, had married a woman of Frankish birth, fair and fierce. Her quarrels with John Chrysostom ended in his death, but not before the struggle had convulsed Constantinople and threatened revolution. The Golden-mouthed could not restrain his denunciations of the corruptions of the Byzantine court, thundering out against Eudoxia, even to the length of likening her to Herodias, and himself to the Baptist.

Her family took a very different direction, and were noted for their piety. However, feminine influence did not cease at Byzantium, but became more powerful than ever. Pulcheria entirely ruled her brother Theodosius; and when he married the daughter of the philosopher Leontes, the struggle between these two ladies became desperate, and the Empress had to retire defeated to Jerusalem, a neighbourhood much resorted to by pious ladies of the higher ranks. Her daughter married Valentinian III., who, in the West, was nominally the emperor, but really the puppet of his mother, Placidia, the daughter of Theodosius the Great. The history of Placidia is a commentary on the times. Taken prisoner by the Goths, this Roman princess was carried round Italy in the Gothic camp, and then married to Ataulf, Alaric's brother. He was assassinated, and Placidia was dragged in chains by his murderer. Finally, she was married to Constantius, the general who delivered her from the barbarians; and when, at six years of age, her son became Emperor of the West, she assumed the rule, and maintained it for a quarter of a century.

Thus at the period to which our landmarks point (A.D. 449–50), two women ruled the Roman world. Pulcheria in the East, and Placidia in the West.

The wicked plots of Ætius to undermine and destroy Boniface led to the introduction of the Vandals into Africa. They landed in A.D. 429, a host of fifty thousand men, under the cruel and ambitious Genseric. Boniface found that he had made a terrible mistake, for the Vandals soon showed that they meant to be masters. The Roman general retired into Hippo, where he was consoled by the presence of his friend the celebrated Augustine. The great Bishop expired during the siege. The fate of Africa was decided in a great battle, in which the Romans had to fly, leaving Genseric to complete the conquest at his leisure.

BUT a far greater calamity than any that had preceded was about to befal the whole Empire. The Huns, a Turanian people from Asia, had found a great leader. Although his Tartar features, large head, swarthy complexion, deep-seated small eyes, flat nose, and beardless face gave Attila the appearance of a savage, he was a man of extraordinary ability, and in honour superior to his Christian enemies. He believed himself called to a great devastating mission, and took the name of the Scourge of God. The Scythian and Germanic nations poured over the Eastern Empire; and from the Adriatic to the Euxine the whole land was at once invaded, occupied, and desolated. The imperial armies were vanquished in three successive engagements, and Byzantium was at the mercy of the Hun; being only saved from the ruin that had befallen seventy cities of the Empire by Attila's not understanding how to lay siege to its walls.

Ætius, the former general of the Empress Placidia, having found a refuge among the Huns, now appeared in the Western Empire at the head of sixty thousand barbarians, and solicited pardon. Forgiven and reinstated, he assumed the imperial authority in everything but the name, made a treaty with Genseric the Vandal, helped the British, maintained the imperial authority in Gaul, and kept on the best terms with the Huns. A quarrel now broke out between Theodoric, the King of the Spanish Visigoths, and Genseric, the Vandal. Theodoric had entered into an alliance with Ætius, who was to supply the Goths with arms, ships, and treasures for the African war. The Franks of the Lower Rhine were just then divided between the claims of two of their long-haired princes, Meroveus, who was supported by Rome, and his elder brother, who was the ally of Attila.

Suddenly the King of the Huns announced his intention of coming to the help of his friends the Vandals and the Franks. Accordingly in 451 he marched to the confluence of the Rhine and the Neckar. From this point the Huns and the Franks poured in myriads into Gaul, fixing their camp under the walls of Orleans. Ætius and Theodoric now appeared. Attila raised the siege, and made his way to the plains of Chalons. Here the contending hosts fought; and if the number of the slain be at all near the truth, then the numbers engaged are not to be paralleled. Theodoric was slain, but the Visigoths triumphed, and the approach of the night only saved Attila from total defeat.

In the spring of the following year Attila invaded Italy. He appeared before Aquileia, which he reduced and destroyed. As he passed through Italy his trail was marked by a line of fire and blood. It was a favourite saying with Attila that the grass never grew on the spot where his horse had trod. At last he approached Rome.

It was only forty-two years since the sack of Rome by Alaric, and the horrors of that time were fresh in the recollection of many. Old people would have often referred to that awful time, when the streets of Rome were filled with dead bodies; and in the greater houses there must have been a vivid recollection of the fear lest the slaves should take the opportunity of revenging themselves on their masters. Marks of the destroyer were visible all around: pedestals without statues, ruined arches, broken vases; and public rumour could tell of palace after palace which had been sacked of the treasury of generations. One blackened ruin, the palace of Sallust, still remained to testify to the terrible work of Alaric the Goth. But a worse enemy was at their gates. Alaric professed Christianity, but Attila was a pagan, and bore the awful name of the Scourge of God. They could not fail to connect that name with their own unworthiness, they could not fail to believe that the wrath of God was being manifested against a world that professed the truth in unrighteousness; and if they did fail, there were many excellent Christians in Rome who would not allow them to do so. In their terror and their sorrow, in their utter hopelessness of any human assistance, the people turned towards the man who represented God in their midst—the Pope Leo. He was not only brave, but had ever shown himself skilful in the management of men. People remembered that when the Roman generals Ætius and Albinus quarrelled, it was Leo who composed their differences; and now all Rome implored him to go forth and appease the Scourge of God. Although Leo was undoubtedly as brave as his name, he had that inward shrinking from effort which often accompanies true greatness. We may well believe that the words with which he expressed his feeling on hearing that he was raised to the bishopric of Rome were just those with which he would contemplate so great a task as facing the terrible Attila:

"Lord, I have heard Thy voice calling me, and I was afraid: I considered the work which was enjoined me, and I trembled. For what proportion is there between the burden assigned me and my weakness, this elevation and my weakness? . . . O Thou who hast laid upon me this heavy burden, bear it with me, I beseech Thee: be Thou my guide and my support: give me strength, Thou who hast called me to this work: who hast laid this heavy burden on my shoulders."

Accompanied by men who had filled the old Roman dignities of Consul and Prefect, the most eminent representative of the New Society went forth to save the city of the Cæsars from its terrible foe. Could Julian have foreseen that day, well might he have exclaimed, "O Galilean! Thou hast conquered."

Attila's camp was at the foot of Lake Benacus, now called Lago di Garda. Leo, like so many of his episcopal brethren, had a profound reverence for Virgil; and it could not fail to add poignancy to his grief to see the land sacred to the Muse of the greatest of the Latin poets trodden down by Scythian hordes.

The Scourge of God was impressed by the venerable form and the religious dignity of the chief ruler in Christendom, and he listened placably to the entreaties of one whom he recognised to be a servant of the Most High. Leo pleaded not only for Rome, but for Italy, and was empowered to offer the immense dowry of the Princess Honoria, whose hand the King of the Huns grimly claimed. Attila accepted the terms, and evacuated the country. Rome in its gratitude declared that their Bishop had been directly assisted by the apostles Peter and Paul, who had appeared to the barbaric invader, and threatened him with instant death if he did not listen to their successor; and this myth has been immortalised by the pencil of Raphael.

Attila's work was finished, for returning home he broke a blood-vessel and died. Ætius, the only general who had withstood the Huns, was murdered by Valentinian, while the weak and dissolute murderer fell himself a victim to the revenge of some of the followers of Ætius; and thus ended the last of the Roman Emperors of the race of Theodosius. Thus the avenger of blood pursued the author of the massacre of Thessalonica and the persecutor of Arians and Pagans.

And now the unhappy Empress Eudoxia was compelled to marry the new Emperor, the assassin of her husband. She in despair secretly implored the aid of the King of the Vandals. Nothing loth, Genseric equipped a fleet of Vandals and Moors, and cast anchor at the mouth of the Tiber. The position of Rome was awful: it had no general upon which it could rely, and its own Empress had invited the foe. The people rose, killed Maximus, and threw him into the Tiber, and again implored the intervention of Leo. The Bishop went forth in solemn procession from the gates of Rome to the camp of the haughty and cruel Genseric. He promised to spare the people, to protect the buildings from fire, and not to put captives to the torture; but he had little of the religious awe or the nobility of mind that distinguished Attila. Rome and its inhabitants were given over to the licentiousness of his African troops, and Carthage was avenged. For fourteen days and nights the sack went on, and the vessels of the Vandals were loaded with every treasure that they could find. As to the unhappy daughter of the second Theodosius, who had invited this terrible calamity, she was stripped of her jewels, and with her daughters carried to Carthage as the lawful prey of the ruthless Vandal.

From these two overwhelming disasters Rome has never recovered, but has remained for fourteen hundred years a city of ruins. And the fate of Rome is but a picture of what is happening everywhere during this century. Goth, Vandal, Hun, Frank and Saxon, all the new untried races have fallen like a flock of vultures on the dying Roman Empire. Ruin came so completely that many great and populous cities disappeared so entirely that their very sites have become doubtful.

LEFT to themselves, the Romanised Britons had sought to rule and defend themselves. But the civilisation of Rome had no real power. It gave an outward polish, it could produce an admirable system of police, rendering life, property, and justice tolerably secure, but it could not make men or patriots. So when its military power failed, its work came down with a crash.

The Britons, without any Roman legions to defend them against the Picts and Scots, began to imitate the example set at Rome and Byzantium, and to pay barbarian to fight barbarian. It was a ruinous policy anywhere, and in Britain turned out worst of all. The allies the Britons sought lived at the base of the Danish peninsula, in the provinces now known as Schleswick-Holstein and Jutland, and were called Angles, Saxons and Jutes, according to the particular province from whence they came. They were distinguished by great independence of spirit. Bound only by the customs of his tribe, each man went where he pleased, and did what he pleased. Nothing was so agreeable to these people as to shed blood and to plunder; nothing so hateful as to stay at home, lead a quiet and peaceful life, and die in their beds.

These men accepted the invitation of the British, and the first detachment arrived in A.D. 449, four years earlier than Attila appeared before Rome. They landed at Ebbsfleet, in the Isle of Thanet, under two leaders more or less mythic, the celebrated Hengist and Horsa. Once in the country, the Angles began to show their determination to be masters. Disputes soon rose over the terms; more and more Saxons arrived, and at last the barbarians felt strong enough to attack the British in a pitched battle, which took place at Aylesford, on the Medway. The Saxons were victorious, massacred every Briton that they caught, and became masters in East Kent. This, henceforth, became the style of their warfare: dispute, battle, victory, extermination. The unhappy Britons had no place of refuge, for the churches, generally respected by Arian Goths, had no sanctity for the worshippers of Odin.

THE same influence at work through the barbaric world, agitating the hearts of all men with some great hope, some undefinable effort to form a new world, filled the hearts of Christians. They too must go forth to war and to conquest. In this chaotic age we see that light that illumines the kingdom of heaven shining on and through Roman imperialism, and Eastern and Western asceticism. Pope Leo illustrates Roman imperialism animated by the new life; in the history of Patrick we see it irradiating the spirit of migratory conquest; in that of Simon Stylites struggling with and piercing through the spirit of fanatical asceticism. The kingdom of heaven was seeking to leaven the whole lump.

Sometime towards the beginning of this century a band of Irish pirates came into the estuary of the Clyde, and making a raid along its shores, carried off a number of captives. Among them was a boy and his two sisters, the children of a man called Calphurnius, said to have been both a Christian deacon and a Roman decurion. Succat, for so the lad was named, soon found himself the slave of an Irish chieftain, one Michul, or Milchu. For the next six years, exposed to the drenching rains and biting frosts of the bleak mountains of North Dalriada, the modern Antrim, Succat kept his master's sheep. In this life of solitude and slavery the influence that was fermenting in the world moved powerfully in his heart. He gave his whole being to God, praying often in the day, and interrupting his sleep in the night, that he might hold communion with his heavenly Friend.

At the end of the six years he made his escape; and after various adventures, in which he was able to show the pagans that his God answered prayer, Succat once more found his parents and his home. But the influences abroad would not allow him to be still, and, animated by the new life, he determined to return again to the land of his captivity, that he might preach the Gospel to the Irish.

"The Divine voice," he says, "frequently admonished me to consider whence I derived the wisdom that was in me, who once knew neither the number of my days nor was acquainted with God; and whence I obtained afterwards so great and salutary a gift as to know and to love God." One night he had a dream, in which he saw a man from Ireland with a number of letters. He gave him one to read, and at the beginning were the words: "The voice of the Irish." As he read it a voice cried, "We entreat thee, holy youth, to come and walk among us."

But it would seem that Patrick thought it necessary to be better instructed in the faith before he undertook his mission, for he appears to have gone to France, and to have passed through the monastic schools of Tours and Auxerre. It is said that Martin, Bishop of Tours, was his uncle; and there seems to have been some relationship. If it were so, then it helps us better to estimate the class of missionary Patrick was—the only kind, probably, fit for the work that he was meditating. Martin of Tours was a Pannonian soldier, who, having felt the power of Christianity, had become a missionary among the Armorican Gauls. His gaunt form, clad in a sheep-skin, his wan face, wild looks, and straggling beard, his fierce eloquence and still fiercer manners impressed the nerveless Roman world with a religious dread, while the pagans looked on with amazement at the daring prophet-like figure, who rushed in a sort of religious fury through the land, destroying their idols, their dolmens, and their sacred trees. His religion became their religion. North-west Gaul became obedient to an ascetic Christianity whose holy places were the cloister and the tomb of Martin of Tours.

Patrick is a figure grander and more shadowy than Martin; but we cannot greatly err in believing that he conducted his mission amongst Celtic tribes, wilder and more heathenish than those in Armorica, in much the same fashion as his friend and teacher. Thus, on his arrival in the country, he is mistaken by a chieftain named Dichu for a pirate leader; but when discovered to be unarmed, the simple pagan explains his inward awe at Patrick's appearance on the ground of a Divine mission. Dichu becomes his convert, and gives him the ground upon which his barn stood. Here the missionary built the celebrated church called *Sabhall Patriac*, the Barn of Patrick.

The apostle does not win his way among these wild, hot-tempered Irishmen by mere gentleness and persuasion, but, like Martin, outrages their beliefs, and by a defiance of their superstitions and of their gods impresses them with a sense of his own superiority. Thus he goes to Tara to a great religious festival, at which King Laoghani and all his tributary chieftains, Druids and Bards, are present. The great act of the festival was the kindling of the sacred fire by the king's own hand; and there was no greater enormity than for anyone to light a fire before the smoke ascended from the palace of Tara. Patrick, regardless of results, erects his tent, and commences to take some food. Of course he is denounced, and the Druids try to arouse the king by telling him that if the stranger's fire is not extinguished, to him will belong the sovereignty of the land. Patrick is brought before the king, and speaks so fearlessly that the king can do nothing. Next day he is again brought before the king; all are impressed, and Patrick has won the day; the youngest brother of the king is converted and baptised.

But all does not go so easily. The demonstrative apostle has many risks, has hairbreadth escapes; but at last the gospel is so generally received that he feels himself strong enough to proceed to the daring act of destroying the great idol Crom-Cruach, on the plain of Magh-Stech. Thus it was clearly Patrick's belief that argument alone would not root up superstition. Its objects must themselves be destroyed. Connected with this incident is a story which well illustrates the character of the man, and the personal devotion he called forth. One of the chieftains vowed to slay him for overthrowing the idol. Oran, Patrick's charioteer, heard of the vow, and when they were passing near the chieftain's fortress he induced his master, on some pretext, to resign to him his place. The chief, casting his javelin with deadly aim at the person he supposed to be Patrick, pierced the faithful Oran, who had thus the satisfaction of saving his master's life by sacrificing his own.

Gradually Patrick rose higher and higher, and became not only in name, but in deed, Bishop of Ireland. Once a Welsh prince named Coroticus, a professor of Christianity, made a raid on Ireland, and carried off some of Patrick's own converts. With what fiery indignation did the old bishop pour out his wrath on the marauder, threatening him with the greatest of penalties—excommunication—if he did not forsake his piratical habits! To daring courage Patrick united a simple, pictorial manner of preaching, of which we have an example in his well-known illustration of the Trinity from a sprig of trefoil. Instead of falling a prey to the heathen, as so many a less daring missionary has done, Patrick founded a church, from whence sprang such a host of learned and holy persons that Erin gained the name of Isle of Saints.

FROM Hibernia to Syria is to measure at one bound the limits of Christendom in the fifth century, and to see illustrated the all-penetrating power of the kingdom of heaven, arousing into action the most opposite forms of human temperament and human thought. As Martin and Patrick illustrate the wild energy of the West, Simon Stylites is an extreme example of the mysticism of the East. As the former had the conquering energy and joyous courage of Western pirates, the latter was kin in thought and action to the Indian fakeer. Yet through this strange figure shone a gleam of heavenly light; and his courageous contempt of every possible comfort was a most striking protest against the fearfully seductive luxury of such a city as Antioch. If pen might describe with plain, unvarnished truth the scenes that had publicly gone on in that city, if it were possible to English Christians to understand the nature of these Syrians, who for ages had been worshippers of the most polluting of all religions, then should we understand why an earnest Christian, profoundly ignorant, and therefore entirely under the peculiarities of his age and race, would make this extraordinary protest against all indulgence to the weakness of the flesh. Like the acts of Martin and Patrick, the life of Simon only produced religious awe; his fellow-countrymen saw nothing mad or preposterous in his living like a stork on a pillar sixty feet high. Learned bishops thought it right to test his sincerity and humility by commanding him to come down and live as other men; but when they found that he was ready to do so, they permitted him to continue his singular life, only taking pains to put a rail round the pillar, and to shelter him with some awning.

Simon commenced life as a poor shepherd in Paul's own country, Cilicia. At thirteen his heart was much moved by hearing the Beatitudes read at church, "Blessed are they that mourn; blessed are the pure in heart." He longed to know how he could attain this happiness; but there was no Paul to teach him the way. Instead, he was instructed in the lore against which the apostle so much contended; and in his earnestness he became the most striking example of where justification by works leads. Far be it from us to deride this weary seeker after holiness! By the intensity of his efforts we may measure the intensity of his soul. Simon was no madman, but one who felt in the profoundest depths of his being the awful impurity of his race. Fallen into darkness, he exemplified the hopelessness of his method, yet was he a great and terrible sign. But it was too late, as the next century will plainly show.

SIXTH CENTURY.

CONTEMPORARY EVENTS IN THE SIXTH CENTURY.

Italy.—Brutal manners of the Lombards.
England.—Anglo-Saxon slaves in Rome.
France.—A Merovingian punishment.
Scotland.—Columba's prayer.

Sixth Century.

A.D. 561-580.

A New Europe—The Teutons—The Merovingians—Their Crimes—Punishment of a Merovingian Prince—The Lombards—Alboin's Victories and Cruelty—Gregory's Desire to Convert the Anglo-Saxons—Columba, the Apostle of Scotland.

HE scythe of war had passed again and again over the old world, hordes of savage feet had trodden down what remained, and now it suffered under long-continued pestilence. At one period as many as ten thousand persons died each day at Constantinople; but though this extreme malignity gradually abated, the plague continued active in the East, along the coast of Africa, and over the continent of Europe for no less than fifty-two years (A.D. 542-594).

Among the ruins of this dying world the new earth began to appear. In the temples the Cæsars had built, the lizard and the toad, the spider and the ant, were now the sole inhabitants. Sometimes a grotto or a fountain were seen, but the nymphs and the fawns had fled, and all to be heard there was the song of birds, the rush of some forest creature, or the sullen roar of a beast of prey.

Such was especially the condition of England and the border-lands of the Empire, once well-nigh as civilised as Rome itself. At Byzantium, and in the region which still called itself the Roman Empire, the same condition of things existed. There are still spaces where civilisation lives on, where culture is preserved; but every year the wilderness encroaches, and the cities are becoming smaller.

There are souls in these oases, there are souls in the wilderness that cannot bear the sight. Inward voices speak to them, angels beckon to them, "Go win this wilderness to the Lord." Has He not said that "the desert shall rejoice and blossom as the rose"?

History relates the story of many heroes who, in the spirit of aggressive patriotism, went to win new realms for the glory of Rome; but what are they to the heroes who, in the midst of this moral ruin, despaired not of this spiritual republic, but in the might of the Holy Ghost stood up bravely for the kingdom of heaven, and determined not only to maintain its conquests, but to add new ones to its realms? Meed of praise, then, for men who, like Gregory of Rome and Gregory of Tours, maintained, according to their light, the law of righteousness.

Let those who dream of Saxons or of Franks as races of Nature's nobility, who see all virtue in the Teuton, all vice in the Roman, study the annals of this century, and they will see that the contrast lay not so much in moral worth, but rather that the Roman belongs to the dead world of the past, the Teuton to a world just born.

In the Roman Empire there is ever the disciplined army to restrain and oppose the Teuton and the slave; and even when it fails, its prestige is awe-inspiring—the mere shadow of the Empire fills savage hearts with terror. But in Britain, where the legions are known to have gone for ever, where the very signs of Roman authority have disappeared, where the sea cuts off the unfortunate inhabitants from succour, the Teutonic pirates know no mercy. Mercy was not in them, and battle and rapine were their very breath. The Saxons well-nigh exterminated the Britons.

In their kindred, the Franks in Gaul, the same qualities are exemplified. Take the story of Clother and his four sons, and where in human records can we find a series of more brutal tales? Moreover, these long-haired princes were not just fresh from the savage wilds of their own forests, but half-tamed, baptised Christians, owning obedience to the laws of the kingdom of heaven.

Clother dies, and his four sons have no sooner buried him, than the third, Hilperik, posts away to Braine, the royal farm, near Soissons, that he may secure the treasury. The other three unite, and Hilperik has to submit and take only his portion. He becomes King of Neustria, Neoster-rike; Sigebert has Austrasia; Haribert, Paris; Gonthramn, Orleans.

Hilperik is the prototype of our Henry the Eighth; coarse, humorous, overbearing, selfish, intellectual, freethinking, theological; at once a ruffian and a coward. He is married, but, like all his race, has many mistresses. One of the women, Fredegonda, of Frankish origin, plays a part in the history of the day which matches that of the worst of Roman or Oriental women. A domestic in the house of Andowera, Queen of Hilperik, she outwits her simple mistress, and supplants her in Hilperik's graces. But one of the brothers, Sigebert, has married a real princess, Brunehilda, daughter of Athanagild, King of the West Goths. Hilperik must have her sister, the gentle Galeswintha. He promises to reform his life and to treat her with the greatest kindness, if he can only obtain a woman so worthy his hand. Athanagild is a statesman, and would sacrifice his daughter; his Queen, Goïswintha, is a mother, and weeps over her child. The gentle girl is almost dragged to Gaul; her mother cannot make up her mind to leave her, but travels with her for more than a hundred miles. Every day she said, "I will go so far;" and still she went farther. "Know you," she cried, "that where they are carrying my daughter there will be no mother for her?" And when at last the Gothic nobles refused to allow their Queen to proceed another mile, she parted from the weeping bride, saying, "I tremble for thee; take care, my child, take care!"

Her forebodings were too true. The wily Fredegonda had submitted with the most docile obedience, begging only that she might be allowed to retain her old place as a servant. King Hilperik was very pleased with his new wife; he was vain of her grandeur, and highly gratified with the money and valuables that she had brought him. But when the first fascination wore off, Galeswintha's moral beauty, her humility and charity, had no charms for the coarse-minded Frank. The treacherous Fredegonda saw her opportunity. Galeswintha wept silently, and begged to be divorced; but one morning she is found strangled in her bed.

The Queen of Sigebert of Austrasia hears the news. As proud and vindictive as her sister was gentle and timid, Brunehilda urges her husband to revenge. Sigebert summons his brother to answer for the murder. Hilperik is cited to appear in a solemn council of the three kingdoms called the Malberg. The trial takes place before Gonthramn, King of Orleans, who sits on a high seat, with the principal chiefs and great proprietors on a low bench before him. Hilperik comes into court, but does not seek to defend himself. Gonthramn adjudges him guilty, condemning him to pay to Brunehilda the *morgengabe* of his murdered wife—namely, the cities of Bordeaux, Limoges, Cahors, Bearn, and Bigowe.

But Hilperik has no intention of really making expiation, and waits a favourable opportunity to seize something in exchange for the towns he has had to surrender. Tours and Poitiers seem good prey, and he takes them. War ensues, and Sigebert makes Hilperik give up Tours and Poitiers, and forgives him, to the great discontent of his army, bent only on plunder. Hilperik soon resumes his evil conduct, and this time his brother is so enraged that he wishes to fight him in single combat, and to put him to death. However, all Sigebert can do is to blockade him, and to wait until he falls into his hands. Then Fredegonda comes to her husband's relief. She calls two young Franks, plies them with strong liquor, gives them each a long knife in a sheath, and bids them go and murder Sigebert. They profess to be deserters, are allowed to see the King of Austrasia, and both at the same time draw their knives and stab him.

Brunehilda is in despair, but determined to preserve her little son. She lets him down at night from her palace in a basket, and a friendly arm bears the precious burden out of the town by night. The little prince is taken to Metz, and, in a great assembly of the Austrasian nobles and warriors, proclaimed King Hildebert the Second. Brunehilda, with her daughters, now falls into the hands of Hilperik, who is so delighted at all the fine things he has obtained by the murder of his brother that he does not trouble himself about his chief foe. Meanwhile the captive Queen observes that her beauty and misfortunes have made an impression on Merovig, Hilperik's son and heir. To serve her own ends, she encourages the prince, and the affair ends in a clandestine marriage. The priest who was willing to brave the authority of both the Church and the King was the bridegroom's godfather, Prætextus, Bishop of Rouen—since canonised, notwithstanding his contempt for canon law.

The couple have to fly, take sanctuary in a church, are wheedled out of it, then separated, Merovig being put in prison. After the prince has been some months in captivity, Fredegonda, who hates all her step-children, induces her husband to inflict a punishment on his son which amounted to disinheritance. Merovig's long floating hair, the sign of his royalty, was cut off, and he was left with a head cropped as close as that of a Roman and a priest. However, he was probably consoled by the family saying, "The wood is still green, the leaves will shoot forth again."

The young Frank had all the impulsive passion of a savage. Freed by the courage of some of his own vassals from the prison to which his father meant to send him, he clad himself in a warrior's dress, only covering his shorn head with a hood, and fled to Tours. There he rushed into the church, where mass was going on. He sat down near the door when they were distributing the holy bread to the congregation after the Eucharist, and the deacons in mistake passed by the hooded stranger. Marching straight up the aisle to where Gregory sat clothed in his pontifical robes, the prince said, in an excited tone, and crimson with rage, "Bishop, why are not the elogies given to me as to the rest of the faithful? Tell me if I am excommunicated." Bishop Gregory tried to calm the angry man, but it was no use, for he burst out saying, "If you dare on your own authority to treat me as an excommunicated person I will act as such, and kill some one on the spot."

It is not surprising that a character of this sort fell an easy prey to the snares of Fredegonda. After a time she contrived so to drive him to despair that he was fain to ask a faithful vassal to kill him. The man obeyed, and his too faithful loyalty was rewarded by the most barbarous death; his feet, hands, nose and ears were cut off, while another companion of the unhappy prince was broken alive on the wheel.

Fredegonda is not yet satisfied. Like some human tigress she pursues everyone who has in the least offended her. Such an one was the Bishop Prætextus, who had dared to pronounce a blessing on the marriage of Merovig and Brunchilda. He is cited before a council, held under the presidency of a truculent Frankish bishop, Berthramn of Bordeaux, and is finally worried into throwing himself on the King's mercy. He is deposed and driven into exile, from whence, however, when Hilperik himself falls a victim to the treachery of Fredegonda, and is assassinated, Prætextus comes back.

This Jezebel does not long leave the Bishop in peace. She plots with his clergy, and finally hires assassins to murder him in his church as he kneels in prayer. When he lies dying she has the insolence to pay him a visit of condolence. Prætextus gathers up his strength to tell the Queen that for centuries she will be an object of execration, and that Divine justice will avenge his blood on her head. However, that does not happen in this world, for every attempt to bring her to an account fails. A Frank who had the daring to go to the palace and denounce her is inveigled and poisoned.

Finally, Fredegonda comes to her end in peace, while Brunchilda, incomparably the better woman, is always in difficulties. Being proud and rash, she drives her son's vassals into such a state of desperation that they give her up to Clother II., son of Fredegonda; and he takes the aged enemy of his mother—then nearly eighty years old—ties her to the tails of two wild horses, which tear her to death.

The Frankish atrocities just related took place A.D. 561-578, during the progress of the Saxon conquest of Britain. The Roman towns all over Britain were in flames, so that nothing remained but ruins to tell the tale. We have seen how Roman Gaul was turning into Teutonic France, how Roman Britain was quickly made into England; and now, at the very same time, Northern Italy is becoming Lombardy, while in the East of Europe appear for the first time the Turks. The fifth century is the springtime of modern Europe; the nations that are to make its future history are in the bud.

CONTEMPORANEOUSLY with the tragedies going on in the house of Clother, events of a similar nature are occurring among the Lombards, also a Teutonic race. With their long battle-axes the Lombards had fought their way from the Lower Elbe to the Danube, and had become masters of Pannonia. Their king, Alboin, was contracted to a Merovingian princess, but having seen Rosamund, daughter of Cunimond, King of the Gepidæ, he demanded her hand. Cunimond, however, refused him, whereupon he entered into an alliance with the Avars, a race related to the Huns, fell on the Gepidæ, defeated and almost exterminated them, killed Cunimond, and made a drinking-cup of his skull (A.D. 566). Whether Rosamund could not help herself, or whether, as is not improbable, she rather admired the fierce wooing of her lover, she was married to the brutal and passionate savage. However, Alboin knew how to lead his followers, and having whetted their appetite for conquest by the slaughter of the Gepidæ, he brought them into Italy. The degenerate inhabitants allowed him to conquer the whole of the country from the Alps to the Apennines without a battle or a siege. The only city that was defended was Ticinum, or Pavia, and when that fell Alboin made it his capital (A.D. 567). But before the conqueror had time to regulate his new kingdom, he fell the victim of a domestic conspiracy. Intoxicated with the wine of his fertile domain, he one day called for the skull of Cunimond. The cup of victory was brought amidst the thundering roars of the drunken chiefs. "Fill it to the brim!" cried the drunken Lombard; "take the goblet to the Queen, and bid her in my name rejoice with her father." Rosamund sipped from the horrid cup, and cursed the monster who compelled her to so vile an act. Ere long she took her revenge. One day when the King was heavy from drink, she admitted her lover and another warrior into the room where he was lying, and urged them to kill him. When Alboin was attacked he half rose and tried to draw his sword, but his wife had already rendered that impossible; he seized a stool, but the assassins had spears, and the conqueror of Italy was quickly despatched while Rosamund stood exulting over his fate (A.D. 577).

From these examples we may judge the character of the new peoples who by sheer force had supplanted the old. It was a new form of human nature, possessing new characteristics. The chief of these characteristics was the importance attached to the individual, the family, the tribe. Ages of vagabond life had impressed on these Teutonic peoples the value of a settled habitation. To become at last rooted in the soil, to have a certain dwelling-place, an assured food and shelter, seemed to these wanderers the great object of life. Only the landed proprietor was the true freeman. He alone was king upon earth, and the master of himself. All others were the slaves of those stronger powers of Nature.

It was the discovery of the fact that there were untold acres of rich land to be obtained by a little hard fighting that attracted such myriads of these landless Teutons over Europe. Each man came, his whole soul concentrated on the one idea of getting a piece of this precious earth for himself; but to keep it he well understood the necessity of belonging to a society. First and foremost were their own kith and kin; each had sprung from some valiant ancestor. With their uncles, and their brothers, and their cousins they had ever wandered, and with them had made this new migration. These families, all equal, were linked in tribes, following the head of the most powerful family among them. He was always a great warrior, and attained this distinction, first by hereditary descent, but chiefly by the force of his own individuality. Whoever was strongest and wisest in the ruling family became chief of the tribe. These Teutons worshipped Nature, and were her true children, for good or evil. Their society was formed by the Nature in which they lived, moved, and had their being; and there was little in it that contradicted its laws. This is why their appearance in the Roman Empire has all the characteristics of natural phenomena. They sweep like cyclones over vast areas; they devastate like wild and irresistible storms; their appearances are sudden as the wind, and they come from all quarters; yet the stormy spring-time turns into a radiant summer, and the few seeds dropped into the exhausted earth rise up in autumn a wealthy and a noble harvest.

THE centre of the battle was Rome. The bishops were the only hope of a dying Italy. The people called for strong men, and such men were those who first of all knew how to rule themselves. Such a man was Gregory I., who, after Leo I., did more than any pope to strengthen and solidify the Papacy. And at this moment the Papacy was all-important to Europe. For it represented, better than any other institution, a universal Christian civilisation, a faith which regarded all men in Christ as equally dear to God, as brothers and co-heirs of the same liberty. Threatened by the intense individualism, clanship, and tribalism of the conquering power, what would local Churches have become, had the visible Church of the day represented less powerfully the idea of an universal religion?

In Gregory centred all that, in the eyes of his fellow-citizens, was most respectable. He was of noble senatorial family; he had himself attained the dignity of Prætor of the city; a pope had been his ancestor in the fourth degree; his aunts were holy virgins. He had inherited considerable wealth, but had devoted it all to religious uses. His charity was unbounded, his asceticism pushed to the last degree. It was reported that he had been only saved from starving himself to death by compulsory feeding. Finally, he gave away the last bit of property he possessed—a silver vessel that he had preserved for the use of his mother. His monastery was surrounded in popular esteem by an atmosphere of wonder-working.

Gregory ruled his monks as he ruled himself. He was stern to cruelty. A physician who had attended him in his illness with affectionate solicitude entered his monastery. On his death-bed Justus confessed to Gregory that he still possessed three pieces of gold. The abbot determined to make him an example. No one might approach the bedside of the dying man, or speak a word of comfort; his brother alone was commissioned to tell him that he died detested by all the community. His body, together with the three pieces of gold, was cast upon a dunghill, the whole convent exclaiming, "Thy money perish with thee!" and it was only after thirty days of fiery burnings that Gregory permitted mass to be said for his soul.

There is nothing really out of harmony with the character of the man capable of this almost incredible sternness in the oft-repeated story of the way in which Gregory was first led to desire to be the instrument in converting our ancestors. His Christianity, as that of the age, was militant; and these Romans of the higher classes were generals by nature. His desire of dominion was elevated by his love of God and of souls; but it remained part of his nature, nevertheless.

Deira and Bernicia, two of the new Saxon kingdoms, were always at war, and some pretty little captives from the territory of the former had been brought to the slave-market at Rome. Poor little creatures, more unhappy than orphans, they stood exposed for sale. Gregory asked from whence they came. "Britain." "Are they still pagans? Alas, that the prince of darkness should possess forms of such loveliness!" He asked their nation. "Angles." "Truly they are angels," he said. "From what province do they come?" "Deira." "They must be rescued from De Ira," he went on, with his quaint punning. "Who is their king?" "Ælla." "Alleluia!" he exclaimed. "Alleluia must be sung in his dominions."

The abbot was so in earnest that he went to the pope, and told him that he must go on a mission to preach the Gospel in England. The pope unwillingly consented; but the people would not hear of it. Gregory had only got three days' journey from Rome when he was pursued. The people, no doubt, thought of him as their future pope, and were unwilling that his life should be wasted on a people for whom they had nothing but loathing.

But the spirit that moved Gregory was rising fast in the Churches; and ere long the missionary spirit became the chief characteristic of the new society. At present it was outside the Roman Church that the finest examples of it were found.

As in the previous century a native of Caledonia became the instrument of winning pagan Ireland to the faith of Christ, so now a native of the isle of Erin carries the Gospel to Scotland. What more beautiful example of that reconciliation among the nations which is made by the blood of the cross? Patrick and Columba are exalted instances of that heavenly citizenship, that membership of a Divine kingdom, which was now to struggle with a selfish, grasping society, whose noblest ideas were founded on self-love, whose highest idea of self-sacrifice was to die for one's kith and kin.

Columba possessed this feeling intensely. The spirit of clanship is strong in him. It is the first source of his sorrows, for it is to them he runs in his anger at an adverse sentence of King Diarmid, arousing them to do battle on his behalf; an act of vindictiveness for which he falls under censure, and in expiation of which he is condemned to perpetual exile. How his heart ever mourns after his dear old home!

> Were all the tribute of Scotia mine,
> From its midland to its borders,
> I would give all for one little cell
> In my beautiful Derry. . . .
> My Derry, my fair oak grove,
> My dear little cell and dwelling.
> O God in the heavens above!
> Let him who profanes it be cursed!
> Beloved are Durrow and Derry,
> Beloved is Raphoe the pure,
> Beloved the fertile Drumhome,
> Beloved are Sords and Kells!
> But sweeter and fairer to me
> The salt sea where the sea-gulls cry.
> When I come to Derry from far,
> It is sweeter and dearer to me,
>   Sweeter to me.

And this dear little cell at Derry the bard and lover of old writings had to leave, through his obstinate love of a manuscript that he had copied out by night in the church. His vindictiveness, leading to the death of so many of his countrymen, was deeply sorrowed over, and led to a thorough conversion, so that he became little by little the gentlest and sweetest of human beings.

But he had to leave the land of which he passionately said, "Death in faultless Ireland is better than life without end in Albyn." He tells his relatives, "An angel has taught me that I must leave Ireland, and remain an exile as long as I live, because of all those whom ye slew in the last battle which you fought on my account, and also in another which you know of." And as he goes he exclaims, "The noble sea now carries me to Albyn, the land of ravens. My foot is in my little boat, but my sad heart bleeds. There is a grey eye which ever turns to Erin; but never in this life shall it see Erin, nor her sons, nor her daughters . . . My heart is broken in my breast. If death comes to me suddenly, it will be because of the great love I bear the Gael."

With twelve companions, in their long osier boat covered with leather, Columba came to the Hebrides, but would not settle until he had found a little island from whence he could not see the shores that filled him with such intolerable craving. At last he established his little colony at Iona; and from that humble monastery went forth in all directions such streams of life that before Columba died he had founded one hundred and fifty kindred institutions in various parts of Scotland. Traces of fifty-three remain, thirty-two of which are found in the Western Isles and the country occupied by the Irish Scots, while twenty-five mark the stations of his labours among the Picts. The former were to some extent his own people, and already Christianised; the latter, who lived to the north and east of the Grampians, were originally a Scythian people, and the ancestors of the Highlanders. Columba was the first to preach the Gospel to them, and his mild but forceful manner won him a rapid way among the barbarians. Even their Druids offered him but little opposition, and were awed by his presence and manner.

The secret of Columba's power lay in prayer. He was one of the most prayerful men that ever lived, and in the exercise of this pure and simple power he wrought many wonders; wonders, no doubt, exaggerated and distorted by popular legend, but which were most real.

Living in an archipelago of islands, and amidst friths and forths, his monks lived almost as much on sea as land. Their risks were often great, and Columba's heart, rendered sensitive by prayer, was ever with his children. He seemed to know whenever they were in danger. Suddenly he would have the bell of the monastery rung and the monks summoned. Columba knew that certain brethren were in danger; and he and the whole community would remain imploring the Lord with tears to help the distressed mariners, not rising from their knees until the leader knew for certain that their prayers were granted. This often happened; and the saved ones returned to testify to their escape, and to thank him for the aid he had thus obtained.

These stories of his prevision of the trouble into which his friends had fallen are so numerous and peculiar that it is certain that they rest on a solid groundwork of fact. Whatever happened, his remedy was always the same. By prayer he reconciled husbands and wives, and restored health to their children.

The Mor-maer, or chief of the district now known as Buchan, refused to permit Columba and his missionaries a place on his lands. His son fell dangerously ill, and he hasted after the missionaries, offering them land for their church if they would pray for his boy. They prayed, and the youth recovered. Columba left Doostan to carry on the work, who, when he learnt that he was to be separated from his master, shed many tears. For not only the monks of Iona, but all kinds of people, old and young, had the profoundest reverence for Columba, so great were his care and unremitting zeal on their behalf. Even over animals he exerted a strange and powerful influence. This great and noble figure rises like another Elijah from among the mists and clouds of old Caledonia, consoling the poor, and bringing them blessings in return for their hospitality. The bearer of all kinds of joy to their humble dwellings, in their defence he was capable of a wrath that carried with it the Divine vengeance.

Thus a certain princely riever had three times landed and robbed a poor friend of Columba. Laden with spoil he met Columba, who entreated him to restore his booty, and not ruin the man. It was useless; the pirate made his way to the sea, and placed his booty in the boat. As he was about to make off, the apostle plunged into the water, and, laying hold of the boat, made a final appeal to the sea-king's mercy. The pirates pushed off, and left the old man with his arms uplifted to heaven. Returned to the shore, Columba told the people that he who thus disregarded Christ in His servants should never more land upon the shore from whence he set out, but that a tempest should swallow him up, and not one on board his vessel live to tell the tale. And so it happened, for a storm gathered between Mull and Colonsay, from whence the crew and all their spoils were seen to sink and perish.

How was society founded in the British Isles? Who planted it in the Rock of Ages, giving it a life and progressive force which it otherwise never could have had? Did the Kings of Tara? or the wild tribes of Picts and Scots? Was it Hengist and Horsa, and the customs they and their followers brought from Jutland? All these varied tribes—Gaelic or Saxon—would have finally exhausted themselves in endless wars, or would at least have remained barbarians little more advanced than the hordes of Central Asia, had it not been for men like Patrick and Columba, Augustine and Paulinus. These are the true founders of the British nation and of British society.

Columba was the first to found a Christian state in Scotland. When Aïdan was chosen King of Scotia, Columba, though his friend, opposed his election. An inward voice declared the choice a right one, and bid the abbot consecrate the new king, which according to Scottish national tradition he did, Aïdan being seated on the Stone of Destiny; and on this same stone the subsequent kings were inaugurated, until Edward I. carried it away to Westminster, where it remains beneath the British coronation chair.

Once, but on a solemn occasion, Columba returned to Ireland. A parliament was to be held at Drumceat, in Ulster, not very far from where he had embarked, and from his dear monastery of Derry. The question to be settled was the position in which the new King of Scotia stood to the King of Ireland, with regard to his hereditary patrimony, which lay in the latter country. Columba was asked to settle the difficulty, but on his refusal, Colman, another monk, decided for the absolute independence and freedom from all tribute of the Albanian Scots.

Columba, however, had another cause to plead—that of his friends the Bards, who in many ways had made themselves obnoxious to the kings and nobles of Ireland. The new king wanted to abolish the order altogether, but yielded to the eloquent expostulations of Columba, on condition that the Bards were limited and placed under rules to be determined by Columba himself.

At last this true prophet of his people came to die. He knew, it is said, four years before that his end was near, and on the day he died, a Saturday, he said to his attendant, "This very night I shall enter into the paths of my fathers. Thou weepest, dear Diarmid, but console thyself; it is the Lord Jesus Christ who deigns to invite me to rejoin Him; it is He who has revealed to me that my summons will come to-night."

As they went on their way the old man stopped to rest at a spot still pointed out. At this moment his old white horse came towards him, and put his head on his shoulder, as if it wished to bid its master a last farewell. The poor brute's eyes wore a most pathetic expression. Diarmid was too occupied with his own thoughts, and would have driven the horse away. "The horse loves me," said Columba; "leave him with me, let him weep for my departure. The Creator has revealed to this poor animal what He has hidden from thee, a reasonable man." Then putting his arms round the horse, he gave the faithful animal his last blessing.

This done, Columba climbed a little hillock, where he could see the whole isle with its monastery, and pronounced upon it a prophetic benediction. When he reached home he tried to go on with his work of transcribing the Psalter, but he was fatigued, and said, "Baithen will write the rest." Then he sat down on the naked stones which had served him so many years for bed and pillow, and entrusted to his only companion a last message of peace and charity to his dear monks. As soon as the midnight bell rung for matins for the Sunday festival, he rose and made his way in the dark to the altar of the chapel. There he was found by his faithful attendant, lying before the altar. Diarmid lifted Columba's head upon his knees, and called for lights. The whole community were soon gathered in deep affliction round their dying father, who, with a face full of radiant joy, looked first on one side and then on the other. He tried, with the help of Diarmid, to raise his hand to bless them, but it dropped, and the last sigh came from his lips, his face wearing the inexpressible sweetness and calm of one who in sleep has beheld a heavenly vision.

SEVENTH CENTURY.

CONTEMPORARY EVENTS IN THE SEVENTH CENTURY.

Arabia.—Ali recognises Mohammed's claim to be THE Prophet of God.
England.—The Witanagemot of Northumbria discussing the truth of the Christian religion.
Rome.—Phocas, Emperor of the East, recognises the claim of the pope to be universal bishop.
China.—Nestorian missionaries preaching the Gospel in China.

Seventh Century.

A.D. 607-636.

The Eastern Church—Nestorian Mission in China—Corruption of Christianity—Asceticism—Image Worship—Veneration of Relics and of the Clergy—Pope Recognised as Universal Bishop—Mohammed—His Recognition as Prophet of God—Mohammedanism—Triumphs of Christianity in England—Paulinus and Northumbria.

F the salt have lost its savour, wherewith shall it be seasoned? It is neither fit for the land, nor yet for the dunghill, but men cast it out." At the beginning of this century, Christendom had reached such a point of degeneracy that it would not have been difficult for any true seer to predict its coming fall.

The Jews had been found unworthy to be the instrument of the kingdom of heaven; the Greek world proved still less deserving. Antioch was the first city illumined by its light, and Antioch was the capital of Syria, a land whose religious traditions were the most dangerous on the face of the earth. All around Syria were regions long under the influence of religious subtleties: the Greek cities of Asia Minor, the Magian lands of Persia and Babylonia, the schools of Alexandria. Wherever the new spiritual influence came it aroused new thought and conscience; and those Oriental speculations that had taken generations of philosophers, many ages, and varied religions to evolve, all came springing up again, full of new life, in the minds of the Christian philosophers of cities like Ephesus, Antioch, and Alexandria.

To think of God rather than man, to speculate on His nature rather than do His will—this was peculiarly characteristic of the Eastern world; and this disposition, so wide-spread and deeply engrained, now fastened itself on the Gospel, and found in it abundant material.

The nature of Jesus Christ was a favourite subject of discussion from the first. Cerinthus and the apostolic Church of Ephesus had their minds full of questions as to His Divinity and His humanity, their nature and their relations. In the next century came the Sabellians with their view, followed by Arius with the extreme opposite, arousing one of the fiercest theological struggles ever known. Arius and Athanasius contend like two stars of the first magnitude, drawing in their train not only the smaller stars, but suns, planets, constellations. Athanasius finally conquers, but not until the strife has agitated whole nations and ranged them into opposite camps.

Even the defeat of Arius and the decrees of the Council of Nice could not stop the ineradicable desire of the mind of man to think for itself, and to believe according to the inner light; for in the next century Nestorius and Eutyches maintained opposing views of the same subject. Nestorius was Bishop of Constantinople, and taught that there were not simply two natures in Christ, but two persons: the Man Jesus and the Son of God, that Mary therefore was not the Mother of God, but of the Man Jesus. Cyril of Alexandria vigorously opposed this view, and procured its condemnation at the Council of Ephesus in A.D. 431. However, the view held by Nestorius pleased the Eastern mind, familiar with the Persian principle of Dualism; and six days after the Council of Ephesus, forty-one Oriental bishops, headed by the Patriarch of Constantinople, held another Council, in which they excommunicated Cyril. In the end, Nestorius gave his name to an important branch of the Eastern Church, which sympathised with his doctrine, and even more with his sufferings as a confessor against the interference of the popes of Rome and Alexandria.

That the peculiar view they held was the result of their Persian tradition is further proved by the fact that when the Emperor Zeno (A.D. 477–491) called upon all Christian sects to forget their dissensions and subscribe the Henoticon, or articles of faith, Barsumus, Bishop of Nisibis, placed himself under the protection of Firouz, King of Persia; and some of the earliest of the Chaldean or Nestorian bishoprics are found to have been established in that land. Babæus, Bishop of Seleucia or Ctesiphon, was the first to declare himself openly in favour of the Nestorian sect; and from his accession may be dated the first recognised establishment of the Nestorian Church and the promulgation of its doctrines in Asia. Cosmas Indicopleustes, who visited Asia in the early part of the sixth century, says that the Nestorians had representatives in India, Arabia Felix and Socotra—bishops, martyrs, and priests—and that they had even penetrated as early as the fifth century into China.

THE statements of this early traveller have been confirmed by the discovery, in 1625, of a remarkable inscription in the walls of the city of Se-gan-foo. This inscription, generally allowed to be authentic, proves that a Christian mission of some importance reached China in the early part of the seventh century, establishing not only a Christian Church, but in a certain portion of the country a Christian state. The inscription purports to be composed by a bonze of the Temple of Taçin, and contains not only a history of the origin of the mission, and the names and titles of the missionaries, but a short account of the tenets and ceremonies they preached and practised.

The leader of the mission is described as a man of shining virtue, a native of Taçin, named Olopen. Having observed the heavens and paid attention to the winds, Olopen, it says, brought the true Scriptures to China. In the ninth year of Chim-Kuan (A.D. 635), he arrived at Se-gan-foo, and was met in great state by a minister of the Empire, Fam-hivin-lim, who, by order of the Emperor, brought him to the palace. In the Hall of Books Olopen began to translate the Scriptures. When the Emperor heard their doctrine, he declared that it ought to be published, and he promulgated an edict to the following effect:—"The doctrine has no limited name, the Holy One has no limited substance; He institutes religions according to lands, and takes, in crowds, all men into His vessel. Olopen, of the kingdom of Taçin, of rare virtue, bringing the Scriptures and the images, has come to offer them in the Supreme Court. Examining the spirit of this religion, it is mysterious, excellent, peaceable. Reflecting on its venerable origin, it produces the perfect and establishes the necessary. This discourse is free from all tiresome verbiage. Reason throws all past snares into oblivion, and brings all things to an happy end. It is useful to men; it ought to be published throughout the earth. Let those who are in office construct without delay in Canton, called Y. Nien of the Imperial City, a temple of the kingdom of Taçin, and cause twenty-one bonzes to go there."

In these singular expressions we have a glimpse of the way in which the Chinese of the seventh century regarded the doctrine of the kingdom of heaven. What the missionaries actually taught is better told by the account given in the inscription of their faith and practice.

It opens by a declaration of faith in the Triune, the true Lord without beginning, the Elohim. He created the world in the form of a cross. He bestowed on His first men interior peace, but Satan soiled their pure and clean hearts with his lies, whence arose a vast number of sects, who wove a web of false religions, wherein to entangle men. The darkness and misery into which the world fell is well described. Having exhausted all its means of self-help, the Triune came to its relief; the Unity in Trinity communicated its substance to the Messiah. The Messiah hid the true majesty, presenting Himself to man as a man. The heavens rejoiced at His nativity, a woman brought forth the Holy One, a constellation announced His birth; Persia saw the light, and sent Him tribute. He has fulfilled the old laws, and by His precepts regulated families and kingdoms. He has given being to the true faith, opening the way of life and destroying that of death. This great work accomplished, He has shown Truth in full daylight, leaving twenty-seven Scriptures. He has extended the primitive conversion, in order to set free the energy of intelligence. By the washing of water and the Spirit this new law carries away the floating flowers and makes clean the whitened void. Its seal is a cross, which, tying together the four parts of the human race, makes them one. Striking a piece of wood, it causes a voice of love and goodness to sound forth.

It then proceeds to speak of the customs of turning to the east and of the tonsures, and declares that the reason that they do not have slaves is that their religion asserts the equality of all men, and that it will not allow them to accumulate wealth. Fasting is good, if carried on in the spirit; its reality consists in tranquillity and attention. Seven times a day they adore God, but only offer the sacrifice once a week, purifying the heart and returning to simplicity. Finally, it declares that the doctrine without the

Holy One cannot extend itself, and that the Holy One without the doctrine cannot be magnified.

That those who preached this simple doctrine were Nestorians or Chaldean Christians appears from the fact that the inscription contains in the ancient Syriac character seven lists of missionaries who preached the Gospel in China from the year 636, the names being Syriac, Persian, and Chinese. And this is made additionally certain by the nature of the doctrine, as well from the fact of the missionary character of the Nestorian Churches, testified to by Cosmas Indicopleustes.

Thus we find at one and the same time in Caledonia and China, the extreme limits of the known world, a comparatively pure and simple form of Christianity, while all around the Mediterranean Christianity is growing unbearably corrupt. The worship of images, a belief in miracles, in the sanctity of relics and of the priesthood, more and more obscures the apostolic doctrine, while the wilder forms of asceticism are rapidly changing its practice into a form of Indian fakeerism. The pillar-saints continue to flourish. One, who not only adopted the fanaticism of Simon Stylites, but took his name, died in 592. We are not surprised to find that he wrote in favour of image worship.

As examples of the diseased condition of Eastern Christianity, the following may suffice:—Theodosius of Cappadocia, wishing to impress his monks with the idea that the remembrance of death is the foundation of religious perfection, had a great pit dug sufficiently large to bury the whole community. Then he said: "The grave is made; who will first perform the dedication?" A priest, named Basil, fell on his knees, saying, "I am the man; be pleased to give me your blessing." The abbot caused the prayers for the dead to be offered up for him, and in forty days Basil departed in peace. Another man, Simon the Foolish, was so animated with a desire for humiliation that he determined to affect the manners of those who want sense, and to pass for a fool. His biographer says that his love for humility was not without its reward, for he was honoured with the gift of miracles.

Asceticism and voluntary torture had become that which in previous centuries martyrdom had been—the high road to fame. Not only was a great saint mobbed in life, but after death it was necessary to resort to stratagem to preserve his remains. Hilarion, to get away from adoring worshippers, wandered on foot from Syria to the Egyptian desert, across the pathless waste to the Oasis; then to Sicily, to the Adriatic, and at last to a distant island of Greece. Afraid that when he was dead his body would be carried off, he entreated those around him that within an hour of his death they would bury him just as he was—in his haircloth shirt, hood, and cloak—in the lonely garden in which he lived. It was done. Nevertheless, an admiring follower discovered the spot, and though the place was carefully watched, managed, after ten months, to carry off the body to Palestine.

Not only a saint's corpse but his clothes were eagerly sought after. Saints themselves left their filthy garments as an invaluable treasure to other saints. Thus Antony left his two sheepskins, the only clothes he had worn for years, the hair next a body that he made a merit of never washing— one to the Patriarch Athanasius, the other to the Bishop of Serapion. "And each," says Athanasius, "having received the sheepskins of the blessed Antony, and the cloak which he had worn out, keeps them as a great possession. Still more they counted it a joy to wear these loathsome garments."

There were degrees of sanctity attached to these holy relics, for, when Simon Stylites died, an awful punishment befel the Patriarch of Antioch, who in his veneration for the saint attempted to possess himself of a portion of the beard. The patriarch's hand immediately withered up, and was only restored at the intercession of the faithful.

Even Gregory the Great was given up to this infatuated idolatry. Having been petitioned by the Empress Constantine for the head or some portion of the body of St. Paul, he writes to tell her that such is the awful sanctity of these relics that those who had only tried to place the scattered bones together had fallen down dead, in one case to the number of ten persons. The utmost that could be afforded would be a cloth that had been permitted to touch the relics, and even such a cloth had been known to bleed. Gregory considered a nail which contained some minute filings of the chains of St. Peter a present worthy a king. A golden nail from these same chains which the pope presented to a distinguished official bore the following singular story:

A certain profane Lombard, a companion of King Autharsis, beholding the chain, was tempted by the sight of this said nail. The knife with which he tried to sever it sprung up and cut his throat. The Lombard king and his officers were in terror, and none dared pick up the nail; at last an orthodox catholic came, and the sacred nail allowed itself to be lifted and replaced.

This absurd idolatry extended to everything that could be supposed sacred, and of course included the persons of the clergy. The most direful calamities befell those who were guilty of disrespect to these favoured individuals. This veneration for the clergy was fostered by the whole Church, but especially that portion acknowledging the supremacy of the Bishop of Rome.

Another sign of corruption was the growth of image worship. Pictures of Bible histories and statues of Bible personages were set up in the churches of Italy as early as the fourth century. After the condemnation of Nestorius in the next century, pictures and statues of our Lord, of His mother, and of the saints, began to be introduced in the churches, especially in Italy and the East. In the sixth and seventh centuries their religious veneration had reached such a height that it was usual not only to keep lights and burn incense before them, but to kiss them reverently, and to kneel down to pray before them, some even making them their godfathers and godmothers in baptism, and mixing the colouring matter which they scraped off them with the eucharistic elements in the communion! Christianity had entered the downward path of Brahminism and Buddhism.

Its earlier corruptions had resembled those of Brahminism, in the formation of a priestly caste and a mass of tradition which, weighing on the people, drove them deeper and deeper into a religion of abject submission, ignorance, and idolatry; later on the course of corruption was more akin to that of Buddhism. Matter with all its laws was contemned, as something under the control of the Evil One; the great effort of life was to get free of this earthly evil, and to reduce its area as much as possible. The highest of all virtues was the monastic life and perpetual virginity.

Pope Gregory's protests against the anti-Christian pride of the Bishop of Constantinople, in assuming the title of Universal Bishop, were far too violent to be disinterested; and the conduct of the man who represented him at that time in the imperial court is a commentary on the spirit in which the protest was made.

Phocas, one of the most detestable beings that ever exercised authority in the world, headed a sedition of the army against the Emperor Maurice. He caused five of the Emperor's sons to be slain before his eyes, closing the tragedy by the execution of the unfortunate monarch himself. The Empress Constantina having twice conspired against the tyrant, was tortured and then beheaded with her three daughters. The brutal usurper who perpetrated these horrors was eulogised by Pope Gregory, who had a private spite against the Emperor Maurice. This want of righteousness will ever be remembered to the discredit of the founder of the Papacy and of the Anglo-Saxon Church.

Phocas, however, knew where his friends lay, and what would most please them; and hating the Patriarch of Constantinople for the protection he had afforded to the Empress and her daughters, this Emperor of the East recognised the Pope of Rome as universal bishop. This recognition appears to have been obtained by Boniface while papal legate at Constantinople; at any rate, he was the pope who was the first thus to style himself (A.D. 607).

Such was the point to which Christendom had now arrived. Chastisement after chastisement had fallen upon it: Goths, Vandals, Huns, Saxons, one after the other, had overrun Europe; again and again Rome itself had been in the hands of the barbarians, but those who professed to be representatives of the kingdom of heaven had appeared to learn nothing by these judgments. Like the Hebrews, whose history was doubtless a type of that of Christendom, the history of times which resembled the epoch of the Judges ended in the Christian Church openly giving up its theocratic government, and surrendering its liberties into the hands of a visible monarch, enthroned, like the ancient Cæsars, in the metropolitan city.

MEANWHILE, in a portion of the globe which hitherto had been little thought of in Christendom, from a people divided and wandering, arose a mighty power which in little more than a hundred years deprived the Roman Empire of all its provinces in Asia and Africa, took Spain and Narbonese Gaul, and all the larger islands in the Mediterranean, absorbed the kingdom of Persia, and finally extended its sway from the Atlantic to the Indus. This power was more to be dreaded than the invasions of the barbarians. These had come against old Rome—force against force. This power was evidently raised up against Christendom—religion against religion.

Mohammedanism has existed more than one thousand two hundred years, and still maintains the greater part of its conquests. No student of history who believes that God reigns over the earth can imagine that this religion arose, and is permitted to exist in vigour, without its having some real mission then and now. If we place Islamism in direct contrast with the religions it supplanted over so large a portion of the earth, we shall see its significance. Brahminism, Buddhism, Magianism, and Christianity in its corrupt form, had all, though so utterly opposed to each other, concurred in leading men away from the worship of the one ever-living God to that of His creatures. Against this universal degradation of the elements of religion, Mohammed emphatically reiterated the Mosaic doctrine : " The Lord thy God is one Lord;" "Thou shalt not make unto thee any graven image; thou shalt not bow down thyself to them and serve them." This was the Arab prophet's one great testimony, the Alpha and Omega of his religion; and in its strength he founded a number of mighty nations, which, for everything that marks civilisation—manners, laws, commerce, art, science, literature—were, for the next five hundred years, the first in the world.

This mighty force had its spring in the soul of one man. An earnest, faithful, meditative man, Mohammed has given sufficient proof that his first efforts were made in the utmost sincerity. An orphan boy, beloved by his grandfather, the head of the powerful tribe of Koreishites, the hereditary keepers of the holy Kaaba in Mecca, the lad was brought up by his uncle Abu Thaleb, and going with him to the fairs of Syria, eventually became steward to Kadijah, a rich widow, for whose business he travelled (A.D. 595). He married her, she bore him many children, and for years the pair lived as quiet and as happy a domestic life as could fall to the lot of the most undistinguished individuals.

Mohammed might have died one of the wealthiest and most respectable of his tribe had there not been in him a strangely disturbing force; he had a deeply religious nature. Every year he spent the month Ramadhan in the solitude and silence of the desert. Thought deeper than usual stirred his soul on one occasion—it was the fortieth year of his life—and he withdrew to a cavern in Mount Haran, near Mecca (A.D. 609). When he emerged again from this retreat he came as one conscious of a message to his fellowmen. Simple enough in itself, to Mohammed it was very awful, since it involved the denial and overthrow of the religion of his family, his tribe, his people. All these three hundred and sixty-five idols in the Temple of Mecca were vanity; their worship was a sin. There was but one living God, and His worship the only one worthy a reasonable man. He sat down by Kadijah, told her that the angel Gabriel had revealed this to him, and not only this, but that he, Mohammed, was appointed the prophet and teacher of this the only true doctrine.

Kadijah was a prudent woman. She knew what such an enterprise involved, yet she declared herself at once a believer in her husband's mission, a proof of affection Mohammed never forgot. "Am I not better than Kadijah?" one day said Ayesha, a young and beautiful wife the prophet took to himself after the death of that faithful spouse. "She was a widow, old, and had lost her looks; you love me better than you do her?" "No, by Allah!" replied Mohammed; "she believed in me when no one else would. In the whole world I had but one friend, and that was Kadijah."

Her faith is a most remarkable testimony to Mohammed's sincerity, since the slightest doubt on that score would have made her anxious in a course certain to excite the fiercest enmity, and perhaps to lead to the destruction of all she held dear. She knew the terror the idols inspired. Her countrymen regarded the anger of God as nothing in comparison. For their sakes the people constantly defrauded Him. When they planted fruit trees or sowed a field, they divided it into two parts, one for their idols and the other for God. If the fruits fell from the idols' part into that which was God's, they were careful to make restitution; but if it was God's portion that suffered loss, they made none. If the water with which they watered the ground ran over from the idols' ground into God's part, they dammed it up; but if it ran from God's portion into that of the idols', they let it run away, saying that the idols wanted what was God's, but God wanted nothing.

It was against this devil-worship, for it was nothing less, that Mohammed felt himself called upon to protest. In a gathering of his kindred he declared to them his doctrine and pretensions, and concluded by asking who would be his vizier (A.D. 609). The company sat silent, until Ali, a young lad, sprang up, and in fierce and passionate language declared that he would. Ali's father, who was none other than Abu Thaleb, the head of the Koreishites, was incensed against Mohammed, and, taking up a stone, said to him, "Mayest thou perish! Hast thou called us together for this?" The rest of the kin, however, seem to have regarded the matter as rather a joke, and breaking out into laughter, rose and went to their homes. So, too, did Mohammed, but in a spirit of bitter resentment against Abu Thaleb, a resentment which has left its mark in a chapter of the Koran, in which he fiercely curses his misguided uncle and aunt. This vindictiveness, so characteristic of his nature, but which as yet had had but little to arouse it, rapidly developed.

Abu Thaleb was not much to blame, since such pretensions must soon bring the house of Hashem into trouble. There were parties in the Temple of Mecca. A man who was at once a zealous idolater and a mortal foe of the house of Hashem, became its chief ruler, convened an assembly of the Koreishites, and they determined on the death of the prophet. Mohammed escaped, aided by the heroism of his devoted young vizier. Ali lay on his bed, covered with Mohammed's garments, expecting every moment to feel the swords of the Koreishites plunged on all sides into his body. Mohammed meanwhile lay hid in a cave with his friend, Abu Bekr. The Koreishites explored the neighbourhood, and came to the very cavern. "We are only two," said the trembling disciple. "There is a third," said the prophet: "it is God Himself." At last they reached Medina; and this terrible journey is commemorated in the Mohammedan Era, which commences with the Hegira, or flight from Mecca. From this moment the fortunes of Mohammed turned. Medina embraced Islam, and sixteen days after the prophet's flight he made a public entry into Medina. The contempt, suffering, and danger Mohammed had endured brought out the fierce side of his nature; every man's hand had been against him, now his hand should be against every man. He had fled from Mecca, trembling for his life; he came forth from Medina breathing vengeance. He preached to his own people, mounting a rough pulpit or planting his back against a palm tree; but in the conversion of the world he relied on the sword rather than the word.

"The sword," he told his followers, "is the key of heaven and of hell.

A drop of blood shed in the cause of God, a night spent in arms, is of more avail than two months of fasting or prayer; whosoever falls in battle, his sins are forgiven; at the day of judgment his wounds shall be resplendent as vermilion and odoriferous as musk, and the loss of his limbs shall be supplied by the wings of angels and cherubim." It was perhaps the most terrible doctrine that had ever been preached. It appealed to the lowest propensities of humanity; the beast of prey sprang up in men's hearts, and the Saracens flamed forth from the East like hordes of raging lions. Nothing could withstand them; the Persians, who for centuries maintained war with the Romans on equal terms, were defeated in the great battle of Nahavend, in which one hundred thousand Persians were slain, and Persia became Mohammedan (A.D. 639). The Roman Empire resisted for a time, but it was useless. Asia Minor was lost, Africa was lost, then Spain; and the Saracens were yet advancing. For centuries they will stand hovering over Europe, a deadly nightmare, which nations so remote from its influence as our own will feel, so that even the English language will bear to the end of time traces of the loathing terror with which Christian Europe regarded this deadly foe.

The seventh century would have been dark, if this great judgment were all that had to be recorded of its history; but while the centre of the civilised world is thus suffering an eclipse, light is breaking out along the circumference, declaring that the kingdom of righteousness still shines, and will maintain itself. We have seen its rays faintly touching the far East, now we see it lighting up with radiant dawn the islands of the West.

Abbot Gregory had, notwithstanding all his false notions, the heart of a Christian apostle; and when he became pope he sent a mission to preach the Gospel to the Anglo-Saxons he had so much pitied.

We know something of the hearts of our forefathers, for a thousand years cannot destroy the unity of a race. It wants no imagination on our part to realise the suspicion with which the new doctrine was at first regarded; a suspicion, however, not inconsistent with a willingness to listen, to consider, and finally to accept, any change, on good reason shown and solid fact proved. It needs no imagination to picture the obstinacy of some compared to the readiness of others; to feel that after tremendous strife the new doctrine would win its way, and find its staunchest supporters in the very quality that had most opposed it. Thus it was when Ethelberht ruled Englishmen in Kent, and Eadwine in Northumbria.

Gregory, with the statesmanship of a Roman pontiff, divided the English Church, making York a second centre; and Paulinus, a noble and truly saintly man, went forth to the work of converting Northumbria. A tall, stooping form, a long aquiline nose, with black hair falling round a thin worn face; these features suggest the man of loving, untiring devotion. These pagan Teutons had one natural virtue : they honoured woman, and they were not slow to see how much the spirit of the Christian religion elevated and purified that in her they so much admired. Their chiefs sought Christian wives, and it was in the train of such a princess, the daughter of Ethelberht of Kent, going to be wedded to heathen Eadwine of Northumbria, that Paulinus came to the North of England.

Eadwine was a good type of our race. He honoured his wife, he honoured Paulinus, but neither he nor his friends would give way until they had had some solid experience that they could understand. A child was born to Eadwine, and Paulinus assured him that it was the gift of God; but that did not touch him. At last he promised that if God would grant him victory over the King of the West Saxons, that he would renounce his idols. Eadwine was victorious, but still he hesitated. Then Paulinus, recalling a romantic incident in his life, pressed home such a scene of the providence of God in his career, that the King was sincerely affected. He determined to call together his councillors, and propose to them the question of the adoption of Christianity.

The question being asked: "Which religion was the true one?" Coifi, a heathen priest, replies : "None of your people, Eadwine, have worshipped the gods with more zeal than I, yet there are many more favoured and fortunate; if they were good for anything they would help their worshippers." "So seems the life of man, O King," says an Ealderman, " as a sparrow's flight through the hall, when you are sitting at meat in winter-tide, with the warm light on the hearth, but the icy rain-storm beats without. The sparrow flies in at one door, and tarries for a moment in the light and heat of the hearth-fire, and then flying forth from the other vanishes into the wintry darkness, from whence it came. So tarries for a moment the life of man in our sight, but what is before us or what after us we know not. If this new teaching tell us aught of these, let us follow it." Paulinus then proclaims the Gospel; the priest is the first to declare himself a convert, and to propose at once to destroy the idols. Leaping on his horse, he rides to the neighbouring temple of Godmanham, and striking the wall with his lance, as if to defy the gods, he sets fire to the building, and both temple and idols are quickly a heap of ruins.

Eadwine and his thanes submit to baptism (A.D. 627), and Paulinus becomes first Archbishop of York. Suddenly the preachers of the Gospel find all Bernicia and all Deira open to them. Paulinus and his assistants hardly know how to baptise their converts; and the Swale becomes another Jordan, so many press down into the stream. Eadwine and his land Christian, he sees the dream of his exile fulfilled.

In a very short while the Northumbrian kingdom became the most powerful as well as the most perfectly governed of all the Anglo-Saxon monarchies. If the dignity of Bretwalda was not yet known, Eadwine bore a position not unlike it. Wherever Eadwine went he was preceded by the royal standard of purple and gold; when he walked in the streets a lance with a feather-tuft was borne above his head. "So free was the land from all wrong-doers that a woman with her babe might walk scathless from sea to sea in Eadwine's day." The very traveller was cared for, the springs by the roadside being marked with stakes, and a cup of brass placed by their side. To realise the greatness of the change, one must compare it with the rough and terrible times by which it was preceded and followed, with the stormy pagan world that was bearing down upon it, and beneath which for a time it was submerged. But it was like the early dawn, the few pure moments that herald the light, too often to be quickly overclouded.

EIGHTH CENTURY.

CONTEMPORARY EVENTS IN THE EIGHTH CENTURY.

England.—Founding of Crowland Abbey.
Constantinople.—Images destroyed in Constantinople by order of Leo the Isaurian
Germany.—Boniface cutting down Thor's Oak.
France.—Defeat of the Saracens by Charles Martel.

Eighth Century.

A.D. 716-732.

Faith in Christ the Foundation of the English State—Guthlac and Crowland Abbey—English Missionaries—Boniface—He Destroys Thor's Oak—Mohammedanism in Western Europe—Charles Martel—Leo the Iconoclast.

HE work of Columba, of Augustine, of Paulinus, is seen not only in the conversion of individual souls, but in the birth of a new nation, destined to be one of the very greatest in the history of the human race. Faith in Christ made the English state.

Its birth is an event contemporaneous with that of the Saracenic empire. The preaching of Gregory's missionaries synchronizes with Mohammed's first efforts in Arabia. The three hundred and sixty-five idols of the Caabah were destroyed, and Mohammed was enthroned prince and prophet in Mecca, within two or three years of the time when Coifi, the Northumbrian high-priest, destroyed the heathen temple at Godmanham, and King Eadwine embraced the Christian faith. We shall have an opportunity further on of seeing what the discovery of its God did for Arabia; this is the moment to speak of what it did for our own country.

Milton has somewhere declared his contempt for the history of the Heptarchy, as little better than a history of the quarrels of kites and crows. Until the cross was preached, such it was; but no sooner is the kingdom of Christ set up amongst these murderers and deep drinkers, than a gentleness, a loving-kindness, an enthusiasm for humanity appears amongst them. A form treading closely in the footsteps of Christ Himself is seen passing from kingdom to kingdom, and at last, in the largeness of its love, crossing the sea, and preaching the everlasting Gospel to still more savage and heathen brothers.

Where in the history of the world shall we find kings more truly Christ-like than those who in the hour of England's first love appear to convert and strengthen their people? Superficial indeed must the historian be who imagines a coarse and vigorous warrior like Penda, the Mercian, to be a greater king than Oswald, whom he conquered and slew.

Oswald, the saint of the Lord, pupil in the school of the holy Columba, was called to the throne of Northumbria in 635. All was anarchy within; a fierce heathendom ranged without. Oswald had to march to the defence of his people against Cadwallon, the Welsh king. He met the foe near the Roman wall. Oswald carried the standard: it was a cross. He planted it in a hollow, his men ranged themselves around it, and the battle of heaven's field was fought and won. Then the king set about restoring order in his own dominions; and one of the first things he did was to send for a teacher from Iona. Colman came, but found the task too much for his patience. "Brother," said a gentle voice, "did you forget God's word, to give them the milk first, and then the meat?" All eyes were turned on the speaker—the monk Aidan—and he was sent to help Oswald. The Gaelic missionary could not speak English. So the king accompanied him everywhere, interpreting his words. By reason of his constant habit of praying or giving thanks to the Lord, Oswald was wont, wherever he sat, to hold his hands upturned on his knees. Aidan and Oswald were very dear to one another. One day Oswald sat at meat with Aidan at his side, and someone said that a crowd waited at the gate fasting. The king ordered his untasted food to be given to them, and his silver dish broken up and divided piece-meal among them. Aidan seized the hand that had given the dish, and fervently said: "May this hand never grow old!" Oswald's subjects never forgot the tale; and when at his death, at Maserfeld, fighting for the Christian King Sigeberht of East Anglia, Penda mutilated Oswald's body, and put the fragments on poles, the legend went forth that the hand that Aidan had blessed remained white and uncorrupted.

Few combined such energy with so devoted a faith; but amongst the kings and nobles of the Heptarchy there were many who, filled with the love of God and a gentle life, could not endure the brutal brawls that raged around, but fled for peace to the repose of some monastery, the form religious life had then taken. For this spring-time was full of fierce blasts and wild elemental war. In the course of a century fourteen kings ascended the throne of Northumbria in a manner as irregular as their descent was rapid and tragical. Six were murdered by their kinsmen or other competitors, five were expelled by their subjects, two became monks, and only one died with his crown on his head. So truly were Christ's words verified: "I came not to bring peace, but a sword."

AT times the struggle seemed hopeless, and faithful souls fled, like the prophet of old, into the wilderness. Thus it was with Guthlac, a youth of the royal race of Mercia. In early manhood—probably in the first enthusiasm of his conversion—fearful lest he should fall, he fled, not knowing whither. He wandered on until he found himself on the margin of a vast swamp. Reeds and rushes, flags and sedge, divided by numberless meres and sullen streams, the home of myriads of wild fowl, and of such countless birds that when they rose the air was black with their presence and resonant with their screams,—this was the scene he beheld.

On these dreary shores he met some poor forlorn fishers, and from them he learnt that far in the centre of the swamp lay an island which none dare inhabit, since it was the abode of horrid, uncouth monsters, too fearful for human eyes to behold. Guthlac received the news with joy. He feared nothing so much as temptation and sin, and so, enlisting the aid of these poor fishers, he soon reached the haunted isle, and built himself "a hut in a hollow on the side of a heap of turf." In his early days, all alone in his dismal retreat, enduring frightful cold in winter, and an atmosphere laden with malaria in the summer, he fell a victim to disease, his mind grew clouded, and he fancied himself visited in the dead of night by black troops of unclean spirits. They seemed to come out of the sky and from under the earth, until they filled the air like dark clouds. Of form and appearance the most horrible and distorted it was possible to imagine, their cries and shrieks were even more terrible, as they rushed by his dwelling and round about it. At last they came creeping in under the door, and through every chink and hole in the walls or roof, and setting upon him with open mouths, bound him, pulled him out, cast him head-over-ears into the dirty fen, and then dragged him over the roughest parts, seeking, if possible, to tear his limbs. It was the delirium of a fen fever, and there was no human hand to assuage his sufferings. But God did not leave him to perish in solitude. The secret of his retreat was noised abroad, other men like minded followed in his wake, and the little company worked so lovingly to disenthral the dismal isle, that, with worship and with work, the solitary place was gradually turned into a garden of the Lord.

Ere long the turbulence of the age conceded to it an immunity only granted to the most holy spots. It became a sanctuary for all in distress. King Ethelbald, driven from Mercia by his cousin Ceolred, fled to Guthlac, who strengthened him, promising him his kingdom and victory over his foe. The king vowed, if it should prove true, to build a church on the island in place of Guthlac's wooden chapel. He was triumphant, and righteously performed his vow. From the distant uplands he caused earth to be brought in boats, first making a secure foundation by driving piles of oak and alder into the mud. And so in the year of grace 716 began to rise the Abbey of Crowland, causing such fame and glory to attach to the little island that men flocked to it, and soon a village sprang up. Causeways and embankments were extended farther and farther into the fen, drains were dug and sluices erected, to let off the water from the standing pools; more and more land was reclaimed and tilled, until the wilderness began literally to rejoice and blossom as the rose.

And thus from this and other islands in the fens arose above the sound of work the hymn of praise, touching alike the hearts of fierce kings and lonely fishers, producing within their rugged souls yearnings after a peace and a beauty of which they had otherwise never conceived. And what was thus begun was in like manner carried on. Abbeys and churches sprang up everywhere, centres of energy and life; around each grew up a community of men bent on the subjugation of the wild waste in the midst of which they lived.

No one can fully understand an age who has not himself lived in it. In this new-born England of the eighth century, the monastery was not only the retreat of the children of God, but the spring from whence flowed civilisation, literature, and art. Columba, Cuthbert, Cædmon, Bede, what do these names import? They are the true founders of English civilisation and English literature, and their lives were spent in the monasteries of Iona and Lindisfarne, Whitby and Jarrow.

From whence came their inspiration? Cædmon, the Anglo-Saxon Milton, the earliest of English poets, is a cowherd to the monastery of Whitby. He does not dream of writing poetry, he cannot even join in the festal song, so little is there in him of the tuneful. One night as he is sleeping in the stable with his cattle, he dreams that One appears to him, who says: "Sing, Cædmon, some song to me." "What shall I sing?" "The beginning of created things," is the reply. And hereupon Cædmon commences, until he has thrown the Bible history into verse, and into such verse that astonished men cry: "Cædmon learnt not the art of poetry from men, nor of men, but from God."

The new nation is alive, it moves, and England cannot contain it. What unaccountable enthusiasm is this that makes men restless in the midst of honour and comfort, that drives them forth from peaceful dwellings to spend their lives among idolaters, knowing well that a violent death may be their fate, that in every case suffering and privation will be their lot?

WHAT a history was that of Boniface and his friends! They were the most highly placed people in Wessex. Boniface was a relative of Richard, a man of royal birth, if not a king. Richard believed in prayer, and his influence is seen in his children, who were all three devoted preachers of the Gospel. Winebald and Willebald, his two sons, were fellow-labourers with Boniface, and so was his daughter Walpurga. All followed their father in devotion to the cause of the kingdom of heaven. Boniface, or Winfrid, as he was called in England, was their leader. He was born about A.D. 680, and had every advantage: birth, education, reputation for learning, ability, and sanctity. But he had heard how Willebrod, the Northumbrian, had evangelised the Frisians, and his ardent soul was on fire to enlarge in like manner the kingdom of heaven. At last he obtained permission from his abbot to go to Friesland; but, a war breaking out, Boniface was obliged to come back. Abbot Winbercht dying, Boniface, to his dismay, was chosen in his place. However, he succeeded in obtaining the interference of the bishop, and was permitted to follow his bent. He made his way to Rome, was cordially received by the pope, who gave him permission to preach the Gospel in Germany whenever and wherever he found opportunity.

Boniface commenced labouring in Thuringia. Willebrod, who had received many marks of honour from Pepin of Heristal, now ruler of France, wished to have Boniface as his successor in the Archbishopric of Utrecht; but this was not the work his intrepid soul felt called upon to fulfil. He plunged into the wilds of Hesse. Two chiefs were converted and baptised, and a monastery founded at Amöneburg, near the Ohm. Ere long his success was great, and multitudes, both in Hesse and on the borders of Saxony, were baptised. The pope heard these things, sent for Boniface to Rome, and having satisfied himself that all was going on according to rule, consecrated him a bishop with a general jurisdiction over all whom he might convert from paganism.

On his return, Boniface found the mission had declined. His converts were mingling their old and new faiths, and he felt it necessary to deliver them at once from the snare of idolatry. From England, Daniel of Winchester wrote, urging him above all things to show a spirit of patience and moderation in dealing with the popular superstitions; but Boniface felt as many other missionaries, that where the spirit of Christ is there is liberty. As burning the pope's bull did infinitely more to shake the papal system than offering to argue the matter in all the churches in Christendom, so cutting down the sacred oak of Thor appealed to the consciences of these old Teutons with a thousand times more force than the patience and moderation counselled by the good English bishop.

This oak stood at Geismar, in Upper Hesse, and for ages had been the rallying-spot for all the tribes, and was believed to be under the special protection of Donar or Thor, the god of thunder. Boniface had often declaimed against the superstition of attributing a divine character to a tree, and he now declared his intention of cutting it down. Thousands assembled to behold the daring deed, all prepared to regard the result as a manifest proof of the power or weakness of their ancient god. The blows of the axe were heard, and at each stroke the beholders waited for the vengeance of heaven. At last the tree fell with a crash, and the sacrilegious woodmen were standing before it unhurt. Then the multitude changed their minds, and went home satisfied that Thor was no god, and that even if he was, the Christ of Boniface was more powerful.

The result fully justified the resolution of the heroic missionary, for from that time the Word of Truth in Hesse had free course and was glorified. Churches sprang up everywhere, and by their side monasteries for the Christian workers. Boniface wrote to England A.D. 733, begging his countrymen to remember them in their prayers to God and our Lord Jesus Christ, that He would vouchsafe to convert the hearts of these heathen. "Have compassion on them, brethren; they often say, 'We are of one blood with our brothers in England.' Remember that they are your kinsmen according to the flesh." Boniface fell a martyr in his great work, Whit-Sunday, A.D. 755.

———◆———

THE Saracenic power, which at the beginning of the previous century could scarcely be said to have an existence, had in about a hundred years become larger than the world Alexander conquered, and almost equal in area to the empire that Rome had taken five hundred years to subjugate. So much for the force of a new religious principle animating a yet unexhausted race. It appeared during the early years of this century about to close upon Europe, and to overwhelm the nascent Christian civilisation. Two men were sent to save it from this catastrophe—Leo the Isaurian, and Charles Martel.

Persia, Syria, Egypt, Africa, Spain, having been successively conquered, the Mohammedans appeared before the capital of the Empire. From A.D. 668 to 675 they had ineffectually attempted to besiege Constantinople; now in A.D. 717, the year after Crowland Abbey was founded, they appeared again, a host numbering no less than one hundred and twenty thousand, Arabs and Persians, with a fleet of one thousand eight hundred ships. The Emperor who had just ascended the throne was a brave and able ruler: Leo, called the Isaurian, from the mountain district in which he began life as a peasant boy. Leo managed to allure the enemy into the Bosphorus, and to launch Greek fire-ships amongst them, by which means the Saracenic fleet was destroyed. The secret of this destructive material was only known at Constantinople, and was regarded as the palladium of the state. It was belched out from the prows of galleys, shaped like the mouths of savage monsters, and seems to have been mainly composed of some inflammable earth-oil, like petroleum. The Arabs, moreover, had the misfortune to lose their Caliph during the siege; and his successor being his enemy, the work was pursued with indifference. In addition, the winter proved unusually severe, so that the Arabs and Egyptians were almost torpid from cold. Famine and disease now appeared, and Leo fell upon them with an army of Bulgarians, and defeated them with great slaughter. Thus at the end of thirteen months the Arabian commander, Moslemah, was obliged to raise the siege and retire; and only five galleys out of eighteen hundred ships entered the port of Alexandria to tell the tale of this disastrous campaign.

Eighteen years after, the Saracens heard the same voice in Western Europe, saying to them in even sterner tones: " Hitherto shalt thou come, but no farther; and here shalt thy proud waves be stayed."

The Pillars of Hercules, now Ceuta and Gibraltar, but then Abyla and Calpë, were in the hands of the Gothic kings of Spain, the fortress on the African coast being held by the Gothic general, Count Julian. For some private reason he surrendered the place to Musa, the commander of the Saracens. In A.D. 711 Tarik, one of Musa's generals, gathered together five thousand soldiers, and embarked for Calpë.

> And like a cloud of locusts, whom the South
> Wafts from the plains of wasted Africa,
> The Mussulmen upon Iberia's shore
> Descend.

Calpë henceforth loses its name in history, and—

> ——is doomed to bear
> The name of its new conqueror, and thenceforth
> To stand his everlasting monument

Gebel-el-Tarik, the hill of Tarik, immortalises in the name of the famous rock of Gibraltar the Moor who conquered Spain. Roderic, the Gothic king, assembled a formidable army; but a battle at Xeres decided the fate of the kingdom, and Spain passed into the hands of a new race, who kept their grasp upon the land for more than six hundred years. Tarik advanced to the royal city of Toledo, which soon capitulated; from Toledo he spread his conquests to the north of the peninsula, and Spain was a Mohammedan province.

From Spain the Moors pushed along the Mediterranean into Narbonese Gaul, then called Septimania. They were everywhere victorious; and when Musa related his campaign to Abdelmerik, he was able to say, "Never was my army defeated; never was a battalion beaten; never did the Mussulmen hesitate to follow me when I led them forty against fourscore."

The stories connected with these invasions have become legendary, and the prowess and numbers on all sides exaggerated. El-Samah, an Arab chieftain, meets Eudes, Duke of Aquitania, under the walls of Toulouse, and is badly defeated—so badly, that one of his own historians speaks of the entire army as perishing, and the spot is mentioned in the Arab chronicles as the Martyrs' Causeway.

But the loss of one great army was not sufficient to deter the impulsive hosts now pouring across the Iberian peninsula. In A.D. 725 they again appeared in Septimania, and even ventured beyond the Rhone. Duke Eudes began to think friendship with such a people better than war. He entered into alliance with a chieftain of renown, Abi-Nessa, and, by the gift of his daughter, detached him from the main host. Abdel-Rhaman, Governor-General of Spain, informed of the treachery, soon appeared at the foot of the Pyrenees. Abi-Nessa was killed, his bride sent to Damascus, to the harem of the Commander of the Faithful, and the Moors were in full march on Bordeaux. Duke Eudes tried to save his capital, but was utterly defeated, and the Moors loaded themselves with its plunder.

The Aquitanian was now obliged to sue for assistance from the Franks. Charles Martel, who ruled that people as Duke of Austrasia, took an oath from Eudes to acknowledge his suzerainty, and with a great army set out for the Loire. It was time, for the Arabs had crossed that river, and had penetrated Burgundy as far as Autun and Sens, ravaging the whole country like vast troops of wolves, destroying towns and monasteries, and massacring the inhabitants. Tours and its abbey was the rich morsel that attracted their avidity, and with greedy haste they hurried on; but as they arrived beneath its walls they heard that the Duke of Austrasia was rapidly advancing with a large army. Abdel-Rhaman fell back and concentrated his troops, who were spread about, dragging from all directions the immense booty that they were collecting. This booty was so embarrassing that the Moorish commander was on the point of having it burnt, but, abandoning that idea, he waited his foe.

It was late in the very year (A.D. 732) in which Boniface had been refreshed by the arrival of some dear old friends from Wessex, that the fate of Christian Europe was determined in a battle, the very field of which is not certain, beyond that it was somewhere between Tours and Poitiers, and of whose importance neither the combatants nor any one else at the time appears to have had an adequate idea. For a whole week the contending hosts watched each other, but at last the battle began. For some time it was doubtful which way it would go, when, some Franks penetrating into the Arab camp either for pillage or to take the enemy in the rear, the Saracens became alarmed for the safety of their booty, and rushed back pell-mell into their camp. It was their ruin, for the fight soon became a confused mêlée, in which those who had nothing to lose had the advantage. There was great slaughter, Abdel-Rhaman being himself among the slain. Night fell, and both armies drew off to their tents. Next morning the Franks came out to the fight. But as they approached the Arab camp all was silence. They entered; it was deserted. The Saracens had fled during the night, leaving behind the greater part of their booty.

By this important victory Charles won his surname of Martel, or the Hammer; and he further vindicated his right to such a title, for in the course of the next seven years he drove the Mussulmen out of Provence. However, they still retained possession of the towns on the sea-shore of Septimania—Agde, Maguelone, and even of some in the interior, as Nimes.

———◆———

THE fate of Spain, as well as that of Syria, Egypt, and Africa, seems to have in no way touched the consciences of the rulers of the Latin Church. They were ready enough, at all times, to see the judgments of Heaven in every calamity that befel a heretic or a misbeliever. Only one man seems to have had any insight into the case, and, being the most powerful layman in Christendom, he felt it his duty to attempt a reform.

Brought up in the mountains of Isauria, among a people who had retained much of the simplicity of early Christianity, the Emperor Leo was offended with the religious frivolities he witnessed in all the great cities of his Empire. Never having been blinded by a false and pharisaic Christianity, the conquests of the Saracens made their due impression on his mind. He could not but see that the accusation of idolatry against the Christians was true; and if this were once admitted, then it was a sufficient explanation of the terrible judgment that had fallen on Christendom.

The Roman Emperors in becoming Christians did not give up their position as supreme regulators of the religion of the Empire. Constantine had exercised the office of Pontifex Maximus, and he and his successors never for a moment supposed that their right to direct the religion of their people was in the least degree lessened by their adoption of Christianity. On the contrary, they used their power vigorously to extirpate paganism, and never allowed any bishops or councils to suppose that they had any independent right or authority. The Church, by a thousand acts, had recognised this, and it would have been strange indeed if Leo had not deemed himself able to make any decrees he chose concerning public worship. Of course he ran the risk of being called, as Julian was, a persecutor; but that he had a prescriptive right of seven centuries, and of more than seventy reigns, in his favour, there could be no doubt. Whether he had a plan for a thorough religious reform cannot be known, since he has had only enemies for his historians; but, in any case, he commenced with the error with which Christendom was chiefly charged—image worship.

He had been ten years on the throne before he gave any sign of his intentions, and then he only issued a decree prohibiting the worship of all statues and pictures of the Saviour, the Virgin Mary, and the saints. Statues and pictures were to be raised so high from the ground that they could not be kissed.

One of those volcanic eruptions so common in southern Europe took place about this time in the Ægean. A new island arose, and the adjacent ones were strewn with clouds of dust. The Emperor and the monks both saw in this earthquake the sign of Divine wrath, but with opposite views. Leo attributed it to the religious habits of his subjects; the monks to the sacrilegious edict.

However, the power lay with the Emperor, and forthwith came a much more severe law against idolatry (A.D. 728). All images were to be destroyed, and all the pictures on the walls of the churches whitewashed. Leo was inflexible; the most venerated idols were not to be spared. A statue of the Saviour in Constantinople, renowned for its miracles, was expressly doomed. The imperial officer mounted a ladder and struck it with his axe. The people waited, hoping, no doubt, that Heaven would interfere; but as no supernatural aid appeared, the women in the crowd seized the ladder, pulled it down, and beat the officer to death with clubs. An armed guard came to suppress the tumult, and a great number of the mob were killed.

As the iconoclastic edict was carried out through the Empire the insurrectionary spirit spread. Greece and the Ægean islands were in flames. Another Emperor was proclaimed. A fleet was raised, and Constantinople was menaced. The clergy, and especially the monks, were its chief instigators. The Patriarch of Constantinople and the Pope of Rome were one in their defence of image worship. The patron of the man who cut down the oak of Thor, Gregory II., was unbounded in his denunciations of this effort to destroy a more dangerous form of idolatry. The ignorance which Pope Gregory displays in his address to the Emperor is only equalled by his insolence. He argues with the Emperor in the following style :—

"'Where the body is,' says our Lord, 'there will the eagles be gathered together.' The body is Christ, the eagles, the religious men who flew from all quarters to behold Him. When they beheld Him they made a picture of Him. Not of Him alone, they made pictures of James, the brother of the Lord; of Stephen, and of all the martyrs; and so having done, they disseminated them throughout the world, to receive not worship, but reverence." It is evident that Hezekiah's grand act—when he destroyed the brazen serpent believed to have been made by Moses at the Divine command, calling it Nehushtan—was used as an argument in favour of iconoclasm, for Pope Gregory, mistaking Hezekiah for Uzziah, denounces him as a wicked, self-willed king, the true brother of Leo, since, like him, he dared to offer violence to the priests of God.

But the pope had an argument which made up for all his ignorant rhapsody; popular clamour was with him, and the great mouthpiece of the doctrine of passive obedience does not disdain to use the common argument of the demagogue. "But for the statue of St. Peter, which all the kingdoms of the West esteem as a god on earth, the whole West would take a terrible revenge." Boniface was living when his spiritual father thus made himself equal to the lowest pagans in thought and temper.

Leo was a simple, stubborn man, who no more cared for the monks than he did for the Saracens. He not only persevered in his own way, but indoctrinated his son and successor. Constantine was a more violent persecutor than Leo, and the monks of the East, among whom were found certain "lewd fellows of the baser sort," managed to make the mud stick on the son where it fell off from the father. The name they gave him, and which has become historical—Copronymus—sufficiently indicates the degradation of the men by whom it was invented. They raised a rebellion against him; Constantine fled to the ancestral mountains, and descending, followed by his faithful Isaurians, suppressed the insurrection with cruel severity. He put out the eyes of the Patriarch of Constantinople, and paraded him on an ass with his face to the tail.

Religious persecution is said to be ineffectual. It was not so in this case. Notwithstanding such acts as the one just mentioned, and many similar, the people of Constantinople, who knew their emperors better than any other people in the Empire, became strongly attached to the Isaurian dynasty, and were devotedly loyal to the son of Constantine, Leo IV. Moreover a Council was convened at Constantinople (A.D. 754), numbering no less than three hundred and thirty-eight bishops, and they were unanimous in declaring that all visible symbols of Christ, except in the Eucharist, were either blasphemous or heretical; that image worship was a corruption of Christianity and a renewal of paganism; that all such monuments of idolatry should be broken or erased; and that those who should neglect to deliver up the objects of their private superstition were guilty of disobedience to the authority of the Church and the Emperor. And, as a matter of fact, while pictures have been retained, the Eastern Church has given up the worship of statues.

However, for the time, the great protest of the Isaurian dynasty was set aside by the woman whom Constantine Copronymus married to his son. The Empress Irene was a Greek, and in her mingled ambition and fanaticism committed the atrocity of seizing her own son, and in the very chamber in which she brought him into the world putting out his eyes, and that in so cruel a manner as to threaten his death. Nature, it was said, appeared to sympathise with the unhappy monarch, for an eclipse of the sun took place, accompanied by more than usual darkness. The act was in all respects a symbol of the way the Church was treating its children.

NINTH CENTURY.

CONTEMPORARY EVENTS IN THE NINTH CENTURY.

Rome.—Coronation of Charlemagne.
Bagdad.—Denunciation of Haroun al Raschid.
Spain.—The Mosque at Cordova.
England.—Ecgberht makes himself over-lord.

Ninth Century.

A.D. 800-827.

Divisions of Mohammedanism—The Ommiades in Spain—Abder Rahman—The Mosque of Cordova—The Abbassides in Bagdad—Story of Haroun Al Raschid—Charlemagne —His Coronation as Emperor of Rome—Ecgberht, First King of the English.

O deal justly with Islamism and mediæval Christianity, we cannot do better than compare the spirit of these religions, as developed in the lives and characters of the two most famous men of this age: Charlemagne and Haroun al Raschid.

Mohammedanism split into parties from the moment of the prophet's death. In the end those parties concentrated round two powerful dynasties, the Ommiades and the Abbassides. Both were descended from the same race as Mohammed, but the Abbassides were the nearest of kin. After the first four caliphs, the Ommiade family reigned at Damascus until the middle of the eighth century, when a revolution occurred, and Abdallah, one of the Abbassides, obtained the caliphate. He inaugurated his reign by treachery and murder. Having invited seventy of the Ommiade family to his palace, under promise of an amnesty, he caused them all to be put to death, and spreading the leathern trays used at executions over the bodies, mounted the ghastly pile, and there sat, eating and jeering at the groans which still came from the victims. This monster, surnamed El Saffáh, the Bloodshedder, was great-uncle to Haroun al Raschid.

His only justification lay in the fact that the man he deposed had an equally cruel heart. Merwan, the last caliph of the Ommiade family, had destroyed the brother of Abdallah by having his head tied up in a bag of quicklime.

ONE of the Ommiades, Abder Rahman, escaped the general massacre of his house, and reached Barbary, from whence he was invited by the Moorish chiefs of Spain to be their caliph. Thus Spain became an independent Mohammedan kingdom, and the new ruler assumed the title of Caliph or Emir of Cordova.

To his garden at Cordova Caliph Abder Rahman had transplanted an African palm-tree, the first of its kind ever seen in Spain. It seemed to him a type of his own fortunes, and he addressed to it a little poem, which became very popular: "Fair palm-tree, thou also art a stranger here. The gentle airs of the Algarba court and kiss thee. Thy roots are fixed in a fertile soil; thy head is erected towards heaven; but thou, too, wouldst shed tears of bitterness if, like me, thou couldst look back."

Abder Rahman could not only compose touching verses, but his reign was mild and benignant; he was even merciful towards those of his subjects who remained Christian. The great bulk of those over whom he ruled had lived for centuries under Roman civilisation and Christian influences. For ages they had had constant relations with the Phœnicians and Greeks, the great artists of the old world, and now, under the fostering care of an intelligent despotism and the energising influence of a new faith, they made extraordinary advances in civilisation.

Among the finest monuments of this period the Cathedral of Cordova still remains to testify to the magnificence of its civilisation. When lit up by its 4,700 lamps, it was the wonder of its age. This great mosque, founded by Abder Rahman, was completed by his successors, and may be supposed to have just attained perfection when this century opens.

As the Ommiade dynasty established themselves at Cordova, the Abbassides made Bagdad their residence, and in the days of Haroun al Raschid the Eastern city began to vie with its rival in the West.

Haroun attained the caliphate through the loyalty of his friend Yahya the Barmecide, and the subtlety of his mother, who, having heard that the reigning Caliph intended to poison her, caused El Hadi to be smothered by some of his own slave-girls.

The new Caliph of Bagdad was a clever, humorous man, with a disposition naturally kind, just, and pious. He was very orthodox in his opinions, and strict in the performance of all the duties of his religion. He rose early to say "the prayers of dawn," made a hundred prostrations during the day; every other year he made a pilgrimage on foot to Mecca, or engaged in a "Holy War;" yet he was far from a bigot, being singularly tolerant of other people's religious opinions and religious pretensions. He had a great taste for literature and art, and liked to be surrounded by wits, poets, and musicians. Thus he attracted to Bagdad men of genius and learning from every country and of every creed. He employed agents in Armenia, Syria, and Egypt to collect books, and did not at all restrict himself to those that were Mohammedan. All that appeared instructive were translated for general use from the Greek, Hebrew, and Persian into Arabic.

Haroun himself was not much of a student. He preferred to cull the results of other people's fatigues. With his favourite, Jaafar, and his executioner, Mésur, without whom he seems never to have moved, he indulged in many whimsical adventures, the legend of which has come down to us in "The Arabian Nights." From the days of the first Abbasside caliph, El Saffáh, state affairs had been under the influence of, if not personally managed by, a powerful Persian family called the Barmecides, and on Haroun's accession Yahya, the son of the Bloodshedder's vizier, became with his sons, El Fadhl and Jaafar, the Governor of the Caliphate of Bagdad. They were clever administrators. They fortified the frontiers, attended to the wants of the provinces, and kept the treasury overflowing with money.

Not that Haroun was in the least degree incapable of ruling, for when he chose to take a matter in hand he showed himself as capable as the Barmecides, and ready for any emergency.

In this way things went on very prosperously for thirty or forty years. Jaafar was the Caliph's especial favourite; in fact, Haroun was so much attached to him that he wanted him always to be at his side. The Caliph was equally fond of the Princess Abbassah, and in order to secure the society of both without breaking the Mohammedan etiquette, he united his friend and his sister in marriage. As, however, such an union was impossible to one belonging to the family of the prophet, Haroun extracted a promise from them that they would never see each other except in his presence. This promise was broken, and after some years the Sultana Zobeida discovered that Jaafar had two sons, who were being brought up in Medina.

Meanwhile the magnificence of the Barmecides had begun to arouse his jealousy, a feeling their enemies were not slow to perceive. In this humour, Zobeida revealed to him what she had learnt. Haroun's resentment was appalling, and throws extraordinary light on the nature of Mohammedan ideas, and the kind of character they tend to form. He called his executioner, and said, "Mésur, when it is dark bring me ten masons and two servants." Night came, and Mésur appeared with the ill-starred workmen. Haroun led the way to the private apartment of his sister. Without speaking one word to her, he ordered the servants to kill her. He had her body put into a large chest, which he locked and took the key, and then ordered the workmen to dig down under the floor until they came to the water. They did so, smoothed the soil, and repaired the floor, the Caliph all the time sitting in a chair and looking on. The work done, he turned them all out and locked the door, merely saying to Mésur, "Take these people and give them their due." They were sewn up in sacks with weights inside, and their bodies thrown into the Tigris.

The Caliph then told Mésur to set up a Turkish tent in the middle of the palace. This he did, and the Caliph entered it before dawn. Among the persons who came to salute him was Jaafar. Haroun welcomed him cordially, and laughed and joked with him. Jaafar then produced the letters that he had received from various quarters, and the Caliph decided upon their answers. After this business was concluded, Jaafar requested leave to go that day to Khorassan, but Haroun observed that the day was unlucky, and that he fancied something serious was going to happen. This was all the warning the doomed man had. He went home, transacted his business, sent the crowds away, and retired to his apartment. He had hardly done so, when Mésur appeared with a message to say the Caliph wanted him immediately. Jaafar dressed himself, put on his sword, and went with Mésur. When he got through the first gate of the palace he found soldiers posted; at the second gate were slaves; and in the third court he found himself alone with the executioner. Mésur brought him into the tent, and made him sit down. Jaafar asked what was the matter. "You know well enough," was the reply; "your time has come. The Prince of the Faithful has ordered me to cut off your head and take it to him at once." Jaafar began to weep, and to kiss Mésur's hands and feet, saying: "O my brother, my Mésur, you know how good I have been to you, and how I have always done what you asked me day and night. I have here two hundred thousand dinars; I will produce them for you immediately if you will only let me get away from here." Mésur was obdurate, and Jaafar continued to beseech, promising everything, even to making him Commander-in-chief of the army. At last Mésur appeared to relent, and even went so far as to say, "Well, it may be managed." Taking off Jaafar's sword and sword-belt, he set forty black slaves to watch the tent. Then he went to the Caliph, whom he found furious with rage. He had a cane in his hand, with which he was digging in the ground. "What hast thou done in the matter of Jaafar?" "What you ordered." "Where is his head?" "In the tent." "Fetch it at once." Mésur went back, found Jaafar in the act of prayer, drew his sword, and smote off his head; then, taking it by the beard, he took it out and threw it before the Prince of the Faithful. Haroun heaved a deep sigh when he beheld the head, and wept profusely. Digging his stick into the earth after each word, he thus apostrophised the head: "O Jaafar, did I not put you on equality with myself? How have you requited me? You have not reflected on the vicissitudes of fortune. O Jaafar, you have deceived me in my family, and disgraced me before men. O Jaafar, you have done evil to me and to yourself."

Haroun sent to Medina for the two sons of Jaafar. They were handsome lads, and the Caliph admired them, and made them talk. "What is your name, my darling?" he asked of the elder. "El Hassan." "And yours, my dear?" he said, turning to the younger. "El Hassem," replied the boy. The Caliph looked at them and wept. "Mésur," he said, "what have you done with the key of that room?" Slaves and workmen were sent for, the pit opened, the children killed, and buried with their mother. All the time the Caliph was weeping, so that even Mésur thought that he would have pity on them; but he wiped his eyes and bid those about him never again mention the name of the Barmecides. This tragedy happened in the year 803, thirty-five years after Charlemagne had begun to rule the Franks, and three years after he had become Emperor of the West.

Yahya, the vizier, and El Fadhl, both died in prison, while the mother of the Barmecides was found years after in poverty. No one, however, dared to utter a word against all this cruelty; but a certain woman one day presented herself before Haroun when he was in the midst of his court, and thus addressed him: "O Commander of the Faithful! may Allah give repose to thine eye, and make thee rejoice in what He has given thee, for thou hast judged, and hast been just." "Who are you?" asked the Caliph. "A woman of the sons of Barmek, whose men you slew and whose wealth you have taken." "As for the men," Haroun replied, "they suffered what Allah decreed; as for their wealth, it has been restored to whence it came."

But her words went home to the Caliph's conscience, and he was compelled to announce his own judgment. "I do not think," he said to his courtiers, "you quite understood that woman. When she said, 'May Allah give repose to thine eye,' she meant, literally, may it cease from motion—that is, in blindness or death. When she said, 'May He make thee rejoice in what He has given thee,' she alluded to the words of the Koran: 'And when they rejoiced in what was given them, we punished them on a sudden!' And when she said, 'Thou hast judged, and been just,' she used the last word in the sense of trespassing, in which it occurs in another passage, 'And as for the trespassers, they are fuel for hell!'"

Haroun sank into misery after having thus given place to the devil, and died about three years after the last of the Barmecides, a frightened and a broken man. Such was the contradiction of his nature, that while he was dying he betrayed touching anxiety lest the friend who sat with him should feel the cold, and yet a few hours before he had had a man hewn to pieces in his presence; while the terrible Mésur, the remembrancer of all his evil deeds, stood by his bedside to the last. However, he had the satisfaction of hearing a choir of priests gabble all the chapters of the Koran at one and the same time, a charm which he, no doubt, thought would greatly benefit him in the last moments of mortality. Strange fascination of idolatry: the men who destroyed all idols made new ones of the words of a book!

SIDE by side with the gorgeous and prolific Mohammedan civilisation of Cordova and Bagdad, Christianity put forth an effort which deserves study, in order that the intrinsic difference in the root and genius of the two religions may be understood.

In the Empire of Charlemagne we see the blossom of feudal Christianity. Bitter winds and icy days soon destroyed it; but the bloom had set, and its beauty aroused the poetic sentiment almost crushed out by Goth and Vandal; and in due course the fruit appeared.

Pepin, son of Charles Martel, with the inveterate Teutonic disposition to sacrifice everything to family considerations, divided his kingdom between Charles and Carloman. However, Carloman soon died, and Charles became sole monarch of the Gallo-Franco-Germanic monarchy. It was a great, unwieldy realm, covering, as it were, the torso of Europe, but all undefined and broken at the north-west. It was Charlemagne's first care to make himself really master of his dominions, and to secure them against further barbaric and Mohammedan invasion.

This is the meaning of his wars against the Saxons, whose piratical, filibustering tendencies had destroyed the old Roman civilisation, and threatened to reduce all Europe to their own barbaric condition. This fear, quite as much as any real desire for the salvation of their souls, gave such vigour and intensity to the missions directed by Willebrod and Boniface. Pepin, Charlemagne, and the popes of the day supported these missions from political motives. While Charlemagne was determined to stop at nothing in order to reduce the Saxons to subjection, he felt all his efforts would be useless unless he could bring them over to his own religion.

One of his very first efforts, therefore, was directed against their national idol, Irminsul. Whatever this was, whether it was a figure of the great Arminius, who destroyed the legions of Varus, or of one of the Teutonic deities, it represented the national religion of the Saxons, and its fall was felt through every tribe. In revenge they rose and destroyed the church at

Fritzlar, built by Boniface. Charlemagne had made it clear that what he designed was not only the conquest of the Saxons, but of their gods.

The Saxons, alarmed, held a general assembly of the people at Paderborn, and agreed to submit to his rule and be baptised. But a national leader arose, Wittikind, who collected his forces and beat Charlemagne's lieutenants, nearly destroying his army. Charlemagne himself hurried to the frontier, Wittikind flying at his approach. The Saxons gave up all who had helped their leader, and Charlemagne in one day cut off the heads of four thousand five hundred men at a place called Werden, on the river Aller. "Saxony," he said, "must be Christianised, or wiped out." So he settled for a time on the frontier, determined to terrify them into submission (A.D. 782).

Wittikind finally submitted and received baptism, making no further attempts, but continuing faithful to all his engagements. Charlemagne gave him the title of the Duke of Saxony, but without any right of sovereignty. Wittikind died two years before Haroun al Raschid.

In A.D. 773 Pope Adrian invoked the aid of Charlemagne against Didier, King of the Lombards, who was besieging Rome. It was a repetition of the position in 754, when Pepin had come to the relief of Pope Stephen against Astolf the Lombard, and had compelled the latter to cede to him all the lands in Italy belonging to the Roman Empire. These lands Pepin presented to the pope, and they have since been known as the Patrimony of St. Peter. Charlemagne appeared at the call of the pope, and his mere name seemed to inspire terror. He and his Frankish warriors seemed to the enervated Italians as some enormous engine of war, moving on to inevitable conquest. They saw his hosts pouring through the Alps and along the roads, and when they told the story to their children's children, they said, "The fields and the highways were covered with steel; the points of steel reflected the rays of the sun; and this steel, so hard, was borne by a people with hearts still harder. The flash of steel spread terror throughout the streets of the city. What steel! alack, what steel!"

When Charlemagne arrived within three miles of Rome he was met by the magistrates and the banners of the city; the municipal bodies, and the pupils of the schools, with palm-branches in their hands, and singing hymns, greeted him as he approached within a mile of the city. At the gate they brought out the cross, at the sight of which Charlemagne dismounted, and proceeded on foot to the basilica of St. Peter, where he was received by the pope. From all the streets arose the chant, "Blessed is he that cometh in the name of the Lord!"

Charlemagne confirmed the gift of his father to the pope, and styled himself King of the Franks and of the Lombards. Three years after he conferred the latter title on a son who was born to him.

The Governor of Saragossa, Ibn-al Arabi, rebelled against Abdel Rhaman, and offered to give up the city to Charlemagne. The King of the Franks seized the opportunity to inflict a blow on the Spanish Moors, and began to pour through the Pyrenees as he had poured through the Alps; but the Moors were a different foe to the Lombards. They rose on all sides to succour Saragossa, and Charlemagne, hearing that there were fresh troubles in Saxony, was not unwilling to accept the overtures of the Saracens and draw off his troops. On its return the army of the Franks had to go through the passes of Roncesvalles. The defile was so narrow that the soldiers went in single file. The Basques, apparently for plunder, hid themselves along the crests of the mountain, and when the main part of the army had passed, they fell on the baggage-train and the troops in the rear-guard, and killed them almost to a man. In this disaster the celebrated Roland fell, and no action of so slight an importance has ever been enshrined by such splendid legends and such beautiful poetry.

Charlemagne knew how to turn even a mishap of this kind to his advantage, for he immediately hung Duke Lupus, of Aquitania, to whose treachery he attributed the destruction of his army; and seizing Aquitaine, of which he had lately become the new sovereign, he made his infant son, Louis, the new king.

Just as the eighth century closed news came of an ecclesiastical revolt in Rome. Adrian had died leaving two of his nephews in high office. These two persons waylaid the new pope, Leo III., and tried to put out his eyes and cut out his tongue. They only partially succeeded in their object, although no one interposed to prevent them. Urgent letters were at once despatched to Charles as Patrician of Rome. The pope was summoned to Paderborn in Germany, where he was courteously received by the king, although his enemies accused him of some mysterious offence. A synod was held, the late pope's nephews were condemned, and Leo III. declared upon oath, holding the Gospels in his hand, that he had never perpetrated or caused to be perpetrated the wicked deeds laid to his account.

Christmas A.D. 800 soon followed, and Charlemagne and all his court were present at the Festival of Nativity at Rome. After the mass the pope arose, and advancing towards the king, who was bowing down in prayer, placed a splendid crown on his head, the people shouting, "Long life and victory to Charles Augustus, the great and pacific Emperor of the Romans!" This done the pope prostrated himself before the emperor, as had been the custom in old times. Charlemagne accepted the new dignity, and became the anointed Emperor of the Romans.

The alliance of Church and State is generally spoken of as commencing in the days of Constantine, but it was not until these days that the alliance assumed the dignity of Christian wedlock. The Church, according to Teutonic customs, was endowed with a material gift by her new husband, and solemnly promised obedience to her lord and master. These transactions between the popes and the first monarchs of the Carlovingian race were the true beginning of that constitution under which we still live, and which prevailed throughout Europe until the French Revolution.

In this new contract between the Church and the State both parties mutually affected each other. The democratic and imperial institutions which had hitherto characterised the Church became leavened with feudalism, while the feudal institutions of the state became leavened with autocracy and democracy. The pope lost more and more the character of a Roman emperor, who beneath republican institutions arrogated to himself despotic power; he became the sovereign pontiff, to whom the bishops of Christendom owed fealty and homage. On the other hand, the Teutonic states, which knew nothing of the principles of autocracy or democracy, received them through the Church. Charlemagne was the first great example of the Teutonic autocrat, the first German Cæsar. In a century or two we shall see the same turbulent democracy that was for ever surging in Rome, pagan and papal, rise in England and France, never to be really laid to rest until it brings about a new era in the history of humanity.

THE same work that Charlemagne did in Europe was done on a smaller scale in England. This revolution followed, as those we have been tracing in continental Europe, mainly in the wake of the Church and by her agency.

The normal condition of the Teuton was tribal independence, with perpetual war and its attendant pillage and slavery. When Christianity began to be preached new ideas seized men. The poor began to be cared for when kings took the cowl, and laboured with the mattock and the spade or kept sheep. Labour began to have dignity and even rights when princesses knelt by the bedside of a dying slave or bound up his wounds. Chiefs, who had hitherto only thought of themselves as the greatest freemen in the tribe, began to regard themselves as the father of the orphan and the protector of the poor and the oppressed. This gave them courage to assert themselves against the proud, overbearing freeman; and the true idea of monarchy arose. But these kings, driven on by their own ambition and tribal feuds, were ever at war, and would have worn themselves out at last, had not the Church instinctively planted in the English mind the thought of one kingdom under one shepherd. The thought did not come from Germany, but was strictly a Christian idea, coming from the homes of early Christianity, Rome and Greece.

In A.D. 668, the see of Canterbury having remained vacant for four years, the kings of Kent and Northumbria sent Wighard, a Saxon, to be consecrated at Rome. He died there, and the kings begged the pope to send someone in his place. Vitalian's choice fell on a learned and pious monk, Theodore of Tarsus. With the Roman genius for organisation, Theodore commenced to put the Church of England in order. The bishoprics resulting from the conversion of the kingdoms were conterminous with them. Thus the sees were in some cases enormous, and Theodore's first work was to make them more symmetrical as to size, and to group them round the one centre of Canterbury. This was the origin of his contention with Wilfrid of York. In the end the organisation of the parishes followed that of the bishoprics. England became ecclesiastically one, and the sight of this formal unity of the Church, with its manifest advantages, accustomed Englishmen to the idea of political unity. Theodore not only showed the way to political unity, but the general councils that he and his successors held familiarised the people with the idea of national parliaments.

The land was thus prepared for the advent of the man who should be endowed with strength enough to complete the work. This took some generations, and would have probably been deferred still longer, had not Charlemagne effected in his own person the greater unity of Western Europe; for it would have been contrary to the spirit of feudalism, which taught that all good flows from the highest, that a little country like

K

England should have been its exemplar. It was for Charles Augustus, crowned of God the great and pacific Emperor of the Romans, to give the new society the law upon which it was to be regulated.

And, as a matter of fact, not only the example, but the final impetus which made England one came from the court of Charlemagne. Again and again had the Frankish kings attempted to interfere in the struggles of the Heptarchy, but without success. In Charlemagne's time, Offa, King of Mercia, held him at defiance, and almost succeeded in obtaining supreme power in England; but it was reserved for Ecgberht, a refugee from Wessex at the court of Charlemagne, to be the first to attain that position. The death of Offa, in A.D. 796, and still further of the king that Offa had set up in Wessex, opened the way to Ecgberht, who came over from France in the year of Charlemagne's coronation at Rome (A.D. 800), and was welcomed by the West Saxons as their king. In A.D. 823 the King of Mercia invaded Wessex, but was defeated by Ecgberht at Ellandune. After this all England south of the Thames submitted to his sway. East Anglia rose against Mercia and twice gained the victory. Ecgberht thus found the way open to march north. He compelled Mercia to recognise his lordship, and then Northumbria. Thus England was gathered under one ruler, and Ecgberht became first King of the English (A.D. 827).

It is only after his coronation at Rome in A.D. 800 that Charlemagne seems to have attained a full conviction of his calling as a legislator. Out of sixty-five Capitularies attributed to his reign, fifty-two are comprised within the years A.D. 801 and A.D. 804.

Charlemagne did not attempt the impossible task of reducing all his enormous territories to one law. He allowed the varied forms to go on at the same time, his chief work being to keep them from clashing, and to enforce certain general rules. One of these was the universal obligation to military service in proportion to the possession of land. The distinction between clergy and laity, which became so marked a feature of mediæval Christianity, received legal recognition in the exemption of the clergy from military service, to which they had previously been liable. Their property was also placed under special protection; but churches were no longer to afford asylum against the sovereign authority. In the national assemblies, of which Charlemagne held thirty-five during his reign, the places of meeting were divided into two parts, so that clergy and laity might meet without mingling together.

These national assemblies are the models of early feudal parliaments. They do not appear to have been assembled on any principle. Certain persons were expected or commanded to be there, others had a traditionary right to be present, most felt it a burden. The emperor regarded these assemblies as a great help in government, since he learnt in them the wants and discontents of his empire. He listened to complaints, petitions, and proposals, but the initiative of new laws proceeded from him alone as from one *inspired of God;* and when they had passed the ordeal of discussion, the result was submitted to the great prince, who, with wisdom received from on high, adopted a resolution.

The laws thus passed and promulgated resembled the ordinances of the founder of a society rather than those enacted by modern authority. For example: the second article of the Capitulary of the year 802 says: "It has pleased us to ordain that everyone shall endeavour in his own person to keep himself fully in the holy service of God and of His promises, and according to his intelligence and strength, for the lord emperor cannot make each individual sufficiently careful to preserve him therein."

Again: "Covetousness doth consist in desiring that which others possess, and giving away naught of that which oneself possesseth; according to the apostle, it is the root of all evil."

More than three-quarters of Charlemagne's Capitularies are composed of similar moral and religious precepts; according to Sismondi, they are only reiterations of the Decalogue and Leviticus. Here we have an indication of the foundation of that great and noble society of which Charlemagne was the principal founder. Religion, we do not say the pure religion of Jesus Christ, but Christianity as understood eight hundred years after His advent, formed the very basis and soul of the new feudal system, which under Charlemagne was foreshadowed rather than realised.

Terribly corrupt as we have shown mediæval Christianity to be, it had enough of truth in it to maintain the most active and civilised nations of the earth for a thousand years, and to bring them up to the point of the French Revolution. If mediæval Christianity could do this, what is there that pure Christianity cannot do?

Charlemagne was fond of reading Augustine's "City of God." Was it not from that book that he drew the inspiration which made him seek to realise a true "City of God" in his empire? The mediæval poets thought of him as the Hebrews thought of David. His kingdom was the typical one, his ideal the one they ever sought to realise. In their legends they more and more disfigured his portrait, reducing him to their own level. For the true Charlemagne, as we know him, was nobler far than anything that appears in romance.

Haroun al Raschid's love of learning was that of the *dilettante;* Charlemagne was a philosopher, in the true sense of the word. Like Haroun, he surrounded himself with wise and learned men, but not for mere amusement. These men formed a learned and industrious society, at times advising him on important questions, at times giving to him and to his court regular lessons in grammar, rhetoric, logic, astronomy and geometry, and even theology. "If your zeal," said the learned Englishman, Alcuin, who was the principal of this royal college—"if your zeal were imitated, perchance one might see in France a new Athens far more glorious than the ancient—the Athens of Christ."

A beautiful picture has been left us of the great warrior striving hard to instruct himself, that he might be equal to all his duties. Latin he knew well, and could speak easily. Greek he understood better than he could express himself in it. He devoted much time to rhetoric, logic, and astronomy. He learnt arithmetic, and in his old age studied grammar. He tried to learn to write, and in order to improve himself kept a little book of tablets, in which he would occupy his hours of rest by trying to form letters.

Towering above every other form in the Middle Ages, this grand old man was its true prophet. Looking out one day from a window in a certain town in Narbonnese Gaul, he descried some strange craft in the harbour. Those with him had no idea what they were, but Charlemagne, perceiving by the lightness of their build that they were not made for merchandise, rose from the table and looked at them a long while, his eyes filling with tears.

"Know ye, my lieges," he said, "wherefore I weep so bitterly? Of a surety I fear not lest those fellows should succeed in hurting me by their miserable piracies; but it grieveth me deeply that whilst I live they should have been nigh to touching at this shore. I am a prey to violent sorrow, when I foresee the evils that they will heap on my descendants and my people."

TENTH CENTURY.

CONTEMPORARY EVENTS IN THE TENTH CENTURY.

England.—Murder of Eadward at Corfe Castle.
Spain.—Its commercial prosperity.

Normandy.—The peasants driven to revolt.
Russia.—Idolatry overthrown.

Tenth Century.

A.D. 975-999.

Christian Europe harried by the Northmen, the Slaves, and the Magyars—Degradation of the Papacy—Pope Gerbert—Dunstan—Murder of King Eadward—Sufferings of the Peasants in France—Horrors and Calamities all over Christendom—Expected End of the World—The Truce of God—Robert of France—Prosperity of Mohammedan Spain —Mohammedanism in India—Conversion of Russia to Christianity.

URING the tenth century Christendom reached the lowest depth of darkness, misery, and despair. Both within and without it was harassed and oppressed by cruel foes. The prophecy of Charlemagne was fulfilled: the Danes or Northmen became the scourge of his descendants and their people. War conducted by large armies, such as those with which the Saracens invaded Europe, was not half so hard to bear as the war carried on by these piratical Northmen. Their barks covered the Northern seas, and had long penetrated far into the Mediterranean. All the coasts of Northern Europe lay open to their ravages, and they were so numerous and so active that no maritime town or village could reckon itself safe from their attacks. Audacious beyond all former invaders, they ran their light vessels up the great rivers under cover of night, making raids on inland towns and villages; setting them on fire, and carrying off the property and the children of the inhabitants. Saxon England they well nigh conquered. Even Alfred the Great was

obliged to leave them in possession of almost half the country, while in France the descendant of Charlemagne was compelled to make a virtue of necessity, and to give up to them one of the finest provinces of France, which henceforth was called Normandy. King and people alike dreaded these pitiless foes, and to the Litany a new petition was added:—" From the terror of the Northmen, good Lord deliver us!"

Meanwhile the East of Europe suffered from enemies whose very name was hardly known in the West. The Slaves, a people occupying the regions now called Bohemia, Poland, and Russia, were a constant source of trouble to the Byzantine emperors. Four times during this century the Slaves of Russia made attempts on Constantinople.

The German Empire, which began its existence in the early part of this century (A.D. 911), had to struggle with a foe still more formidable than the Slaves. Towards the close of the ninth century a Turanian race called the Magyars, numbering two hundred thousand warriors, led by a chief called Almos, fell like hordes of wild beasts upon Europe. By the beginning of the tenth century, under Arpad, son of Almos, they had conquered all that now forms the kingdom of Hungary. The Germans found it hard work to keep these terrible Asiatics back, but at length in A.D. 955 they were defeated in a great battle by Otto I.

The misery of the unhappy people of Christian Europe, who thus lived in continual dread of being invaded on all sides by remorseless pagans, was aggravated by the weakness and wickedness of their own rulers. The bulk of Christian men and women in the days of Charlemagne were serfs, reduced to that unhappy condition chiefly by war, and its certain consequence—poverty. The clergy, though so corrupt, were still Christian in thought and feeling, and constantly used their influence in favour of the poor. They set an example in the way they treated their own serfs; and when wealthy men were dying, they were sometimes induced by the suggestion of the priests to give freedom to their bondmen.

But in an age so wretched in all its circumstances, even freedom was hardly a boon to those who had kind masters, while its acquisition by large numbers served to depress the remnants of the only class who might have defended the original liberties of the Teutonic race—the free farmers. What with the terror of being carried off by the pagans, and the poverty engendered by a continual state of war, many of these ancient freeholders had bartered their independence for protection. Placing themselves under some powerful lord, they became his men, and held their lands from him.

While, by this kind of voluntary surrender, the land thus gradually came into the hands of the lords, the domains of the more powerful nobility were continually enlarged by the oppression of the weaker, and by the gifts of the king. When, as in France, the royal house was feeble, the great landowners rapidly increased in power, and became almost absolute in their own domains. In France, towards the end of the tenth century, there were fifty such petty states. Frequently at war among themselves, their subjects did not enjoy even a slave's freedom from anxiety, for anyone who owned a castle, or could arm a sufficient body of men, thought himself at liberty to attack his neighbours whenever he imagined that he had received an insult or an injury.

One of the greatest evils brought about by the general terror and anarchy of the age, was the rapid extinction of the light which had appeared in the days of Charlemagne and Alfred. The grossest ignorance prevailed, and in its train came vice and superstition. Nowhere did wickedness appear more rampant than in the lives of the so-called heads of the Church. The Papacy never sank so low. The election fell into the hands of any power that happened to get the mastery at Rome: the neighbouring prince, the demagogue, or some daring and infamous woman. Theodora, a woman of aristocratic birth but disgraceful life, succeeded in placing her paramour and illegitimate sons on the papal throne. Octavian, her grandson, thus became pope at the age of twenty-one, under the title of John XII. His life was such an outrage that Christendom could endure the scandal no longer. The emperor was compelled to hold a synod at Rome, at which John was cited to answer a strangely mingled series of charges: adultery, incest, hunting, cruelty, drinking, gambling, neglecting matins and vespers, invoking Jove and Venus, celebrating mass without communicating, never signing himself with the sign of the cross, going about with sword, lance, helmet, and breastplate. Instead of answering his accusers, John declared that if they elected another pope, he would excommunicate all concerned, and forbid them to confer orders or to say mass. Happily he died after he had been supreme pontiff for eight years. Though a signal instance of the degradation of the times, he was by no means a peculiar one. The papal succession for many years fell to men of vicious life.

Under these auspices the condition of the Mediæval Church was such that it would have been a reproach to the heathen. In England the Church was torn by implacable contests between the secular and regular clergy. The religion of the common people seems to have chiefly consisted in collecting and worshipping relics. The universal ignorance and superstition were so great that when, in the last year of the century, a really learned man, Gerbert, Archbishop of Ravenna, was made pope, under the title of Sylvester II., he was accused of being a sorcerer, and the most absurd stories of his magical powers were circulated and believed.

How brutal in their ignorant hatred of all learning were the English lords, we may learn from the story of Dunstan. He, like Gerbert, had a passion for knowledge which nothing could suppress. While yet a youth the fame of his learning caused him to be summoned by King Eadmund to his court. But the courtiers were more than a match for the king; they not only drove Dunstan from the royal presence, but dragging him off his horse, as he passed through the marshes, they trampled him in the dirt as a sign of their contempt. With the decay of religion and learning violence became rampant. In A.D. 975 a young Saxon prince, about fourteen or fifteen years old, became King of England. His stepmother, Elfrida, wanted the throne for her son, a young child. By the influence of Dunstan young Eadward was crowned, and maintained in his position for three years. Hunting in the neighbourhood of Corfe Castle, where his stepmother lived, he paid her a visit. He was welcomed and invited to dismount. Wishing to rejoin his companions, the king declined more than a cup of wine. This was brought, and just as he was about to drink, one of the queen's servants treacherously stabbed him in the back. He spurred his horse, but fainting from loss of blood, fell, and was dragged by one foot in the stirrup over the rugged road until he was dead.

———

In such a miserable state of affairs it is not surprising to find that the patient, suffering people began to wish to get rid of their rulers. In Normandy the labouring people met after their hours of labour to talk over their sufferings. "The lords," they said, "do nothing but evil; we cannot obtain either reason or justice from them; they have all, they take all, they eat all, and make us live in poverty and suffering. Every day is a day of pain; we gain nought by our labours, there are so many dues and services. Why do we allow ourselves to be thus treated?" So they swore to stand by each other, and soon there was formed a vast association which spread over the country. Before, however, they had committed any overt act of rebellion, the lords found out what was going on. Their leader, Count Raoul of Evreux, sent out spies in every direction, and in consequence of their report he was able to arrest in one day all the principal men of the association. In order to strike terror into the hearts of the people, Count Raoul tortured his unhappy prisoners by cutting off their hands and feet, and putting out their eyes; some he impaled alive, while others had their legs burned, or melted lead poured over them. Those who survived were sent home to their respective villages as a warning.

No wonder that, borne down by this awful load of wretchedness, men everywhere began to believe the end of the world was at hand. As the year A.D. 1000 approached horrors seemed to accumulate. Famine ravaged the East, Greece, Italy, France, and England. Corn rose so high in price that even the rich became thin and pale; as to the poor, they were glad to gnaw the roots they found in the forests, and men grew so desperate with hunger that they tore the food out of their children's hands. Horrible stories were rife of widespread cannibalism. The weak, it was said, were attacked on the high roads, torn to pieces, roasted, and eaten. A man who had dared to offer human flesh for sale in the market had been burnt; another, found digging up the dead, had shared the same fate. In the Forest of Maçon a hut had been found containing the skulls of forty-eight men, women, and children, the victims of a wretch who murdered every wayfarer who sought his hospitality.

These famines occurred year after year, and plague and pestilence followed in their wake. In Aquitaine the epidemic took a frightful form. The flesh of the victims seemed as if it had been burnt, and fell from the bones and became gangrened. The people crowded to the churches. At St. Martin's, in Limoges, several were stifled, and their bodies fell in a heap upon each other. Still the crowds pressed on. Many of the bishops came, and the relics were brought out. It was no use, the people thronged more than ever; the infection spread, and the victims fell dead on the relics of the saints. To these was added a new horror: so many corpses remained unburied, that wolves appeared, and began to attack the living as well as the dead.

Christendom was paralysed with terror; it sank crushed before God. The great robber-nobles were touched. They hastened to the churches, and swore to live peaceable lives; they would no more infest the highways; at the very least, they would respect all who travelled under the care of priests or monks. War was only to be allowed between Monday morning and Wednesday evening; during all the rest of the week there was to be peace, a peace later on called "the truce of God."

Men fled to the church and the cloister, making a gift on the altars of their lands, their houses, and their serfs. Often they gave not only their goods, but themselves. The monks had the greatest trouble to prevent kings and dukes from becoming members of their orders.

The author of several beautiful hymns, King Robert of France, though his name does not appear in the Roman Calendar, is the typical saint of this age. He had the greatest pity for all classes of sinners, but especially for thieves, whose temptations at this dreadful time he seems to have thought insurmountable. He allowed himself to be robbed with a gentle smile; he even shut his eyes to sacrilege rather than punish theft. In order to lessen the crime of lying, which he hated, he had recourse to a pious fraud. The reliquaries on which he administered oaths to his people contained no relics. The one in use for the nobles was a mere ball of crystal richly gilt; that for the poor, a plain ball containing an egg. It was under the rule of this good and simple-hearted man that France passed such dark and awful days. At such a time the highest quality in life was the power to endure. He who in such an age could still believe in God and love man was worthy the title of Robert the Wise.

THE helpless misery and dark despair into which Christendom had now fallen was intensified by the fact that vast tribes, animated with boundless energy and hope, encircled the Christian countries. In the Mohammedan countries learning and commerce flourished. Large cities sprang up, the depôts for the exchange of the multifarious industries which the energy of a people animated by a faith in an invisible God, and governed with some reference to public good, brought into being.

Mohammedan Spain was governed during this century for nearly fifty years by one monarch, the famous Abder Rahman III. Under his sway the resources of Spain were developed in a marvellous manner. Agriculture, manufactures, and commerce all flourished vigorously. The culture of rice, of the fig, and of the sugar-cane was introduced, a great system of drainage and watercourses carried out. At Seville, Cadiz, Tarragon, and Almeria large ports grew up, which brought untold wealth to the merchants of Moorish Spain. The warehouses of Syria, Egypt, and Constantinople were piled with Spanish manufactures—leather, cotton, linen, and especially silk. Leather was called, throughout the Middle Ages, cordwain or cordovan, and workers in leather were known as cordwainers, from the great centre of its manufacture, the Mohammedan city of Cordova. In addition to these more useful commodities, the Spanish merchants drew great wealth from the export of Andulasian coral, Catalonian pearls, Carthagenian amethysts, and rubies.

Cordova, the capital of Moorish Spain, contained at this time two hundred thousand houses, six hundred mosques, nine hundred baths, fifty hospitals, and eighty schools. Seville and Granada rivalled Cordova in the number of academies, colleges, and libraries. Authors in every branch of literature appeared, so that while the rest of Europe sat in darkness, Spain was a focus of intellectual light. Thus it was that lovers of learning like Gerbert stole away into Spain, and purchased, at the risk of all kinds of imputations, the key of knowledge from the infidel Moor.

While in the West Mohammedanism gave itself up to peace, learning, and progress, it found in the East a new champion in Mahmoud of Ghuznee, surnamed the Idol-breaker. The father and grandfather of Mahmoud were both slaves, who, with the aid of the Afghans, had reigned successively in Ghuznee as independent rulers. Mahmoud had obtained the throne in A.D. 997, and two years after had assumed the title of Sultan. His reign was mainly spent in invasions of India, destroying idols and plundering temples; but as it extended to A.D. 1030, historically it belongs to the next century. Yet it is interesting to recall the fact that, both in India and Europe, the Aryan peoples were suffering from the same spiritual malady— idolatry. Beautiful temples everywhere, filled with idols, their shrines resplendent with precious stones ; society governed by a priestly caste, supported by kings and warriors, who attained a character for piety in proportion to their obedience to ecclesiastical behests ; myriads of toilers bound fast in the darkest superstition, and dying at times like rotten sheep from the folly and imbecility of their rulers—the condition of Europe and India presents at this time and during the early Middle Ages a singular external resemblance.

If intellectual energy distinguished Christendom's southern foe, energy, both mental and physical, distinguished its northern enemy. The Northmen were the most restless and ruthless of invaders; but wherever they conquered a civilised people they soon mastered all that their new subjects had to teach them, and showed themselves capable of a higher civilisation still. Thus they became a ruling race in Europe. The very qualities that rendered them so terrible to the English and to the French aroused the admiration of the Slave, so that at the very time when Alfred and his brothers were struggling to get England out of their grasp, the Slaves of Northern Russia were entreating them to come, as the only persons capable of giving them protection, order, and unity. "Our land," they sent word to the Northmen, "is great and bountiful, but there is no order in it; come and rule over us."

Accordingly, in A.D. 864, Rurik came with his brothers to undertake the task. Their kingdom at first appears to have been confined to the North, but Isor, Rurik's son, took Kiev, which then became the chief city of the new kingdom of Russia.

It is not until the middle of this tenth century that we hear of Christianity penetrating the land. Although it was accomplished in a way consistent with the darkness of the age, it is a gleam of light on its horizon, and must have comforted some sad souls in the apparent wreck of Christendom.

Olga, Isor's widow and successor, was the first to embrace Christianity, but her subjects did not follow her. Her grandson, "the sunny Prince Vladimir," was a thorough pagan when he ascended the throne, A.D. 980. The manner of his conversion is curious and characteristic. Deputations of the various religious sects came to try and persuade him to adopt their faith. The first who came represented either the Paulicians, the dissenters of the East, or the Western Church of Rome, for the answer he is reported to have given them suits neither wholly. The next were the Mussulmen. He dismissed them, as it was quite impossible for him to give up pork and wine. Then came the Jews, whom he derided as people forsaken by God on their own confession. Lastly, came a representative of the Greek Church —a philosopher, who discoursed to him very learnedly on the whole scheme of revelation, relating the history of the Church from the earliest times to the seventh Council.

Vladimir seems to have been impressed, but, cautious in all his proceedings, he determined to send ambassadors to see how these various religions appeared in practice. The embassy brought a very poor account of the Jews and Mohammedans and of the Christian denominations. Having been to Constantinople, they declared themselves convinced that the Eastern Church was by far the most glorious and worthy of confidence. Rude, uncultured barbarians of Asiatic origin, they were smitten with the grandeur of the ritual at St. Sophia's. The artful Greeks had taken every care to make the display as scenic as possible; and the Russians went home firmly believing that the deacons and acolytes they had seen emerge in a mysterious manner from behind the altar with torches and flying lappets to their shoulders were actually angels who constantly participated in the services.

Vladimir, however, was not prepared to give up his old faith too readily. Like Clovis, he wanted to be sure he should still be a successful warrior. So he made war against the Greeks, and besieged Cherson. The city fell into his hands, and then he made another demand. He would become a Christian if Anna, the emperor's sister, would marry him. The princess made the sacrifice, wedded him in A.D. 988, and reaped her reward; for Vladimir, in the sequel, seems to have become a changed man, leading a new life, and exhibiting a character every way the reverse of that which he had hitherto manifested. His first act after his baptism was to induce his people to follow his example.

In order to convince them of the futility of their old religion, he caused the great idol they worshipped, Perim, the god of thunder, which he himself had set up at Kiev, to be dragged by horses twelve miles across the country, and whipped ignominiously all the way, and finally pushed into the Dnieper, and sunk there. After this his people gave way, and were baptised in crowds. Thus strangely was Russia brought under the power of Christianity; and thus fitly concluded a cycle of contemporary events characteristic of this singularly interesting century.

MOORISH BRIDGE AND GATE, CORDOVA.

ELEVENTH CENTURY.

CONTEMPORARY EVENTS IN THE ELEVENTH CENTURY.

Germany.—Henry IV. at Canossa.
Spain.—The Cid entering Toledo.
England—Making Domesday Book.
Palestine.—Peter the Hermit in Jerusalem.

Eleventh Century.

A.D. 1079-1095.

The Age of Construction—The Norman Genius for Building—The Abbey of Bec—Lanfranc—Anselm—William the Conqueror—Hildebrand, founder of the Mediæval Papacy—The Cid—Peter the Hermit and the first Crusader.

S the closing years of the tenth century were passing away, the two most potent rulers in Christendom sat at Rome in council. One was an ancient priest, his face furrowed and weary ; the other, a handsome, daring knight, just turned twenty. The world without said that the elder man was a wizard, for, in spite of universal suspicion, he had become pope, fascinating alike king and priest, Moor and Christian. Pious King Robert was his friend, and still more this brilliant young stripling, who was no other than the Emperor Otto II., called by his fond admirers "the wonder of the world." And remarkable indeed he was for precocious talent, as his old tutor and friend, now Pope Sylvester II., very well knew. For had he not done deeds, the like of which had no parallel, save in sacred history? Scarcely fifteen years of age, he had come to the rescue of the pope, had defeated the patrician Crescentius, and had restored order in Rome. Charlemagne was Otto's ideal hero, and with Sylvester's help he hoped to work out the great Carlovingian idea : Christendom under a double head, the Holy Roman Empire side by side with the Holy Roman Church.

L 2

But pope and emperor worked alone; the Romans suspected and disliked them both; and when, after a pilgrimage to Jerusalem, in the solemn year A.D. 1000, and a visit to the grave of Charlemagne, from whose corpse he took the golden cross, Otto returned to Rome, he fell victim to a foul plot and died, apparently of poison. As Pope Sylvester mourned his hopes for the future of Christendom thus sadly frustrated, he might well say, "I have observed the higher men are placed the greater their inward anguish." A year after, he, too, had gone.

But it became the work of the eleventh century to realise the ideal that Charlemagne had pictured forth, and that Otto and Gerbert had hoped to establish. A gift of constructive energy had been granted it, the results of which are apparent to this day. The castles, cathedrals, abbeys, and monasteries, whose ruins cover Europe, for the most part date their foundation or reconstruction from the eleventh century. The men who were thus able so marvellously to express in stone an image of the order that reigned in their minds were equally gifted in founding great societies. Some of these remain, to testify, like their ruined castles and their magnificent cathedrals, to a genius peculiar to this age, and undoubtedly a gift from on high. Some have passed away, as, for example, the free municipal institutions of Spain and Italy; but this age saw the foundations laid of the English Constitution and the Mediæval Papacy.

───◆───

THE chief agents in this work were the members of that race which in the last age had ravaged all the coasts of Europe—the dreaded Northmen. Settled in France, converted to Christianity, mingled with their neighbours, the Normans developed a strong character. A determination to make their way in the world was their chief characteristic. To make it by fighting, if they could, but, if fighting did not suffice, then by chicanery and art. In them was combined the soldier and the lawyer, the tiger and the fox, in nearly equal proportions. They seemed at once patriotic and cosmopolitan, but they cared little for their own country or for men. Wherever their interests lay, they found their country, and if a good thing was to be had, the Normans were always ready to put in a claim.

They could not ravage Europe in armed bands, as their fathers had done, but they took up the trade of the pilgrim, which answered nearly as well. With staves in their hands and shells on their capes, and a drawling, snuffling accent, they passed where men-at-arms would have been challenged; but when the opportunity occurred they knew how to draw the sword, and what they acquired they kept. Thus some of these pilgrims, being in Naples, helped the people to drive away the Saracens. The reward they obtained attracted others; among them came a poor gentleman from Hauteville named Tancred, the father of twelve sons. In A.D. 1042, one of these sons obtained the sovereignty of Apulia, and soon added Calabria to his possessions. His brother Roger became Count of Sicily, and Roger's son, uniting all the Norman dominions in Italy, and subjugating the republics of Naples and Amalfi and the principality of Capua, an important Norman kingdom was established in the very centre of the Mediterranean.

Rarely men of genius themselves, these adventurous Normans, so energetic and unscrupulous, had an extraordinary faculty for finding out men who were. They esteemed them, learnt of them, and rewarded them well. Moreover, the Normans were religious, obedient, temperate, capable of much culture. Thus they and the lands they occupied became, during this eleventh century, the centres of the intellectual life and energy of Europe.

Not that the Normans or the men they attracted were the well-spring of that life and energy. That, as ever, sprang from the eternal Source of every good and perfect gift. The honour and wisdom of the Normans consisted in their recognising that fact, and making themselves its instruments. Selfish and ambitious they may have been, but it was the selfishness and ambition of Jacob. An ardent faith in God was mixed up with it; and it was this which gave them power with God and men, and made them prevail.

Proofs of this are abundant. All the historians have remarked the different manner in which the Normans and Saxons spent the night before the battle of Hastings. While the latter were drinking, the Normans were confessing their sins, listening to the chant of litanies, and in the early morning they received the sacrament. No land in Christendom was so covered with churches and abbeys, nor were they anywhere so beautiful and magnificent as in Normandy. William the Conqueror never refused permission to anyone who wished to found a church. Normandy, says the same authority, William of Poitiers, rivalled the Thebaid for the multitude of its monasteries. Accordingly, the learned and pious from all parts, but especially from Italy, were drawn to Normandy, and gave it their spiritual wisdom and genius.

The story of the Abbey of Bec is a striking illustration of all this. Herlouin, a Norman warrior, moved by the love of God, threw aside the girdle of military service and became a monk. In one of those pleasant valleys so characteristic of this bright and beautiful land, where pure and rapid streams make their way through peaceful meadows shut in by wooded hills, Herlouin founded a monastery. Its beginnings were humble enough, but God attracted to it men of such ability that it was afterwards said of this simple soldier-monk, "With the torrent of the wisdom of thy sons hast thou filled the world."

But Herlouin had no learning himself—his sole strength lay in his faith in God and in prayer. Obliged constantly to leave the cloister to procure provisions, he had no one to watch over the religion of his household while he was absent, and he therefore often prayed that God would send someone to preside over the monastery. And his prayers were answered.

The son of a rich citizen of Pavia, led by love of letters, quitted his home to come to Normandy. He taught for a time at Avranches, but, moved by that inner craving for God that nothing earthly could satisfy, he determined to go to some place where there were no literary men who would hold him in honour and reverence. Late one evening, going through a wood near Rouen, he was stopped by a band of robbers, who took away all that he had, bound his hands behind him, and left him in a dark part of the forest. Having bewailed his misfortune, he tried to pay his accustomed praises to God, but could not. He wondered at his stupidity, and cried, "Deliver me, O Lord, from this tribulation, and with Thy help I will so study to correct and establish my life that I may be able to serve Thee and know Thee." Before daybreak travellers passed through the wood, who untied his hands and set him free. "Tell me," said he, "of the poorest monastery in this neighbourhood to which I may betake myself." They knew of none more lowly and abject than one which a certain man of God had built hard by. And so Lanfranc, one day to be Archbishop of Canterbury, came to Bec.

The abbot was lighting a fire when the learned young doctor presented himself. Herlouin looked at him and rejoiced, for he believed that God had answered his prayers. Lanfranc became a monk, and henceforth there was a pious contest between the two, the abbot full of veneration for the new brother's learning, Lanfranc scrupulous in his obedience to the abbot's slightest word. His light, however, could not be hid. Dukes, and the sons of dukes, as well as the most distinguished masters of the Latin schools, flocked to Bec to sit at Lanfranc's feet.

Lanfranc aroused William's anger by siding with the pope in a strife that arose about his marriage with Matilda, and was banished. Riding on a lame horse, the only one the abbey could obtain, he was overtaken by William, eager for his departure. "Give me a better horse," said he, "and I shall go the quicker." The ready reply changed wrath into amusement, and Lanfranc became William's chief counsellor.

Reading one day at table, he was corrected by the presiding monk for saying "docēre." He immediately shortened the middle syllable, "knowing that it was not a capital crime to violate prosody, but that it was to disobey one who commanded him in the name of God." This story throws much light on the principle that guided Lanfranc's life. He had a difficult path to tread, with William on the one hand and Hildebrand on the other; but the facility with which he could throw away his scruples to save his principles, was in full harmony with the spirit of the society he served. "Certainly," says one of the ablest of his critics, "a very sagacious man, with a wonderful faculty for managing the things of earth, but with little, if any, of the finer sensibility, or the stern love of truth, which we are taught to look for in one who seeks the kingdom of heaven."

But Bec sent another Italian to be his successor of very different mould, one who had a deeper love of righteousness, a more tolerant mind—Anselm, of Aosta, the philosopher of the eleventh century. From Theophilus of Cilicia to Thomas Cranmer, no two men did more to found the Church of England, and to give it a tone and a character, than these two subjects of pious Herlouin, the prayerful Norman, who founded the humble monastery of Bec.

But if that Norman monastery is a fine example of the sources whence flowed the stream of new life into the world, the sovereign lord of Normandy is a good illustration of the kind of agents by whom the new society was raised. Notwithstanding certain startling facts to the contrary, the genius of William was constructive rather than destructive. While only Duke of Normandy, he earned the title of "the Builder."

None of his predecessors ever erected so many castles, churches, and monasteries. He was, however, to work with grander materials than quarried stones.

William the Norman laid the foundations of the English Constitution. He began the conquest of our land, as we all know, in the decisive battle at Senlac, near Hastings. Daring and ruthless, he was clever in getting the utmost out of his efforts, and keeping all he had gained. His head was never turned by success, but immediately after victory he was ready to grant the best terms to all who would submit. To master England he stopped at no bloodshed, but once secure on his throne, he ruled wisely. Preserving the framework of the old laws and customs, he established in England the feudal system in its most thorough form. The king became the centre and source of everything, the lord of all the land, and the fountain of justice and honour. Since all land was henceforth held on feudal tenure, that is, with the obligation of so much military service, William caused an exact inventory to be taken of the extent and value of every estate in the kingdom. Commissioners went through the country summoning before them all who could tell what each estate, small and great, had been and then was. Their register was called "the Domesday Book," in the despondent language of the conquered Englishmen, and it exists to this day a most complete monument of Norman England (A.D. 1086).

With the help of Lanfranc, William reformed the Church of England, which had sunk very low. "In choosing abbots and bishops," we are told by one who lived at the time, "he considered not so much men's riches and power as their holiness and wisdom. He called together bishops and abbots in any vacancy, and by their advice inquired very carefully who was the best and wisest man, as well in Divine things as worldly, to rule the Church of God."

ABOUT the time that the grandson of the Norman tanner was scheming how to obtain the succession to the English crown, the son of a Tuscan carpenter was dreaming of a far greater task—how to reform the Roman Church, which for centuries past had been disgraced by the grossest scandals, and saved from dissolution only by the still grosser ignorance and servitude of the people it professed to direct. The bishops, almost as warlike as the barons, were constantly at feud with their neighbours, harrying and oppressing their own people. Kings and other rulers were in the habit of seizing the bishoprics and great abbacies, and appointing their relatives or their courtiers, who were sometimes mere youths, to fill the most responsible offices. Simony and concubinage were common among the clergy. The whole ecclesiastical fabric was going to ruin, when a monk arose, gifted with all the Conqueror's mental qualities—courage, perseverance, insight into human character, adroitness in intrigue, pertinacity in keeping an advantage once gained, freedom from all scruple. He was also possessed by an idea to which he was absolutely ready to sacrifice himself and every one else. Such was Hildebrand, cardinal and archdeacon of Rome. Leo IX. found him at Cluny some time during his pontificate, 1048-1054, and brought him to Rome. Hildebrand's idea of Church reformation was a thoroughly monastic one. He proposed to reform the Church by making the Papacy not only independent of all secular authority, but supreme over it. The emperors of Germany, as successors of Charlemagne, claimed the title of Emperor of the Romans, and in that capacity to have the final voice in the election of the pontiff. In the anarchy into which all things had fallen in Rome for a century past, the German emperors had deposed and instituted pope after pope.

Hildebrand worked as long as he could behind other men's shadows. Thus, in A.D. 1059, Nicholas II., at his instance, published a decree which has been the method of the papal election ever since. It took the election of the pope out of the hands of the people, and confided it to a conclave of cardinals. However, in A.D. 1073, Hildebrand was himself elected and forced into the papal chair by popular enthusiasm. He refused to assume the tiara without the sanction of the emperor. Henry IV. gave it, little dreaming how great a foe he was raising. Once secure in his position, Gregory VII. set about the great work of his life—the emancipation of the clergy from all secular control, and their complete subjection to the papal power. He began by asserting his own independence of, and supremacy over, the emperor himself in all ecclesiastical matters. He struck at once at the right the emperor claimed of intervening in the appointment of every bishop. Chosen, in the first instance, by the people or chapter, the bishops were always obliged to look to their sovereign for permission to take possession of the temporalities of the see; the granting of this permission was called the right of investiture, and was accompanied by the presentation of the ring and crosier from the sovereign's hands. This claim had come to be so abused that investiture really meant nomination, and bishoprics were freely sold to the highest bidder. To get rid of this scandal, which had become inveterate, Gregory determined to deny altogether the right of investiture by the secular power. He summoned a Council at Rome. This Council decreed that all persons guilty of simony should be excommunicated, that all persons guilty of immorality should be expelled from the ranks of the clergy, and none admitted for the future unless they took the vow of celibacy. In reply to these decrees from Rome, the emperor seized the first plausible opportunity that presented itself to depose a bishop nominated by the pope, and to put his own man in his place. The pope, knowing Henry's subjects were very discontented, stirred them up to revolt, and after a time sent a summons to the emperor to appear at Rome and answer the charges brought against him. Henry was enraged at the pope's assumption, and assembling a Council at Worms he procured a sentence of deposition against Gregory. Whereupon the pope, in solemn council in the Lateran Palace, issued a decree of excommunication against Henry, depriving him of his kingdoms of Germany and Italy, and forbidding his subjects to obey him any longer. The pope's audacity was completely successful. Rather than lose his kingdom, Henry consented to humble himself in the most abject manner. In the middle of the winter of 1077 he crossed the Alps with his wife and a few servants, and presented himself at the Castle of Canossa, in Lombardy, where Gregory was staying with his devoted partisan, the Countess Matilda. For three days the pontiff refused to see him, compelling him to spend the time shivering in an outer court of the castle without shoes and with no clothes but a single woollen garment. On the fourth day he was admitted to the papal presence, and on confessing his errors received absolution, but could not get the pope to restore him to his kingdom.

The only ruler in Europe who dared to repudiate Gregory's claims was William the Conqueror. "Fealty," he replied to the papal summons, "I have never willed to do, nor do I will to do it now. I never promised it, nor do I find that my predecessors did it to yours."

Henry, absolved but still deposed, found support in his Lombard subjects, who hoped to turn the quarrel to their own advantage. The great cities of Northern Italy had for some time emerged from the state of servitude into which they had sunk during the decline and fall of the Roman Empire. In the seventh century, they began to rebuild their walls, and this once effected, they soon became asylums for all the oppressed. Such persons were always welcomed, as it was soon discovered that the wealth and power of a town increased in proportion to its inhabitants. As the spirit of freedom arose, the dukes, marquises, counts, or prelates, who had hitherto regarded these cities as their own property, found the atmosphere anything but agreeable, so they quitted them to live in castles in the open country, making friends of their rural bondsmen by enfranchising them and giving them arms.

The cities thus to some extent having disposed of the great noblemen, began to try their strength with the emperor himself. During the early part of this century we find them refusing the bishops he had appointed. From this they proceeded to assert their right to elect their own magistrates. Such, however, was the reverence of the Italians for the shadow of the Roman Empire, that when they saw in distress the man who claimed to be its head, they rallied to his aid, so that he was able to recross the Alps, defeat his rebellious subjects in Germany, and win back the crown, Rudolph of Suabia, his rival, having been slain.

In 1081 Henry IV. returned to Italy, and held a Diet, in which he declared Gregory deposed, and appointed Guibert, Archbishop of Ravenna, as his successor, under the title of Clement III. Such was the magic force of the words, "splendour of the Roman Republic and Empire," that Gregory's defeat would have been complete, had he not found a powerful ally in the new Norman Duke of Apulia and Sicily, Robert Guiscard.

For three years Henry hovered about Italy, advancing twice to the walls of Rome. At last in 1084 he succeeded in getting into the city. Gregory shut himself up in the castle of St. Angelo, and Guibert was elected pope by the people. Then the new pontiff crowned Henry Emperor of the Romans in St. Peter's. But the cries of the people had scarcely died away when Henry heard that the Duke of Apulia was marching on Rome. The emperor made haste to escape before the arrival of the redoubtable son of Tancred of Hauteville. Robert Guiscard entered Rome, followed by a horde of wild troops, among whom were a number of Saracens. Gregory was set free, but his people were given up to the tender mercies of a ruthless army of Normans and Saracens. At a council then held, Gregory again excommunicated both Henry and Guibert, but fearing to stay in Rome, he returned with Robert to Salerno, where he died, A.D. 1085. But he had done his work. Gregory VII. is the Charlemagne of the Papacy. It may sink again, but he had given Christendom an ideal to which his successors ever sought to attain.

The invasion and subjugation of England by the Normans, and the invasion and subjugation of the secular power by the clerical, were simultaneous with the invasion and subjugation of Asia Minor by the Turks, and with their first appearance in Europe.

Early in the century the Turcomans, a people coming from Central Asia and settled on the Caspian Sea, conquered Massoud, the Sultan of Eastern Persia. Their leader became a Mohammedan, and showing himself a great slayer of Christians, was accepted as protector and temporal sovereign of the Moslem world by the Caliph of Bagdad, the successor of the Prophet. Henceforth we find his descendants enlarging the Turkish conquests in the East. The year before the battle of Senlac, Palestine was invaded and conquered by the Turks; and just about the time that William had completed his conquest, Asia Minor was sold by a Greek general to the Turks, as the price of their help to seat him on the imperial throne, the Sultan being entertained at Scutari on the occasion. The new Turkish kingdom of Asia Minor was called Roum, and extended from the Black Sea to Syria, from Constantinople to the Euphrates.

WHILE Islamism was thus pressing again into Eastern Europe, efforts were being made in the West, which were eventually successful, to deliver Spain from its grasp. A thin strip of territory, running from the Bay of Biscay along the southern base of the Pyrenees, had always remained Christian land. At the beginning of the eleventh century this strip of Christian country was divided into four diminutive monarchies—Aragon, Navarre, Leon, and Castile. To this last asylum of Christianity fled all those Spaniards who preferred independence to the tolerant but still alien rule of the conquering Saracen. The refugees were men of all ranks of society; but a common calamity developed a liberty, equality, and fraternity among them, which gradually produced, in this narrow territory, a noble Christian society, recognising the dignity and worth of its members, regarded either as individuals, or as organised states or cities. In this society duty went hand in hand with freedom; every citizen, without exemption, had to render military service, the rich as horsemen, the poor as foot soldiers.

This society, alive to the great principles of freedom and duty, reconquered Spain, and made it once more part of Christendom; and as the foremost leader in that work, and as its typical hero, the Cid shines forth an example of the higher type of manhood produced by Mediæval Christianity.

The chronicle of the Cid tells that the hero arose in the days of that Fernando who united into one monarchy the four kingdoms of Christian Spain; that he was born in 1026 (a year later than his great contemporary, William of Normandy), and that his name was Rodrigo Diaz. His first exploit was an act of filial piety. His father, Diego, was old and infirm. Don Gomez, a great nobleman, the first councillor in the Cortes, and a mighty man in arms, grievously insulted him. The proud old man, unable to revenge himself, falls into deep dejection. Rodrigo, though a youth, offered to be his champion. Armed with his father's sword and blessing, he defied the great lord, and slaying him, returned with the gory head fastened to his saddle-bow, "in order," as the chronicle tells us, "that the old man's drooping eyes might glitter once more with the joy of vengeance."

Then Ximena, daughter of Don Gomez, goes to King Fernando, and, casting herself at his feet, beseeches him to compel her father's conqueror to marry her, "for," says she, "I am certain he will one day be greater than any man in the king's dominions." The king sends for the young hero, who consents. But Rodrigo refuses to enjoy his felicity until he has proved himself worthy of it, and so sets himself the task of winning five battles over the Moors before he will think of domestic ease. But the battles he proposes to fight seem to have been as much with his own selfishness as with the Moors. His first adventure, manifestly mythical as it stands in the chronicle, is no doubt truly characteristic, as setting forth his humanity and simple faith in heavenly guidance. Rodrigo is represented as succouring a poor leper whom he found struggling in a quagmire, as lifting him upon his horse, and as making him share his plate and his bed. The leper disappears in the night, to reappear in vision as St. Lazarus, telling Rodrigo that since, for the love of God, he has been so pitiful, he will henceforth succour him in moments of difficulty, so that he shall be successful in whatever he undertakes, and prevail over all his enemies, dying an honourable death in his own house. "Go on," said the saint, "and persevere in doing good."

Rodrigo soon after gains his first victory over the Moors, and is knighted in the great mosque of Coimbra, the queen herself holding his horse, and the Infanta his spurs. From that day forth he was called Ruy Diaz. Afterwards he has for vassals five Moorish emirs, and it is they who give him the title of Cid—El Seid, the Lord.

King Fernando dies, and leaves three sons. Sancho, the eldest, soon follows his father; and the Cid believes there has been foul play. The new king banishes Rodrigo, and no one is allowed to help him. When he reaches his castle, he finds it has been sacked, and he is reduced to borrow the means of living from the Jews.

He next goes to war on his own account against the Moors, taking their castles and burning their towns, his morality being in no respect higher than that of the age. In process of time Alfonso gets into difficulties, and sends for the Cid, granting him permission to return to Castile. But the Cid refuses, unless the king respects for the future the privileges and charters and good customs of any town or other place possessing them, and promises never to impose taxes against their rights, and if he did, that it should be lawful for the land to rise against him until he amended the misdeed.

In a defeat which Alfonso's army suffers about this time the Cid loses his son; but shortly after, in the year A.D. 1085, Toledo is taken, the first Christian banner that enters the town being carried by the Cid, who becomes the first Christian Alcayde.

Banished again a second time, and again restored, the Cid adds Valencia to his conquests; but here again his morality is no better than that of his age. The promises made before the surrender are ruthlessly broken, and the town ravaged. He brings his wife and daughters to Valencia to take up their residence in the city. Soon after her arrival he takes Ximena up a high tower, and shows her a vast Moorish army spread over the plain. Her alarm is soon turned into admiration. The Moorish host is defeated, and the Cid takes great spoil.

The Cid henceforth, when not engaged in war, lived in great honour at Valencia; and when he died his corpse was placed in his ivory chair on the right side of the altar of the church, and a grand tabernacle made over it, richly wrought with azure and gold, having thereon the blazonry of the Kings of Castile and Leon, and of the King of Navarre and the Infanta of Aragon, and of the Cid, Ruy Diaz, the Campeador. From this half-mythic history we gain a better idea of the spirit and life of the age than can be obtained by the mere recital of the dry facts of more authentic history.

THE work in which the Cid spent his life now became the occupation of Christian Europe. Sylvester II. had dreamt of a great war against the Saracens, which should restore unity to Europe and deliver it from an ever-pressing danger. Gregory VII. preached a crusade, but without effect. It was reserved for a French monk to be the man who should arouse Christendom to this great enterprise.

Of the origin of Peter the Hermit nothing certain is known but that he was born at Amiens, in Picardy, at what date does not appear. There was nothing, we are told, noble or imposing in his appearance; but he was consumed by an ardent spirit, which gave him no rest. He passed through every condition of life: letters, arms, celibacy, marriage, the ecclesiastical state; and in no condition could he find rest. Disgusted with the world, he became the most austere of hermits. He believed that he held converse with Heaven, that he was the instrument of its designs, the depositary of its will. His zeal and his fervour knew no obstacles, and all he desired to accomplish seemed easy. He went on a pilgrimage to Jerusalem, and was by turns filled with adoration, with terror, and with burning indignation. Having followed his fellow-pilgrims to Calvary and the Holy Sepulchre, he paid a visit to the Patriarch of Jerusalem. The white hairs and venerable figure of Simeon, and the persecutions he had endured, aroused his sympathy. They wept together. Could nothing be done to stop such calamities? "Yes," replied the patriarch, "when our afflictions shall be accomplished, and God shall be touched with our miseries, then will He soften the hearts of the princes of the West to come and succour us." The suggestion was enough for the ardent Frenchman; the patriarch must at once implore the help of Europe through the pope, and he would go as his messenger to arouse Christendom.

Ere long he was in Italy with Simeon's letter at the feet of the pope. Urban II. received him as if he were a prophet, and heartily promised to second his design. Crossing the Alps, he passed through France and the greater part of Europe, filling all hearts with the passionate zeal with which he himself was devoured. He rode a mule, a crucifix in his hand, his feet naked, his head bare, clad in a long frock bound round the waist with a thick cord, and covered with a hermit's mantle of the coarsest stuff. He went from village to village, mounting the pulpits of the churches, or preaching in the roads or public places. With fervid eloquence he recounted the profanation of the Holy Places, and described the blood of the Christians as flowing down the streets of Jerusalem, working himself as well as his hearers into a passionate excitement by striking his breast and shedding floods of tears. All classes were equally affected, and the chivalry of Europe was on fire with enthusiasm.

In 1095, Urban held a Council at Clermont, and his eloquent sermon before the assembled clergy and laymen fell on ears thirsting to receive it; for at the conclusion the whole assembly cried out with one voice, "Deus id vult! Deus id vult!" "God wills it! God wills it!"

The poor were the first to go, and Peter himself led an enormous rabble of men, women, and children across the Continent, until at length he reached Constantinople, his army reduced to a condition of abject misery. The emperor was glad to send them across the Bosphorus. There they became so ungovernable that Peter quitted them in despair, and returned home.

Four expeditions were thus successively led to destruction. Of a quarter of a million of human beings not a tenth survived. Later on an organised army set out, the flower of European chivalry, led by Godfrey de Bouillon. Even this splendid host experienced terrible sufferings. Peter accompanied them, and at one time, during the siege of Antioch, he fell into such dejection at the misery of the army that he suddenly determined to turn his back on the whole enterprise and fly. He was overtaken, brought back, and severely rebuked. However, he was permitted to see the great object of all his passionate efforts completely successful. Antioch was taken, and in the last year of the century Jerusalem was delivered. The Turks were driven out of the Holy City, and a Christian throne set up where David and Solomon had reigned. Henceforth Peter disappears from history. His work for good and for evil was done.

TWELFTH CENTURY.

M

CONTEMPORARY EVENTS IN THE TWELFTH CENTURY.

England.—Baronial oppression.
Italy.—Arnold of Brescia entering Rome.
France.—Bernard of Clairvaux and Abelard.
Germany.—Surrender of Weinsberg.

Twelfth Century.

A.D. 1137–1155.

Baronial Oppression, especially in England—Bernard and the Monastic Life—Abelard and the new passion for Learning—The Council of Sens—Arnold of Brescia and the Roman Republic—The Guelphs and Ghibelines.

OTHING gives a more striking impression of the character of this period of European history than the fact that peace and justice were only possible under the sternest and most remorseless rulers. Kings who dared to lay waste with fire and sword the possessions of their robber-barons, to raze to the ground their castles, and to doom the criminals themselves to have their eyes torn out, or to be imprisoned for life in subterranean dungeons, were the kind of monarchs the age regarded with admiring awe. For it was only under such vigorous government that the mass of the people found any ease. As soon as the strong hand was withdrawn, a thousand tyrants sprang up, and the whole country became a scene of bloodshed and misery.

Such was the case in our own land when, in 1135, Stephen of Blois succeeded Henry I. on the English throne. Stephen was strong neither by character nor position, and the Norman barons of England, taking advantage of his weakness, soon made the country a place of torment, in which every iniquity and cruelty possible to man was practised.

The Saxon Chronicle, under the year 1137, says, "Every rich man built castles, and defended them against all, and they filled the land full of castles. They greatly oppressed the wretched people by making them work at these castles, and when the castles were finished they filled them with devils and evil men. Then they took those whom they suspected to have any goods, by night and by day, seizing both men and women, and they put them in prison for their gold and silver, and tortured them with pains unspeakable, for never were martyrs tormented as they were. They hung some up by their feet, and smoked them with foul smoke; some by their thumbs, or by the head, and they hung burning things on their feet. They put a knotted string about their heads and writhed it till it went into the brain. They put them into dungeons wherein were adders and snakes and toads, and thus wore them out. Some they put into a crucet-house, that is, into a chest that was short and narrow, and not deep, and they put sharp stones in it, and crushed the man therein, so that they broke all his limbs. There was a hateful and grim thing called *sachentage* in many of the castles, which two or three men had enough to do to carry. The *sachentage* was made thus: it was fastened to a beam, having a sharp iron to go round a man's throat and neck, so that he might no ways sit, nor lie, nor sleep, but that he must bear all the iron. Many thousands they exhausted with hunger. I cannot, and I may not, tell of all the wounds and all the tortures that they inflicted upon the wretched men of this land; and this state of things lasted the nineteen years that Stephen was king, and ever grew worse and worse. They were continually levying an exaction from the towns, which they called *Tensery*, and when the miserable inhabitants had no more to give, then plundered they and burned all the towns; so that well mightest thou walk a whole day's journey, nor even shouldest thou find a single soul in a town or its lands tilled.

"Then was corn dear, and flesh, and cheese, and butter, for there was none in the land. Wretched men starved with hunger; some lived on alms who had been erewhile rich; some fled the country: never was there more misery, and never acted heathens worse than these. At length they spared neither church nor churchyard, but they took all that was valuable therein, and then burned the church and all together. Neither did they spare the lands of bishops, or of abbots, or of priests, but they robbed the monks and the clergy; and every man plundered his neighbour so much as he might. If two or three men came riding into a town, all the township fled before them, and thought that they were robbers. The bishops and the clergy were ever cursing them; but this to them was nothing, for they were all accursed and foresworn and reprobate. The earth bare no corn: you might as well have tilled the sea, for the land was all ruined by such deeds, and it was said openly that Christ and His saints slept. These things, and more than we can say, did we suffer during nineteen years because of our sins."

This dreadful picture of the misery of England from 1135 to 1154 gives some idea of the condition to which mediæval Europe tended, wherever and whenever the hands of its chief rulers became weak. In Southern Europe the people of the towns had learnt the power of combination, and were ready to defend themselves. But north of the Alps and west of the Danube, Europe was under the power of an immense number of petty masters who owed feudal obedience to an over-lord, who was called king or emperor; and the happiness or misery of the people at large depended mainly on the courage and ability displayed by the Emperor of Germany and the Kings of England and France, in enforcing order and justice throughout their dominions. In this work their most effective allies were the clergy; the Church, as a rule, being ever ready to discountenance all tyranny but its own. It is only when we realise to what an extent Christendom was in the hands of a semi-savage aristocracy, who could dispose of the lives and fortunes of the people almost at will, that we can do justice to the kings and priests of the twelfth century. The fear is, that when we do, we shall too readily condone the cruelties and usurpations of which both were guilty.

HAPPILY the course of history, even in the darkest times, is full of light, and there has never been an age since the Christian era when the kingdom of heaven has not asserted itself as the most powerful, as well as the most purifying, influence of the time. In the twelfth century, under forms quite opposed to our ideas, and which, being human, necessarily ended in death and corruption, this blessed influence worked. Souls were smitten with an intense hunger and thirst after righteousness, with an intense longing after peace, and, despairing of being able to attain either in a world full of violence and sensuality, they separated themselves from it, and vowed to take up a life of obedience, poverty, and chastity. It is true that they constantly missed their aim, and that the great monastic orders which such persons founded and supported, ended in evils as great as those which caused their formation; but in the twelfth century they were still comparatively pure, and the balance of good done was greatly in their favour.

Scattered all over Europe, sometimes hidden in wild glens or among savage rocks, sometimes sheltered by the walls of a town, these religious communities were both literally and metaphorically—

> "Little gardens, walled around,
> Hallowed, and made peculiar ground."

At the very time that we find in England, perhaps, the most extreme example of the misery to which the unbridled tyranny of a mediæval aristocracy could reduce a country, we have in the neighbouring land of France one of the brightest examples of the antidote which Christian faith offered to the endless strife and brutal iniquity of the age. As the one is typical, so is the other; both must be thought of side by side, in order to realise in any degree the social life of the time.

In a valley near the Aube in Champagne, a valley not famous for picturesque beauty, but rather as its name, Val d'Absinthe, indicates, dismal and savage, rose a number of conventual buildings grouped around an unpretentious-looking abbey. On all sides were signs of human skill and labour. There was the farmyard, here the carpenter's shop, there the farm, the orchard, and the well-cultured fields. On the river, divided into many channels, stood several mills. Save the occasional tap of the carpenter's hammer, the singing of the birds, the ringing of the convent bell, or the blast of the swineherd's horn, scarce any noise ever disturbed the solemn stillness of this valley. Yet here dwelt a large community, many of whom had been among the fiercest and most passionate of men. Noblemen and knights whose early career had been one of riotous wickedness might there be seen working in poverty and in fraternity with the peasant over whose body they would once have ridden, or to whom they would have applied the lash without mercy. Within this abbey their lives are spent according to strictest rule. They have no will of their own, but obey with a satisfaction more or less real one who is to them father, bishop, and teacher. At his bidding they come and go, at his feet they sit, his voice stirs them to spiritual effort, consoles them in failure. A lean, pale man, with fair hair and red beard, both turning white, with haggard cheeks and soft, dove-like eyes, he seems weaker and more emaciated than any of his monks. Within this feeble frame burns, however, an indomitable energy which has made him more truly the master of Christendom than either pope or emperor. Kings and peoples, bishops, and even popes, all bow before the influence of him whom they call the "man of God." No position, except that of the Hebrew prophet, can give any idea of the place occupied by Bernard of Clairvaux in this twelfth century. At his rebuke a haughty ruler had fallen insensible to the ground in the sight of his subjects. The highest and most self-willed gave up, at Bernard's command, their dearest projects. Mothers tried to prevent their sons, and wives their husbands, from listening to his sermons, lest they should follow him into a cloister. Kings and princes at his bidding left thrones and palaces, and wandered perilously in Oriental lands. Contending popes submitted to his arbitration; and the sight of this venerated monk leading by the hand the pope of his selection turned the recalcitrant people of Italy into a crowd of adorers.

Through his whole life Bernard contended daily for what he believed to be truth and righteousness. Sometimes he was signally wrong, as when he urged Europe to the Second Crusade, an expedition disastrous to all concerned. Far less really a lover of righteousness than Anselm, he was especially intolerant of all disobedience to authority. Seeing that the cause of all the violence and all the iniquity which raged around him was self-will, he thought it the first duty of life to curb that will and bring it into subjection.

And the self-will which was then raging in England and elsewhere in so brutal a manner was, under a stronger government and more culture, developing itself in France under mental forms. The Crusades, in arousing religious enthusiasm, had quickened religious thought. The spectacle of such myriads undertaking a journey to the East had enlarged the general knowledge of Europe. Western Christians came in contact with Greeks and Saracens, and learnt with astonishment of worlds that had existed before and outside their own. The pagan authors began again to be studied, and the old world, with its love of liberty and philosophy, broke on mediæval Christendom as something quite fresh. The Vaudois translated the Bible into the vulgar tongue. The Institutes of Justinian were also translated; law and theology were confronted at Orleans and Angers. In place of the longing for a religious life, a passion for learning seized the intellectual youth of Europe. The schools were thronged, universities began to rise, and became centres of power.

In the north of Europe the most frequented was the University of Paris; and at this particular time, when England was groaning under baronial tyranny, and Bernard exercising his greatest influence, it had become especially famous, in consequence of the appearance of a great intellectual luminary—Peter Abelard. Conscious of his intellectual power, and concentrating in himself the rising spirit of free thought, Abelard cared not whom he offended. He became at last so puffed up with pride, that he fell into a sin which made the rest of his life terribly bitter. To Bernard the career and teaching of Abelard must have been very repulsive, for it not only represented human pride and individual licence, but dealt with Divine things in that cold, analytical way which to a man of his fervent nature was especially painful. To Bernard, love constituted the very being and nature of God, and he who professed to understand theology untouched by this Divine passion must go profoundly astray.

However, Abelard was followed, even when in deepest disgrace, by admiring crowds. He represented earnest and sincere thinking against formal, dead teaching. He had begun as a dialectician, but he was far from being a mere manipulator of words. The students of the day felt that there was all the difference in the world between him and those sophistical teachers, whom John of Salisbury describes so wittily:

"Those creatures who live in words had rather seem wise than be wise. . . . They stir up little questions; they make words into nets, that they may catch the sense of other men and their own; they are always more ready to raise a wind of argument than to winnow a question, if any difficulty hath arisen. . . . They succeed in making themselves not understood rather from the weight and multitude of their words than from any difficulty in the things, and when they have accomplished this high object, they think they deserve to be reckoned philosophers above all others. . . . Play with words, tell stories with words, dispute with words, that is the business of the learned man. So long as he can speak, it is no matter where he gets his thoughts, or what they are, or about what."

It was a young world, this mediæval Christendom, and Bernard's passionate love and Abelard's free thinking indicate that it had just arrived at that age when life begins to move and blossom. Thus the twelfth century, notwithstanding much wretchedness, suffering, and cruelty, is in some aspects beautiful as an orchard in spring-time. That note of Divine love that Bernard struck so tunefully re-echoed in feebler and more earthly tones through uncloistered hearts. Human love was purified and exalted by the new ideal of God; woman was no longer treated as a superior animal, but rather as an inferior angel. Women sat side by side with their husbands, even on the judgment-seat; and this new position will never be lost, for its roots are in the kingdom of heaven.

This elevation of the position of woman, due to the idealisation of human passion in the light of Divine love, affected not only the cultured and cared-for ladies of the palace and the castle—it extended to the lowest and most degraded of the sex. Robert d'Arbrissel, a Breton monk of a spirit like Bernard's, and perhaps of a more tender charity, was smitten with intense pity for those poor outcasts of whom history rarely speaks. In the name of his Master he dared to enter the most evil places, and to claim the miserable inmates as the redeemed of Christ.

It is recorded that on such an occasion in Rouen a company of women gathered round him, and their mistress said, "Who are you, to tell us such things? Twenty years ago I entered this house in order to commit these crimes, and be ye sure no person has ever come here who spoke of God and His goodness. If but I knew that these things were true!" Robert d'Arbrissel built an abbey at Fontevrault, where he might receive those who were penitent. There were soon many Fontevraults in Christendom. The order had thirty abbeys in Brittany alone. Some were for men; and the spirit of the founder and the age is seen in the peculiar fact that these were ruled over by ladies of illustrious families, who were subject only to the pope.

Once, and once only, did the heart and the intellect of Christendom appear in open contest. Bernard avoided a personal struggle with Abelard as long as he could. Abelard, on the other hand, more than once tried to bring on a battle. But Bernard thought it safer to repress heresy than to argue with it, and made appeals to the powers of Europe to put down this audacious thinker. Bernard, however, had enemies, and they, of course, favoured Abelard. The Archbishop of Sens was one of these. He was to hold a synod of his province, at which the king, Louis VII., and a crowd of bishops, abbots, and priests from the north-eastern parts of France were to be present. This was in the year 1140. Abelard thought it a good opportunity to defend himself from Bernard's attacks, and induced the archbishop to invite the Abbot of Clairvaux to come and dispute with him. Bernard at first declined the contest, but, being urged by his friends, consented. On the day appointed the assembly met in solemn conclave in the church of St. Stephen, in Sens. Bernard was in the pulpit with a pile of Abelard's books at his side, in which were marked the passages he intended to read, and to demand the writer's explanation, recantation, or condemnation. But the reading had scarcely commenced when, to the surprise of all, Abelard arose, refused to hear any more, or to debate a single point. He appealed, he said, to Rome.

That a freethinker like Abelard should reckon it easier to win a victory in the court of Rome, rather than in the Council of Sens, may astonish us, as perhaps it did some simple-minded people in the year 1140. But Abelard knew, and Bernard knew, that the Papacy at this time had very little independence, and that money and influence could do more for a cause in Rome than any proofs of truth and justice. Rome was ever gentle to the offences of the powerful, if they would only acknowledge her authority. Had Abelard thought and talked as freely about the Papacy itself as he had done about the theology of which Innocent II. was supposed to be the divinely appointed exponent and defender, his appeal to Rome would have quickly brought him to the fate of his more earnest disciple, Arnold of Brescia.

This man was a monk who had learnt from his master the new art of thinking for himself. He formed a very strong opinion about the corruptions of the clergy, and was specially opposed to their temporal power. His doctrine on this point was branded as the heresy of the politicians. His pure life, his knowledge, his eloquence, combined with the righteous object he had in view, won him great popularity, so that his opinions soon spread far and wide. He was cited before the second Lateran Council, and ordered to leave Italy. He took refuge at Zurich, under the protection of Cardinal Guido, then Bishop of Constance. Bernard tried his best to induce Guido either to drive him away or to imprison him, but the bishop would not heed his advice.

Arnold was centuries in advance of his age, or, perhaps it would be truer to say, centuries behind. He was smitten with the idea which has carried away all the great Italians: the belief that the Roman Empire was a golden age. He preached a resumption of all the political rights and liberties the Italian cities had then enjoyed. The times seemed really ripe for such an effort. The cities of Western Christendom—in Spain, in France, in Germany, and even in England—were feeling their way to self-government. By various means, but mostly by purchase, they were obtaining charters from their sovereigns. For more than a century past a spirit of independence had especially distinguished the cities of Northern Italy, their peculiar position under a German emperor giving the effort unusual stimulus. In Rome this tendency had been encouraged by the schisms at the Vatican. During the hundred years prior to the preaching of Arnold, there had been eight or nine anti-popes, and two periods in which there was no pope at all. The Papacy had just emerged from such a contest. Thanks to the advocacy of Bernard, Innocent II. had been acknowledged the real pope, and his rival, Anacletus, became a usurper. Tivoli, a city near Rome, continued, however, to adhere to the cause of Anacletus. The Romans attacked them, and were defeated, but returning again the next year, they finally reduced the city, and wished, in their jealousy, to impose such conditions as should ruin the inhabitants. Innocent interposed, and granted milder terms. This incensed the Roman people against the pope, and they rose in insurrection. The nobles, affected, no doubt, by the teaching of Arnold, went amongst the people, and instigated them to elect a Senate which should sit in the Capitol, and govern Rome as in the olden time. The people acceded to the proposition, a Senate was elected, and Innocent died of chagrin.

His successor was the friend and protector of Arnold, Cardinal Guido, who became pope under the title of Celestine II. He did not, however, live long enough to take any steps of importance one way or the other, and was succeeded by Lucius II. This pope was most unfortunate, for, imagining that a display of his pontifical grandeur would awe the people into submission, he marched surrounded by his priests and his partisans to the Capitol to dismiss the Senate; the people poured a volley of stones on the procession, one struck Lucius, and so hurt him that he died in a few days.

Eugenius III., a disciple of Bernard, now obtained the tiara, but quickly left Rome to its real ruler. In 1145, Arnold of Brescia made a triumphal entry into Rome, accompanied by two thousand Swiss mountaineers. He sought to reproduce the whole polity of the Roman Republic. He wished not only to have a Senate, but consuls to preside over it, tribunes to defend the people, and an equestrian order to stand between the patricians and the plebeians. The pope he proposed to exclude from all temporal authority, and to limit the imperial power as much as possible.

For eight years Arnold's influence was supreme in Rome, but Pope Eugenius dying, the papal throne was filled after the short reign of Anastatius IV. by an Englishman named Nicholas Breakspeare, but known in history as Adrian IV. This English pope was a man of strong will, with notions about his prerogatives as high as those of Hildebrand. One of his first acts was to lay Rome under interdict, an act so unprecedented that the new Senate became frightened, and begged Arnold to quit the city, in order that they might propitiate the pope. Arnold retired to the castle of one of his friends in the Roman Campagna.

His efforts had succeeded as long as the ruling powers in Italy were weak, but now that both the Papacy and the Empire were in the hands of determined men, the cause of liberty began to be in bad case. Frederick Barbarossa, who has left a name in German history only second to Charlemagne, had succeeded his uncle, Conrad III., as emperor. He crossed the Alps at the head of a great army, determined to recover all the lost prestige of the Empire. Arnold had hoped to enter into alliance with him against the Papacy, but instead, Barbarossa made common cause with the pope, and treated the Senate of Rome with contempt. Getting possession of Arnold, the two rulers of Italy had him put to death. Very early one morning, before the city was awake, the patriotic Brescian was led to the front of the Gate of the People, and there, at a point to which three of the principal streets converge, he was first hanged and then burnt (A.D. 1155).

GERMANY meanwhile was the scene of a civil commotion which, though only a chapter in a great national struggle which had been going on for more than a century, has European interest, since it gave names to the contending parties in Italy.

The three great emperors of the Franconian dynasty—the third, fourth, and fifth Henrys—all pursued the same policy; namely, to curb the insolence and repress the despotism of the spiritual and temporal princes of Germany. Sometimes they sought to do it by entering into direct conflicts, sometimes by working out more completely the wise initiative of Henry the Fowler, who laid the foundation of the great middle or burgher class in Germany.

As far back as the middle of the tenth century, this emperor sought to provide a new military force, by offering inducement to the smaller nobles and the *ingenui*, or superior freemen, to quit their rural homes and come and dwell in fortified towns. Here they were to know no master but the emperor and those whom he should appoint. Free from the rule of the feudal aristocracy, such towns became virtually independent, and soon attracted a large class of mechanics, artificers, and men of commerce, who gradually obtained privileges in return for the strength they gave to the town. These cities became the best and most reliable friends the emperors had. But the imperial policy, though calculated greatly to strengthen the State, was viewed with jealousy by the spiritual and temporal princes, and they were ever seeking to depress and weaken the imperial power. Unfortunately, Henry IV., as we have seen, entered into a contest with the Papacy, and then Rome ranged herself on the side of the malcontents, stirring up the strife whenever she thought she could gain by it.

The enemies of the house of Franconia drew their chief support from Saxony, for there they were more disliked than in any part of Germany. On the death of the last male member of the house, Henry V., the papal-princely party obtained the election of the Duke of Saxony, who ascended the imperial throne as Lothair III. To secure this position,

Lothair consented to hold his dominions as a fee of the pope. Innocent II. had a picture painted of the ceremony of swearing fealty, under which he wrote, "Rex homo fit Papæ." But the pope could not give him a son, and Lothair was therefore obliged to plan and plot to secure the throne to his son-in-law, Henry the Proud, a nobleman of great possessions, descended from a distinguished family, called the Welfs, of Altorf, in Suabia. Lothair's hopes were deceived, for instead of electing Henry, the friends of the house of Franconia, in a very unconstitutional manner, proclaimed Conrad von Hohenstauffen. The new emperor and his family thereupon gave a new name to their race, calling themselves the Waiblinger, after the Castle of Waiblingen, in the Reimsthal, which Henry V. had left them. Henceforth the struggle between the rival factions in Germany was carried on under the names of the Waiblinger and the Welfs.

Henry the Proud yielded his claims to Conrad; but when the latter wished to despoil him of his possessions, and put him under the ban of the Empire, the Welfs arose, and in Suabia, in Bavaria, and in Saxony they raised the standard of war. In the course of the struggle it happened that Conrad was brought into direct conflict with a brother of Henry the Proud, who bore the ancestral name of Welf. This was at the siege of Weinsberg, near Heilbron, which took place in A.D. 1141. Doubtless the circumstance of the chief of the Waiblinger besieging the Welf in person moved the soldiers on both sides to drop their usual battle-cries, and to shout, "Hie, Waiblinger!" "Hie, Welf!" Henceforth these uncouth names became the badges and rallying-cries of the two factions, and travelling with the emperors into Italy were softened into Guelph and Ghibelin, and so handed down to posterity.

But this siege has become additionally famous for a most curious and ludicrous incident with which it closed. Conrad, when he saw the city about to fall, offered to let all the women go out before his army entered, and to permit each one to bring with her all she could carry. Welf's wife accordingly appeared at the gate carrying him on her shoulders, all the women in the city following her example, each bearing her husband or her lover. The emperor does not appear to have been either annoyed or amused at the spectacle; it rather seems to have astonished and touched him. To those of his followers who thought that he ought not to permit himself to be thus outwitted, he simply said, "An emperor keeps his word."

THIRTEENTH CENTURY.

CONTEMPORARY EVENTS IN THE THIRTEENTH CENTURY.

Constantinople—*The Doge of Venice leading the besiegers.*
France—*The Albigenses defending Beziers.*
England—*King John signing Magna Charta.*
Italy—*An Incident in the Preaching of Francis.*

Thirteenth Century.

A.D. 1204-1216.

Feudal Europe—Effort to Found a Feudal Theocracy—Innocent III.—His Struggle with John of England—Magna Charta—Persecution of the Albigenses—Constantinople taken by the Venetians—Enrico Dandolo—Dominic and Francis.

EUROPE in the nineteenth century is separated into distinct nations, each one divided from the others by recognised boundaries, by a different language, and by a special history. Hence it is very difficult to gain a clear conception of the Europe of the beginning of the thirteenth century. The map appears a chaos, and can only be understood when we recollect that the leading principle upon which the society of that day was founded was feudal rather than national. Thus there was a time in the latter half of the twelfth century when the King of Scotland was the vassal of the King of England; the King of England himself doing homage for the French half of his dominions to the King of France. Yet the King of France was not necessarily over-lord of the whole of France, for at the accession of Philip Augustus several of the great lords in Provence and Languedoc held their lands of Pedro of Aragon as supreme suzerain. England was ruled by men French in blood, speech, and interests; Italy by Germans, the German Empire itself

being a type of all Christendom, an unwieldy mass of incoherent interests in a condition of perpetual strife.

The institution which, in the midst of all these conflicting interests, maintained the idea of a brotherhood of nations united under one visible head, was the Latin Church. While all the secular rulers were weak, the Papacy was strong. In the thirteenth century it arrived at the zenith of its power. The great fact of this age is the effort made by the bishops of Rome to found a feudal theocracy. This effort commenced with the accession of Innocent III. (A.D. 1198), and ended with the pontificate of Boniface VIII. (A.D. 1303), so that it entirely covered the century. The universal tyranny the Papacy thus sought to establish, and the audacious claims it put forth, gave a great impulse to the germs of national unity and the desire for civil and religious liberty.

The man who made the world understand what the Papacy really claimed to be was Innocent III. He aimed to make it a Christian Republic, of which the pope was the divinely-appointed ruler and head. He, as Vicar of Christ, claimed to be "King of kings, lord of lords, the only ruler of princes," appropriating to himself the word of the Lord to Jeremiah: "See, I have this day set thee over the nations and over the kingdoms, to root out, and to pull down, and to destroy, and to throw down, to build and to plant." In the first sermon he preached after he was seated in the chair of St. Peter, he described himself as "standing in the midst between God and man; below God, above man; less than God, more than man."

His first effort to enforce these lofty pretensions was in Germany. The year before Innocent became pope Henry VI. died, leaving a young son, Frederick. The electors were at variance, some supporting Frederick's uncle, Philip of Suabia, others Otto of Saxony, son of Henry the Lion. Innocent, in supporting the latter, "declared that he had authority to examine, confirm, anoint, crown, and consecrate the elect Emperor, provided he should be worthy, or to reject him, if unfit by great crimes—such as sacrilege, heresy, perjury, or persecution of the Church; in default of election, to supply the vacancy, or, in the event of equal suffrages, to bestow the empire upon any person at his discretion."

Every ruler in turn was made to feel there was one over him who claimed his obedience. The King of France was living in adultery. Innocent compelled him, sorely against his will, to put away his mistress and restore his wife. The Kings of Castile and Portugal were forced to keep the peace under pain of excommunication and interdict; while the King of Navarre was threatened with a similar penalty, on account of certain treaties he had made or was suspected to be making with the Saracens. In Norway, a pretender to the throne was excommunicated, a legate being sent even to Iceland, in order to warn bishops and nobles not to recognise the usurper. But the circumstance which most brings home to us the full meaning of the papal claim to be the new Cæsar of Europe is the contest into which John Plantagenet entered with Innocent III., and which ended in a King of England acknowledging himself the vassal of the Pope of Rome.

John ascended the English throne in the last year of the twelfth century. His father had ruled over one of the finest realms in the world, his sovereignty extending from the Orkneys to the Pyrenees, from the Atlantic to the German Ocean. John Sans-Terre succeeded to this inheritance, less the lordship of Scotland, which Cœur de Lion had sold for a consideration, and with some doubt about the French portion, which was claimed by Prince Arthur. But by skilful generalship he defeated and captured his young rival, who shortly afterwards died a prisoner in his hands. Cynically selfish, his detestable lust, falsehood, and meanness brought him into collision with all classes in his kingdom, until the whole people were united against him in common hatred. His impiety caused him to drift into a contest with the pope before he had time to realise its danger. In a fit of rage with the monks of Canterbury for electing an archbishop without his knowledge, he put his own man into the see, although he had already placed the matter in the hands of Innocent for decision. Innocent seized the opportunity to assert his lofty pretensions in England, and caused his friend, Cardinal Langton, to be elected.

Of Langton's early life little is known, beyond the fact that he was a fellow student of Innocent at the University of Paris, of which important institution he became Chancellor in 1209.

He accepted heartily a maxim popular at Rome: "As the sun and the moon are placed in the firmament, the greater as the light of the day, and the lesser of the night; thus are there two powers in the Church: the pontifical, which, as having the charge of souls, is the greater; and the royal, which is the less, and to which the bodies of men only are intrusted." Innocent must have believed Langton to be thoroughly at one with himself on this all-important maxim of his policy when he chose him as the papal candidate for the headship of the English Church. How erroneous were their views, the history they helped to make, and all the subsequent history of Europe, has served to show. Their claim to our respect is that, notwithstanding the grossness of their view of the kingdom of heaven, they did really believe that there was such a kingdom, and that it was their duty to make the kingdoms of this world obedient to it. This faith ennobled them, and lifted from the blind contentions of human interest and passion every cause they took in hand. Thus, directly Langton came to England he elevated the discontent which was seething throughout the nation into a real struggle for law and liberty. But, before Langton could take this position, Innocent had to use all the weapons in his spiritual armoury against the recalcitrant king. John was furious, and offered every possible resistance. Expostulation he answered with expostulation, threat with threat. "Stephen Langton at his peril should set his foot on the soil of England." Innocent proceeded to his usual resort, and laid the kingdom under interdict.

We may form some idea of the reality of the papal power in the thirteenth century from the following account of the effects of this interdict by an old English chronicle: "Oh, how horrible, how pitiable a spectacle it was in all our cities! To see the doors of the churches watched, and Christians driven from them like dogs; all divine offices ceased; the sacrament of the body and blood of the Lord not offered; no gathering together of the people, as was wont at the festivals of the saints; the bodies of the dead not admitted to Christian burial, but their stench infected the air, the loathsome sight of them appalled the living; only extreme unction and baptism were allowed. There was deep sadness over the whole realm, while the organs and the voices of those who chanted God's praises were everywhere mute."

Never, however, did interdict do greater good. During the four years it lasted it brought home every day and every hour to the great body of the people the worthless character of their king, and prepared them to sympathise with and support the champions of English law and liberty when the time came. The royal power had found in the people and the clergy its chief support against the barons. John had alienated the people by his indifference to their religious sufferings; and he now added the clergy to his enemies by his cruelty to those who dared to obey the pope. One unfortunate clergyman, the Archdeacon of Norwich, he loaded with chains and afterwards cased in a surcoat of lead—cruelties which soon terminated his existence.

A universal loathing took possession of the land, a feeling quite apart from any sympathy with the pope's action in reference to Langton. Innocent, on the other hand, did not regard the opinion of the English people; he was simply determined to assert his own pretensions, and to have them acknowledged. His punishment of the contumacious king rose step by step in intensity. From an interdict on his kingdom he passed to a personal excommunication. When that proved unavailing, he absolved John's subjects from their fealty; and, finally, using the last weapon in his armoury, he deposed him from his throne, declaring his domains the lawful spoil of whoever could wrest them from his hands. Philip Augustus, nothing loth for such an adventure, began to levy an army, and to enter into correspondence with the English barons.

John was one of the cleverest of a clever race. He could show himself wonderfully bold and rapid in the execution of military plans, and marvellously subtle in weaving plots and counter-plots. As he had no principle, and no real self-respect, he could turn at any moment and offer his alliance to the man he most hated, if thereby he could crush a greater foe.

At first it appeared as if he were about to defend his rights by force of arms, for he collected a large army on Barham Downs, in Kent. In the army appeared a hermit named Peter of Wakefield, who prophesied that by the next Ascension Day John would cease to reign. Rightly interpreting this prophecy as an expression of the universal discontent, and receiving from Pandulph, the pope's legate, who landed in England shortly after, proof that nearly all his barons had deserted him, he suddenly and absolutely conceded all the demands of Innocent. Not only did he promise to acknowledge the full right of Langton to the see of Canterbury, and to reverse all his prosecutions against the clergy, making them full restitution for all that they had suffered, but he further agreed "to bestow and yield up" "to our Lord the Pope Innocent and his successors all our kingdom of England, and all our kingdom of Ireland, to be held as a fief of the Holy See."

This humiliating surrender of his crown took place on the vigil of Ascension Day, so that the hermit's prophecy was, in a very real sense, fulfilled. The barons and the people of England were amazed; but very soon they saw that, degrading as it might be for his subjects, the king's act was a master-stroke of policy. It broke up the army of the French king, and disconcerted his plans; it prevented the pope from giving his influence to the rising tide of popular discontent, and it set John himself free to complete a great plot he had been weaving against Philip Augustus.

In the following February John's schemes were ripe, and he passed over to Poitou. One point, however, failed — the English barons would not trust him, and refused to follow. However, his great league was a reality; he had managed to combine all the foes of the King of France into one large army. Philip Augustus met them, and defeated them at Bouvines, a battle in which an English king and an English army and its allies were defeated, to the lasting benefit of England. To it we owe the Great Charter; for John returned shorn of all prestige, so that Langton and the barons had to deal with a monarch who had fallen in every way into contempt.

Innocent's archbishop was now advancing on a path which he must tread alone, although it was the path the pope himself desired to tread —the assertion and establishment of the kingdom of righteousness. Yet the archbishop's method transcended Innocent's experience, or even his comprehension. His conduct in this great transaction proves Langton to have been an honest, brave, and God-fearing man. He proceeded cautiously, but resolutely. He produced in a council held in St. Paul's a charter of Henry I., and the barons agreed to make that the basis of their demands. They went on from step to step until they forced the king into a corner, compelling him at last to sign a charter, which was founded on this ancient grant of King Henry, but so enlarged as to include the many new grievances of the late reigns, and especially important, since it embraced in its various provisions all classes of the community, testifying at once to the national character of the struggle and the consequent legal and binding character of the charter.

Innocent was astounded at this exhibition of the spirit of freedom in England; and what doubtless added to the sting was the fact that his own man should have been the leader of the movement. He fulminated anathemas against the Great Charter, and excommunicated the barons, the citizens of London, and of the Cinque Ports. Langton, refusing to publish the excommunication, was suspended, and summoned to answer for his conduct at Rome. The signing of Magna Charta took place May 15, 1215; and rather more than a year later Innocent died.

THE period during which Englishmen were thus compelled to feel the inhumanity of their spiritual father, and to experience his bitter animosity against their civil liberties, was exactly contemporaneous with that during which the unfortunate inhabitants of the South of France were passing through similar trials intensified a hundred-fold. No part of Europe contained a population so varied in its origin as the South of France. Greek, Roman, Phœnician, Basque, Gaul, Goth, Frank, and Moor: all had contributed their blood to form its brilliant and versatile people. From the earliest times they had been accustomed to the most diverse sentiments, and to exercise, therefore, a freedom of thought and of choice in religious matters utterly unknown to the more northern parts of France and the rest of Europe. While this habit of mind rendered it easy for every teacher of a new creed to get a hearing, it made it impossible to impose such creeds on mere authority. The clergy were despised, partly because they were not worthy of respect, but chiefly through the strong anti-sacerdotal spirit which prevailed through the land. In the twelfth century this freedom of thought had taken form, and had established itself in positive institutions. The republican spirit which pervaded Italy was equally strong in Languedoc and Provence. Their cities were governed by magistrates called consuls, chosen by the citizens. Avignon, Arles, Nice, Tarascon, at the beginning of the thirteenth century, were fully enfranchised from their feudal lords, and had become independent little states, within the limits of their municipal jurisdiction. In the other cities the situation was not quite so advanced, but as a rule the people had possession of real power, and paid but nominal homage to their lord.

To a ruler entertaining such a notion of his mission as Innocent III., the religious and political condition of the South of France must have appeared like a cancer in Christendom, which nothing could cure but extirpation. However, the pope hesitated before attempting so terrible a remedy. He sent a number of missionaries, mostly Cistercians (1200–1203), to convert the people to the orthodox faith. These legates travelled about in great pomp, but made little impression on a people who themselves revelled in every luxury. They were on the point of giving up the effort in despair, when they fell in with two Spanish priests, the Bishop of Osma and his sub-prior, Dominic Guzman. They advised them to sow the good seed as the heretics did the bad. "Cast off," said they, "those sumptuous robes, renounce those richly caparisoned palfreys, go barefoot without purse and scrip, like the Apostles, out-labour, out-fast, out-discipline these false teachers." The Spaniards did more than advise, they offered to set them the example. Ere long they began to teach and preach in this new fashion with the utmost zeal and energy, Dominic finding it necessary to form the preachers who rallied round them into a new order.

But the people jeered and ridiculed. The legates called upon the Count of Toulouse to punish these contumacious heretics. Raymond VI. showing no sign of obedience, Innocent, who was then in the thick of the controversy with King John, poured out on him the vials of his wrath in a furious epistle. This letter was written about a month before the pope consecrated Langton Archbishop of Canterbury. In the November of the same year (1207), Innocent followed up his letter by action. He called upon the King of France and all the nobility and faithful Christians in the land to take up arms for the suppression of the heretics in Languedoc and Provence, granting all the estates and goods of the heretics to those who should join in this holy war, and the same indulgences they would have on going on a crusade to the Holy Land. Between three and four months after Innocent had thus "framed mischief by a law," he laid England under interdict. He had evidently yoked Raymond and John in his mind, and was bent on chastising both them and their dominions. Unfortunately for the former, one of his hot-headed subjects replied to Innocent's incendiary proclamation by the assassination of the papal legate.

This act was the signal of one of the most atrocious wars the world has ever seen. "Up," wrote the pope to Philip Augustus, "up, soldiers of Christ! Up, most Christian King! Hear the cry of blood; aid us in wreaking vengeance on the malefactors." He wrote in the same strain to the noblemen, counts, barons, and knights of the provinces of Narbonne, Arles, Embrun, Aix, and Etienne, declaring the Count of Toulouse excommunicated, and all his vassals and subjects released from their oath of obedience. Then he called upon the Archbishops of Lyons and Tours to publish this ban, and charged particularly the Abbot of Citeaux and his monks to preach the crusade which he thus proclaimed. This man, Arnould d'Amauri, sent out twelve abbots and twenty monks to arouse France. The report of the numbers who responded to their call is almost fabulous, some putting it as high as half a million, at least fifty thousand being men-at-arms. The crusaders found a military leader in Simon de Montfort, an adventurer connected with the nobility both of France and England. He entered the war, no doubt, in the spirit of Dominic and of Innocent. Ere long the spirit of a murderer and a robber took possession of him, and we find even the pope himself reproving his legates and Simon for their wolfish rapacity.

Before this took place five years of fearful horrors were allowed to devastate the doomed land. Ten years longer they continued, until nearly all the towns and strong castles between the Rhone, the Pyrenees, the Garonne, and Dordogne were taken, lost, retaken, given over to pillage, sack, and massacre, and burnt. Scenes of cynical cruelty marked the progress of the crusade. At Béziers, the first town which fell, Abbot Arnould d'Amauri, the pope's legate and chosen instrument, gave the frightful command: "Slay them all. God will know His own." Neither age nor sex was spared. At the lowest computation, twenty thousand fell in the remorseless carnage. At the fall of Lavaur a general massacre ensued: the very children were cut to pieces, four hundred of the garrison being burned on one pile, to the hideous joy of the crusaders. The Lady of Lavaur was cast into a well, and heavy stones thrown down upon her. Everywhere heretics were burned, and it was the special business of Dominic Guzman to talk with them, and to undertake the dreadful task of convincing them of their errors, when they were about to be led to the stake.

The total number of human beings that perished in this terrific war can never be known. By the prolonged massacres, the numerous executions, and the subsequent work of the Inquisition, the Albigensian sect was entirely extirpated—so entirely, that it has ever since become a most difficult thing to say what they really believed, and what kind of people they were. With them perished thousands of others who never had any idea of separating themselves from the Catholic Church; many quiet, simple persons, who desired nothing better than to serve God according to their own consciences. Doubtless there were many enlightened believers among them, such as have existed in all ages. All that went before and came after assures us that the good seed was thickly sown in this unhappy land.

If anything could have brought home to Innocent the falsity of his idea of the kingdom of heaven, this fearful issue of his efforts ought to have opened his eyes. But it does not seem to have done more than shock and bewilder him. He called a council at the Lateran in 1215, the year of Magna Charta. Innocent's bull, annulling the foundation of English liberties, and excommunicating the barons who obtained it, was issued about the time he was summoning this council to help him out of these terrible difficulties in Languedoc. It must have been as a foreshadowing of judgment to come for Innocent to listen to the awful accusations which some of its members dared to make against the crusaders in that holy war of which he had been the great instigator. He seems to have been appalled, to have tried to excuse himself, and to have attempted to salve his conscience by taking up the cause of the younger Raymond. But it was too late: the whole matter had got beyond his grasp. He had dared, in the name of Christ, to call together an army of human tigers and wolves, and now he was powerless to restrain them. The Lateran Council decided, in spite of the pope's faint opposition, to endorse the results of the crusade, and to give the lands of the Count of Toulouse to Simon de Montfort. Innocent died the next year of a burning fever, and a nun, since sainted, is said to have seen him in vision with a belt of fire round his loins, condemned, as he told her, to torment for three great sins until the day of judgment.

As the only permanent result of forcing Langton into the see of Canterbury was to help the advent of constitutional liberty, as the only permanent result of the crusade against the Albigenses was to burn into the hearts of Christian men an ineradicable hatred of sacerdotalism, so Innocent's feverish desire to bring on another crusade in the East only resulted in developing the infantile commerce of the Middle Ages. Thus Divine Providence compelled him to become largely responsible for the existence of the very forces which were destined to prove the three greatest opponents to the aim of his life.

THE second and third crusades had been such failures that the secular mind of Europe had become weary of the effort. Not so Innocent, who, absorbed in his one idea, took little heed of the loss of life and dreadful misery each of these efforts had occasioned. As soon, therefore, as he was seated on the pontifical throne he began to preach a new crusade. He found in a French parish priest, Fulk, of Neuilly, near Paris, another Peter. This enthusiast preached with such fervour, that ere long the noblest portion of the French baronage declared themselves ready to take the cross and go the rescue of the Holy City. The maritime states of Italy alone had the means of transport; the French crusaders therefore deputed six of their number to go to Venice and negotiate for the necessary ships.

When the French envoys arrived in Venice in 1201, its chief ruler was Enrico Dandolo, a venerable man in his eighty-seventh or, as some say, in his ninety-second year. He had already been Doge nine years, having served the Republic in various capacities all his life. He was the incarnation of the spirit of Venice; of a Republic conscious of possessing a power far greater than had yet appeared—a power owing nothing to fortune or favour, but much to the long-continued exercise of the virtues of self-denial and probity, prudence and industry; of a Republic therefore careful never to give unnecessary offence, but jealously maintaining its independence of every influence, imperial or papal; of a Republic remorseless in its endeavours to crush its competitors, but generous in dealing with its own clients; of a Republic, in fine, accustomed to self-restraint, and therefore able to veil boundless ambition and the most romantic spirit of adventure under the garb of the humble pursuit of commerce.

Such was Enrico Dandolo, and such was the Republic he served. Although half blind, his mental eyes appear to have been keen indeed. In the proposals of the French envoys he saw the possibility of great advantage to Venice, and in a great public assembly of the citizens held before the Church of St. Mark, he recommended that the Republic should provide the crusaders with a sufficient number of ships, that it should supply the fleet for nine months with provisions, and further aid the expedition with a squadron of fifty galleys, the French on their part agreeing to pay 85,000 marks, and to share all their conquests with the Venetians. But when the time came for payment, the crusaders could only raise 35,000 marks, whereupon Dandolo proposed to his fellow citizens to accept this instalment, on condition that the French army helped them to reconquer Zara, a fortified town owing allegiance to Venice, and which the King of Hungary had seized.

The proposal took the crusaders by surprise, and greatly incensed the pope. Dandolo, however, overcame their reluctance by himself offering to take the cross and to go with them. By so doing he led them to suppose that he was animated by similar motives to themselves, and at the same time by his presence secured the fulfilment of the treaty. But Innocent refused to allow the arrangement. He sent the Cardinal of St. Marcel to forbid even the Venetians to attack Zara. But when the papal legate attempted to take the command of the fleet, the Venetians quietly interposed, and told the cardinal that if he came as a preacher he was welcome to accompany them, but not otherwise. The legate retired in dudgeon. The great bulk adhered to Dandolo, and after a short siege, Zara was taken; and then the Doge was able again to divert the destination of the army, in order that it might effect the end he had in view.

The Eastern question is a very old one, since it had begun to require settlement in the thirteenth century. The Byzantine empire had arrived at the final stage of corruption and decay. The last of the Commenian house was succeeded by a weak prince, named Isaac Angelus. Alexius, his brother, deposed him, and put his eyes out. The son of Isaac, a younger Alexius, escaped in the guise of a common sailor, and, supported by his uncle, Philip of Suabia, who had at that time obtained the imperial crown of Germany, presented himself both at Venice and Zara, and tried to enlist the sympathy and help of the crusaders on behalf of his unfortunate father. Dandolo and the Venetians favoured the cause of the young prince, since they saw in the proposal new wealth and power for Venice. The adherents of the pope were entirely opposed to the diversion. However, the terms offered by Alexius were so advantageous, that the leaders of the crusade decided to take their armies to Constantinople. By these terms it was agreed that on recovery of their position, Isaac and Alexius would terminate the Eastern schism, and recognise the pope, that they would help the crusaders in Palestine for one year with an auxiliary force of ten thousand men, as well as to maintain a guard of five hundred knights for the Holy Sepulchre, and finally to divide between the crusaders a sum of twenty thousand marks.

Innocent, who had excommunicated the Venetians for their conduct at Zara, evidently was at a loss what to do. The spirit of commerce was more than a match for him; indeed, he seems himself to have been somewhat fascinated by the idea of the submission of the Byzantine Church to the Roman see; for his imprecations grow feeble, and at last die away. "Faithful among the faithless," Simon de Montfort withdraws from the crusade, preferring a more orthodox way of growing rich.

A prosperous voyage brought the allied French and Venetians to Scutari, from whence after nine days they crossed the Bosphorus and attacked Constantinople (A.D. 1204). The French took the land, the Venetians the sea. The vessel which bore the Doge, who by this time was at least eighty-two, led the attack. Clad in complete armour, the standard of St. Mark before him, his galley was the first to strike the shore, and he the first warrior to land. Ere long the banner of the Republic was waving from the ramparts of Constantinople. Learning, however, that the French were in danger of being overpowered, he went to their rescue, and before dawn the metropolis of the Greek empire was in the hands of the Latins. Isaac was brought out of his dungeon, and with his son Alexius crowned in the Church of St. Sophia.

Alexius now feared to lose the help which had re-seated his father on the throne, and besought the crusaders to stay. Again Dandolo supported his proposal, and for a consideration of sixteen hundred pounds of gold the French barons and knights consented to put off their campaign in the Holy Land. To the Greeks, however, the presence of their Latin conquerors was a daily degradation. A few drunken crusaders made an attack on some Jews, and were unexpectedly repulsed. In their retreat they set fire to certain houses, causing a conflagration, which burnt down part of the quarter. Immense indignation was aroused in Constantinople, and Alexius, at his wits' end, became the dupe of a wretch named Mourzoufle, who pretended to be his friend, and then murdered both the prince and his father.

As the crusaders were encamped outside the city, in the suburb of Galata or Pera, they lost their hold on Constantinople by this revolution, and were obliged, unless they intended to lose all they had bargained for, to undertake a fresh siege of the city. This proved a far more formidable work than on the first occasion. Nearly three months were consumed in skirmishes and preparations, and it was only after a severe struggle that at last the city was taken by storm, and two thousand of its defenders slain. Constantinople was given over to rapine and plunder, and the booty, which was enormous, repaid all the Crusaders' demands over and over again. The property equally divided between the French and the Venetians was computed at nine hundred thousand marks of silver, or one million eight hundred thousand pounds sterling, while the secret plunder is computed by Gibbon to have represented about four million pounds sterling. Much of this was in priceless works of art, gems, vases, sculptures, paintings, frescoes, mosaics, which were thus scattered all over Europe. Down to a recent period the Cathedral of St. Mark and the Hall of the Great Council were decorated with trophies and enriched with treasures taken at the sack of Constantinople. To this day the doorway of St. Mark's is ornamented with the four famous horses which Marino Zeno brought from Constantinople.

But the Republic acquired other advantages more considerable than all this treasure. The Morea, the Illyric Isles, a large portion of Thessaly, the Sporades, the Cyclades, Adrianople, and three other cities, Servia, and the coasts of Hellespont, fell to its share. Dandolo himself might have become Emperor of the East; but the Venetians were too wise to allow their Doge to accept such a position, even if he had wished it. The crusaders, however, conferred on him the singular title of "Despot of Roumania, and Lord of one-fourth and one-half of the Roman Empire." Baldwin of Flanders was elected emperor; but the Latins soon showed they were incompetent to manage the people they had conquered. Baldwin fell into the hands of the King of Bulgaria, who shut him up in prison, where he died. To crown their misfortunes, Dandolo, who, though now bidding fair to become a centenarian, was still regarded as their best man, intellectually, succumbed to an attack of dysentery. He was buried with great pomp in the Church of St. Sophia, June 4, 1205.

To counteract the spirit of anarchy, of secularism, of luxury and inhumanity likely to result from a too rapid development of civil freedom, anti-sacerdotalism and commerce, another movement arose, which, though it may appear to us a travesty, was a most sincere attempt to realise, according to mediæval ideas, the life recommended in the Sermon on the Mount. The instruments through whom this new force came into being were two obscure men, possessing natures totally different, and passing lives diametrically opposite, yet one in their belief in the supreme importance of the religious life, and in witnessing with all their might for the principles of poverty and obedience.

The one was Dominic Guzman, a Castilian; the other was Francis Benardone, an Umbrian. The former was born in 1170, the latter in 1182.

We have spoken of Dominic, the ardent, exalted Castilian; stern, ascetic, relentless as the bare, burning mountains of his early home. We have noted how the religious licence of the land of the troubadours shocked him, how it led him to found an order of itinerant preachers, who, poor, but learned, might contend with the flood of heresy and immorality which seemed to him to deluge the South of France. Dominic founded his order in the year memorable for Magna Charta (1215). It rapidly made way in France, Italy, England, and even Scotland. Within fifteen years after its foundation it had obtained a chair of theology in the University of Paris, and within six years of the same date it had established a monastery at Oxford. In Scotland it possessed a powerful friend in Alexander II., who is said to have met Dominic at Paris in 1217. A welcome still more enthusiastic was given by the common people of the great towns, who were always struggling with poverty and oppressed by ignorance and disease. The advent of the *Frères*—the brothers—was hailed like a new dawn. And Christendom was not deceived, for in England the future witness for civil and religious freedom—the Friars, Black and Grey—were workers in the cause of liberty and light.

It may seem strange how a man coming from a land where Christianity was Mohammedan in spirit, and who himself was the most intense representative of this extraordinary fusion of its antagonistic creeds, could in any degree promote the cause of light and liberty. It is evidence that the least spark of faith in a God of Righteousness is powerful towards these ends in counteracting misanthropic bigotry. In the soul of Dominic the passion for righteousness burnt like a furnace seven times heated.

But side by side with these funereal-looking messengers of wrath appeared a gentler brotherhood, full of mercy for the fallen and suffering. The founder of the order of Grey Friars was a man even more remarkable than Dominic, and a thousand times more loveable. Francis of Assisi was the son of a cloth merchant in that town, a handsome, gay, light-hearted youth, who loved nothing so much as fine dress and merry company. Yet, in the midst of his mirth, Francis had serious thoughts. In the course of one of the little Italian wars he was taken prisoner, and had a long illness. He had a very prayerful spirit, and came to the conclusion that it was his duty to give up every worldly consideration, in order that he might take up his cross and follow Christ. He now obtained, and ever after manifested, an intense love to Christ. Being a man of great simplicity of spirit, he did things which some will regard as childish, others as childlike. He determined to be absolutely poor, and to possess nothing. He clad himself in the dress of a shepherd —a rough coat, girt about with a cord. He carried this devotion to poverty further than anyone before him, since he had no idea of becoming a hermit and living on roots, but of living entirely for the conversion of his fellow-men.

Both he and Dominic had similar ideas at the same time, but the Spaniard's great idea was learning in the garb of poverty; the Italian raised the standard of poverty, ever working, loving, giving. The soul of Francis was filled with the love of God. He had a poetic gift, and made sweet songs expressive of his passion. Although so simple a man, and of the most unbounded faith, he had great common-sense, and a quaint humour which kept his mind healthy. As he meant his friars to work and live among the people, he would not let them give up common food, but ordered them to eat flesh, as the seculars did. He won his disciples by his evident love to God, and kept them by his tender love for themselves. He did not, however, spare them, and sometimes ordered them the most outrageous penances; but then he took care to suffer with the brother in disgrace. When he was near his end, he seems to have thought that he had not treated his body quite fairly, and in his odd, simple way, he asked pardon of "Brother Ass," which was his cognomen for his poor burden-carrier.

His love to animals and his influence over them were great. One story which perhaps approaches as near the literal truth as any, relates that, preaching near the town of Alvia, Francis was continually interrupted by the swallows, which, flitting about over the heads of the people, kept up a perpetual twittering. Turning round, the preacher thus addressed the noisy birds: "My sisters, it is now time that I should speak. Since you have had your say, listen now to the word of God, and be silent until the sermon is finished." Of course, his little sisters were not less obedient than penitent Brother Wolf, who, after having been a terror to the town of Gubbio, was converted by Francis, and led an exemplary life.

These popular legends, and they are numerous, show how great an influence Francis obtained. He sent forth his friars two and two; and though at first their rough garb and singular simplicity caused them to be mocked, the simple faith and earnest love of souls with which Francis imbued his disciples won all hearts. They were welcomed throughout the little castellated towns of Italy, and their preaching was listened to by every class, from the proud noble to the humblest artisans. At last Francis himself became alarmed at the results of his preaching. On one occasion a whole castleful was so moved that everyone, lord and lady, officers and retainers, wanted to follow him, and renounce the world. This caused him to institute an outer order, requiring no sacrifice beyond that of the heart.

Even with these efforts to render the revival reasonable, the fraternity increased so prodigiously that, at a great chapter of the order held A.D. 1219, more than five thousand attended. At this meeting Francis had made no provision for his brethren, relying entirely on the bounty of Providence. Dominic had come as a visitor, curious to watch the working of an experiment so nearly akin to his own, and was amazed at such indiscretion on the part of Francis. He, far from fearing, exhorted his brethren to give no thought as to what they should eat or drink; and, if we are to believe the old chronicler, his faith received a great and manifest reward, for the people of the various cities on the Umbrian plain appeared by one consent to have taken upon themselves to supply all necessaries. Suddenly men appeared with asses, horses and carts, laden with bread, wine, beans, and game, and everything requisite for the tables; and he was considered happy who could carry most things, and could serve most humbly; and even the knights and barons who came to look on began humbly to wait on the poor friars. Dominic now was even more amazed, and going to Francis, humbly confessed his sin, saying, "Truly God has a special care of this poor family, and I knew it not."

MAGNA CHARTA ISLAND.

FOURTEENTH CENTURY.

CONTEMPORARY EVENTS IN THE FOURTEENTH CENTURY.

Italy.—Dante in the Streets of Verona.
Switzerland.—The Death of Geissler.
Scotland.—Robert Bruce and the men of Galloway
Italy.—Pope Boniface and Colonna.

Fourteenth Century.

A.D. 1303–1315.

Dante—Comparison between the Gothic Cathedral and the Divina Commedia—Rise of the Spirit of Independence—The Temporal Power defies the Spiritual—Philippe le Bel and Pope Boniface—Struggle of the Swiss Cantons against Austria—William Tell —The Battle of Mortgarten—Struggle of the Scotch against England—Robert Bruce—The Battle of Bannockburn.

HEN the women of Verona beheld Dante moving like a shade through their streets, his head bent, his aspect grave and severe, bitterness and melancholy written in every line of his face, they saw the man who most of all was possessed with the thought of the epoch; and when they whispered one to another, "This is the man that has been to hell," they said that which was to a great extent true of the Middle Ages. The poet and the people each built monuments in which they enshrined all their thoughts. The Gothic cathedral and the *Divina Commedia* are the best commentaries on the Middle Ages. He who passed from the fresh air and from under the clear blue sky into a cathedral, felt as one who had entered a home of sadness. Through the vaulted aisles came the low wailing of the priests chanting masses for the dead. In the confessionals and before the altars knelt sad-eyed penitents. On the

cold stones lay pale, prostrate figures agonising in silence. In the far distance was the symbol of the birth-thought from whence had sprung the whole structure—the Christ on the cross, mute and dead.

Each returning Easter Day told the worshipper how this dead Christ had arisen, and would come again to judge the world. There was life in the thought. The heavy vaults of the Anglo-Saxon cathedral lifted their roofs, the columns shot upwards, arch rose upon arch, window after window began to open, until the clerestory was full of light. The walls began to be radiant with colours that spoke of heaven : gold, purple, and azure blue. Through painted windows looked in the transfigured forms of saints and martyrs who, when the full notes of the hosanna rose, appeared to take up the song, so that the mystic roof, ever soaring higher and higher, seemed to become at last a visible heaven. Then a living presence—human, maternal—entered to overshadow the saints, and to embrace in its arms the dead, mute Christ. The Lady Chapel rose behind the high altar, and looked down upon and enveloped the crucifix; but, as if the mediæval artist had an intuition of what was coming, he opened his great rose window exactly opposite the crucifix and the Lady Chapel, like some new eye whose light should dissipate the shadows of the tomb.

Such was the architectural monument of the Middle Ages : the counterpart is to be found in the great poem of the sad Florentine. The *Divina Commedia* speaks the same language as the cathedral. Suffering, eternal anguish for the many, purification through suffering for some, beatitude at once for the elect few. But death and judgment, hell and purgatory, are its realities. Heaven is only a blaze of monotonous light : the God who reigned over all, the Christ who had redeemed the Church, and the saints who had entered glory, exercise no real influence over the drama. The real goddess of Dante's universe is a woman. Beatrice occupies in the *Divina Commedia* the same position as the Virgin did in the Church of the Middle Ages.

"Except a corn of wheat fall into the ground and die, it abideth alone ; but if it die, it bringeth forth much fruit." Thus was the Middle Age the seed-time of the modern world. In it were the germs of the national life, the languages, the civil and religious liberty, the science, literature, and art of to-day.

The fourteenth century marks the close of this long period of germination; the blade has appeared above the earth, and all who seek the first developments of national life, modern language, civil and religious liberty, science, literature, and art will find them living and breathing the free air in this fourteenth century.

THE previous century had seen the climax of the papal power. Towards the close (A.D. 1294) Boniface VIII. became pope. His inauguration was the most magnificent that had ever been known. He rode through Rome on a white horse, richly caparisoned, a crown on his head, his bridle held by two kings, the nobility of Rome in his train. The streets were so crowded with masses of kneeling people that the procession could scarcely force its way; suddenly a furious hurricane burst over the city, every light and every torch in St. Peter's was extinguished, a riot arose among the population, and forty lives were lost. Boniface believed in display, and at the turn of the century he determined to hold a jubilee in Rome. Every pilgrim who for thirty days should visit the tombs of the apostles was promised a plenary indulgence. The pilgrims streamed in from all parts; the houses, and even the churches, were insufficient to accommodate them, and they had to camp out in the streets and squares. The pope was elated with his success. He appeared in the sight of these vast multitudes attended by the signs of imperial power. A herald went before him crying, "Here are two swords; Peter, thou seest here thy successor, and Thou, O Christ, Thy vicar!"

Like many proud dreamers, Boniface little knew what the future was bringing. The cup was full, the statesmanship of Europe was bitterly resentful, and the superstitious reverence which had so long supported the Papacy was fading away, as its scandalous selfishness and preposterous ambition became more and more manifest. The blow that was to humble it came from a quarter and through an agency that the Papacy had itself prepared.

One of the fruits of the Albigensian persecution was a dispute between the pope and the King of France as to the suzerainty of Narbonne. The pope took upon himself to carve out a new bishopric from that of Toulouse, and appointed a man of his own, one Bernard de Saisset. The

new Bishop of Pamiers was a descendant of Raymond of Toulouse, and
hated Philippe le Bel. He plotted against the king, was arrested, found
guilty, and a demand was made to the pope for his degradation. This
was the origin of the dispute between the pope and the King of France,
but it soon took larger dimensions. Boniface claimed the bishop, and
convoking the French clergy to an assembly in Rome, asserted his right
to tear up and pull down, to destroy and to build up in the might of his
own power and teaching.

But a new force had arisen—the instinct of national life; and against
this force the theories of Hildebrand, of Innocent and of Boniface were
destined to defeat. A new race of rulers had appeared, neither
mailed barons nor cowled monks, but astute lawyers. The Roman law
was their Bible. *Scriptum est*, settled everything. With texts, citations,
falsifications, they demolished the theocracy, the feudalism, and the chivalry
of the Middle Age. They ventured even to seize the body of the pope,
and to send the crusaders to the stake, in the persons of the Templars.
They were the founders of modern civil order. In France they were devoted
friends of the monarchy, and worked for the ruin of the Church and the
nobility. They covered the land with a web of legal officers of all kinds,
in the centre of which was the grand council called the "Parlement."
This body was established at Paris A.D. 1302, and no priest was allowed
to take part in its proceedings.

To these lawyers Philippe le Bel committed his quarrel with the pope.
He sent two of them to Rome; and Boniface soon discovered that lawyers
were quite as perfect as priests in the art of invective. They stormed
against the abuses of the papal court, and even denounced the papal
conduct. But this was not all. Italian priests found themselves outdone
in fraud. The French lawyers forged a bull, in which they made Boniface
claim not only the spiritual but the *temporal* power in France. To this
a short answer was published, purporting to come from the king, in which
Boniface was addressed as "thy very great self-conceitedness," and his
claims flatly denied. Philippe sanctioned all these proceedings by appearing,
surrounded by a crowd of lords and knights, and in the presence of the
people of Paris burning this false bull. To bring the people into the
quarrel, the king convoked the States-General, but instead of calling the
estates of the north and south separately, and the clergy and the nobility

of each separately, he convoked all in one body, and added humbler personages, citizens, mayors, sheriffs, consuls of cities.

For a moment Philippe appeared to receive a violent check in the battle of the Spurs, in which his chancellor fell, together with vast numbers of the nobility of France. But in reality it was a defeat much to the interest of the French monarchy, since it freed France from its most turbulent subjects. It is further noteworthy, as a sign of the rise of the people, that the chivalry of France had been totally defeated by the Flemish burghers.

Boniface thought to profit by the occasion, and threatened Philippe with excommunication if he refused to allow the French bishops to come to Rome. The lawyers replied by an ordinance for the reform of the kingdom. Good administration, equal justice, protection of priests, consideration of baronial privileges, security of individuals, goods and customs; gentleness was promised, and force shown. The king made peace with England by the sacrifice of Guienne, and then by his new chancellor, Nogaret, denounced the pope. Boniface was a Balaam, who loved the wages of iniquity; the chancellor, the ass who rebuked the madness of the prophet; the king, the angel with the drawn sword, standing ready to prevent the pope from doing the harm he intended to God's people.

The legate left the excommunication in France and fled; the king appealed to a council. The French government expected that Boniface would at once follow up his excommunication by delivering the country into the hands of Albert of Austria. The bull was in fact ready; and in order to weaken the effect, Nogaret determined to present the appeal for a council to Boniface in person. Boniface fled to his native town of Anagni, where he was among his own people. The French chancellor proceeded rapidly and steadily to effect his purpose. He took with him a deadly enemy of the pope, Sciera Colonna, a man who knew so well what would be his fate if Boniface could get him, that, rather than fall into his hands, he had served as a galley-slave for years. These two went to Anagni, and Nogaret hired Sapino of Ferentino, a captain of a neighbouring city, to deliver up the pope to him, dead or alive. Sapino suddenly appeared before Anagni, whose captain betrayed his trust, and joined his troops to those of the enemy, so that Nogaret and Colonna had the pope in their power.

The palaces in Anagni were given up to pillage, the cardinals escaping by the most ignominious of all exits, the pope's own nephew making terms for himself. Thus Boniface found himself alone, confronted by his most deadly foes. The palace was in flames, the crowd were pressing in: "Abdicate," they cried, "and yield at discretion." Boniface, eighty-six years of age, could not restrain his tears. "Here is my neck," he said, "here is my head." Colonna, so the story runs, struck the old man a blow in the face with his mailed hand. Nogaret told him to look now only to the King of France, and to his protection. Boniface turned fiercely on the chancellor. "You come," said he, "of an heretical family; it is from you that I expect martyrdom."

Colonna wanted to kill him, but the man of law would not permit it. Moreover, Boniface seemed likely to settle the question himself, for he refused to eat. Suddenly, however, the people of Anagni rose, and the foreigners were forced to give up their prey. But the fright had driven the aged pontiff out of his wits. He went into the square, and told the people that he was poor as Job, and had nothing to eat nor drink. If any poor man would give him a bit of bread or a drink of water, he would bestow on him the blessing of God and his own. If anyone would give him the smallest thing, he would absolve him from all sin. He was taken to Rome, but his friends did not dare to show him. He raved and refused food, he foamed and ground his teeth, and when at last they attempted to give him the viaticum, he repelled it with a blow, dying without confession or communion. Finally, he was condemned to everlasting punishment by the self-constituted Rhadamanthus of the age, the greatest poet of Catholicism.

In an age in which a pope was thus treated, we are not surprised to find English barons bearding their king, even though that king is Edward I., or Flemish burghers rising against their nobles, or Swiss mountaineers and Scottish clansmen daring to resist all the forces of their feudal superiors. The times that produced Wallace and Bruce and Philip von Arteveldt, and that have given us the half-legendary story of William Tell, are the natural sequence of the spiritual freedom which now burst forth, and of which Nogaret and Dante are such striking examples. A spirit of independence had taken possession of all classes.

Far, however, from tending to anarchy, it was in the highest degree constructive; for it was truly religious, having a deep respect for law and order, individual and social rights. The Black Friars of Dominic, the Grey Friars of Francis, had produced a religious revolution. Notwithstanding the opposition of all interested in supporting the old order of things, and perhaps in consequence of it, the friars were welcomed everywhere. The common people heard them gladly, for they came poorer than the poorest into their dark, close, filthy lanes and houses. Instead of seeking out the sweetest and most retired spots, as the monks had done, the friars went at once to the densely-populated and fever-haunted districts in the great towns. Thus, in London, they came to live in the shambles of Newgate, and at Oxford, in the swamps between the city walls and the Thames.

They won their way among the lower classes by their coarse wit and fervid appeals, among the more cultured by their learning and thought. The mendicant friars were the great teachers of the fourteenth century. Albert Magnus and Thomas Aquinas among the Dominicans; Roger Bacon, Duns Scotus, John Ockham, and Adam Marsh among the Franciscans.

Under the latter the Franciscan school at Oxford became one of the most noted in Christendom; indeed, the teaching of the friars soon rendered the English University only second to that of Paris, where the intellectual giants, Aquinas and Duns Scotus, aroused the intellect of all Christendom.

The work of the friars had been done amidst much opposition, not only of the regular clergy, but of learned bodies like the Sorbonne. The friars were therefore on the side of freedom. In England their university was among the chief opponents to papal exactions and royal tyranny; and the towns in which they had the most influence were the best supporters of the barons in the struggle for freedom. Their great doctor, Adam Marsh, was the friend of the leading reformers in Church and State, Grosteste and De Montfort.

Thus the little rill of faith which had sprung up in the hearts of Dominic and Francis became a universal flood which watered the roots of liberty throughout Christendom. This religious faith, this sense of personal responsibility to an unseen Judge, rendered eminently constructive the new spirit of independence. It took form in confederated societies, of which the members bound themselves by oath to defend each other's lives and properties against whosoever should molest them, singly or collectively.

A NOTABLE example is that of the Swiss, who, in defence of such a contract, defeated an invasion of the Duke of Austria, supported by the armies of other German nobles, thus laying the foundations of a free national life which has now endured for more than half a millennium. The Old League of Germany was the name the Swiss gave their confederation, indicating their belief that they were only defending ancient laws and privileges. However, A.D. 1291 is the first time in which this league gives any sign of existence.

The Swiss Highlands and the towns on the Lake of Geneva existed under a rule composed of all the contradictions of feudalism: the empire, independent lords, and prince-bishops. This state of things was endurable as long as the rulers were just and free from ambition; but when a sovereign appeared grasping, tyrannical, and a known foe to popular liberties, the Swiss became agitated, and more than ever determined to preserve their independence. Such was the feeling when Albert of Austria became King of Germany, A.D. 1298. His Swiss subjects, determining that nothing should be done which should give colour to the idea that they had surrendered their independence, asked that the usual imperial commissary should be appointed. Albert sent Herman of Brunck, near Hapsburg, and Beranger of Landenberg, as imperial bailiffs.

These men appear to have been instructed to pursue the wicked policy of arousing revolt by insult, that ground might be given for the suppression of the popular liberties. Not only were the laws cruelly administered, and trade impeded by tolls and other difficulties, but the people were wounded in their family life by the licence permitted to the Austrian soldiers. Herman built a castle in the valley of Altorf, which he called Twing or Zwing Uri: the curb of Uri. His oppression gained him the name of Geissel, the scourge of the country; or Geissler, the tormenter of its inhabitants. But tyrants always misunderstand the genius of the people they attempt to coerce. Yeomen living on their own small estates, a peasantry enjoying a free and natural life, on good terms with their richer neighbours and employers: such were the Swiss mountaineers;

and in all ages societies thus composed have been the most determined defenders of their independence.

The first effort to put a stop to the rising tyranny was made by three men : Werner Stauffacher, a magistrate held in much honour by the people, his friend Walter Furst, of Uri, and a youth named Arnold Melchthal, whose father, for a trifling offence, had been blinded. They held their meetings at midnight in a meadow called Grütli, in a sequestered vale at the foot of the rock Mlytenstein. Here by agreement, on the night preceding the 11th of November, 1307, they came, each bringing with him ten trusty comrades. These thirty-three confederates agreed that none should be guided by his own opinion, but that all should jointly live and die for the common defence, and that each in his own neighbourhood would promote the great object of their league—namely, to hand down, undiminished, the liberties that they had received from their fathers. They concluded by clasping each other's hands, and then lifting them up to heaven in solemn attestation of their bond.

Geissler, no doubt, had some inkling of what was going on, and, in order to disarm the conspirators, he determined to make the people take what was tantamount to an oath of allegiance. He set up the symbol of feudal authority, the ducal hat, in the market-place of Altorf, causing his officers to summon the people to the courts. The confederates came, and treated the hat with due respect; one man alone, William of Burglen, said to have been a son-in-law of Walter Furst, marched before it without bending his head. He was arrested, put on board a boat, to be taken by Geissler himself to the Castle of Schwanau. The boat had scarcely started before a terrific wind came rushing down one of the mountain gorges, and Geissler was fain to trust the helm in his prisoner's hands, knowing him to be an experienced boatman. William steered the vessel close to a projecting cliff, and, seizing his arms, sprang on shore. Then, taking his cross-bow, he deliberately aimed an arrow at the bailiff. It pierced his heart, and he fell dead.

This act, which was not in accordance with the deliberation and prudence otherwise shown by the confederates, gained for William of Burglen the epithet Telle, or Tolle, one who was thoughtlessly bold, rash. However, the act raised the country. Soon after this the Castle of Rossberg was taken by a stratagem. Zwing Uri and

Schwanau were both seized, and the insurrection was so complete and methodical that Beranger of Landenberg, the other bailiff, fell into the hands of the confederates. They conveyed him to the frontier, and took an oath from him that he would never re-enter the three cantons. He had not long rejoined his master before Albert was himself assassinated by his nephew.

This effort for civil liberty is all along mixed up with disputes with clerical authority, showing that a spirit of religious independence was arising. The dispute centred on a money question. The people demanded that the clergy should pay taxes like other people; the clergy, accordingly, were against popular liberty. After the three cantons had effected their revolution this ill-feeling continued to fester, until one day it broke out into actual warfare. Some canons of Einsidlen insulted two men of Schwitz, and drew their knives upon them. The Swiss attacked the abbey, and carried off four canons and the schoolmaster, The Bishop of Constance excommunicated the audacious mountaineers, and the Abbot of Einsidlen obtained against them an imperial edict. But the new King of Germany had no desire to enter into a contest with men who knew so well how to defend their liberties, and both interdict and excommunication were revoked.

But the indignation of the higher classes in Germany was aroused; this insolent herd of burghers and rustics must be put down; and Duke Leopold of Austria, the son of Albert of Hapsburg, does not seem to have had much difficulty in raising several armies of counts and noblemen to assist him in reducing his Swiss territories. Three separate attacks were to be made. Otho, the young Count of Strasbourg, was to lead an army of four thousand men through the Oberland to the frontiers of Underwalden. Another thousand were to invade Underwalden on the side of the lake, while the duke himself was to conduct the main army towards Zug, followed by all the ancient nobility of Hapsburg, Lenzburg, and Kyberg, and by Beranger of Landenberg and the kinsmen of Geissler.

But the Swiss had the inestimable advantage of knowing every yard of a difficult country, and being led by an experienced veteran, Rudolph Reding de Biberick. He chose a meadow above the heights of Mortgarten as the place to await the invaders. And here, with prayerful hearts, stood the thirteen hundred who had gathered to defend this Swiss Thermopylæ and the rights of many generations.

Early in the morning of the 13th of October, 1315, the armour of the Austrian troops was seen glistening in the first rays of the sun. Ere long the whole pass was full of a long line of knights and men-at-arms. Some fifty Swiss, posted on an eminence, now gave a sudden shout, and threw down heaps of stones and fragments of rocks on the crowd filing below. The confederates, watching the moment when the confusion was greatest, rushed down from the mountain, and fell on the flanks of the disordered column. Duke Leopold was caught in a trap, and his unfortunate followers were almost massacred by the enraged mountaineers, who attacked their enemies with their massive clubs and long pikes. The cavalry fell back on the infantry, who, not being able to open their ranks from the nature of the country, were trampled to death. The rout was general, and the carnage great. Leopold barely escaped, a peasant leading him along a by-path across the mountains to a place of refuge. Thus in three hours the Swiss gained the decisive victory of Mortgarten.

For the other armies, hearing of the disastrous result, quickly beat a retreat; and the Swiss had leisure to thank God for thus supporting them against their foes, and helping them to maintain His cause.

IN turning to the contemporaneous effort for the maintenance of the liberties and independence of Scotland, that country must not be considered as an organised nationality. England was only just becoming such, and prior to the struggle we are about to relate, Scotland was a mere *omnium gatherum* of all the people whose land was contiguous, collected together by circumstances and the policy of the Scotch and English kings. Four peoples may be distinctly seen. The Lowlanders, who were to all intents and purposes Englishmen. Their land had formed the northern half of the old kingdom of Northumbria, and went by the name of Saxony. It had suffered the fate of Saxon England, for its nobility were chiefly men of Norman race. The peninsula between the firths of Solway and Clyde was inhabited by the descendants of the ancient Britons, and was still called Cumbria. The Highlanders were the old Picts, the only people whose settlement was pre-historic. They, as the most ancient inhabitants, should have given their name to the country; but that honour was reserved for the descendants of certain Scots, who in the early ages had emigrated from Ireland, and had founded a kingdom on the western shores of

Caledonia. Their king, Kenneth MacAlpine, having succeeded by marriage to the Pictish kingdom, his descendants finally gave the name of their first possessions to the whole land.

In 1286, Alexander III., the last male of his race, fell over a cliff and was killed. His little granddaughter, the Maid of Norway, dying on her passage to Scotland, the direct line became extinct. So many claimants to the vacant throne appeared that it was determined to refer the decision to Edward I., a certain kind of over-lordship in the King of England having been frequently acknowledged since the time of Edward the Elder. The claimant adjudged the rightful heir to be John Baliol, but when he had accepted the position it was found that King Edward had so fettered him that the King of Scotland had become a vassal of the English crown. The Scottish nobles, however, offered little resistance to Edward's claims, but the commons were obstinate. Thus the same determined obstinacy in maintaining their liberties possessed both the Scotch and Swiss peoples in the last decade of the thirteenth century. Baliol soon found his position untenable, and being forced to head an insurrection, he was deposed, and Edward marched triumphantly into Scotland. The earls, barons, and gentry did homage to the King of England. The sacred stone upon which all its monarchs had been crowned was carried to Westminster. The conquest of Scotland seemed complete.

A deliverer, however, appeared; a man whose daring courage and ardent patriotism more than equalled that of Tell, and who remains, moreover, a far more substantial figure in history. A young athlete—generous, humorous, full of fiery daring and patriotic enthusiasm—William Wallace had every characteristic of the typical champion. His life was romantic in the highest degree. With a chosen band of followers he led the life of a guerilla chief in the recesses of Clydesdale, issuing forth from time to time, and committing terrible deeds of vengeance on the English garrisons, running every risk, and passing a life full of adventure. He fell in love with a gentle girl, Marion Bradfute, the orphan daughter of Sir Hew Bradfute. Wallace secretly married her. The English governor of Lanark, having on one occasion discovered that she had sheltered the outlaw, had her hanged. When the news reached her husband, he set off for Lanark, slew the governor that same night, and drove the English out of the town.

So many gathered round the heroic patriot, and his exploits became so famous, that several noblemen joined him, among others Robert Bruce, who had hitherto been an adherent of King Edward. In 1297 or 1298, Wallace assumed the title of Guardian of Scotland. His regency, however, did not last for more than a year, for in 1298 King Edward came with a large army into Scotland. A battle was fought at Falkirk, in which, notwithstanding a noble defence, and great skill on the part of Wallace, the Scots were defeated. Their leader escaped with difficulty, and became again an outlaw. In 1305 he fell, through treachery, into the hands of the English, and was taken to London. He was tried in Westminster Hall, and condemned to the atrocious death mediæval cruelty inflicted on traitors. He suffered at Smithfield, and his head surmounted by a laurel crown was exposed in derision on London Bridge. Thus perished the champion of Scottish independence.

The germinating power of the blood of the martyrs is an universal truth. The death of Wallace sent a pang through every noble heart in Scotland, and its patriotism, up till then mixed with much alloy, became a pure and disinterested flame, which through all the ages since has kindled itself again and again at the memory of William Wallace.

Bruce, who at first appears as a commonplace self-seeker, the descendant of the grasping Normans, now steps forward as the successor of Wallace, and in the pursuit of a great and noble cause is gradually changed into one of the finest characters in history. A claimant for the throne, he tried at first to win Edward's patronage, then in passionate resentment he murders the Red Comyn, whom he suspected of betraying his wavering allegiance to the English king. The deed could not be forgiven, and in self-defence he seized the throne.

Scotland rejoiced at his daring, and King Edward saw that unless he was prompt and terrible the new possessions would be lost. He marched north with a great army, but Bruce had already fled. All who sympathised were seized, and every noble was hanged. Bruce took refuge in the Western Isles. Here and in other wild regions of Old Caledonia he wandered so long, that the world might well have thought him dead. However, he gave evidence of life by appearing now and again with his followers, and doing some daring deed. Sometimes he was reduced to one man, and at times he was entirely alone, always living in fear of sudden surprise, a great reward being offered for his capture.

On one occasion two hundred men of Galloway track him with a sleuthhound. Bruce is aware of what they are doing; he goes to a morass beside a stream, and selects a place where there is a ford. He sends his two followers for help, and waits there alone. He watches, he hears the baying of the hound, he sees the foe coming in the clear moonlight. He determines to make a stand. Only one can attack him at a time. The first who comes is struck down; he slays five on the ford. His pursuers fall back, but their leader exhorts them to advance, and they all come on together; he fills the water with the slain. Fourteen men has Robert Bruce struck down with his own hand.

Another time John of Lorn and a band of followers are again on his track with a sleuthhound. Bruce finds a stream in a vale. But at last, being over-tired, he can go no farther; then his foster-brother, who is his only companion, cheers him and urges him forward. The king wades down the stream some distance farther, the scent is lost, and John of Lorn returns without his prey.

Such were the perils in which Bruce lived; but tyranny endures not for ever. The old King of England died breathing vengeance against Scotland, and leaving the completion of his work as a sacred duty to his successors. But the master spirit gone, the conquest flagged, and Bruce gradually became strong enough to invest Stirling Castle.

The danger aroused England, for Stirling was the key to the country. Edward II. advanced to its relief with thirty thousand horsemen. The battle of Bannockburn owed its success very greatly to the skill with which the ground was chosen, and its result showed, as also at the battle of the Spurs, how effectually free forces were learning to overcome the feudal. As at Mortgarten and before Bruges, ruse was largely employed. Bruce posted his troops where there was a wood on the right and a stream on the left; in front was a meadow, in which he dug pits, which he carefully covered with brushwood and turf. The English came strong in numbers, the Scotch in faith and patriotism. Success was not on the side of the big battalions. The rout was thorough. The English knights were soon floundering in the pits or flying in hot haste to the border. The cause was gained, and Scotia's independence won.

FIFTEENTH CENTURY.

CONTEMPORARY EVENTS IN THE FIFTEENTH CENTURY.

America.—The Landing of Columbus.
Italy.—Savonarola's Martyrdom.
Africa.—Bartholomew Diaz doubling the Cape of Good Hope.
England.—Caxton's printing press in Westminster.

Fifteenth Century.

A.D. 1476-1498.

Invention of Printing—Caxton's Press at Westminster—Revival of Classic Literature—Lorenzo de Medici—Savonarola, the Prophet of Italy—Great Navigators—Prince Henry of Portugal—Vasco de Gama—India reached by Sea—Columbus—Discovery of the New World.

It is night, and three small ships are ploughing in solitude the waves of the ocean thousands of miles beyond all known navigation. On the poop of one stands a figure looking intently into the darkness. He has seen a light on the horizon, a light that comes and goes, flashes for a moment, and is extinct. Is it real, or only delusion? He is sure of its reality, for it is the sign of a land he alone has believed in; for faith in which he has fought a long and painful battle, and endured many sufferings and much reproach. He will see on the morrow the glorious fruition of all his labours, but only for a moment, for the clouds will gather over him again, and he will die heart-broken. October 11, A.D. 1492, Columbus discovered America. This was the typical fact of the age, declaring its character and the character of its greatest men.

The spirit of independent thought, which the faith and preaching of Dominic and Francis aroused, had long overshot their mark, and was producing results of which they little dreamed. Learned monks or friars no longer meditate in cells on fate and freewill, on perpetual motion and the philosopher's stone; the spirit of research has seized the laity, and princes and traders, sailors and artisans, moved by it, make discoveries which are rapidly dissolving the old times and bringing in the new.

The stories which attribute the simultaneous discovery of printing by moveable types to a sacristan at Haarlem and a mechanician at Strasburg may be little better than popular myths; but at least they show that this "almost divine benefit," as a writer in the next age calls it, sprang directly from the people. Manuscript copyists and other interested folk may have surrounded the name of Faustus with dark legends, but the age welcomed discovery, and very soon every learned city in Europe had its printing-press. It was brought into our own land in 1476 by William Caxton, a man of versatile genius. Caxton set up his press in the precincts of the Abbey of Westminster, and met with great encouragement from the English court and the English nobility. The Wars of the Roses had taught them in a very terrible manner that old things were passing away, and in this ingenious invention they saw the hope of a wiser and a more peaceful society.

The first effect of the printing-press was to make the world better acquainted with the treasures of classic antiquity. And the taste for antiquity which, by means of the press, became every year more universal, received an immense impetus when, in 1453, a few years after the discovery of printing, Constantinople finally fell into the hands of the Turks. The scholars fled, bringing with them into various parts of Europe, but especially into Italy, many ancient manuscripts. A rage arose for collecting old manuscripts, and men spent their lives and fortunes in the search. Wiser men studied what others had so zealously collected. Some of these students were polyglots; as, for example, Pico, Prince of Mirandola, who was said to be acquainted with twenty-two different languages. One great monument of this period is the Complutensian Polyglot, printed at Complutum, or Alcala, in Spain, under the direction of Cardinal Ximenes. This munificent statesman spared no expense in collecting the ancient MSS. of the Bible, and in bringing together scholars from all countries to carry out his design. It cost him no less than eighty thousand ducats, and contained, besides the Hebrew text, the Septuagint, Greek, and the Chaldee (each with a literal Latin version), and the Vulgate. This was the first printed Greek text of the New Testament.

That the age, however, was one rather of learned research than literary taste is manifest from the fact that such a man as Mirandola considered the *Canti ˌCarnascialeschi* of Lorenzo de Medici superior to the *Divina Commedia*. These poetic efforts were ballads intended to be sung by the younger nobility during the carnival at Florence, and are described by Villari as of such a character that the lowest rabble in the present day would be disgusted, and that, if sung in the streets, they would be such an outrage on public decency as to call for punishment. But it was the policy of Lorenzo to make Florence corrupt, in order that it might forget that it had ever been free. In his time, Florence became a scene of orgies and revelling. Probably, as a man of the world, he considered no other policy possible. When the heads of Christendom set the example of crime, and turned Rome into a city of harlots, what could a layman do except to cultivate the tastes of the hour in a manner sufficiently grand to earn him the title of the Magnificent?

The Papacy sunk low enough in the tenth century, but never did it reach such a depth of infamy as at this period. The tiara was stained by every possible crime, until the Vatican became a hell upon earth. The downward progress was rapid. Sixtus IV. was bad; Innocent VIII. was worse; Alexander VI. surpassed all his predecessors in wickedness. No man, however holy, could approach Rome, and not be infected by the moral pestilence. The plague raged from the centre, and all moral power in Italy rapidly died.

"When, like the plague-struck with their hands of lead,
None care for cure, but easy take death's snare."

ONE soul at least was living—a youth in Ferrara, who wept alone. Girolamo Savonarola was but twenty years of age when he wrote the poem entitled *De Ruinâ Mundi*. His heart was broken by the cruel vice that raged around. He fasted, prayed, hardly spoke, spent long hours reading the Bible and Thomas Aquinas; often he was so overcome with sorrow that he could find no relief except in church, where he lay at the steps of the altar imploring comfort from God amidst the evils of a dissolute age. To add to his grief, he experienced a scornful rejection from one in whose heart he had trusted. He determined to enter the order of Dominic. One day his mother heard him playing mournfully on his lute; she looked sadly at him, and said, "My son, that is a sign we are soon to part.". The next day he fled to Bologna, and went straight to the Dominican convent.

"Dearest father," he wrote, "the cause which led me to adopt this resolution was this: that I could no longer endure the gross corruption of the age, and witness throughout Italy vice triumphant, and virtue in the dust."

In a writing that he left for his father to read, after describing the habits of the time, and comparing them to those of Sodom and Gomorrah, he exclaims: "There is no one, not even one, remaining who desires that which is good; we must learn from children and women of low estate, for in them only yet remains any shadow of innocence. The good are oppressed, and the people of Italy are become like the Egyptians who held God's people in servitude. But already we see famines, and inundations, and pestilences, and many other signs of coming evil that will announce the anger of the Almighty. Part, O Lord, part again the waters of the Red Sea, and drown the wicked in the waves of Thy indignation."

The year in which he thus renounced the world he wrote another poem, *De Ruinâ Ecclesiæ*. He describes the Church as a chaste virgin, who shows him her body covered with wounds; and when he asks her who had brought her to this sad state, she points to Rome: "*Una fallacia superba meretrix*" — a deceitful and a proud harlot. "Would to God, O Lady, that I could break those soaring wings!" is the fervent ejaculation of his righteous soul.

Thus this young man not only saw that the old world and the old church were in ruins, but that Rome was the cause; and he felt that it was his mission to bring down her cruel pride. From Bologna he was sent to Ferrara; from Ferrara he came to Florence, where he went at once to the Convent of St. Mark, famous for its library, its paintings by Fra Angelico, and for the reputation of its founder. He began to preach, but his audience was small. His rough diction and sincere thoughts were disagreeable to a people who would not read the Bible, lest its incorrect Latin should corrupt the purity of their taste! For a time he thought of giving up preaching. He prayed earnestly, and he expected an answer. One day he was conversing with one of the monks, when suddenly the heavens seemed to open, and he saw as in a vision the future calamities of the Church, a voice at the same time commanding him to declare them in the face of the people.

He uttered his message for the first time at San Germiniano during Lent 1484-1485. "The Church," he said, "will be scourged, then regenerated, and that quickly." Towards the end of 1486 he was sent to preach in the different cities of Lombardy. His sermons in Brescia were long remembered, and when, in 1512, that city fell into the hands of the ferocious soldiers of Gaston de Foix, and six thousand persons were slaughtered in the streets, the people recalled to mind the prophetic words of the preacher from Ferrara.

These sermons made him famous throughout Italy, and won him the friendship of the accomplished Prince of Mirandola, who never rested until he had induced Lorenzo de Medici to have Savonarola recalled to Florence. When he recommenced preaching in that city, he suddenly found himself popular, so that St. Mark's became too small for the crowds that pressed to hear him, and in 1491 he began to preach in the cathedral. Here, beneath the grand dome of Brunelleschi, itself one of the signs that the world had passed out of the Middle Age, Savonarola took his stand, and ere long proved himself the greatest power in Florence. Lorenzo thought it would be easy to win the austere friar, and to add him to his court. But Savonarola was the personification of the nobler spirit of the age: independent towards man, aspiring to be the friend and the messenger of God, he cared nothing for the wiles of a cultured court, and regarded a magnificent tyrant like Lorenzo as the worst enemy of Florence.

When messengers were sent to warn him, that if he continued to use such strong language he would be exiled, he told them, "It is I, Savonarola, who will remain, while the Medici will have to leave the city." Elected prior of St. Mark's, he refused Lorenzo the customary visit. The Magnificent thought him moved by excessive ambition and pride, and to win him often went to hear mass at St. Mark's, and walked about in the garden. Then he sent rich presents to the convent, and large contributions to the poor. But none of these things moved Savonarola, who could scarcely disguise his contempt. Thus foiled, Lorenzo set up another monk to preach him down; but the effort recoiled on both, and increased the popularity of the prior of St. Mark's.

In 1492 Lorenzo fell ill, and, notwithstanding certain marvellous draughts of distilled precious stones, it was evident that he was about to die. He was a prey to remorse; but not having the least faith in any human being, he could not believe in the sincerity of his confessor. "No one," he said to himself, "ever ventured to utter a resolute 'No' to me." Suddenly he thought of the inflexible prior. "He is the only honest man, send for him." Savonarola came. Three things he required of the dying man. To the first, that concerned his faith, Lorenzo gave a hearty assent. At the second, in which he was called upon to restore all that he had unjustly taken, he seemed surprised and grieved; however, he agreed; but when, finally, the confessor, rising up, said, "And, lastly, you must restore liberty to the people of Florence," Lorenzo turned scornfully on his bed without saying a word. So Savonarola departed without giving him absolution.

A few days after another great sinner passed to his account: Pope Innocent VIII. followed the ruler of Florence. Three unhappy boys had been sacrificed, in order that by the transfusion of their blood vitality might be restored to this bad old man. All failed, and the Roman Conclave, as if to crown all its iniquity, gave the tiara to Roderigo Borgia. Dismay seized all Italy. Men who had not even wept over their dead children, shed tears at the news. It was clear Savonarola was right—the Church was to be scourged. The prophet himself saw still more dreadful visions. The sword of the Lord was in the air, it turned towards the earth, the atmosphere grew dark with showers of swords and arrows, whilst the whole earth became a prey to wars, famines, and pestilences.

In 1494, dwelling on the approaching judgments, he spoke of a new Cyrus who would pass through Italy as a conqueror without breaking a lance. Before he had completed the course he was preaching, his words were realised. News came that Charles VIII., King of France, had crossed the Alps, and was on the high road to Florence. The agitation was great. Piero de Medici went to the French camp, and surrendered everything; the Florentines, enraged, drove him from their city.

All depended now on Savonarola. He enjoined charity and faith on the people, and was sent as an envoy-extraordinary to obtain terms for the city. He attempted no diplomacy, but briefly informing Charles that his mission was to deliver Italy and reform the Church, he told him that if he was not just and merciful, if he forgot the work for which the Lord had sent him, then another would be raised up in his place, and he would be punished with awful scourges. Charles was filled with awe, and determined to act honourably to the Florentines. Savonarola preserved his influence over the king to the last; but Charles was of so vacillating a nature that he utterly failed to fulfil the mission of which Savonarola had spoken.

The French gone, Savonarola was consulted as to the future government of Florence. He told them that their reform must begin with things spiritual, since the temporal ought to be subservient to morals and religion, on which it depends. "If you wish to have a good government," he said, "it must be derived from God." But he had to deal with a subtle, deceitful set of men, educated under the Medici, and acting on political principles which Macchiavelli was later on to reduce to a system. It was at this time and amid these scenes that Macchiavelli gained his first political ideas. He was a Florentine, just twenty-five years of age, and held a subordinate post in the office of the Chancellor of Florence.

The Medici had many friends in Florence, and these men hated Savonarola. They sought by every means to get rid of him. At last they induced the pope to summon him to Rome. Savonarola excused himself, and was then forbidden to preach. However, the new Florentine government so represented matters to Alexander that he, impressed with the power of the friar, sent him the offer of a red hat. Savonarola was shocked at the proposal, and only said to the messenger, "Come to my next sermon, and you shall hear the answer."

Beneath the great Duomo, surrounded by an immense multitude packed in rows on the steps of a lofty amphitheatre, which they had erected inside the cathedral to accommodate these vast audiences, the prophet stood up, his eyes flashing like living coals, and amidst such profound silence that the very breathing of the preacher could be heard, so troubled was he by his contending feelings. He delivered several sermons before he could fully explain his attitude to Rome. As long as it was a question of faith, he contended for his orthodoxy, but when he came to morals, his invectives against Rome were terrible. "O Rome," he said at last, "great will be thy punishments. Thou shalt be put in irons; thou shalt be put to the sword; fire and flame will consume thee. . . . The law of the priests will perish, their dignities will vanish, the princes will put on hair-cloth, the people will be crushed by tribulations."

While he was thus denouncing woe on the sinners of Italy, he was doing his utmost to reform Florentine manners. He began with the children, whom he induced to give up their indecent behaviour and brutal amusements at the carnival, and to sing hymns and psalms instead of foul songs. In 1496 he preached to a vast number of children in the great amphitheatre of the Duomo. At the conclusion he turned to the rest of the congregation, and holding up the crucifix, exclaimed, "People of Florence! this is the King of the Universe; He would be your King —will you have Him?" To this appeal all assented with loud voices, many shedding tears. Determined to purify the city, he induced the people to make a great bonfire of all the obscene pictures, books, dresses, and masks that could be gathered together. The pile was said to be worth twenty-two thousand florins; and many have regarded Savonarola as little less than a Vandal for so barbarous an act. But if a work or two of art perished, and a valuable MS. here and there, much old filth and garbage was cleared away, and the city made more wholesome.

By this time he had earned the implacable hatred of Pope Borgia. He was not greatly incensed at Savonarola's denunciations of the vice and corruption of the age. That was a preacher's business, and might be utilised for the benefit of ecclesiastical corruption. The college of cardinals would have been delighted to welcome a man of Savonarola's reputation into their midst. He might have preached such terrors as he chose in the evil atmosphere of Rome; he might have pushed asceticism to the utmost limit, in order to protest against the carnality of the ecclesiastics, if he would only have walked with them and supported their rule. Then they could have given him every honour during life, and sainted him after his death. But Savonarola refused to become a mere tool in the hands of the wicked, and his love of liberty made the Medicis and the Borgias alike his foes.

At length he was excommunicated. This troubled him little; but the effect on Florence was deplorable; profligacy was re-established in a day. A terrible tragedy occurred in the pope's family. One of his sons murdered the other, and the deed pointed to darker crimes. Alexander seemed to feel for a moment the enormity of his wickedness, but his remorse was transient, and he shortly returned to his murderous projects against Savonarola. A seigniory hostile to the prior came into office, and he was ordered to desist from preaching. He took leave of the people, saying, "We shall effect by prayer what we cannot effect by preaching." His hopes now centred on a General Council, and to this end he wrote letters to the Kings of France, Spain, England, Hungary, and the Emperor of Germany. "The Church," he wrote, "is full of abominations from the crown of the head to the soles of the feet, and not only do you fail to apply any remedy, but you worship the very source of all the evils by which it is contaminated." His letter to King Charles of France fell into the hands of the pope.

Borgia would have had little power against him, had the people of Florence remained true to their prophet. Savonarola was often challenged to show a miracle in proof of his authority. It was a great temptation, for he believed that the Lord would as assuredly work one on his behalf as for the prophets of old. At last a Franciscan challenged him to the ordeal of fire. Savonarola did not reply; but Fra Domenico, one of his friars, accepted the challenge. Savonarola reproved Domenico, and did what he could to restrain him, but all seemed bent on pushing the matter to a conclusion, and the appointed day arrived. Savonarola accompanied Fra Domenico. All Florence was in the square, but the opposing party managed so to arrange matters that the day passed without anything being done. The people turned on Savonarola, whom they accused of deceiving them. Even his own followers, the Piagnoni, said he ought to have gone into the fire alone, and so have given an unanswerable proof of his supernatural power. The Arrabbiati said that now his imposture was exposed, for it was clear that he was afraid to enter the fire; and the Minorites shouted victory, although their champion had hid himself all the day.

In this temper it was easy to move the populace to a tumult, in which Savonarola might be crushed. Accordingly, the next evening a cry was raised in the streets of Florence: "To St. Mark's! to St. Mark's! set it on fire!" A furious mob surrounded the church, which was full of people attending vespers. In a few minutes it was emptied of all but a few followers of Savonarola, determined on a defence. Expecting an attack, they had, unknown to their master, brought in a quantity of arms. Savonarola and Fra Domenico tried to persuade them to refrain; but the effect of these divided councils was ruinous; the mob got possession of the convent, driving the monks from point to point. The prior terminated the struggle by surrendering himself to the macebearer of the seigniory, who had arrived on the scene, and amidst a crowd furious with rage he was led away. It was dark, and the torches lit up with weird lights the tumultuous sea of helmets, cuirasses, swords, and spears, and showed every now and then some diabolical mouth, from which curses and insults streamed forth. The rabble scorched and burned the prophet's face with the flambeaux, and beat and kicked him, so that if the guards had not crossed their swords over him he would hardly have arrived at the prison alive.

There was great joy among the princes and prelates of Italy. The pope wrote to tell the seigniory that he considered them true sons of the Church, that he granted them full absolution, the powers they desired, and every benediction. The Duke of Milan was equally congratulatory, promising them his hearty support. And, to crown all, letters were received saying that on the very day of the ordeal the King of France, the only monarch in whom Savonarola trusted, had died in a fit of apoplexy. It was indeed an hour of darkness and the power of Satan. The seigniory, with that mediæval cruelty which it requires a vivid imagination to realise, proceeded to put the friars to the question. Savonarola was bound to the hoisting rope—a torture capable of being so used as to produce delirium and death. His delicate frame, made weak and nervous by such years of excitement and anxiety, succumbed at once. His mind began to wander, he became incoherent. For a whole month he was subjected to these trials. He knew that his enemies wanted his humiliation. To escape the horrible torture, something must be admitted. He would rather die a thousand deaths than deny his faith; he could not forsake the cause of liberty, but his prophecies might be admitted doubtful; and we can well imagine that in this hour of deep despondency all confidence in his own career may have departed. In moments of anguish he contradicted himself, and admitted far too much. It was the last nail in his cross to know and feel himself thus humiliated. But the trial over, he had a month's solitude and repose; his old force returned, and his *Meditations* in prison are amongst the most powerful of his writings.

The day came in which the prophet of Italy was to die. The pope's commissioner, afterwards Cardinal Romolina, had told the magistrates four days before, "We shall make a famous blaze; I have the sentence already prepared." Yet after this Savonarola was again cruelly tortured in the presence of the papal commissioners and the Florentine authorities. On the 22nd of May, 1498, sentence of death was passed on him and the friars Silvestro and Domenico. They were permitted to see each other that same evening for an hour. After passing the whole night in prayer, they met again in the morning, and Savonarola administered the sacrament in the chapel of San Bernardo, in the Palazzo Vecchio. He was permitted to pray in his own words: "Lord, I know that Thou art that perfect Trinity, invisible, distinct, in Father, Son, and Holy Ghost; I know that Thou art the Eternal Word, that Thou didst descend into the bosom of Mary, that Thou didst ascend upon the cross to shed blood for our sins. I pray Thee, that by that blood I may have remission of my sins, for which I implore Thy forgiveness, and for every other injury or offence done to this city, and for every other sin of which I may unconsciously have been guilty." Then they were called into the Piazza, where they had to pass in succession before three tribunals—that of the Bishop of Varsona, where they were degraded and cut off from the Church militant; that of the papal commissioners, where they heard their sentence and received plenary absolution; lastly, that of the Otto, where their sentence was put to the vote and carried unanimously. They were then led to the gibbet amidst the insults of the populace. A priest approached Savonarola and said, "In what state do you endure martyrdom?" "The Lord," he replied, "has suffered as much for me."

These were the prophet's last words. Fra Silvestro was the first to ascend the ladder. When the halter was fixed, he exclaimed, "Into Thy hands, O Lord, I commend my spirit." He was thrust off, and Fra Domenico ran up quickly, his countenance radiant with joy. He had chanted the *Te Deum* on the way, and had said, "Remember that the prophecies of Savonarola must all be fulfilled, and that we die innocent!" Lastly came Savonarola, who was directed to take the vacant place between the two corpses. From the top of the ladder he cast one look upon the crowd below, otherwise he appeared already to have left the earth. In the midst of the silent horror with which the populace seemed suddenly smitten, a voice cried, "Prophet, now is the time to perform a miracle!" To amuse the rabble, the executioner began to play with the body before it had ceased to move, and in so doing nearly fell off the scaffold. He was reprimanded by the magistrates for his brutality. The fires were then lit, the bodies were burnt, and the ashes thrown into the Arno.

VILLARI, than whom no one has studied more diligently the life and times of the prophet of Italy, tells us that Savonarola's celebrated *Conclusions* show that he was "the first to feel that a great re-organization of the human race was about to take place; that the religious sentiment was about to be revived in the hearts of men to regenerate them; that after passing through sanguinary conflicts, society would recover its wonted vigour. He continually repeats, "The infidels will be converted, Christianity will be triumphant over the whole earth; before long there will be but one sheepfold and one Shepherd;" he is confident that the human race is about to recover its lost unity, and that Christianity will become, ere long, the sole religion of all civilised nations.

In this hope he is instinctively followed by the great souls of the age. While many are looking back to times anterior to Christianity, the nobler minds are looking for great triumphs of the faith in unknown lands. Prince Henry of Portugal was one of the earliest of these watchers. From his observatory on the promontory of St. Vincent he was ever looking across the South Atlantic, obstinately believing, against all maritime authority, that there were good lands and deep seas over which an easy path might be found to the Indies. He sent out several expeditions, founded a school of navigation, and inspired many with his own ardent spirit of research. He believed that God had moved his mind to these attempts, and that it would be ingratitude in him to desist from them, or to be negligent in the work. One of his friends passed the dreaded Cape Bogador, and brought back with him a barrel of new-found plants; and when the prince saw them he rejoiced, and gave thanks to God, as if they had been the fruit and sight of their promised land; and he besought Mary that she would guide and set forth their doings in this discovery to the praise of God, and to the increase of His holy faith.

The faith Savonarola entertained of an enlarged and renewed Christendom took, in some minds, the form of a belief in a hidden Christian kingdom in Asia, ruled over by a Christian prince named Prester John. This was the origin of the efforts of King John II. of Portugal, who, about the time that Savonarola first began to be known as a preacher in Italy, fitted out expeditions by land and sea, in order to discover the realm of Prester John, and to gain information about the Indian ports.

The belief in the existence of this mythical personage had existed for more than three centuries in Europe. Its origin is traced to the conversion of a Tartar khan by the Nestorians, the report of which reached Christendom, clothed in oriental hyperbole.

John II., sharing not only the enterprise but the superstition of his age, had his curiosity aroused by an account he received from a certain negro ambassador, sent to Portugal by the King of Benin, of a great potentate existing some two hundred and fifty leagues from Benin, called Ogané. This ruler was represented as exercising supreme authority over the other kings of the country, so that on the accession of any one of them, an embassy was despatched to procure his confirmation to the territory inherited or acquired. The ambassadors never saw Ogané, who remained veiled by a silk curtain; but, on going away, a foot was thrust out, "to which they did homage as to a holy thing."

The King of Portugal and his council were of opinion that this mysterious Ogané could be no other than the long-sought-for Prester John. Animated, therefore, by the double desire to enlarge the limits of the Christian faith, and to promote Portuguese commerce, they determined to send an expedition to find him out and seek his alliance. The first expedition failed owing to its leader, a Franciscan friar, not understanding Arabic. Two more were fitted out—one by land, the other by sea. The command of the latter was given to Bartholomew Diaz, who, steering due south through the Atlantic Ocean, and, losing all sight of land, was driven by heavy gales into the Indian Ocean. When Diaz descried the coast he was really on the eastern side of Africa; but he did not find out his mistake until, upon his return, he arrived at the very promontory he had been so

Q

long seeking in vain. He called it, remembering the tempests in which he had first passed it, Cabo Tormontosa (the Stormy Cape); but the king, with a happier faith, gave it the name of the Cape of Good Hope. The discovery of this route to India by sea reunited the east to the west, and opened up a new era in the history of the world.

The great discovery of Bartholomew Diaz (1486) is somewhat obscured by the voyage of Vasco de Gama, who, twelve years later, again doubled the Cape, and succeeded in reaching India. It is this voyage which Camoens has taken for the subject of the *Lusiad*—that epic of commercial enterprise and geographical discovery, as the *Divina Commedia* is of mediæval Catholicism. Vasco de Gama set sail in 1497, and arrived, in March, 1498, at the city of Mozambique. The fanaticism of the people, who were Mohammedan Arabs, had well nigh proved fatal to the Portuguese; however, they escaped in safety, and finally, on May 20th, three days before the martyrdom of Savonarola, Vasco de Gama landed at Calicut, then one of the richest and the most commercial of the cities in India. He was received at first with great pomp by the Zamorin, but the Mohammedans again aroused the animosity of the people, so that the Portuguese commander was obliged to use all his address to get back to his ships. Doubtless the ill-feeling of the Mohammedans was due to the belief they entertained that the strangers represented a country in which Mohammedanism had been conquered, and was now depressed and persecuted.

The last Moorish kingdom in Spain was that of Granada; it had endured down to 1492, just six years before Gama's voyage. For two hundred and thirty-three years it had recognised the supremacy of the Kings of Castile; but in 1481 a quarrel broke out, and after eleven years' war Granada was conquered, and the Mohammedan authority entirely destroyed in Spain.

This occurred under the Catholic Kings, as they were called—Ferdinand and Isabella. These two rulers having united Aragon and Castile by their marriage, in conquering Granada achieved the unity of Spain.

The Portuguese navigators had not yet found the new earth, but they had seen a new heaven, and its brightest constellation was in the form of a cross. Seven years later a new earth is in reality found. And of this King John might have had the glory, had he not meanly tried to filch the whole scheme of the discovery from the author, in order to carry it out independently.

FIVE years before the conclusion of the war in Granada, and about a year after Diaz doubled the Cape of Good Hope, a Genoese sailor had arrived in Spain offering the Catholic Kings a far greater heritage than they would possess even when their conquest was complete. Columbus believed that the direct route to India was across the Atlantic, and he offered, if they would give him ships, to make the territories of Spain vaster than that of any other empire, and to give her the inestimable privilege of fulfilling all the prophecies, and covering the earth with the knowledge of the Lord, as the waters cover the sea. But the actual conquest of Granada seemed worth many such nebulous worlds, and Isabella, who as the more generous and large-minded of the two, listened to the project, always pleaded the drain of the treasury to support that war. Columbus having in sheer despair determined to leave Spain, one of Isabella's counsellors, Luis de Santangel, made a last appeal to the Queen, representing that it was the part of great princes to ascertain the secrets of the world, and that so great an enterprise ought not to be abandoned for so small a sum as a million of maravedi (about three hundred and eighty pounds). Isabella was moved to offer to pledge her jewels, but Santangel said he would advance the money, whereupon Columbus was overtaken, brought back, and the expedition launched.

This incident was the happy conclusion of a series of trials by which the heart of the greatest man of the age was nearly worn out by the stupid blindness of nearly all the authorities of the day.

The lives of Christopher Columbus and Girolamo Savonarola were almost parallel. The latter was born when Columbus was still a very small boy, dreaming, perhaps, even then of worlds unknown, as he looked wonderingly on the crowded port of his native city of Genoa. Columbus married a few years before Savonarola entered the cloister, and they may both be said to have began their life-work at the same time, for it was in 1482—the very year Savonarola came to Florence—that Columbus first unfolded his schemes to John of Portugal. Then both passed through a period of neglect and opposition. Columbus was not only shamefully treated by the King of Portugal, but, applying to the authorities of his own

Republic, his scheme was treated as the silly project of a visionary brain. A murrain was on the intellect of Italy, for the Venetian Republic, once so astute, treated the greatest of all Italians in the same contemptuous manner.

Columbus, however, did not despair, for his faith was rooted in God. "Reason, mathematics, atlases, were of no service to me in my enterprise to the Indies." Such was his testimony. Who, then, in his opinion, sent him there, and what were the means by which he accomplished his mission? "It has pleased our Lord to grant me faith and assurance for this enterprise. He has opened my understanding, and made me most willing to go." No profound studies in science awakened the thought of another hemisphere. It was one of those great ideas which are revealed to a whole generation, but which, seizing on one mind, forces it to become its organ. Columbus nurtured his faith not so much on geographical studies, though he neglected nothing which seemed to bear on the subject of his thoughts, as upon the oracles and prophecies of all nations, but especially upon those of the Bible. He collected them into a volume, which he called the *Book of the Prophecies*, and dedicated it to Ferdinand and Isabella.

It was this faith which supported him even when begging his bread. Wandering in Spain, he one day stopped at the gate of the Convent of La Rabida, and asked for a little bread and water for his child. While they were eating this humble fare, the prior, Juan Perez, happened to pass by, and being struck with the look of the stranger, began to talk with him. This casual meeting ripened into friendship, and the Prior of La Rabida became one of his warmest friends, and the means of introducing him to Isabella.

With three small ships did this man of faith set sail to cross an unknown ocean. The Portuguese discoveries are tentative, gradual; they follow the road of human experience. Columbus seems to proceed by inspiration, his prow shoots in a straight line across the Atlantic. Every evening the log book repeats the same words—"*his course was to the West.*" "Who," as a great historical philosopher has asked, "who told Columbus his course was to the west?"

His companions murmured, but a wind ever blowing from the east rendered return impracticable. Wrapt more and more in meditation as he entered the unknown, he saw from day to day proofs, such as sea-weed and land birds, that he was approaching the object of his faith. He who would not turn aside a hair's breadth for the murmurs of his crew, now made the flight of birds his guide to the new world.

One night, about ten o'clock, the vessel in advance signalled that it had seen a light; the admiral, being on the poop of his vessel, also saw it, but feeble and flickering like a candle. Some thought it a sign of land, but Columbus was sure it was land. At two o'clock in the morning of the 12th of October, 1492, his prevision proved true. The new world was at hand. What a sunrise for Christopher Columbus!.

The crew of the *Pinta*, which led the way, began chanting the *Te Deum*, and the admiral and all who were with him fell on their knees, and, with tears of joy, poured forth their "immense thanksgivings to Almighty God." But he whose faith had brought about this miracle now suddenly felt a great sinking take possession of his heart. Did he whose soul had stretched across the Atlantic, now feel instinctively the sin and suffering that would be the immediate result of his great discovery?

> "Slowly, bare-headed, through the surf they bore
> The Sacred Cross, and, kneeling, kissed the shore.
> But what a scene was there! Nymphs of romance,
> Youths graceful as the fawn, with eager glance,
> Spring from the glades, and down the alleys peep,
> Then headlong rush, bounding from steep to steep,
> And clap their hands, exclaiming as they run,
> 'Come and behold the Children of the Sun!'"

"They are a loving, uncovetous people, so docile in all things that I assure your highnesses that I believe in all the world there is not a better people or a better country." Such was the admiral's enthusiastic opinion of the inhabitants of the new world.

In the spring of the following year he returned to Spain, landing at Palos. He made a public entry into Barcelona, the people pouring out in such numbers that the streets could not contain them. It was a nobler procession than that of an old Roman triumph, and yet resembled it not a little, for here were his captives, the new men from the West, preceded by the wonderful things he had collected on the voyage. The Catholic Kings were on their thrones. Columbus approached, his face beaming with satisfaction. He knelt at the kings' feet and begged leave to kiss their highnesses' hands. Ferdinand and Isabella bade him rise and be seated before them; he related the events of the voyage, concluding by showing them the new men and the new things he had discovered. All fell on their knees and returned thanks to God, the choristers of the royal chapel closing the glorious day with the *Te Deum*.

For the next few years the influence of Columbus was great, and every honour was shown him. It was at the same period that Savonarola was at the zenith of his influence and fame; but the great discoverer, like the prophet-tribune, was to have his name and his honour dragged through the mire. His rule was not always wise, and he stained his laurels by promoting slavery. Like Savonarola, he was ever pursued by jealous and treacherous foes. At last they succeed in having him superseded, and Columbus is sent back to Europe in chains! He insisted on wearing them in the royal presence, and ordered them to be buried in his grave. Age of Columbus and Savonarola, of Richard III. and Alexander VI.! What contrasts of light and darkness!

SIXTEENTH CENTURY.

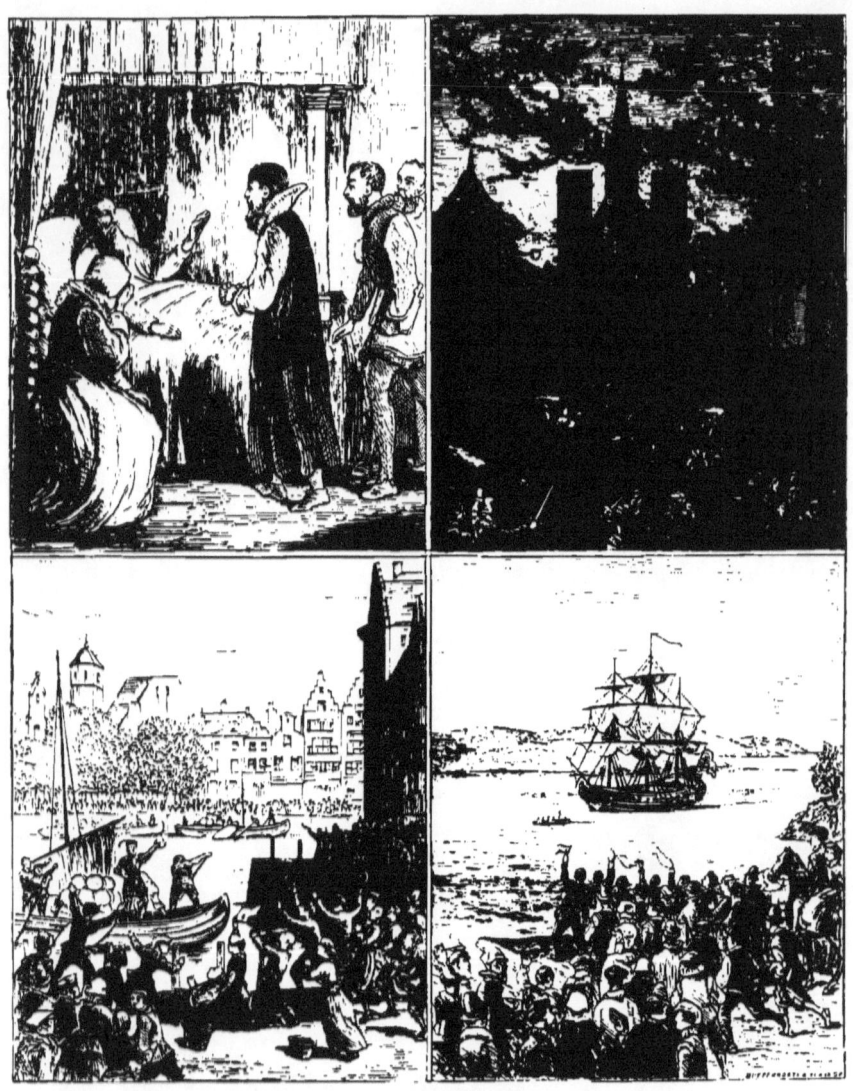

CONTEMPORARY EVENTS IN THE SIXTEENTH CENTURY.

Scotland.—The death of John Knox.
Netherlands.—The relief of Leyden.
France.—The massacre of St. Bartholomew
England.—Drake's return from his voyage round the world.

Sixteenth Century.

A.D. 1521-1580.

The Bible Reopened—A Galaxy of Genius—Appeal from the Church to the Bible—William Tyndale—His New Testament Burnt at St. Paul's Cross—Martin Luther—The Diet at Worms-Spanish Catholicism—Hernan Cortes—His Exploits in Mexico—Ignatius Loyola—His Conversion and Work—The Sack of Rome—Calvin and Calvinism—The Massacre of St. Bartholomew—Death of John Knox—Phillip II. and Alva—William the Silent—War of Dutch Independence—The Relief of Leyden—England's Great Seamen—Drake's Voyage Round the World—Akbur, Emperor of India.

I. A.D. 1521-1530.

A STRONG angel coming down out of heaven, having in his hand a little book *open*." Whatever the real meaning of this Apocalyptic vision, a better symbol could hardly be found of the new power about to move Europe. What the spoken word was to the first preachers of the Gospel, what some visible image of Calvary was to the mediæval missionaries, an open Bible was to the Reformers. The early teacher of Christianity is ever journeying; the mediæval missionary plunges into the wilderness, and builds a church and a monastery; the reformer, hidden in some garret, translates and prints the Scriptures. In a movement which was to give such an extraordinary impetus to mental and spiritual life, it was natural that the instrument should be a Book, and the leaders learned men. Luther himself was a man of no little learning; but among his companions, predecessors, and

successors were to be found scholars equal to those of any age. Erasmus, Melancthon, Bucer, Zwingle, Lefèvre, Tyndale, Calvin, Beza, suggest erudition of the highest order.

In few periods of the world's history has there been such a galaxy of genius as Christendom possessed when the sixteenth century opened. Columbus was still living; Leonardo da Vinci had just painted his "Last Supper;" Raphael, a youth of seventeen, was at work in the studios of Pietro Perugino; Michael Angelo was at Bologna, symbolising in stone the religion of the day; Bramante was just beginning his famous works at Rome; Ariosto had already commenced writing poems; Wolsey had lately become rector of Limington, in Somersetshire; Erasmus had recently visited England, and had made at Oxford the friendship of a "marvellous witty" student, named Thomas More; Albert Durer had just returned from his travels, and had entered into his unhappy marriage; Lucas Cranach had been to Palestine with the Elector Frederick, and was soon to be his court painter; Las Casas was about to start on his first voyage to the Indies; both the Holbeins were living, the younger and greater being still in leading-strings, as also was Philip Melancthon; Gustavus Vasa was beginning to run alone; Hans Sachs was playing in the streets of Nüremberg; Margaret of Valois was an eight years old princess; Thomas Cromwell was watching the hammer in his father's forge; Hugh Latimer was acting as ploughboy; Hernan Cortes was at school; Ignatius Loyala was a page in the court of Ferdinand and Isabella; and Luther had just entered the college of Erfurt.

IT was to this generation, so greatly gifted, that the Reformers appealed. Their object was the same as that of Wiclif, Huss, and Savonarola—the reformation of religion. Learned as they were, the argument they used was plain enough to be understood of the common people. They simply appealed from one authority to another. The Catholic Church had always recognised the authority of Holy Scripture. Were the two in harmony? The Reformers showed that both in doctrine and practice the Church was flagrantly and diametrically opposed to Scripture. Nothing tended to so convince the people that the Reformers were right as the horror with which the clergy regarded the publication of the Scriptures, and the efforts they made to destroy every translation in the vulgar tongue.

Take, for instance, the history of the famous version by Tyndale. Translated and printed at Cologne as far as signature K, the work was spied out by a certain deacon named Cochlæus, who, when he discovered the magnitude of the danger, was inwardly affected by fear and wonder, and cast about in his mind how he might prevent this wicked attempt. He was so far successful that Tyndale had in hot haste to snatch up his printed quarto sheets, hurry them on board a boat, and glide away to Worms, where the remainder of the work could be completed in safety. But the argus-eyed clergy had found out this terrible treason, and in course of time, the King of England, Henry VIII., received a letter from Bordeaux, written by his almoner, in which his Highness was informed "that an Englishman hath translated the New Testament into English, and within a few days intendeth to return with the same imprinted into England. I need not to advertise your grace what infection and danger may ensue thereby if it be not withstanded. All our forefathers, governors of the Church of England, have with all diligence forbid and eschewed publication of English Bibles, as appeareth in constitutions provincial of the Church of England."

Notwithstanding the warning the book entered the country, and was quickly disseminated. The bishops were on the alert, and tried to buy up the edition. Good-natured Archbishop Warham pronounced "the undertaking a gracious and blessed deed." Tonstall, Bishop of London, threw himself heartily into the effort, and employed, as his agent, an Antwerp merchant named Packington. The bishop's agent went straight to Tyndale, and said, "William, I know thou art a poor man, and hast a heap of New Testaments and books by thee, for which thou hast both endangered thy friends and beggared thyself, and I have now gotten thee a merchant, which, with ready money, shall despatch thee of all thou hast, if you think it profitable to yourself." "Who is the merchant?" said Tyndale. "The Bishop of London," replied Packington. "Oh! that is because he will burn them," rejoined Tyndale. "Yes," quoth Packington. "I am the gladder," rejoined Tyndale; "for these two benefits will come thereof. I shall get money to bring myself out of debt, and the whole world will cry out against the burning of God's Word; and the overplus of the money that shall remain to me shall make me more studious to correct the said New Testament, and so newly to imprint the same once again; and

I trust the second will much better like you than ever did the first. So forward went the bargain; the bishop had the books—Packington had the thanks—and Tyndale had the money." Thus the story is related by the old chronicler, Hall, and we see nothing intrinsically improbable; it bears the marks of the humour and simple directness so characteristic of Tudor England.

May 4th, 1530, the Bishop of London made a holocaust at Paul's Cross of the Testaments he had taken such pains to procure. The citizens of London came in crowds to witness the sight. Strange thoughts rose in many a simple mind. If the New Testament contained the Word of God, was it not sacrilege to treat it thus? Could those who did so believe at all in it?

The uselessness of such efforts was soon apparent, and the clergy saw that, instead of burning the translations, the shorter and more effectual way would be to burn the translator. King Henry's agent in the Netherlands did his best to persuade Tyndale to return. "Only on one condition," said Tyndale. "If it would stand with the king's most gracious pleasure to grant a bare text of Scripture to be put forth among his people, be it of the translation of what person soever shall please his majesty, I shall immediately make faithful promise to repair unto his realm, and there most humbly submit myself at the feet of his royal majesty, offering my body to suffer what pain or tortures, yea, what death his grace will, so that this be obtained."

Finally, this disinterested servant of the truth—the man whom the recent New Testament revisers declared to have laid the foundation of the English version of the New Testament—this man was pursued to the death. By the treachery of an Englishman named Philips, his retreat was discovered; he was imprisoned in the Castle of Vilvorde, near Brussels, and in September, 1536, he was hanged, and his body thrown into the flames. His last cry was: "Lord, open the eyes of the King of England!" "If they burn me," he had said, eight years before, "they shall do no other thing than that I looked for. There is none other way into the kingdom of life than through persecution and suffering of pain, and of very death, after the example of Christ."

THE resurrection of the Bible in the fifteenth century is the most important fact in European history between the advent of Christ and the French

Revolution. How completely it had been buried is witnessed by the fact that Martin Luther never saw a Bible until he was twenty years old. He found an old copy of the Vulgate in the library of the University at Erfurt. He perused it eagerly, and it made him think for himself on theological matters, and in a few years he became one of its greatest doctors. He translated the Bible into the vulgar tongue, doing more thereby to affect the minds of his countrymen than any German before or since. Luther's Bible helped to form the German language, filling it with Biblical words and Biblical thoughts. The Bible undoubtedly became in a few years the text-book of the nations; so popular, that people could hardly talk without a Biblical reference or a Biblical expression. Rabelais, amidst the grossest wit, will point a jest or illustrate an argument by a Scripture quotation.

Impatient of every restraint, humorous, intellectual, sensual, at times sweet-mannered, at times brutal, Henry VIII., Francis I., and the Elector of Saxony were types of the average conscience of the sixteenth century. Luther himself is, perhaps, its fullest expression : loving, generous, independent, pious, but occasionally coarse and overbearing, the battle of the age was fought out first of all in his own soul. Of a merry and cheerful disposition, no one was better fitted to enjoy the simple pleasures of life; he had a taste for learning, and still more for music. He makes such progress at the University that his father, a German peasant, hoped to see him a wealthy lawyer. But he had hardly completed his curriculum, when two events happening, one upon the other, altered the whole course of his life. The sudden death of a young friend aroused his thoughts concerning eternity ; in a thunderstorm, as he passed through a wood, he decided to devote his life to God. He collected his friends, they passed a merry evening, and the same night he entered the Augustine monastery at Erfurt.

The door closed, Luther was alone with his own heart. The full tide of carnality returned, and the unhappy young monk struggled helplessly, crying, "Oh, my sins, my sins!" He fasted, prayed, kept vigils so long that he fainted in his cell from exhaustion. The Vicar-General of the German Augustines, visiting the convent, saw the young monk, and said to him, "Instead of making a martyr of thyself for thy faults, throw thyself into the arms of the Redeemer. Confide in Him, in the righteousness of His life, in the expiation of His death. Keep not back; God is not angry with thee; it is thou who art angry with God." "No repentance," Dr. Staupitz went on to tell him, "is true, save that which begins in the love of God and righteousness. If thou wouldest be converted, dwell not upon all these macerations and tortures; love Him who first loved thee!" Luther was consoled for a time, but failed to penetrate the depth of the teacher's words. He almost sank beneath his sufferings. An old monk tried to console him, Luther told him his fears: "I believe in the forgiveness of sins," said the old man, very simply. Luther saw it now, and still more when his friend went on to say, "The thing to be believed is not that the sins of David and Peter are forgiven. God's command is that everyone of us believe that our own sins are forgiven."

He now renounced all idea of a righteousness of his own, and he began to see clearly that there was a righteousness of God revealed in Jesus Christ, and which, being independent of all human merit, was imputed to all who believed. "The just shall live by faith" became henceforth the motto of his life. But many things had to occur before this thought so possessed him as to make him its prophet, and to become in his hands the hammer with which he broke the chains that held Christendom in the thrall of the Roman superstition.

The first was a visit to Rome. As he approached the city he cried out, in the fervour of his piety, "Holy Rome, I salute thee!" Macchiavelli, than whom no one knew better the spirit that governed Italy, was then living at Florence. Speaking of Rome, the great thinker had said, " The nearer you come to the capital of Christendom, the less you find of the Christian spirit." The young German monk soon found this to be simple truth. The scandals were not quite so bad as in the days of the Borgias. The new pope was not a disgrace to humanity, nevertheless he was a veritable heathen. Michael Angelo gave the true idea of Julius II. when he represented him thundering his blessings on Bologna. His very face suggested Jove; he was a priest of Mars rather than a minister of Jesus Christ. Rome was a city of sceptics, the priests mocked at their own religion. The only world that was real was that of art. But the Roman artists were no more Christian than those of Greece were heathen. Of this world Luther saw only the outside. He beheld stately palaces arising, and great preparations for the building of the new St. Peter's. In the crowds that looked on he saw only sullen, contemptuous faces; intellect was there, but otherwise men wore the look of Cain. It froze the heart of the simple, ingenuous German. He took refuge in the churches; but the priests gabbled so fast that he had just reached the gospel when they were elevating the host. He found nearly all he met to be infidels, and heard one say, as he consecrated the host, "Bread thou art, and bread thou wilt remain." The great thought that had completed his conversion had but very partial hold of him, for he actually began to climb Pilate's Staircase, in order to gain the indulgence promised to those who made the effort. As he was painfully crawling up, the words resounded in his ears, "'The just shall live by *faith*." He rose up in amazement, reflected on all he had beheld, and afterward said, "I would not for one hundred thousand florins have missed seeing Rome. I should always have been afraid that I had not done justice to the pope."

The Papacy little dreamt of its danger. The pope, who was more than half a soldier, was succeeded by an epicurean philosopher. Leo X. was the Mæcenas of art, the proper ruler for Rome of the Renaissance. But to call himself a successor of the Apostles was an outrage on good taste, and ought to have shocked his sense of harmony. But religion was the ware he sold, and like many men of culture since, he did not inquire too narrowly into the tricks of the trade by which he lived. He spent his money so freely on high art, that his treasurers were at their wits' end to keep his great works going. Architects, painters, sculptors, and builders would not work for nothing. A bright idea struck some worried official. The pope had an untold mine of wealth in his power to grant indulgences. It might not bring in much in Italy, where the people were beginning to doubt if there was any hereafter; but in Germany and Switzerland there were plenty of credulous people, who would willingly part with their money to save their own souls or those of their kindred from the pains of purgatory. A commission was equipped and sent into Germany, headed by a blatant Dominican, whose white frock was already very considerably besmeared with mire. Tetzel went about the country in a fine carriage, and was received by the authorities with much honour.

When Luther heard of this shameful business, his soul was filled with indignation, and when he was told of the lying words of the indulgence-monger, he said, in his characteristic way, "Please God, I'll make a hole in his drum." Accordingly, on All Saints' Day, 1517, Luther fastened on the door of the church of Wittemberg his famous ninety-five theses. In addition to these propositions, which were negative and polemic, and chiefly related to indulgences, he published nearly at the same time certain dogmatic theses, in which he brought men back to the thought of God as the sole source of grace and pardon, putting forth in the strongest language the Augustinian theories. The soul of Germany responded to the teacher, his efforts were applauded to the echo, and he suddenly found himself one of the most famous men of the day.

Leo at first thought it only a quarrel between the Dominicans and the Augustinians, but, finding out his mistake, he ordered Luther to appear in sixty days at Rome. Luther had no earthly protector but the Elector of Saxony. Happily, the elector was thoroughly in sympathy with Luther, and the Emperor Maximilian dying during the controversy, his power was very considerable, as he became Vicar-General of the Empire.

Meanwhile Luther's conscience was rapidly freed from superstition. He published a book called *The Captivity of the Church*, in which he bewailed the comparative darkness he was in when he wrote the theses, declaring that the booksellers might burn them all, if they would only put in their place this phrase: "The indulgences are rubbish invented by the Roman cajolers." And as to what he said on the papal supremacy, he would put in its place one word: "The pope is the mighty hunter, the Nimrod of the Roman episcopate."

Evidently there was no time to be lost, and Luther was condemned forthwith. When the papal bull arrived, Luther at once flew to the charge with a writing *Against the Execrable Bull of Antichrist*. But, more portentous still, he proceeded solemnly to burn it in the public place at Wittemberg. The enthusiasm was immense. Everything he published was eagerly read, and passed from hand to hand. Hans Sachs wrote one of his finest pieces at this time—*The Nightingale of Wittemberg*. Although Erasmus thought it necessary to disown him, Luther had the heart of Germany with him, and not only its heart, but its intellect. Among his friends were Lucas Cranach, Albert Durer, Philip Melancthon, Ulrich von Hutten, and Franz von Sickengen, the German Cid.

Protected by the Elector of Saxony and the whole force of German opinion, Rome could do nothing with Luther. The only hope lay in obtaining some retractation from the Reformer, which should destroy his credit and make him appear a waverer. Everything was done to entrap him, but all proving useless, it was determined to bring him before the Diet. His enemies thought the very name of the Diet would frighten him; but when the herald who brought the summons asked him if he meant to appear, he replied, "If there were as many devils in Worms as there are housetops, I shall come." But the elector would not allow him to go without a safe-conduct. This was granted, and his progress to Worms became a triumphal procession.

Never had a man appeared before a more august assembly. Not only were there such dignitaries as the deputies of the free towns, the papal nuncios, the ambassadors of England and France, but there were thirty archbishops, twenty-four dukes, and six electors, with the Archduke Ferdinand—quite a crowd of reigning sovereigns, the president being no less a person than the Emperor Charles V., the greatest of the whole line, considering his dominions, since Charlemagne. Martin Luther felt awed at the sight of the assembled authority of his country, and when called upon to retract, asked for a day's grace. That night he wrestled in prayer with Jacob-like earnestness. Next day he was brought to the Diet, and for two whole hours he was kept in the crowd, but his face was unruffled. He was again asked to retract. In a firm and moderate manner he gave his reasons why he could not. Being pressed again, he said, "Unless I am convinced by Holy Scripture, or any other clear and uncontestable writings, I cannot—I will not retract anything. The passages that I have quoted have not been answered; my conscience is bound by the Word of God; no one would counsel a man to disobey his conscience. Here I am, I can do no otherwise. God help me. Amen."

MEDIÆVAL Christianity had received a great blow at the Diet of Worms. A single man, in the name of his individual conscience, had defied all its powers. Luther's spiritual courage emancipated Christendom. Men everywhere began to break their chains, and to assert their right to follow their own ideal of truth. Had Italian Catholicism been left alone to cope with the Reformation, it would have been swept away as completely as the old paganism. But Italy was only the brain of Roman Catholicism; its heart still burnt with a fiery intensity that more than equalled that of the nascent Protestantism.

Islamism and Christianity had for seven hundred years struggled for the possession of Spain. But it had not been all war. There had been long intervals when the peoples mingled, traded, entered into the ordinary relations of life. Thus, notwithstanding their mutual hatred, the religions influenced each other. Islamism became more gentle, Christianity more intolerant. When Mohammedanism was finally overwhelmed, it was seen that the persecuted soul of Islam had taken possession of its conqueror. Mohammedan in heart, Christian in speech, Roman Catholicism found in Spain a champion that had all the fiery enthusiasm, all the stern bigotry of the prophet of Mecca, with not a little of the love of souls, the moral purity, the disinterestedness of Jesus Christ. Thus the two religions of Spain gave birth to a monster whose work has been most disastrous to the world.

Among the eldest of the sons of this hybrid religion were Hernan Cortes and Ignatius Loyola. These two men were contemporaries, Loyola being born six years after Cortes, and dying eight years later. The life and exploits of Cortes read like a reproduction of the fiery course of one of the first followers of Mohammed. Entrusted with the conquest of Mexico, he landed in that vast empire in 1518 with a force of six or seven hundred men, only thirteen of whom were musketeers, and possessing ten field-pieces and two or three smaller pieces of cannon. He burnt his ships, founded Vera Cruz, and marched towards the capital, a city of three hundred thousand inhabitants. Montezuma, the king, was a warrior and a priest of the frightful worship of Huitzilopochtli, the Mexican Mars. Montezuma's auguries had told him that great changes were impending; and when he heard of the coming of Cortes, he believed it to be the fulfilment of an old prophecy which declared that the Children of the Sun should come from the East, and destroy the Aztec Empire. He attempted first by presents, and then by treachery, to prevent Cortes from coming to Mexico. But nothing deterred the indomitable adventurer. He took fearful vengeance on those who had attempted to surprise him, and reaching Mexico, was received by the Emperor with great pomp. An attack, however, being made on his settlement at Vera Cruz, he at once seized the person of the Emperor, and compelled the surrender of the offending general, whom he burnt with three other chiefs in front of the palace. Soon after he frightened the Aztec monarch into ceding his empire to Spain. That an adventurer with a few hundreds of followers should be able, in the midst of a great city containing three hundred thousand inhabitants, to excute its chiefs and lay down the law for its sovereign, reads like a dream; but when we find that the Mexican religion was the worship of remorseless force, the wonder is at once explained. In Cortes the Mexicans beheld one who had no fear of their hideous Moloch, and they bowed before a power which appeared to excel that of the highest.

The deeds of Cortes excited the jealousy of his superior, the governor of Cuba, who sent an army of about a thousand men to compel his obedience. Cortes came suddenly on the opposing force, conquered, and made it his own. In his absence from the capital an insurrection broke out, and Montezuma appearing on the terrace of his prison with a view to appeasing the people, received a wound from a stone, an insult he took so much to heart that he died in a few days. Cortes marched again on the city of Mexico, which he commenced to besiege within a few days of Luther's appearance before the Diet of Worms. He took it in two days' assault after a siege of four months. Famine had assisted the Spaniards, for out of three hundred thousand inhabitants they only found forty thousand alive when they entered the city, which lay in ruins "like some huge churchyard with the corpses disinterred, and the tombstones scattered about."

Faith in the power of remorseless force was the outcome of the Christian-Islamism of Spain. It is the faith which animates Cortes and all the Spanish *conquistadors*. They believe in audacity, in terrorizing, in gunpowder, and in gold. The expedition of Cortes was ruthless, that of Pizarro atrocious. If the accounts of the civilisation of Peru under the Incas be correct, his work was the most infernal the world has ever known.

Pizarro discovered Peru in 1526, and returning to Spain in 1528, obtained from Charles V. and his ministers a recognition of his right to the discovery and conquest of Peru, with the titles of governor and captain-general of Peru. He returned to America with a small but well-equipped force.

By a course of relentless violence and remorseless treachery, he succeeded in conquering the empire of Peru. He happened to arrive just at the time in which the country was a prey to civil war, and its legitimate king had been overthrown by his rival, Atahualpa. By a perfidious stratagem Pizarro got possession of the conqueror and his army. He then caused a priest to explain to him the Christian religion, and the authority that it gave to the pope over the whole earth, finally informing him how this great potentate had made a present of Peru to the King of Spain. Atahualpa indignantly exclaimed that the pope must be a crazy fool to talk of giving away what was not his own. The priest then took up a Bible to show him on what ground the pope claimed this authority, but the Indian monarch dashed the book on the ground. Pizarro now waved a white scarf, the signal agreed upon should Atahualpa prove contumacious. In a moment the artillery opened fire on the terrified Peruvians, while the Spanish cavalry rode down upon them. Atahualpa's army sought only to protect their sacred Inca, and it was only after hours of butchery that the Spaniards succeeded in his capture. After a mock trial he was condemned to be burnt alive, but on his consenting to be baptised the sentence was commuted to strangulation. These deeds, performed in the name of a truly heretical Christianity, were contemporaneous with that terrible outburst of fanaticism at Munster, where the spirit of rapine and bloodshed in John of Leyden and the Anabaptists threatened to take possession of the Reformation and effect its rapid ruin.

That the conscience of Spain was not yet wholly blinded by fanaticism and the lust of gold, is clear from the indefatigable labours of that most excellent priest, the philanthropic Las Casas. This disinterested man spent a long life in contending with the Spanish conquerors. He crossed the Atlantic again and again in defence of the Indians, and succeeded in getting Cardinal Ximenes to issue a commission of inquiry; and, finally, in a council held at Valladolid, chiefly through his efforts, the freedom of the Indians who had been enslaved was recognised. Relying on this decree, he, as Bishop of Chiapa, refused the sacrament to those planters who disregarded it; but in so doing he not only incurred the resentment of the colonists, but the disapprobation of the Church, so that he was finally compelled to return to Spain, where he died in 1566.

In the year, then, that Luther made his grand protest before the

Diet of Worms, the Spanish conquest of America commenced, and in that very same year Ignatius Loyola devoted himself to a life which was to countermine the work of Luther, and to complete in the spiritual sphere the ruin Cortes and Pizarro effected in the New World.

At the siege of Pampeluna, an incident in the war between Charles V. and Francis I., a dashing young Spanish nobleman, Inigo, son of Bertram, lord of Loyola, was severely wounded by a ball in the leg. Carried to his father's castle, he endured with great fortitude the horrible surgery of the times. But the shock was so great that he was considered to be dying. At this crisis he believed that St. Peter appeared and gave him new life.

During his recovery he beguiled the weary hours with two books : one contained the lives of some saints, the other was a life of Christ. A new ambition awoke in him. As his wound incapacitated him for the military life, he determined to emulate Dominic and Francis.

The world was not, however, to be surrendered without a struggle. He threw himself into violent asceticism. He frequented the shrine of the Virgin at Montserrat, and commenced his spiritual knighthood by spending a whole night before her altar : he vowed a pilgrimage to the Holy Land. As his conscience was not appeased, he wore a chain of iron round his loins, begged his bread, and mixed it with ashes. Three times a day he lashed himself; three times a day he went to church; seven hours a day were spent in devotion; once a week he confessed and took the Sacrament. Finding this brought him no peace, he devoted three days to an elaborate confession of all the sins of his life; but satisfaction not arriving, he went carefully over his confession, in order to discover the forgotten sin. His despair grew so great that he contemplated suicide. He began to fast for days together, and was only stopped by his confessor threatening to refuse him the Sacrament.

Suddenly he came to the conclusion that all he was doing was a mistake; these gloomy thoughts, this anguish of spirit, were, he decided, from "the adversary," the evil spirit, and he determined by an effort of will to consign to oblivion once and for ever the delinquencies of his past life. This great effort revealed to him the strength of his own will, and he began to exercise it over himself in a manner truly wonderful. Finding his sleep disturbed by his spiritual experiences, and reflecting that his time was devoted to the service of God and his neighbour, he determined that all these comforts and illuminations were from the evil one, and that he would go to sleep at the proper hour. He now set out on his pilgrimage, begging his way, and enduring every misery. In 1523 he arrived barefooted in the Holy City. As he knelt before the Holy Sepulchre he believed that he had a vision of Christ calling him to convert the Oriental peoples. Understanding from this that his mission was to teach, and reflecting that to teach he must be himself taught, this energetic man hastened back to Barcelona, where he put himself to school at the expense of a devout lady. Here, among boys, submitting himself to the ordinary discipline, he studied the Latin grammar. Meanwhile, he engaged in religious instruction, and began to write his "Spiritual exercises" for his disciples, that "mysterious book" by which he proposes in thirty days to conquer the will and the reason. His first efforts being novel, he did not escape being put in prison, but he was soon found to be a true son of the Roman Church, and his book received the authorisation of the Inquisition. When his course at Barcelona was finished he went to Paris to complete his education; but, no longer believing in beggary and barefooted pedestrianism, he took with him a purse reasonably well-filled, and travelled on the back of an ass furnished with panniers full of books. At Paris he still further reduced the time devoted to pious exercises. Robbed by his companion, he was compelled to make most extraordinary efforts to complete his three years' study. His college companions were Pierre le Fèvre, an enthusiastic young Alpine shepherd, and Francis Xavier, a young Asturian of noble birth. The first he treats with reserve—the second he flatters; both pass through the "Spiritual exercises," and are won. Besides these he attaches to himself several others: Spaniards, Frenchmen, Portuguese, Italians.

On the 15th of August, 1534, this little band met in the crypt of the Church of Montmartre, outside Paris, and vowed themselves to poverty and renunciation of the world, to the service of God and the good of souls, to a mission in Palestine, or any other work which the pope might direct.

Two years elapse, and the same men arrive by different paths in Venice, each carrying in his knapsack "the mysterious book." Loyola meets them; they are prepared to depart to the Holy Land; he shows them that they are called to undertake the conversion, not only of one nation or of one country, but of all peoples and of all kingdoms in the world. Accompanied by two others, he sets out for Rome, in order to make an unconditional surrender of the well-being and energies of the whole band to the Apostolic See, to be used in upholding and promoting the authority of the Church. On the road, "through the favour of the Virgin," Loyola had one of his daring visions. He saw the Father, who presented him to the Son, who said, "I will be favourable to you at Rome." Henceforth the band called itself "the Society of Jesus."

THE Papacy needed some such help, for it had suffered great humiliations since the proud days of Julius and Leo. In 1496 Savonarola had denounced the most terrible judgments upon Italy and Rome. He had declared that God would bring a race of men upon Italy who would bring down the pride of Rome, take possession of her holy places, defile her churches, and turn them into receptacles for horses and hogs; that confusion on confusion should be the fate of Italy, war, famine, and pestilence; that a barbarian people should be heard approaching from one side, and a second barbarian people from another. "The law of the priests," he said, "will perish, their dignities will vanish, the princes will put on sackcloth, the people will be crushed under tribulations. All men will become faint-hearted, and as they have judged so will they be judged in their turn."

During a whole generation these words remained unfulfilled. All things remained as they were. Julius died, Leo was called away so suddenly that he had not time to receive the Sacrament. Adrian departed with a sad consciousness that the evils of the Church were well nigh incurable. Clement VII., a nephew of Leo X., and another Medici, ascended the papal throne. Astute, moderate, and prudent, he had ever worked with the Spaniards, as the power which had done most to extend the States of the Church, and to re-establish the authority of his family in Florence; but after the battle of Pavia, in which Charles V. totally defeated the French and captured Francis I., the arrogance of the Spaniards became intolerable, so that even Clement began to enter into the plots which were forming on all sides against them. When the French king obtained his liberty, the first use he made of it was to refuse to fulfil his pledges, a proceeding for which the pope granted him absolution. At last, in 1526,

Clement VII. ventured to head a league of the Italian cities against the horde of *half-barbarous foreigners*, as the cultured Italian people considered the Spaniards. Although sure of the assistance of the King of France, and the sympathy of the King of England, it was a hazardous undertaking for the pope. His march northwards at once affected his spiritual power in Germany. At the Diet of Spires in 1526 it was openly proposed that the Holy Scriptures should henceforth be taken as the rule of faith. The Archduke Ferdinand, representing the emperor, signed a decree in which it was declared that in matters of religion each state was free to act according to its own judgment. This decree gave legal existence to the Protestant party and the new Reformed Church in Germany.

Meanwhile the imperial troops in Germany were burning to go to the relief of the imperial cause in Italy. They were mainly Lutherans, and their feeling towards Rome was expressed by their leader, George Freundsberg, who said, "When once I make my way to Rome, I will hang the pope."

Rome, filled with the works of the greatest artists the world had ever seen, teeming with riches and every luxury—Rome, the sink of every vice and the source of every infamy, was now threatened by two semi-barbarous armies—one Lutheran from heretic Germany, the other Catholic from orthodox Spain. Italy, the land of artists, of poets, of thinkers, of Michael Angelo, of Ariosto, of Macchiavelli, made no effort to repel the invaders. Without faith, without conscience, there was no national life. Italy was, and remained for centuries, nothing more than a geographical expression.

The imperialists came, they traversed Italy, they arrived at Rome. The pope and his forces were overthrown at the first onset. Unhappily for the Romans, both the generals of the invading armies were absent when the assault took place. The Constable Bourbon was killed at the very moment of fixing the scaling-ladders, and Freundsberg had been seized by apoplexy. Thus unrestrained, the barbarous and savage soldiery, burning for the splendid prize, burst into Rome, and the sack commenced. The slaughter was not very great, for this proud, avaricious, luxurious people did not defend themselves; but the pillage was universal. Not only palaces but churches were emptied of their contents, and booty of inestimable value fell into the hands of the invaders.

In Florence, the city of Savonarola, a strange scene was enacted.

The Medici having been expelled, the Gonfalonière, the chief magistrate of the city, fell on his knees in the midst of the Great Council crying, "Have pity, O God!" Everyone cried, "Have pity, O God!" Then he inscribed over the gates of the palace, "To Christ, the King, Lord of Lords, Liberator, Saviour." But it was too late; the door of mercy, once open, was now shut.

The pope, who had declared war against the Spaniards, who had been invaded by them in his own city, now united with them to crush Florence, in order that it might pass once again under his own family. Its fate was sealed. It was the end of Italian liberty.

The ruin that befel the Italian peninsula may be compared with the contemporaneous events happening in the Scandinavian peninsula. At the beginning of the century Sweden was a wilderness, the prey of a haughty nobility and clergy. Its people, driven to despair by over-taxation and bad government, were ever ready to revolt. By the middle of the century it had become a well-organised state: peaceful, powerful, civilised, prospering in all its interests save those of the nobility and clergy. It was the work of a Lutheran prince, Gustavus Vasa. He had almost alone fought the battle of its independence, and when the people, in gratitude, made him king, he risked all his popularity in his determination to establish the Protestant religion. But the result proclaimed him not only courageous but wise. The rise of Sweden as a civilised state was one of the first-fruits of the Reformation.

II. A.D. 1572-1580.

The sun, which had risen with such brilliancy in the flood of genius that shone over Europe at the commencement of the sixteenth century, now sank in blood. Armies gathered again and again on the battle-fields of Europe, and amidst the clash of swords, the roar of artillery, and the charge of cavalry, the highest welfare of many generations was decided. The cause of national independence, of civil liberty, of the individual conscience, found itself in the grasp of its ancient foes—tyranny and superstition. The struggle was deadly, and the enemy only conquered at last by Divine interposition.

Luther's watchword—"*The just shall live by faith*"—was such a blow to the system of Christian Phariseeism, which had usurped the name of Christianity, that Rome herself was almost persuaded to become Lutheran. Contarini and Pole at one time seemed likely to make Luther's doctrine the creed of Christendom; but Caraffa and Loyola were too powerful, and the Council of Trent declared itself of their opinion. Then came a word as potent as that of Luther, but fraught with consequences even more destructive to the old theology. Calvin proclaimed the sovereignty of Divine grace. God was absolutely free, His will was bound by no human trammels whatsoever. Luther had destroyed the idea of salvation by good works; Calvin levelled at a blow sacerdotalism and sacramentalism. For if the salvation of individual men depended on decrees known only to the secret councils of God, and predetermined before all ages, upon decrees irresistible and absolutely certain in their execution, where was the room for the mediation of a priest, or how could free grace be limited to certain visible channels, such as sacraments?

Mediæval superstition and Renaissance kingcraft might have entered into some compromise with Luther, but with Calvin it was impossible. He cut the ground from under their feet; he held a different conception of the universe; his disciples, therefore, were bound to enter into long and deadly struggle with the old society. A new heaven compelled a new earth; the conviction that God could be approached without priestly mediation made free men. And it is a significant fact that until the French Revolution no nation achieved civil freedom except those which had adopted the Calvinistic creed.

Although Calvin's doctrine may, in the strictest sense, be called transcendental, Calvin was the most practical of theologians. An able statesman, a great lawgiver, he gave proof of his capacity by the way in which he ruled Geneva. From an unimportant city it became in his hands the focus of European liberty—a veritable anti-Rome to all the Protestant nations. It would, however, be too much to attribute this to his ability; it was rather the power of the doctrine of which Geneva became the seat. From that doctrine all the great leaders in "the cause" drew their inspiration—Coligny, William of Orange, John Knox.

———————

FOR a time the fate of France seemed to hang in the balance, since Catharine de Medici and Charles IX. made advances to the Calvinists, as Paul III. and some of his cardinals made advances to the Lutherans. Catharine de Medici brought to France the easy unbelief and crafty tactics of her house; her policy was to destroy one party by the other, and then to circumvent the conquerors by fraud or force. No doubt the position of the House of Valois was a difficult one, and much might be pardoned in a mother struggling for the defence of the throne of her sons. But it was not so much her object as the means she used that condemn her; and yet even in them she was not a sinner above all other sinners. Her disposition and circumstances made her the instrument of the new Catholic society which was coming into being—a society of which Dominic and Macchiavelli were the sponsors, and Ignatius Loyola the schoolmaster. The massacre of St. Bartholomew was not her idea; she only had the chief hand in working it out. As far back as 1559, the Duke of Alva had urged on her husband the extermination of the Huguenots, and Henry II. had entered into a secret convention with Philip of Spain, by which the French Calvinists, "that accursed vermin," were one and all, high and low, to be massacred at the most convenient season. In 1565, Alva again urged its execution on Catharine, at that time a widow. "A thousand frogs," said he, "are not worth the head of one salmon." Not only the King of Spain but the pope himself urged this policy. Pius V., the pontiff whom St. Carlo Borromeo and the new Catholic reformers supported, continually exhorted

Catharine to repress the insolence of the Huguenots, to arrest their progress, and no longer to endure their existence; and he gave an earnest of what he meant when he commanded the leader of the troops, which he sent to the aid of the French Catholics, "To take no Huguenot prisoner, but instantly to kill every one that should fall into his hands."

Such was the advice given by the chief authorities in Church and State; but Catharine was no fanatic, and she waited stealthily until the moment arrived when it should best serve her interest to spring upon the prey. The civil war had gone on for years. Now the Catholics seized the king; now the Huguenots. Now he was compelled to listen to the Guises; now to Coligny. At last Guise, Montmorency, Bourbon, Condé all being killed, and the Huguenots thoroughly defeated at Moncontour, a party appeared in the court favourable to reconciliation. A treaty of peace was made with the Protestants; and Coligny, full of faith in the king, went to court. Charles IX. was by no means the worst of men; he was not without chivalry, and evidently felt impressed by the grandeur of Coligny's character. He was, moreover, sufficiently a King of France to perceive that Coligny's policy was the true one. "Oppose Spain, your hereditary foe, help the Netherlanders in their struggle against Philip, and enter into a league with the German Princes." The king entered into Coligny's policy, and Louis of Nassau received a letter from him, in which he declared his determination to employ all the forces in his hands to rescue the Netherlands from the oppression under which they were groaning; while Coligny wrote assuring the Prince of Orange that there was no doubt of the sincerity of the royal intentions, and expressed a hope that he would shortly be able to join him with a large French army. To crown the reconciliation between the court and the Protestants, a marriage was agreed upon between the king's sister, Margaret of Valois, and Henry of Navarre.

Catharine saw her danger: Coligny would deliver the king from her influence, and rule in her place. The hour had come. She threw herself into the scheme of reconciliation; all the leading Protestants were invited to the approaching marriage, and she and her fellow-conspirators, most of whom were Italians, prepared the arrangements of the massacre.

Suddenly an attempt was made to assassinate Coligny, but it failed; he was only wounded in the right hand and the left arm. Charles was playing at tennis when the news was brought him. He exclaimed, as one in torment, "Am I never to have peace?" He went to see the admiral, assured him of his sympathy and his rage against his enemies; but his mother and his brother went with him, more than ever determined to compel him to do what they wished. The conspirators surrounded him: they appealed to his fears, they told him lies, they baited him with arguments. He appeared stubbornly determined to stand by Coligny. At last his mother insinuated that he was a coward. Worried almost to madness, the king cried out, in a sort of frenzy: "God's death! since you find it good to kill the admiral, I will not only kill him, but every Huguenot in France, so that not one may even reproach me. By God's death, give the order at once!"

The conspirators lost no time. It was decided that on the morning of August 24th, 1572, as the bell of the Palais de Justice rang the dawn, the bloody work should be begin. On the previous evening the king, his mother, and brother sat together in moody silence. Suddenly the report of a gun was heard. The king sprang up, and seemed even then as if he would stop Guise. But it was too late. Catharine had given orders to commence before the time arranged, and Coligny was already dead. When the assassins arrived at his house, he bid his friends save themselves, and, rising from his bed, he steadied himself against the wall. He was quickly despatched, and his body thrown into the courtyard, where it was brutally kicked by Henry of Guise, and then dragged through the streets of Paris.

The scene that Sunday morning in Paris was never equalled until the hour of vengeance came, three centuries later. In the dead of the night, in that hour of stillness and deep darkness which just precedes dawn, frightful noises awoke the city. The storming of houses and the crashing of doors, the cries of men, women, and children suddenly murdered, the sound of tramping feet, the rushing of the victims along the dark streets, pursued by the assassins, armed with torches and daggers: nought was heard through that terrible night but the report of guns, agonising shrieks, sudden splashes. When the sun shone on Paris, the city was filled with dead bodies, which the ladies of the court came out to see, and upon which they levelled their obscene jokes.

As the diabolical work proceeded, the miserable king became as one possessed. He took an arquebuse, and, flying to one of the windows of the Louvre, began to cry, "Kill! kill!" while he himself fired down upon his own subjects. When he saw the Seine covered with corpses, which floated up and down with the tide, he seemed as if he really enjoyed the sight. He even went to see the mangled remains of Coligny, which they had nailed up in a public place. The ladies of the court held their noses. Charles said, "I find the smell of an enemy very agreeable."

Certainly he had yielded to one of the darkest crimes ever perpetrated. The guests he had collected under his roof were nearly all murdered. Among the very few spared were his physician, Ambrose Paré, and Palissy the potter, whom Catharine had employed to decorate the gardens of the Tuileries. Part of the method of the conspiracy was to deliver men up to the vengeance of their enemies. Thus, it is said, the great Protestant philosopher, Ramus, perished through the hatred of a certain Professor Charpentier. The terrible work over, the royal assassins appeared to vacillate, not knowing what the world would think. One day they excused the deed, the next they glorified it. But the example had spread, and the massacre went on through the provinces. In the end, it is computed no less than fifty thousand persons perished.

The news burst on Europe like a clap of thunder; even those who had urged it were surprised at its magnitude. Alva and Philip were never more pleased in their lives. For the first time in his life, so it was said, the gloomy Spaniard laughed. The Roman court was equally delighted. Cardinal Lorraine rewarded the bearer of the news with a thousand crowns. Salvos of cannon thundered from the castle of St. Angelo, and joy-fires blazed in the streets of Rome. The pope, the Sacred College, and the ambassadors of the Catholic monarchs went in procession to return thanks at the church of St. Louis. An extraordinary jubilee was published in Rome in honour of the double victory over the Huguenots in France and the Turks at Lepanto, and a medal struck to commemorate the massacre. Still more, the pope ordered Vasari to paint a picture of the massacre, which was put in a place of honour and inscribed with the legend, "*Pontifex Colignii necem probat.*"—"The pope approves the death of Coligny." With very different feelings was the news received in Germany and the Protestant states. The Emperor Maximilian shed tears when he heard of the crimes of his son-in-law. Elizabeth and the English court would hardly speak to the French ambassador. The city of Geneva ordered a fast, and John Knox, infirm and dying, summoned up all his strength, and had himself carried up into the pulpit in Edinburgh, where he thundered forth, like another Elijah, the vengeance of God against the King of France and his wicked house.

Knox died November 24th, 1572, exactly three months after the massacre. "Here lies he who never feared the face of man," said the Regent Morton, as he stood over the grave of the great Reformer; and truly this grim, stern servant of truth had the bravest heart ever granted to a human soul. Simple as a child, he understood nothing of the fashion of the world. "I have learnt," he said, "to call wickedness by its own terms—a fig, a fig; a spade, a spade. His conduct to the queen is represented as cruel and turbulent, but when it is remembered that Mary Stuart came from among the very people who planned the massacre of St. Bartholomew, that the Guises and the Valois were her own kith and kin, and the court of Catharine de Medici her nursery and her school, and that her tendencies proved to be exactly the same, could it be supposed that a man who had "the utmost sharpness of discernment," and the simplest, truest nature, could force himself to use honeyed phrases and bye-paths of rebuke because the object of his indignation was a beautiful and accomplished woman? Doubtless Knox tended to Republicanism, as all Calvinists did. Students of Macchiavelli, as Catharine de Medici and Philip of Spain, knew this instinctively, knew it better than the Calvinists did themselves. As to the latter, they had no other political system than that of their age; but since they believed and taught a doctrine that cut at the root of the sacramental theory, they were bound in due course to deny the mediæval doctrine of kingship which was essentially mystic and sacramental.

The last days of John Knox mark a new order of holiness. Instead of the painful efforts of the old asceticism to intensify the sufferings of dissolution, the soul of the Reformer is alternately given to rapturous prayer on behalf of the Church, and to thoroughly human interests, even to a desire to add to the simple enjoyments of life. Two friends come to see him unaware; he is so ill. He rises from his bed, insists on their stopping to dinner, orders a hogshead of wine that he had in the cellar to be pierced, and merrily bids one of them send for some as long as it lasted, for, " I will not," said he, " tarry with you until it is all drunk."

On the last day, as he lies the subject of solemn spiritual struggles, he desires them to wet his mouth from time to time with a little weak ale. It is the death of a man, not of a saint. Yet was there in those last days all the characteristics of the prophet and the apostle. In his efforts to bring the captain of Edinburgh Castle to repentance, and the striking prophecy he utters concerning his end, in his address to his fellow minister, elders, and deacons, one seems to be living over again the times of Elisha and Paul. Almost his last words, like those of Coligny, contained an allusion to the great doctrine that animated them both—the doctrine of sovereign grace. " What hast thou that thou hast not received? By the grace of God I am what I am : not I, but the grace of God in me."

AND it was this same doctrine that supported another great contemporary of John Knox—William Prince of Orange.

In a corner of Europe, a spot in which man had fought with the ocean for a dwelling-place, the spirit of the Reformation in Europe made its real struggle with the spirit of mediæval Catholicism. The champion of the cause of the corrupt and dying Church was Spain, then at the very summit of her power. The spirit of Islamism, fatalistic, bigoted, sanguinary, remorseless, had taken possession of Christian Spain, and was now concentrated in the heart of its ruler, a man of narrow but ardent mind, of relentless will and icy heart. Philip II. made it the object of his life to crush the heresy which was misleading the world and destroying the Catholic Church. For this object he spared no pains, grudged no expense, stopped at no crime, from lies and treachery to the most atrocious and wholesale murder. Day by day he sat for long hours in his private chamber planning and plotting all the details of the schemes by which he proposed to annihilate the new-born liberties of the Reformers, and to crush everyone likely to give the slightest trouble.

His instruments were worthy of himself. The chief among them was a man more than equal to his master in ability, in stern inflexibility, in absolute freedom from all remorse, in silent tenacity, in cool daring. Alva was a military genius—probably the greatest of his age, but it agrees with the moroseness of his character that he preferred to win his campaigns by taking advantage of the mistakes of his adversary rather than by dazzling the world with splendid victories. Philip sent Alva to take the place of Margaret, Duchess of Parma, as Governor-General of the Netherlands, in order that he might more effectually repress the free spirit rising in those provinces and exterminate the new heresy. Alva determined to rule by terror; he accordingly appointed a council which, in its manner of working, exactly prefigured the Revolutionary Tribunal of the French Revolution.

This Blood Council, as it was rightly called, commenced a wholesale massacre of the people of the Netherlands. Not only was every possible offence in connection with the Lutheran heresy punished with instant death, but, its action being retrospective, everyone who had shown the least sympathy with reform was hanged. Many innocent persons, who were in reality Catholics, suffered. The Council did not understand finding accused persons guiltless, especially if they happened to have wealth. "To the gallows, to the gallows with him!" was the usual cry of Councillor Hessels, a sleepy-headed Fleming, who had to be woke up every afternoon, in order that he might give his judgment before each prisoner was condemned. The gibbet worked at such a rate that when Alva quitted the country he congratulated himself on the fact that eighteen thousand persons had been put to death while he had been governor.

It took years to rouse the slow, patient Netherlanders into anything like self-defence. Prior to Alva's arrival, many nobles and chief persons had come forward to protest indignantly against the establishment of the Inquisition in the Netherlands, but after a little experience of the terrific severity of the new governor-general, the Netherlanders seemed disposed to submit. Happily for the cause of liberty and of religion, there were a few persons who refused to let such tyranny pass unresisted. Chief among these was William of Nassau, the Prince of Orange. In the midst of appalling catastrophes, and assailed by all possible calamities, this calm, great-hearted man stands out on the canvas of history like the one glowing light in a painting of Rembrandt. Unhappy in his wife, his eldest son filched from him and turned into a Jesuit, his three brothers struck down in war, with no armies but those of mercenaries, which he was at his

s

wit's end to pay, suffering defeat upon defeat, deceived and stunned by the massacre of St. Bartholomew at the moment victory was in his grasp, struggling year after year with the richest nation in the world and the most courageous soldiery, urged by his staunchest supporters to yield, weakened and rendered almost delirious by a fever at the very crisis of the war—what could have sustained this man, and rendered his soul as inflexible as that of the stern despot he came to oppose?

Nothing but his faith. William of Orange was a Calvinist. When the war opened, he was a great prince of the Empire, living in splendour and extravagance. He had been the trusted adviser of Charles V., and retained the confidence of his son. In 1559 he was appointed to negotiate a peace between Spain and France, and became one of the hostages for its fulfilment. It was at this time that he was informed by Henry II. of a secret convention between himself and Philip to exterminate the heretics. The prince, disguising his feelings, determined to do all he could to prevent it. He was not then himself a Protestant; his sympathies were, however, with justice and liberty. The early part of his career was marked by an almost excessive prudence; compared with his friends, he appeared cold and indifferent to the national cause; but his interest grew with every effort, and when, at last, faith in God became a living power in his soul, and he had openly joined the Calvinist Church, he displayed courage, energy, watchfulness, and disinterestedness.

After some years of the most cruel tyranny ever inflicted on a people, the Netherlanders were aroused to a pitch of indignation, which at last reached such a climax that even Alva and Philip had to succumb. Alva was superseded, and a man of milder mood took his place. But the Netherlanders understood their monarch by this time, and though they were not free from a certain superstitious belief concerning his authority, they grew every day more thorough in the support of the man whom they recognised as their God-sent deliverer. William had entered the Low Countries with one army, his brother Louis arriving from another point with a second, and the two were to meet in Holland. Unhappily, Louis was defeated on his route, and he and another brother were slain (1574).

The siege of Leyden by the Spaniards had been raised at the moment of the approach of Louis; but, now that he was defeated, the city was again invested. By an extraordinary error, the people had omitted to use the opportunity to revictual the town. They were therefore in the worst possible condition for another siege. However, William urged upon them the vast importance of standing firm, since to them was committed not only the cause of the Netherlands, but probably that of liberty and religion for many generations. If, he said, they would hold out for three months, he would in that time certainly devise means for their relief. Nothing but a determination to succeed at any cost could warrant this conviction. No help was to be expected from France or England. Henry III. was selfish and treacherous; Elizabeth narrow-minded and haughty. William proposed to cut the dykes and flood the land. The Estates demurred at first, but after a short time heroically determined to sacrifice their property to save Leyden. "Better," said they, "a drowned land than a lost land."

The news of this determination was forwarded to the besieged city, and the dykes were pierced in sixteen places. Ere long the water was high enough to admit the flat-bottomed fleet of Admiral Boisot, consisting of two hundred vessels, manned by crews of Zeelanders, men who called themselves "Sea Beggars," and who, animated by a burning patriotism, had come to regard every act performed in defence of their country, however atrocious, as not only necessary, but meritorious. They wore crescents in their caps, with the inscription, "Rather Turkish than Popish." The fleet passed rapidly over the waters, but soon found that an inland dyke barred the way. Happily, the Spaniards had not made effective preparations for its defence. It was accordingly seized and cut, the fleet entering into the inner space, which had been quickly flooded. A second dyke was now found to bar the way; this was also carried and pierced, and the fleet entered through the aperture. But here it stranded, for the waters thus spread out were not deep enough to float the vessels, a strong east wind blowing them back towards the ocean. The admiral was in despair, and wrote to William that if the wind did not soon cease, the attempt would have to be given up.

Meanwhile, what with the deliberations of the Estates and other difficulties, six weeks had elapsed since the siege began, and the people were on the brink of starvation. They had eaten all their meat except a few cows which had been reserved for milk, and which were now gradually slaughtered, the meat being dealt out in minute proportions. People ate dogs, cats, rats, and even boiled skins. Women and children searched the gutters and the heaps of garbage for some morsel of food. They even stripped the leaves off the trees, and devoured the grass. At last they grew desperate, and a crowd pursued Adrian Van der Werff, the burgomaster, through the streets, crying out against his cruelty. He turned upon the people, and, with face gaunt as theirs, but in tones of calm determination, thus addressed them: "I know that we shall starve if not soon relieved, but starvation is preferable to the dishonoured death which is the only alternative. Your menaces move me not; my life is at your disposal. Here is my sword; plunge it into my breast, and divide my flesh among you. Take my body to appease your hunger, but expect no surrender so long as I remain alive."

These courageous words were received with applause, and being in accordance with the spirit of the majority of the population, no more was said about surrender. In the centre of the city was a mound surmounted by a tower, said to have been erected by Hengist to commemorate his successful invasion of Britain. On this tower the citizens daily assembled to watch for the coming aid. But they knew as well as Admiral Boisot that as long as the east wind lasted it was impossible for it to arrive.

William had watched all the efforts to relieve the city with intense anxiety. At last he fell ill with a fever. His brain was overwrought, and he was on the brink of delirium. Nothing, the doctors knew, would cure him but absolute peace of mind; and as long as the fate of Leyden hung in the balance this was the one thing he could not have.

Suddenly a strong equinoctial gale blew from the sea, and the ocean came sweeping over the dykes. The fleet rose and advanced bravely towards the city. But they soon found that two great forts barred the way. However, the enemy was beginning to lose all confidence; such hardihood was appalling. The people of Leyden were clearly determined to starve rather than surrender, while those who came to their relief were desperadoes, since they had dared to make the ocean their ally, and call in its terrors to their aid. Valdez declared himself conquered by the powers of nature, and fled along the dyke to the Hague. He was attacked, and lost a thousand men in the flight.

The other fort, held by Colonel Borgia, seemed so strong that Admiral Boisot wrote in despair to the prince that if the wind did not change so that the water rose high enough to carry them to the other side of the city, all would yet be in vain. However, Boisot managed to send the besieged a communication informing them of his position. The people gathered on the tower, and Van der Werff, pointing to the fort, said, "Yonder behind that fort are bread and meat and brethren in thousands. Shall all this be destroyed by the Spanish guns, or shall we rush to the rescue of our friends?" "We will tear the fortress to fragments with our teeth and nails," cried the people, "before the relief so long expected shall be wrenched from us!"

It was resolved that at earliest dawn a sortie should be made in support of an assault by the fleet upon the Spanish fort. The night was one of great anxiety to Leyden, to the Spaniards, and to the admiral, for it was filled with strange and alarming noises, and by a long procession of lights which appeared to pass over the dark waters. A large portion of the city wall suddenly gave way, and the horror-struck citizens believed that Leyden had fallen at last; the Spaniards, on the other hand, imagined that the people were coming upon them in the dead of the night.

When morning broke all was silent, the fort appeared empty. What could it mean? The despairing thought arose—the Spaniards have taken the city, all is over. Suddenly a boy appeared at the top of the fort waving his cap, and a man approached wading through the water. The Spaniards had fled in the night, every obstacle was gone, the city was open to the fleet. God had delivered Leyden out of the hands of the Spaniards as surely as He delivered Israel from the hands of Pharaoh.

As the fleet came into the city every individual who could stand was on the quays; bread was thrown in all directions to the famishing crowd, and directly the admiral landed a procession was formed composed of emaciated burghers, women, and children, with the sailors and soldiers who had just arrived. They made their way to the church, and there offered up their heartfelt thanks to the God who, after having permitted so sore a trial, had at last interposed in so wonderful a manner. After prayer the congregation tried to raise a thanksgiving hymn, but everyone broke down in tears, and men, women, and children were sobbing with emotion. This was the greatest event of the struggle. The Spanish power was broken. In a few years William saw his efforts crowned by the establishment of the Republic of the United Provinces, of which he was declared the Stadtholder (1579).

The policy of the age was Macchiavellian, and every monarch acted on the principle that he who did not know how to dissimulate did not know how to reign. No one was less embarrassed in acting on this policy than Queen Elizabeth, since few royal personages were less troubled by conscientious scruples. Had she possessed a spark of disinterested enthusiasm, she would have taken the proud position the Protestants of Europe offered her as "head of the Religion" and "Mistress of the Seas;" but she laughed at such high-flown notions, and preferred a less dangerous rôle. Her highest object was to consolidate the new order of things, and make England a strong and stable state.

Happily, the country had a soul greater than that of its queen. The Reformation in England was not simply made by Act of Parliament. It was a popular movement that had been going on for centuries, revealing its intensity in the Marian persecution. The fires of Smithfield render the old hatred against foreign domination in matters of religion ineradicable, and the blood of the martyrs became the seed of the Church. Never has there been a more widespread religious life than existed in England from the Reformation to the Restoration. It is the great Puritan age—the age to which England owes many of its purest and most energising influences. It gave birth to a literature the most influential the world has ever known, a literature which displayed at once a power and a perfection no later age can hope to rival. The rapid development of English trade, manufactures, and commerce dates from this great period.

The heart of England recognised that its future prosperity was bound up with the Protestant cause. Elizabeth might refuse aid, except in useless dribblets, to the struggling Netherlanders; the London traders voluntarily subscribed half a million sterling—a sum equal to a whole year's revenue of the crown—and sent it to the Prince of Orange. Englishmen left the kingdom secretly that they might fight for the "cause," until there was a regiment of a thousand English volunteers in the Low Countries. England felt that its real foe was Spain, and burned with indignation at the thought of the South Atlantic and the road to India being closed against its vessels.

A vigorous war was commenced and carried on independently of the English Government, and almost in defiance of it. Every port on the southern coast was a cradle for the "Sea Dogs." Accepting letters of marque from Condé and the French Protestants, English sailors fitted out expeditions which sailed to the Spanish main, attacked and sank every Spanish vessel they could find, plundered the Spanish ports, and destroyed the shipping. In strict legality they were pirates, but Puritan England regarded them with pride and admiration. These "Sea Dogs" were the heroes and the paladins of "the cause," and were not unfrequently deeply religious men.

The most renowned of these privateers was Captain Francis Drake, the son of a Kentish clergyman. This daring adventurer made himself such a terror in the Spanish main, that his name was known in every court of Europe. On the 15th of November, 1577, Drake set out on his famous voyage round the world. After having crossed the South Atlantic, he passed through the Straits of Magellan, and was the first Englishman to enter the Pacific. He sailed along the coast of Chili and Peru, seizing whatever he could lay hands on, until he had laden his little vessel with gold dust, bars of silver, pearls, emeralds, and precious stones, so that he had on board a freight worth not less than half-a-million sterling. With these spoils he steered for the Malaccas, rounded the Cape of Good Hope, and entered Plymouth Harbour on the 26th of September, 1580, "after having," to use the quaint words of Fuller, "spent two years, ten months, and some odd days beside, in seeing the wonders of the Lord in the deep, in discerning many admirable things, in going through many strange adventures, in escaping out of many dangers, and overcoming many difficulties in thus encompassing this nether globe and passing round about the world."

It was five months before the queen gave Drake any sign of her approval. But the enthusiasm grew over his wonderful adventures and the vastness of his spoil, until the popularity-courting queen determined to give the bold seaman a mark of her favour. She went on board his famous little vessel, and made him a knight.

Drake's voyage round the world marked a new era. The fraternal sympathy which, in the Middle Ages, was strictly confined to Christendom, is clearly broadening out to humanity. Las Casas was among the first to assert the rights of the heathen to justice and brotherhood.

The reign of Akbur, the great Moghul Emperor of India, is exactly contemporaneous with those of Elizabeth and Philip II. But what a contrast between the moral character of the Eastern and Western rulers, and, above all, between their methods of action! During a long and eventful reign of fifty-one years, full of struggles with his foes, Akbur descended to no deceits, no falsehoods, no shifts, no intrigues. "I can find but one road to the attainment of my purposes," he said, "and that is the straight one—after all the easiest and the best."

Akbur was the grandson of Babur, the Indian monarch of whom the beautiful story is told that when his beloved son appeared dying, he declared he would give his life in his stead, and walking three times round his bed praying, he exclaimed, "I have borne it away, I have borne it away." He died, and his son, Hoomayoon, lived; lived to suffer most terrible reverses of fortune, and Akbur was born under circumstances in the last degree distressing to his parents. Hoomayoon recovered his position, and pushed his boy into public life at the early age of ten. Before the lad was thirteen Akbur had developed such extraordinary character that he was allowed to lead the Moghul troops in the most critical battle in the struggle between his father and his enemies. The victory gained on June 18, 1555, decided the fate of India for some generations, since it established the Moghul dynasty in its empire.

Akbur ascended the throne seven months after, being then only thirteen years and three months old. His position was still critical. He represented a new Mohammedan party, which was so weak, compared to the old, that whereas his opponents could easily muster one hundred thousand horsemen, he could only bring into the field about thirty thousand. Northern and Eastern India were in the hands of his opponents, and the Hindoos of Central India had given no sign as to which Mohammedan party they intended to support. Akbur had for his prime minister a brave and devoted general, his uncle, Beiram Khan. By his decision and ability, supported by the good sense of the young emperor, the Moghul rule was firmly established. But when Akbur found that Beiram wished to rule in his name, and that the rule would be a violent and stormy one, he, though only seventeen years of age, in the gentlest but most decided manner dismissed his prime minister, and took the empire into his own hands. Henceforth his reign was one continued series of successes, both in peace and war.

Akbur himself, though an able and valiant commander, had no taste for war, bloodshed was abhorrent to his nature, and though he was a conqueror, he always aimed at the utmost happiness of his subjects.

In fact, the chief characteristic of his rule was its philanthropy. If any ruler ever practically loved his enemies, and sought to overcome evil with good, it was Akbur. Instead of causing elephants to trample on his defeated foes, or hewing them to pieces, Akbur promoted them to dignity and gave them estates. Instead of allowing his troops to massacre their Hindoo prisoners, and to sell the women and children into slavery, he forbade both under such heavy penalties that the practice became impossible. Though a Mohammedan, he exercised the utmost tolerance towards the Hindoo religion, relieving their temples, places of pilgrimage, and sacred bathing-places from taxation, while he fearlessly put down every practice that was cruel or injurious to humanity: suttee, early marriages, and non-marriage of widows. He encouraged the Christian missionaries, showed the utmost respect for the symbols of their religion, and an especial reverence for their sacred Scriptures. He permitted them to establish schools, missions, and colleges, and promoted theological controversy between them and the Mohammedan priests.

He went further than mere tolerance: he sought in the most effectual way to make India one people. He succeeded in inducing the hitherto inaccessible Rajpoot chiefs to bestow their daughters on himself, his sons, and his grandsons; and he introduced the Hindoos by thousands into the imperial service. His finance minister, Rajah Toder Mul, was a Hindoo. With his aid he perfected a great reform in the assessment of the land revenue of the empire. All the petty means of extortion were abolished, a simple system introduced, bearing a close resemblance to modern reforms in the English rule of the Bengal Presidency.

Akbur was adverse to capital punishment, refusing to allow his subordinates to inflict it except in case of dangerous sedition; and in no case was it to be accompanied with mutilation or cruelty.

That under such a ruler a land should prosper is a foregone conclusion. Akbur had a revenue sixty times greater than Queen Elizabeth, and his court was the most gorgeous India had ever seen. He was never in debt, and the stipends of his officials, as well as the pay of his army, were never in arrear. He was more insatiable of work than Philip II., and was most abstemious in sleep and food. Although he had never taken wine to excess, he gave it up entirely, and abstained from animal food two days in the week. He constantly sat in public, receiving petitions even from the most humble. Every handicraft was a subject of interest to him, and by his fine taste and munificence he greatly promoted the one beautiful art of India—architecture.

That Akbar's beneficent career was in no way due to his race or religion is strikingly proved by the fact that within a year of his death his son Selim, whom he named his successor, in spite of his rebellion, committed an atrocity which equalled the worst cruelties Alva, Philip, or the Inquisition ever devised. Selim was a strict Mohammedan and a drunkard. He had caused a devoted friend and minister of his father to be murdered because he suspected him of advising Akbar to renounce Islam. The eldest son of this drunken bigot rebelled in his turn. Selim pursued him into the Punjab, where he had collected ten thousand men. He was taken prisoner, and brought to his father in chains. To give him a lesson, his father caused seven hundred of his followers to be impaled on stakes in a line from the gate of Lahore; and while many were alive and shrieking in agony, he caused his son to be placed on an elephant and taken along the line.

Thus the spirit of religious bigotry is essentially inhuman, becoming more and more atrocious in its cruelty in the degree that its creed is anti-Christian. If mediæval Christianity chastised men with whips, Mohammedanism chastised them with scorpions.

SEVENTEENTH CENTURY.

CONTEMPORARY EVENTS IN THE SEVENTEENTH CENTURY.

Germany.—Gustavus Adolphus at Lutzen.
Scotland.—Signing the Covenant.
England.—The arrest of the five members.
Italy.—Galileo forced to recant.

SEVENTEENTH CENTURY.

SECTION I.

A.D. 1632-1642.

The Catholic Reaction—The Jesuits—Urban VIII.—Galileo's Recantation—The Thirty Years' War—Richelieu—Gustavus Adolphus—The Solemn League and Covenant—Attempt to Create an English Despotism—Struggle between Charles I. and the House of Commons.

WHEN the Roman pontiff any Easter Day during the third quarter of the sixteenth century ascended St. Peter's, in order to pronounce his famous blessing—*Urbi et orbi*—he must have been either stolid or sublime if, casting his eyes towards the north of Europe, he felt other than depressed. Scandinavia, Great Britain, and the United Provinces had wholly rejected his authority. Nine-tenths of the German people were Protestant; Poland and Hungary, France and the Flemish Netherlands, hung in the balance; no states remained secure save those of Italy and the Iberian peninsula.

Yet from this fallen condition the Papacy rose again, and in the first half of the seventeenth century appeared likely to regain its old domination. We cannot pretend to give the history of this great reaction towards Catholicism, but a few facts will show its extent. In Poland great numbers of the nobility recanted, and sent their sons to Jesuit colleges. Every parish church, except that of Danzig, came back again into the possession of the Catholics. In the year 1624 the Jesuits claimed to have recovered in Bohemia sixteen thousand souls; the Catholic churches in Prague astonished the papal nuncio, filled as they were with two to three thousand persons every Sunday morning. At Tabor, the population, which had been entirely Protestant, became Catholic in the course of a year or two. In Hungary, the principal families abjured Protestantism, and in the Diet of 1625 the Catholics had the majority. In France, Henry of Navarre led the way, and the apostasy amongst the higher ranks of Huguenot nobility was only too general. In the land of the Reformation an almost equal defection was seen. Mayence, which had been Protestant for nearly forty years, became in a short time almost entirely Catholic. It was the same with the cities of Bamberg and Paderborn. In the year 1603 the Archduke of Austria congratulated himself on an increase of forty thousand communicants to the Roman Church in his dominions. In the Netherlands, in the very cities where Philip and Alva had met with such undaunted resistance, the principal families became Catholic. By the year 1622 there were one hundred and fifty thousand Catholics in the diocese of Utrecht, and one hundred thousand in that of Haarlem. In England the Puritans complained to James I. that in a very short time fifty thousand of their countrymen had been allured into Romanism.

To explain fully how all this happened would be to write the history of Europe at this epoch; it is not difficult, however, to indicate the main causes. Such wholesale defections show that the public mind of Europe had never been really penetrated by Protestant doctrine, and that the mass of the people had only yielded for a time to the enthusiasm awakened by the men of faith; now they were gone, it fell back to the old creed. Power is the only god to which the mass of mankind remain true; they follow its star with never-ceasing devotion. Thus, in the seventeenth century conversions always followed in the wake of military successes.

It is the fate of all revolutions: the intense energy of the first period of the Reformation was followed by a time of torpor and moral dissolution; the power temporal and spiritual had passed over to the other side. In place of the religious revivals that marked the preaching of the early Reformers, the Protestant world was torn by acrimonious disputes. Lutherans hated Calvinists, and Calvinists cursed Arminians with even more energy than they did the pope. A people that saw Oldenbarneveld put to death and Grotius imprisoned could not but conclude that "new presbyter was but old pope writ large." In seeking the kingdom of God the Protestant nations had inherited the blessing promised. The "all things" had been added to them; but in the degree that "their silver and their gold had been multiplied" they forgot God and relapsed into hard-hearted Phariseeism and gross worldliness.

The prosperity of the Netherlands in this second age of the Reformation encouraged the development of a great school of painters. What do they tell us of its life? From Gerard Dow, Metsu, and Terburg we learn how richly furnished and how comfortable were the homes of the burghers of the great Dutch cities, while another class of painters, of whom Teniers, Ostade, and Jan Steen are types, show us how coarse and debased were the lower classes. In Rembrandt's meditating philosophers, and perhaps among his Scribes and Pharisees, we may see the Protestant teachers. It is the great age of Protestant theology; the age of Arminius and Gomar, and the Synod of Dort. The philosophers are again at work on the Gospel; and the greatest among them has just come into the world. Spinoza was born at Amsterdam in 1632.

The Flemish school depict a still more luxurious life. Its voluptuousness is of a type so rank that Rubens had to paint in the hot light of an Oriental sun to give it full expression. Gross materialism and sensual enjoyment were evidently the characteristics of a society in which Jordaens spent a long life, and which he worked so indefatigably to represent. Its powers, quickened by the Reformation, had been stimulated into an almost tropical fecundity by the wealth of the East Indies.

In Germany and France, Protestantism had depended too much on royal and noble personages. The generation that had known Luther and Calvin having passed away, their descendants returned in flocks to the old faith, or led such worldly lives that their following lost all heart. What rendered all this the more alarming was that the degeneracy took place in the presence of a new tide of devotion in the Roman Church. The appearance of men and women so disinterested and of fervour so intense as Theresa of Cepida, of Francis de Sales, of Johannes à Deo, and Vincent de Paul, was in itself sufficient to create a religious revolution. Their efforts and their prayers attracted a host of gentle labourers likeminded, who threw themselves into philanthropic works, the care of orphans, of the sick, of the ignorant and the poor. The great societies of the Brethren and Sisters of Charity arose, while the power of the pulpit in the Gallican Church was revived by the brilliant priests of the Oratory.

In a free society all this energy in well-doing would have been an unmixed benefit; devoted to a spiritual despotism, it was so much new capital upon which, and by which, tyranny might trade. The nominal rulers of Catholicism appear to be the pope, the Roman court, and the bishops; its real directors, especially in times of earnestness and energy, are those who are most thoroughly imbued with its spirit. That spirit has developed with ages. In the sixteenth century it took the mould of Ignatius Loyola; and at the time we are considering the Jesuit society was in the full zenith of its power.

It was to this powerful body, at once the janissaries and the generals of the papal army, that all the great conquests of the Catholic reaction were due. Dauntless, unscrupulous, reckless of their lives, pliable in defeat, uncompromising in success, equally ready for the meanest or for the highest work, caring nothing for reputation, if they could only obtain influence, this marvellous society was the real conqueror of seventeenth century Protestantism. It was the Jesuit society that organised the armies, conceived the campaigns, did the hard fighting, took the forlorn hope, pursued the enemy, executed the prisoners, divided the spoil, and sang the hymn of triumph. Their personal disinterestedness made the Jesuits marvellously courageous; but when once they got the upper hand, they scorned no means to make their victory absolute, outdoing the vilest politicians in the arts of bribery and corruption, intimidation and violence. But their greatest conquests were obtained through their educational ability. They set up colleges and laid themselves out for the higher classes, aiming especially at moulding the minds of those who were to be the rulers of the world. The champion of the Catholic cause at this time, a man more papal than the pope—Ferdinand II. of Austria, Emperor of Germany—was a pupil of the Jesuits.

The German Protestants, alarmed at the progress of events, began to take measures to defend themselves. They had formed the Evangelical Union, for the general protection of Protestant interests throughout the empire; but it soon became clear that the opposing party intended nothing short of absolute and unconditional victory. The war commenced by an offer of the crown of Bohemia to the Elector Frederick of the Palatinate; the real meaning of the transaction being that he should take the lead in the Protestant cause in Germany. Urged by his own ambition and that of his wife, the noblest and worthiest of the English Stuarts, and by the advice of Maurice of Holland, and the other Protestant leaders, in an evil hour for himself Frederick accepted the position. A single battle, that of Weissberg, fought November 8, 1620, decided his fate. The Palatinate passed into the hands of Maximilian of Bavaria, who divided the country into twenty stations, in which he placed fifty Jesuits. The churches were given into their hands, and the people appeared willing to accept the result. The fine library of Heidelberg was presented to the pope. This defeat of the Protestants was followed up in France, in Switzerland, in the Netherlands, and everywhere the Catholics were victorious.

To add to the exultation with which these triumphs of the faith were viewed in Rome, came news of the progress of the Catholic Church in all quarters of the globe. In South America cathedrals and monasteries and parish churches innumerable were arising. The Indians were full of reverence for the priests. At San Ildefonso, in Mexico, the Jesuits had a college. In Asia the successors of Francis Xavier boasted of the most wonderful results. Three princes of the house of Akbur had been baptised. Not a year passed in China but they claimed to have converted thousands. In Japan they numbered the converts from 1602--1622 at 239,329. Unfortunately, they were converts to Jesuitism rather than Christianity. The Jesuit preachers were literally trappers of souls. They hid their own religion under the forms of heathendom. If they could only catch men, they felt sure of moulding them to their own mind.

BUT "the wicked is snared in the work of his own hands;" the papal power which the Jesuits had laboured to render supreme became the instrument through which all their indefatigable labours were arrested, and an indelible stain fastened on the intelligence of Catholic orthodoxy. In 1623 Urban VIII. ascended the papal throne. His self-importance refused even the counsels of the Sacred College. In his own opinion, he

T

knew better than all the cardinals put together. He was equally contemptuous of the wisdom of his predecessors. "The sentence of a living pope," he said, "is more than all the decrees of the dead ones." As Cardinal Barberini he had been very friendly with the great astronomer, Galileo Galilei. In 1620 he sent Galileo some elegant verses, in which he celebrated his discoveries. "I beg you," he wrote to him, "to receive with favour this insignificant proof of my great affection." It seemed most advantageous for science and for Galileo when this friend of learning took the place of such thorough ecclesiastics as Paul V. and Gregory XV. Notwithstanding the utmost care on his part to walk circumspectly, and to let light into men's eyes by ocular demonstration rather than by any assertions of his own, the astronomer had been drawn into controversy with the Jesuits, and had defended the new system of Copernicus. Unable to answer Galileo, the Aristotelians declared his teaching contrary to Holy Scripture, and he was recommended to the notice of the Inquisition. Having so many friends at Rome, the astronomer thought it best to go there himself, and see what could be done with the Holy Office. The storm was allayed, but the Inquisition declared, "false and absurd philosophically, and formally heretical, the proposition that the sun is the centre of the world, and immovable from its place, and that the second proposition, that the earth is not the centre of the world, and is not immovable, but moves, and that also with a diurnal motion, to deserve the like censure philosophically, and to be at least erroneous in the faith." Galileo was admonished by the great theologian, Bellarmine, that he was not to hold, teach, or defend such doctrines in any way whatever, either verbally or in writing; which injunction he promised to obey.

Things went on quietly for a few years, when a Jesuit father again attacked Galileo. In his reply, which he called *The Assayer*, Galileo took good care that the truth of the Copernican system should be made manifest, although he expressly declared that, as a pious Catholic, he considered it entirely erroneous. He was so encouraged by the success of this book that he ventured another in the same vein. The new work took the form of a discussion between three persons—Salviati, a Copernican; Simplicius, a Ptolemaist; and Sagredo, an intelligent layman desirous to learn. Salviati is made to put the case for Copernicus in so clear and forcible a manner that no one can doubt its scientific truth, especially as care is taken that Simplicius shall bring forward every argument for the Aristotelian theory. Salviati, however, is never allowed to push the victory to a conclusion, but at critical moments always declares that he has not the least desire to maintain its truth, but regards it all as a mere phantasy. This work made an immense sensation; Galileo was delighted, and the Jesuits enraged. However, they were not long in getting the better of the too clever astronomer. They had found out Urban's weak points, and proceeded gradually to open his mind to the evil nature of the book. The Copernican system, they said, not only endangered the dogmas of the Catholic faith in the highest degree, but Galileo, by entering into theological interpretations, had set at nought papal decrees. What, however, seems to have affected the pope's mind most of all was that they managed to induce him to believe that, under the character of Simplicius, the heretical astronomer had dared to satirise his sacred person.

Suddenly Galileo heard that the pope had ordered a special commission at Rome to investigate the whole affair, and that none of his friends were nominated. He begged his sovereign, the Grand Duke, to protect him, and the Tuscan ambassador at Rome did all he possibly could, but he found the pope in a bad humour. "Galileo," said Urban, "had better take care that he was not summoned before the Holy Office; it was a question of the most godless business that could ever be discussed." Unfortunately, the entry in the records of the Inquisition made in 1616, forbidding Galileo to teach, defend, or discuss the incriminated doctrine, was brought to light, and it was clear that the unhappy astronomer would have to answer for his temerity. Summoned to appear in Rome, Galileo took to his bed. The Inquisitor at Florence visited him, and finding him in a state of nervous depression, forwarded a proper medical certificate. The pope was dissatisfied, and threatened to send a commissioner and a physician from Rome to make a trustworthy report of his condition, and if he were in a state to travel to bring him in irons to Rome.

With a heavy heart Galileo got into a litter and went. He was so broken that he determined to make an absolute submission. Put on his trial, he admitted everything; he had erred, he said; he had gone too far. At the second hearing he made a confession, which he thus concluded, "My error, then, has been—and I confess it—one of vainglorious ambition and inadvertence," and he offered to make this confession publicly. He was remanded, and left for a month in a miserable state of anxiety as to his fate. Then he was informed that it was intended under threat of torture to try him as to his intentions. He was now interrogated whether he held or had held, and how long ago, the opinion that the sun is the centre of the world and that the earth is not the centre, and moves and has a diurnal motion. Galileo replied, "That before the injunction of the Holy Congregation of the Index he had been indifferent, and regarded the opinions both of Ptolemy and Copernicus as open to discussion, but after the said decision, assured of the wisdom of the authorities, he ceased to have any doubt," and held, and still held, as most true and indisputable the opinion of Ptolemy, that is to say, the stability of the earth and the motion of the sun. The Inquisitors were not satisfied, and he was pressed again. He again repeated what he had already said, concluding with the words, "I affirm, therefore, on my conscience, that I do not hold the condemned opinion, and have not held it since the decision of the authorities. I am here to obey, and I have not held this opinion since the decision was pronounced, as I have stated." The Copernican heresy was then fully condemned. Galileo was declared vehemently suspected of entertaining it, and was condemned to the formal prison of the Holy Office during pleasure, and to repeat once a week for three years the seven penitential psalms.

As the sixteenth century had opened with a discovery of the extent of the earth, so the seventeenth commenced with revelation after revelation of the infinite extent of the universe. The discovery that our globe was not the centre of creation, but only a small and subordinate province, began to revolutionise men's ideas. Very soon, however, a new and grander order was seen rising in place of the old; a series of important discoveries in various branches of science made it manifest that the whole system of created things was held together by laws to which our earth was subject in common with remote planets and distant stars.

A passion for scientific research had seized Europe, and there were few countries which did not produce some great invention, or in which some discovery did not take place. The German, Kepler, was coeval with Galileo, dying just before the trial in Rome; he discovered the three great astronomical truths known as Kepler's laws. A London physician, William Gilbert, established the magnetic character of the earth, and suggested the idea, since proved correct, that terrestrial magnetism and electricity are emanations of a single force. Another London physician, William Harvey, demonstrated the circulation of the blood; a Frenchman, Descartes, the laws of motion.

In addition to these discoveries of actual natural laws, the task of future research was immensely assisted by a series of great inventions. Jansen, a Dutchman, invented the microscope, and from the same country, probably, came the telescope; both these instruments were vastly improved by Galileo. The thermometer and the barometer were invented, the latter by Torricelli, an Italian; James Napier invented logarithms, and Descartes originated analytical geometry.

But the whole force of this new direction of mind was summed up and elevated into a new philosophy by two of the very greatest among human thinkers: Francis Bacon and René Descartes. Their originality consisted in the clear view they had of the futility of the old methods, and of the necessity of beginning afresh. Bacon, in all his works, went on the principle that to obtain true knowledge hypothesis must be discarded, and nothing trusted but investigation and experience. Descartes, who had been educated by the Jesuits, resolved, on leaving college, to throw aside books, and efface from his mind all that he had ever learnt. He determined that he would hold nothing true until he had ascertained the ground of certitude. The Jesuits were not wrong in telling Urban VIII. that the works of Galileo were more pernicious for the Church than the writings of Luther and Calvin.

Pope Urban not only gave the world the finest argument against "infallibility" it could possibly have had, but he was instrumental in arresting the progress of the great Catholic reaction with which this century opened. Raised to the papal throne through the influence of France, and of a thoroughly secular temper, Urban sought for far more mundane ends than such monarchs as Sigismund of Poland and Frederick of Austria. He wanted to make the Papal States absolutely independent of Austria and Spain, and to this end he carefully maintained his alliance with Cardinal Richelieu, whose policy it was to ruin Austria and Spain, that France might become the leading nation in Europe. To promote this object, Richelieu stirred up and supported the German Protestants in their wars with Ferdinand of Austria; and thus the pope gave most effectual help to the Protestant cause, and helped to defeat the Catholic reaction.

The Emperor Ferdinard was far too good a Catholic to be affected by the political opposition of the pope. He threatened Italy with an invasion headed by his famous general, Wallenstein, who, among his other eccentricities, had, though a convert to Catholicism, a rooted dislike to priests and Jesuits. However, Richelieu sent his *alter ego*, Father Joseph, to the Imperial Diet at Ratisbon, and he and the papal nuncio managed to induce the Catholic electors to pray for a restoration of peace with Italy and the dismissal of Wallenstein. The pressure was so great that the emperor yielded on both points. Meanwhile Richelieu had been intriguing to arouse the German Protestants, and to provide them with a new leader in Gustavus Adolphus, King of Sweden.

Gustavus Adolphus must be placed with William of Orange and Coligny; he was a man strong in faith and in the love of righteousness. His people were wholly at one with him when he proposed to throw himself into the struggle; hardly a Protestant could be found in Europe who did not wish him God-speed. When he bid the Diet farewell, it was as one who had made his life an offering to the cause; the whole assembly were in tears, and he himself could not speak.

He landed in Germany, June 24, 1630, with a force of fifteen thousand men, and soon learnt not only that the emperor had ten times as many troops in the field, but that the German princes refused to co-operate with him. Strong, however, in faith and in the righteousness of his cause, he pushed on. An army of thirty thousand imperialists, under Tilly, advanced to meet him. On his road the Austrian general took and gave up to sack the great and rich city of Magdeburg. The carnage went on for four days; the cruelties inflicted having been rarely equalled in history. The slaughter was calculated at thirty thousand women and children, and even infants were murdered.

On the 7th September, 1631, the two armies met near Leipsic. The battle-cries were, "God with us," and "Jesu-Maria." Before the battle, Gustavus stepped out in advance of the whole army, and kneeling down prayed that God would defend the right. A loud Amen came up from the troops. The struggle was obstinate, the imperialists were at last defeated, and fled on all sides, and Tilly barely escaped. From Saxony and Pomerania, Gustavus marched towards the Rhine. "With the sword in one hand," says Schiller, "and mercy in the other, he traversed Germany as a conqueror, a lawgiver, and a judge, while the keys of towns and fortresses were delivered to him by the inhabitants as to their native sovereign." All places, however, did not open to him so easily. He had to lay siege to several towns in which there were strong Catholic garrisons; but when he took them there was no retaliation for the cruelties practised on the Protestants. It was a principle with Gustavus to spare human blood, be it friend or foe.

All this time Tilly had been following him, and at last Gustavus met him encamped in a strong position. He gave battle, and the imperialists were again defeated, and Tilly killed.

The Emperor Ferdinand now turned to Wallenstein, whom he implored to come to his aid. The general made terms, as if he were himself a king; he must have absolute authority, the sovereignty of all the provinces he conquered, and no peace was to be concluded without his consent. He gathered an enormous army, cleared Bohemia of the Saxons, and marched against Nuremberg. Gustavus, fearing a repetition of the horrors of Magdeburg, threw himself into the city with a small force. At length Wallenstein and Gustavus met at Lützen on the 6th of November, 1632, at the very time of the prosecution of Galileo. Gustavus Adolphus commended, as was his wont, the issue to God. The combatants met, and the Swedes were victorious; but, just as the battle was about to terminate, the king, having heard that his infantry were giving way at a certain point, rushed to the spot, and while he was riding in advance of his troops, and all alone, he was wounded in the arm. He grew faint, and asked to be led to the rear. As he was going an imperialist colonel recognised him, and shot at the king between the shoulders. Gustavus fell from his horse, and was dragged some distance. The horse, however, got loose, and all excepting one aide-de-camp having fled, the dying hero lay at the mercy of the foe. Three horsemen came up, and demanded who he was. "I am the King of Sweden," feebly cried Gustavus. They shot him through the head, and pierced his body with their swords. The retreating Swedes returned; the battle raged over the dead body, so that when it was sought it was with difficulty recognised, covered as it was with mire and torn with wounds.

THE thirty years' war between Catholicism and Protestantism in Germany took in England the form of a struggle between arbitrary power and constitutional liberty. James I., with all his folly, was a philosophic statesman; he had a complete theory of government, founded on principles which were analogous in Church and State. And this system was essentially that of all the Catholic rulers in Europe. England in this century presents, therefore, a microcosm of Europe; the king and his courtiers in Church and State are pursuing the same ends as Richelieu and the Jesuits; the country party, and its leaders, Eliot and Pym, those of Gustavus Adolphus and the Dutch Republicans.

Reverence for the royal authority was a deep-seated sentiment in the English people when James Stuart ascended the throne. But a time had arrived when radical changes were taking place in men's minds, and inquiry was being made into the grounds of things. At this juncture a king ascends the throne, of foreign extraction, and of most undignified appearance and manners, who openly avows the most despotic doctrines. He threatens to harry the Puritan ministers out of the land; he instructs his judges that "as it is atheism and blasphemy to dispute what God can do, so it is presumption and high contempt in a subject to dispute what a king can do, or to say that a king cannot do this or that." He denounces the House of Commons for daring to deal with mysteries of State, and with his own hand tears its protestation out of its Journals. He not only refuses to gratify the natural desire to help the foreign Protestants, but enters on the most detested of all alliances, proposing to marry the heir-apparent to a Spanish Catholic. In one generation James destroyed in England the work of eight hundred years.

The Spanish match having proved a failure, Prince Charles and Buckingham became violently anti-Spanish. In this state of feeling Charles came to the throne, and enjoyed in consequence a brief popularity. But it was soon found that he was in reality a far more dangerous man than his father. With none of James I.'s personal drawbacks, Charles was quite wanting in his natural shrewdness and witty humour.

Soon after the accession of Charles, Buckingham had led an expedition against France, which had miserably failed. The leaders of the country party, determined to enforce the great principle of ministerial responsibility, called him to account. The king came to the duke's rescue. He would not, he told the Commons, permit his servants to be questioned. The House was resolute, and Eliot denounced the favourite in burning words. Charles came down to the House of Lords, declared himself responsible for Buckingham's deeds, and Eliot was committed to the Tower. Parliament was dissolved, its protest burnt, and Charles tried to govern without its help, raising money on his own authority.

To win popularity, Buckingham stirred up the French Huguenots to revolt, the only result being the fall of La Rochelle and the military ruin of French Protestantism. A Parliament was now called; the court candidates were everywhere rejected, and the patriot leaders triumphantly returned. The new House drew up and presented to the king "A Petition of Right," in which, after formally recounting all their grievances, they laid down the principle that no money or tax of any kind could be levied without consent of Parliament. The king returning an evasive reply, the Commons presented "A Remonstrance on the State of the Realm," and denounced Buckingham as the author and source of all its miseries. The animosity of the nation seemed to vent itself in the knife of the fanatic, John Felton, and after Buckingham's assassination he was spoken of no more.

Charles supplied his place by two men of character far more dangerous. Laud, a man of restless energy, considerable learning, and unselfish devotion to his idea of the Church, soon committed his master to an onslaught on the faith of the most earnest men in England—men, moreover, who had the confidence of the nation. To crush the Puritans, he turned the High Commission and the Star Chamber into an English Inquisition. He had the Puritan clergy expelled from their livings; he caused men's noses to be slit and their ears cropped off, and worried and baited the religious portion of the country. On the other hand, he was seen promoting, as far as he possibly could, a Catholic reaction in the Church of England.

Laud's tyranny drove many Puritan families to seek refuge in North America, in the colony founded at Massachusetts by that little band who went forth in 1620 in the *Mayflower*, and who have received the name of "The Pilgrim Fathers." Three thousand emigrants left England in one year, and this was just about the time that Gustavus Adolphus was pursuing his splendid career. Thus, instead of Protestant England helping the cause which had been nearest her heart for almost a century, she saw her best children driven to seek shelter across the Atlantic.

But Laud was not equal to the task of forcing despotism on an unwilling nation. Charles, therefore, was glad to accept the offer of an apostate from the country party—Sir Thomas Wentworth. The very opposite of the archbishop, Wentworth worked primarily for himself. His mind was powerful and capacious ; he was troubled by no scruples ; the name he gave his policy was "Thorough." He left Laud in England, while he commenced in Ireland, by a system of corruption and terrorism, to prepare in that unhappy country the means to overthrow English liberty. When he had sufficiently "educated" the Irish, he summoned a parliament, who voted the means of maintaining an army of five thousand foot and five hundred horse.

Laud found more congenial work in attempting to extend to Scotland his efforts to Catholicise the Church of England. This work was no freak of the restless archbishop. It was only a portion of a determined and pertinacious attempt, extending over half a century, to enforce prelacy on "the Kirk." "No bishop, no king," had been a favourite maxim with James 1. ; and he had never rested until he had induced an assembly of the Scottish Church to receive some bishops. Three were consecrated at Westminster, and returned to Scotland to consecrate the rest. After this, Laud succeeded in getting another assembly to accept the rites and ceremonies of the Church of England ; however, these changes had been so utterly opposed to the wishes of the people, that they had made no actual way. But Charles had determined on "Thorough" in the three kingdoms. He began by proposing to the Scottish Parliament to regulate vestments, and to introduce a prayer-book that Laud had arranged. The new liturgy was appointed to be used in the churches on the 23rd of July, 1637. But when the day came, Janet Geddes' protest sent dean and bishop flying from the High Church at Edinburgh, and the whole country was boiling over with indignation. The excitement was immense. Charles and Laud, however, remained obstinate; they were determined the Scotch should have a prayer-book, and that all opposition should be treated as treason.

Meanwhile, "Thorough" was commenced in England. In times when no permanent fleets existed, the port towns had been compelled to furnish ships for the king's use, and the maritime counties to supply their equipment. This obsolete custom was now revived, and it was determined to make it extend all over the country; the Earl of Strafford, as Wentworth was now called, arguing that, if this tax for raising a fleet were once recognised, it would be easy to levy one for raising an army.

John Hampden, a leader in the country party, saw how much was at stake, and resolved to resist the payment of this ship-money. He was put on his trial in November, 1637. The case was argued, and all the judges except two decided in favour of the king.

The Hampden judgment emboldened Charles to sterner measures with the Scots. All the winter negotiations had been going on; now arrived proclamations requiring instant obedience. Wherever the king's proclamation was made a protest immediately followed; and it was determined that one held at Edinburgh should be on a national scale. A fast was appointed; the people gathered together at Greyfriars Church; the Covenant was read, and hundreds pressed forward to sign it, and with uplifted hands, and tears falling down their faces, swore to observe its conditions. Such was the enthusiasm that some subscribed with their blood, and the whole nation felt prepared to die in defence of their national covenant.

The Council wrote to England pressing the king to give satisfaction to the people. "I will rather die," Charles wrote to the Royal Commissioner, "than yield to these impertinent and damnable demands." But to gain time he was willing to appear to do so; but in a short time the concessions were all withdrawn, and the Scottish people learnt that the king was not only gathering an army in Yorkshire, but reckoned on the support of the Highlanders. The Scots immediately took possession of Edinburgh and several of their chief towns, and marched across the border.

Charles now summoned a Parliament in London, hoping that national prejudice would work in his favour. The new Parliament took no heed of the war with Scotland, but began at once to consider its own grievances, declaring that their redress must precede all supplies. In three weeks it was dissolved. The king, in fact, very soon found that the English nation was in almost as complete a state of revolt as the Scotch. The war was denounced as "the bishops' war," the very soldiers mutinied, murdered the officers they suspected of papistry, broke the altar rails of the churches they passed on their march, and deserted to their homes. In despair, Charles was driven to summon the Houses again at Westminster.

The resolute looks of the members as they gathered foreboded a severe reckoning for the ministers who had brought the country to such a pass. One by one all the illegal acts were annulled. Laud was sent to the Tower, and Strafford impeached for high treason. When the trial of the latter commenced, the whole of the Commons appeared in support of the charges. When it seemed as if the impeachment might fail, they at once resorted to a Bill of Attainder. The Lords passed the Bill, and in three days Charles gave his assent. Strafford met his doom amidst the unrepressed joy of a whole people. Couriers ran through every town, waving their hands, and crying, "His head is off! His head is off!"

The people now had lost all trust in the king; they believed him capable of any treachery. Even the moderate party advocated a Bill by which it was provided that the Parliament then sitting should only be dissolved by its own consent. The king went to Scotland, and strove to win back the allegiance of the people. Suddenly the news arrived of a terrible insurrection in Ireland—the rebound of Strafford's reign of terror. Fifty thousand Englishmen perished in a few days, and the most dreadful tales of horror and outrage were told all over the country. A kind of panic seized men; it was believed that there was a great plot at work for a counter-revolution, and the House of Commons passed a Remonstrance to the king.

While they were engaged in debating, the king returned from Scotland, and events precipitated themselves with extraordinary rapidity. Episcopacy was very unpopular in England as well as in Scotland, and there was a very general feeling against the bishops sitting in Parliament. They were hooted and hustled as they went to and from the House of Lords. They became alarmed, and joined in a protestation to the king, in which they declared that they should cease to attend the House until they were effectually secured from such affronts, and that all that was done in their absence would be null and of no effect. Half an hour after this protestation was known, the twelve bishops were impeached, and ten sent to the Tower.

The king now determined on an act which proved the most fatal he had yet attempted. The Attorney-General appeared at the bar of the House of Lords, and impeached Hampden, Pym, Hollis, Strode, and Haslerig of high treason, in having held correspondence with the Scots. The king's sergeant appeared at the bar of the Commons and demanded their surrender. The House sent a deputation to the king to say that the accused would be ready to answer any legal charge. This was on the 3rd of January, 1642. That night was a busy one at Whitehall. What really occurred is doubtful, but the five members had an intimation that they would be forcibly arrested next day in the House, and that by the king himself. After meeting in the morning, and making some defensive speeches, the news arrived that the king had actually set out, and was approaching with some four hundred armed gentlemen and soldiers. The House immediately ordered the five members to retire, which they did, and shooting down the river in a barge, they took refuge in the City. The king, leaving his guard outside, entered the House, accompanied only by the Elector Palatinate. The members uncovered and stood up. The king went up the centre, and said, "Mr. Speaker, I must for a time make bold with your chair." Then standing on the step of the chair, he looked a long while about, and then began to make a speech. After declaring his good intentions, he said that he had come to know if any of the accused persons were there. A dead silence followed. "I must have them," said the king, "wheresoever I find them." No answer. "Is Mr. Pym here?" Another dead silence; then the king, turning to the Speaker, asked him whether the five members were there. Lenthall dropped on his knees, and replied that he had neither eyes nor tongue to see or say anything but what the House commanded. Charles felt himself in a wrong position, and said, "Well, well, 'tis no matter; I think my eyes are as good as another." "I see," he said at last, "that my birds are flown; but I do expect you will send them to me; if you do not, I must seek them myself." And so, looking a great deal more discontented and angry than when he came, this badly-advised, unfortunate king left the House, sundry cries of "Privilege! privilege!" being ejaculated as he receded from view.

The king then tried to win the City, but failed; the Commons, on the contrary, being welcomed when they determined a Committee of the House should sit within its precincts. Events proceeded rapidly; the Committee went the length of appointing a guard to watch over the Tower, and still further a small army to take care of the king, the kingdom, and the Parliament. Hampden told the House that thousands were coming up from Buckinghamshire with a petition, in which they declared their readiness to live and die with the Parliament, and in defence of the rights of the House of Commons.

A week had only passed since the great attempt; all had failed, and the king made up his mind to leave London. The next day the five members came back to Westminster in triumph. The king was thoroughly beaten, and had no resource but to submit, or go to war with his people. He chose the latter alternative; and thus began the struggle that closed so tragically on the wintry morning of January 30th, 1649.

BANQUETING HOUSE, WHITEHALL. (*From an old Print.*)

SEVENTEENTH CENTURY.

Section II.

CONTEMPORARY EVENTS IN THE SEVENTEENTH CENTURY.

America.— Penn's treaty with the Indians.
France. The Dragonnades.
Austria.— The relief of Vienna.
England.— Landing of William of Orange.

Seventeenth Century.

SECTION II.

A.D. 1680-1688.

Political Results of the Reformation and Catholic Reaction in France and England—The French Autocracy—Protestantism to be Exterminated—The Dragonnades—Gallicanism —Revocation of the Edict of Nantes—The Restoration in England—James II.— William of Orange—The Revolution—The Turks besiege Vienna—John Sobieski— William Penn—His Treaty with the Indians—Founding of Pennsylvania.

BY their fruits ye shall know them. This simple rule is a better guide to truth than all the disputations of logicians or all the arguments of theologians. And where can be found material so abundant or teaching so safe as in the stream of history, looked at from many points of view?

The latter portion of the seventeenth century affords an opportunity of testing the nature of the two tendencies which commenced in Europe with the Reformation and the Catholic reaction. The histories of England and France are singularly linked; the same struggle is going on in each at the same time, but with what different results! In the former we see the effort to establish arbitrary power finally defeated; in the latter we see it completely triumphant.

MONARCHY in France had been growing with the ages, but it would never have succeeded in making itself absolute, had not the Catholic reaction worked so assiduously to establish the principle of passive obedience, and to destroy all who held the contrary opinion. Nothing tended more to strengthen the monarchy in France than the final defeat of the Huguenots. Henceforth the spirit of servility grew apace. The French nobility, once so independent, became the most abject of courtiers, while the French clergy grovelled before the king. Louis XIV. summed up his own idea of his power in the famous aphorism, "I and the State are one."

About two years before the peace of Nimeguen, he began to feel some remorse for the public scandals of his life, and to be anxious to make atonement. It accorded both with his religious prejudices and his despotic policy to consider the conversion of the Huguenots the best expiation that he could make. He gave himself to the work with his usual energy, his efforts being seconded by those about him, directly they found that religious bigotry was the high-road to favour. But it is clear that he had public opinion with him, otherwise it would not have been possible for a persecution, as widespread as it was atrocious, to have occurred in a country which, in literature and art, gave the law to Europe. This almost universal consent to inhuman atrocities at a time when, to use scholastic cant, "the humanities" were cultivated to such a pitch of refinement, is a proof of the degradation the Catholic reaction had wrought in the national conscience; and this debasement is still further seen in the methods used to convert the unfortunate Huguenots.

One of the earliest was barefaced bribery. A kind of banking-house was opened, under the direction of an apostate named Pellisson, and conversions were bought at so much a head. But it was soon found that converts of this kind were in the habit of being converted several times over; very severe laws were accordingly promulgated against relapsed heretics. As bribery worked so badly, the converters fell back on the old method of terrorising. Governors and officials of all kinds, military and legal, understanding that the king had determined to root out the Huguenots, were seized with a sudden ardour for the work of conversion. Everyone wished to show his zeal by sending up to the Privy Council a list of abjurations, of Protestant services stopped, and temples destroyed. The populace took their cue from authority, and here and there made attacks on the temples.

Gradually the net was tightened, the ordinances growing more and more severe. The Protestants were forbidden to exercise any of the following callings: councillors, judges, consuls, magistrates, advocates, notaries, doctors, apothecaries, publishers, printers. They were not to be employed in the treasury or the post-office, or to be members of the corporations. They were not to be allowed to intermarry with Catholics; they were not to have Catholic valets, lest they should seduce them; then they were to have none but Catholic servants, because the latter were wanted as spies. Protestants were not permitted to send children under sixteen years of age out of the country; but children over seven who wished to become Catholics could go where they pleased. Converts need not pay their debts for three years, and were exempted from taxation, and from having soldiers billeted on them for two years. Medical men were bound to inform the authorities of any Protestants who were near death, in order that they might be visited and induced to abjure. Pastors might not speak of these grievances, and every means was taken to prevent a continuation of the Protestant worship.

The next step was to introduce the military. A regiment of cavalry was sent into Poitou in 1681, and by command of the king the greater number were to be quartered on the Protestants; where there ought to have been ten, twenty were to be sent. The troops were to march as in an enemy's country, demanding the arrears of the taxes. They were to lodge in the houses of the obstinate Protestants, and were permitted, by any means short of killing them, to worry them into abjuration. The horse soldiers put crosses on the ends of their muskets, and if the people refused to kiss them, they forced them against their faces or their stomachs. They spared neither the young nor the old, but beat them sometimes with the flat side of their swords, sometimes with the butt ends of their muskets, and this they did with so much violence that some remained lame for life. They were especially cruel to the women, striking them with whips or with a cane across the face; sometimes they dragged them by their hair through the mud or over the stones. Terror seized the unhappy people, and along the shores numbers of men, women, and children, trembling and half dead, were to be seen hiding among the rocks until some vessel approached to convey them to another land. The Government grew alarmed, and adopted fresh severities to prevent this emigration.

The bishops now threatened the Huguenots with troubles incomparably more appalling than any they had yet suffered. For the "Grande Monarque" was so set upon accomplishing his pious work that he told the Marquis de Ruvigny that to bring back all his subjects into Catholic unity he would give one of his arms, or with one hand cut off the other. The men, therefore, who had just affirmed the four celebrated Gallican articles, and who, according to Condé, would have followed Louis if he had become a Protestant, were just as ready to follow and abet him in the most atrocious tyranny.

In the south of France, an effort having been made to renew the suppressed worship, Louvois immediately ordered his troops to march against those who, under the shadow of the Edict of Nantes, had met to read the Bible and pray. He tracked them to the woods, and killed them by hundreds; those made prisoners had to choose between abjuration and death. Driven to despair, the populations of the Vivarais and the Dauphiny defended themselves with arms. Louvois deluded them with an amnesty. All the ministers were excepted, as well as fifty other persons; and one aged pastor was broken on the wheel. Two years later, the Gallican clergy, in their general assembly, complimented the king on his admirable success in the extirpation of heresy. One bishop said the conversion of the Protestants had taken place without violence and without arms; in fact, their way back to the Catholic Church had been strewn with flowers.

But Rome did not endorse this obsequious intolerance. Innocent XI. said, "It was not of such methods that Christ availed himself. Men must be led to the temple, not dragged into it." Although a pope of exceptional virtue and enlightenment, it may well be doubted if he would have entertained so evangelical a sentiment, had not Louis given him a great deal more anxiety than all the heretics in Europe put together. For the King of France was bent on making himself as absolute in the Church as in the State, and to this end renewed and extended all the claims made by his predecessors with reference to the right of regalia, or royal prerogative to interfere in ecclesiastical things.

In 1682 Louis convoked an Assembly of the clergy of France, and obtained from them the celebrated declaration of the four articles which have ever since been the foundation of Gallicanism. The first asserted that princes were not subject in temporal things to any ecclesiastical authority, nor could they be deposed, or their subjects released from allegiance by the power of the keys; the second affirmed that the authority of a General Council was superior to that of the pope; the third, that the power of the pope is restricted by the canons of the Universal Church, and in France by the rules, customs, and institutions of the Gallican Church; and the fourth declared that the judgment of the pope is not irreformable unless it shall have been confirmed by the judgment of the entire Church. The authorship of these articles is attributed to Bossuet, who exerted his eloquence in their defence.

In reply, the pope refused to institute the bishops appointed by the king, the quarrel going on until there were as many as thirty-five bishops in France who could not exercise a single spiritual function. In order to bring Innocent to terms, Louis occupied the papal territory of Avignon, and it was believed had formed the design of making the Archbishop of Paris Patriarch of France.

A schism with Rome was thus imminent in the Gallican Church, and it was this position of affairs which no doubt rendered both the king and the clergy doubly anxious to prove their orthodoxy by greater zeal than ever in persecuting the Huguenots.

But this necessitated a further progress in cruelty. In 1685 it was determined to effect the conversion of the Bearnese, and the dragoons entered the houses of the Reformed with drawn swords, crying, " Kill, kill!" They seized the unfortunate inhabitants, and tortured them by not permitting them to sleep; they suspended them with cords, they blew tobacco into their noses, they pinched, pricked, and by every possible petty and miserable persecution harassed and worried their prey. The women were subjected to even more atrocious indignities. This treatment was effectual; out of twenty-five thousand, only one thousand remained steadfast, the rest abjured. The clergy celebrated their triumph by a grand mass, and a procession, in which the Parliament of Bearn took part, and in which the newly-converted had to march as captives taken in war. This success encouraged the authorities, and dragonnades went on in Languedoc, Guienne, Saintonge, Aunis, Poitou, the Vivarais, the Dauphiny, the Cevennes, Provence, and the county of Gex. Later on they were continued in the centre and in the north of France. Of those who resisted, the men were thrown into prison, the women sent to convents, and the children forced to abjure. At last terror had so completely done its work that it was enough only to threaten a dragonnade for a population to abjure *en masse*. The converters were able to look forward to the speedy completion of their apostolic labours.

The time now seemed to have arrived to put the legal crown on the work by the Revocation of the Edict of Nantes, which was signed by Louis XIV. on the 18th of October, 1685. By this act the Protestant religion became illegal in France, and all its ministers had to quit the kingdom in a fortnight, unless they chose to be converted, in which case they were to have every possible encouragement. Parents were to have their children instructed in Roman Catholic doctrine, and baptised, under a heavy fine. Emigration was punishable with the galleys for men, while seclusion for life was to be the fate of the women.

Notwithstanding these terrors, the people fled in all directions. Within a year after the Revocation France lost one hundred thousand of her people, not to speak of those who had gone earlier; nine thousand sailors, twelve thousand soldiers, six hundred officers, immense sums of money, and her most flourishing manufactures. Every branch of commerce was ruined, and a fourth part of the country depopulated.

These cruelties were no exceptional acts. They are simply the most flagrant instance of the Ludovican despotism. Before the spirit of Catholicism proceeded to the destruction of its opponents, it had consolidated its own strength, by stamping out every internal influence that might have made it hesitate. Thus in 1660 Louis suppressed the famous society at Port Royal, destroying the school in which Racine had been educated, and dissipating the great and powerful community of Jansenists. Despotism ran through and affected every department of the government and the whole organisation of society. It even controlled the law, the king withdrawing by *lettres de cachet* offenders from its jurisdiction, and imprisoning them at pleasure. Nine thousand such letters were issued during his reign, the most notorious sufferer being the mysterious person known as "the man with the iron mask."

It is extremely suggestive to note that the steps by which this tyranny was established synchronise very nearly with the same effort in our own land, which there can be little doubt would have succeeded, had England, like France, refused and suppressed the Reformation. Richelieu, Mazarin, and Louis play the parts of James and Charles, Laud and Strafford; the great Condé that of Cromwell. In each case the Parliament opposes the arbitrary proceedings of the court, and the contentions turned on fiscal questions. In each case the citizens of London and Paris support the Parliaments, the courts fly, civil wars ensue. Then the great leaders appear on the scene, but with what different results! Condé, a man of war from his youth, is defeated; Cromwell, who had reached middle life before he became a soldier, is triumphant. In the one case all the real opposition and all the great leaders come from the House of Commons; in the other, they come from the *faction des importants*, the powerful classes, headed by the princes of the blood. Without a party at their back, ready to die for God and the liberties of the country, they sink into a mere turbulent faction, which France is not sorry to see suppressed.

Worn out with internal strife, more than ever imbued with mystic ideas concerning the royal authority, the French people yielded themselves to a despotism which assured them peace at home and glory abroad, enlarged their territory, and gave them an opportunity of developing a genius hitherto kept in abeyance by civil contention. After the death of Cromwell, a like temptation presented itself to England; that it escaped the snare must again be attributed to its Protestantism.

"THE worst revolution," some wise man has said, "is a restoration;" and this all will now allow was the character of that brought about by the intrigues of General Monk in 1660. The ideas which had conquered and which had triumphed in the civil war and during the Commonwealth appeared conquered; and for a few years their ancient enemies verily believed that to them the victory belonged. Hence followed the execution of the late king's judges, the Test and Corporation Acts, the Act of Uniformity, the Conventicle Act, the Five Mile Act; a series of laws of the same nature and springing from the same spirit as that which directed the persecutions of the Huguenots in France. Under these laws Richard

Baxter and two thousand of the most pious of the English clergy were driven out of their cures. John Bunyan and many other Nonconformists languished in prison; and of one of their smallest sects, the Society of Friends, fifteen hundred were in gaol at the same time. Sir Harry Vane and other great Englishmen, in the presence of Charles II., suffered the mediæval atrocities of being hung, drawn, and quartered; and the corpse of Oliver Cromwell was dug up from its grave and hanged at Tyburn. As if these acts were not disgraceful enough to England, the period is pilloried in history by the following significant facts:—Dunkirk sold to the French; the Dutch fleet riding triumphantly in the Medway; the plague in London; the metropolis almost destroyed by fire; the Titus Oates' Plot; the king and court the most immoral ever known in England; the head of the Church and State the pensioner of the greatest despot of the time, and himself a secret Roman Catholic.

All this could not have occurred unless the royal authority had had a deep hold on the faith of the mass of the English nation. When Charles II. was dying, the people flocked to church, and groaned and sobbed as the prayer for the king was read; and Lord Macaulay asserts that there was not a housemaid in London who did not find a piece of crape to put on her bonnet when he was dead.

Meanwhile, the cultured classes in England were becoming convinced of certain great political truths. Although the doctrines of Hobbes and of Locke tended in opposite directions, they were alike in bringing all political ideas to the test of reason. The arguments of Hobbes ended in an absolute, those of Locke in a limited, monarchy; but they both agreed that the origin of all power was in the people, and, to whomsoever delegated, ought to be used for the benefit of the people. With Locke, the power never really departed from the people, who had a right to withdraw it when it was abused by the prince. While these doctrines permeated the minds of the philosophic few, a large class throughout the country preserved the Calvinistic tradition in religion and politics.

Over a nation holding these principles, the least gifted of the Stuarts came to reign. James II. ascended the throne with one fixed idea. He was determined that his religion should at least be tolerated in England. To this end he sacrificed his crown; so that, if Charles I. was a martyr for Anglicanism, James II. was a martyr for Romanism. But he was not allowed to reign without a protest, both in England and Scotland. Monmouth in the south, Argyle in the north, paid the penalty of non-success with their heads; the Bloody Assize in the West of England gave the country an impression of the horrors in store if ruled by Catholic kings. Yet, such was the reverence for the crown, that James came out of these insurrections as completely triumphant as his brother after the Rye House Plot. Whiggery seemed completely crushed, and had James preferred his crown to his religion, he might have had a good chance of establishing a Hobbist absolutism supported by Anglican mysticism. But, happily for England, he was too sincere a Catholic and too dull a man to play so fine a game. He openly surrounded himself with Catholics and Jesuits, quarrelled with the Church of England, and even tried to oppress it, absurdly supposing that in so doing he might reckon on the help of the Dissenters. Poor king! he comprehended but dimly the principles which actuated this part of the nation; in offending Tories and High Churchmen he lost the only men who would have struck a blow for his prerogative.

Louis XIV., who maintained the Richelieu policy of keeping up division abroad while he enforced unity at home, did his utmost to induce James to be moderate. He gave material help to the leaders of the opposition, so that James might be coerced into reasonableness, and as he also allowed the King of England a pension, he had the right to give him good advice. Spain and the pope were also anxious that James should be on good terms with his people, since their interests now lay with the policy of a Protestant England rather than with that of a Catholic king. For the whole of Europe dreaded the overbearing French despot. Catholic Spain had suffered more than any country from his rapacity, and, notwithstanding his persecutions of the Protestants, he was far from being a papist. Thus Spain and the pope had actually come to be friendly towards so heretical a State as the United Provinces, and to wish their great stadtholder, William of Orange, God-speed in his struggle against the eldest son of the Church.

The Prince of Orange, like his great predecessor, William the Silent, was a Calvinist, and, like him, he combined personal courage and an apparent recklessness of his own life with the utmost prudence in counsel and the conduct of affairs. Of the most feeble constitution, perpetually ill, suffering from terrible headaches, he was animated by a restless energy; and, having noble ends in view, his career was fruitful of blessing to his own land, and still more to ours. The prince viewed the progress of events in England with interest, for his wife would be Queen of the British Isles at the decease of James. Then he would have the vantage-ground he had so long sought against Louis. Suddenly the news reached the Hague that the Queen of England had given birth to a son. On the first impulse congratulations were sent; but very shortly arrived assurances from all kinds of authorities in England that the birth was a great fraud, that, in fact, an infant had been surreptitiously introduced into the palace, in order to defeat the hopes of Protestant England.

It was felt that the moment had arrived on which the future of England depended. If the country allowed itself to drift on under King James, its fate was sealed. A race of Catholic monarchs would sit on the throne, and all would be lost. Men of all parties began to enter into negotiation with the Prince of Orange : bishops and Presbyterian divines, peers of the realm, and members of the House of Commons ; the conspirators were so numerous that only a man so obtuse as James, and so utterly out of harmony with the whole country, could have remained blind to what was going on. The Prince of Orange, however, had great difficulties to overcome. He could do nothing unless the States of Amsterdam agreed, and Amsterdam was his hereditary foe. Happily, Louis helped him, first by his cruel persecutions of the Huguenots, who came flying into Amsterdam, filling the city with their complaints; and secondly, by his restrictions on the Dutch trade. The stadtholder's own means were small, but immense sums of money came from England, and a great number of Englishmen and Scotchmen flocked to his support.

On the 19th of October, 1688, the Prince of Orange sailed from Helvoetsluys ; but ere the armament had got half across the North Sea, a west wind arose, and blew it back on to the Dutch coast. It had to wait until the 1st of November before it could put to sea again. Meanwhile, the news had reached King James. He was in dismay. The descent, he imagined, would take place somewhere in Yorkshire, and he sent troops to the north; the Dutch fleet, however, made for the Channel. The gale which carried them on prevented the English fleet from coming out of the Thames. At night the Channel seemed all ablaze from the lights of the scudding vessels. It passed the Isle of Wight on Sunday ; it was in full career for Torbay, where William intended to debark. But the next morning was hazy, and the pilot allowed the fleet to go too far. The consternation was great, for Plymouth was in the hands of a friend of the king. "You may go to prayers, Doctor," exclaimed Edward Russell to Burnet; "all is over." Suddenly the wind shifted, a soft breeze sprang up from the south, the mist dispersed, the fleet veered round, and ran safely into Torbay. "Well, Doctor, what do you think of predestination now?" the prince gaily exclaimed, as the impulsive Burnet rushed up to congratulate him on the success of the enterprise. The people ran to the shore; the British regiments were the first to land. William soon followed, and to this day may be seen the piece of English rock on which he planted his foot as he stepped from his boat.

The delivering army marching through the clay of the Devonshire roads seemed like a force raised by humanity itself to protect the chosen seat of freedom. In its ranks were not only Englishmen, Scotchmen, and Dutchmen, but Frenchmen, Swedes, and Switzers. And not only were the representatives of every European nation that cared to strike a blow for civil and religious liberty there, but, with a prophetic glance at a far-off future, the spirit of freedom had mingled among her defenders not less than two hundred negroes, their swarthy features set off with embroidered turbans and white feathers. All eyes were turned towards the prince himself, who, on a white charger, and wearing a plume of white feathers, rode stern and sad. For a moment a smile of satisfaction played on his grave features, when an aged woman, making her way fearlessly among foreign soldiers and careering steeds, touched the deliverer's hand, exclaiming that now at last she was happy.

At the news of William's approach confusion reigned in London. The king wasted time in trying to find out if he were really deserted by the bishops and the nobility. He had an army at Salisbury, but the news came that its leader had joined the invading army. The king set off himself for Salisbury, but only to hear at every step of increasing opposition and fresh desertions. The whole country was rising, and everywhere the insurrection was headed by some great nobleman. Devonshire had left Chatsworth, and had appeared in arms at Derby, Danby in Yorkshire, Delamere in Cheshire; Bath had offered to give up Plymouth. The most inveterate Tories were deserting; but what struck James most of all was the treachery of his private friends and of his own family. None of them uttered a word to him of danger, they ate and drank at his table, they heard all his plans, and undertook to execute them. But, one after the other, they slunk away from their master, their patron, and their father, and were soon seen riding among the victors.

A stronger man than James might, under such circumstances, have betrayed faint-heartedness and depression; none could have acted more foolishly. Petulant with his best advisers, he deceived them all, first by despatching his queen and the heir-apparent to the Continent, and then by suddenly and ignominiously taking flight himself. But all was ordered well; without such a series of terrible blows, blows all administered by the hands of the anointed himself, the belief in Divine right would have lingered on another century, and the English monarchy would have disappeared in the terrible storm reserved for the land then basking in the glowing sunshine of the Ludovican despotism.

CONTEMPORANEOUSLY with the great danger which threatened European liberty during the reigns of the later Stuarts, European independence and the existence of Christendom were threatened by the overwhelming advance of the Turkish power in the East. The Emperor of Germany, Leopold I., had, by flagrantly violating the privileges of his Hungarian subjects, provoked a revolt, and its leaders called in the Turks. Mohammed IV. determined to push this advantage to the utmost point, and prepared to invade Austria on a scale and in a manner more formidable than had ever been known. Vienna having been the residence of so many successive emperors, had become a kind of modern Rome; and its capture would be the conquest of Western Europe, and an augury of the fate of Christendom. Unfortunately, its defences were very weak, and two-thirds of its inhabitants lived in the suburbs. A Turkish army, consisting of three hundred thousand men, with three hundred cannon, now appeared in the great plain to the south of the city; and the governor of Vienna, who had only a garrison of eleven thousand men, was compelled to burn all the city outside the walls. The emperor and his family fled, and in his distress he turned to the only man in Western Europe who inspired absolute confidence, John Sobieski, the King of Poland.

Sobieski was descended from a brave and martial race, and had obtained the throne by force of merit. Seeing the immense danger, he made great efforts to come at once to the relief of the beleaguered city. Knowing the power of his name among the Tartars and the Turks, he separated himself from the main body of his army, and, pushing through a country invested by the enemy, arrived at a small town about five leagues from Vienna. Here he collected his troops, and urged upon them on all occasions to prefer expedition to caution. The army had to cross the hills; and when they arrived at the last, they beheld the plain between them and the city covered with tents, and an immense multitude of soldiers and horses and camels. As to Vienna, the smoke of the cannonading completely obscured all but the tops of the steeples.

At sunrise the Christian army descended from the hills, preceded by its cannon, and stopping at every thirty or forty paces to fire. The Turks were in great commotion, and all the more when, seeing the streamers belonging to the Polish horse-guards, the news flew through the camp that Sobieski had come. The vizier had all the prisoners put to death, and ordered a general assault. However, the infantry of the Christian army rushed forward with such impetuosity that they broke the Turkish lines and made way for the cavalry. About noon the king's brother got possession of some rising ground, and took the Turks in the flank. Sobieski himself now took the lead, and the Polish troops charged. The Cham fled, the bashaws were in despair, the vizier was nowhere to be seen, the consternation was general; had night been farther off, the rout would have been complete.

Next morning the Turkish camp was opened, and to their horror the Poles found that the Turks had butchered all their women. Five or six hundred infants were found alive; the booty was enormous. Sobieski wrote to his queen that he had found in the vizier's tent several millions of ducats. He was welcomed into Vienna by demonstrations of affection scarcely ever equalled. The people prostrated themselves before him, kissed his feet, called him father, saviour, the greatest of princes, and conducted him to the cathedral with shouts of joy. When he arrived there he ordered the crescent, which had been placed there as the condition upon which Soliman had formerly raised the siege of Vienna, to be taken down, and trodden under foot. Then he himself commenced the *Te Deum*.

after which a sermon was preached from the text, "There was a man sent from God, whose name was John."

The year before Christendom was finally secured from Mohammedanism, and six years before England was finally secured from despotism, the foundations of a new State were laid in the Far West on the purest principles ever attempted with practical success. The memory of William Penn has been assailed on the ground of his friendship with the Stuarts, and especially with James II. That friendship—the only fact in the charges brought against him that remains proven—is easily understood, if we recollect the old adage, "Extremes meet." James Stuart and William Penn were as far asunder in their characters and their ideas as the two poles, but they were one in the fact that neither of them belonged to the age in which their lot was cast. William Penn was as much in advance as James Stuart was behind the seventeenth century.

Living in a land where he found himself in constant antagonism to the prevailing ideas, and possessing wealth and energy, it was not strange that Penn should look, as so many other Nonconformists had done, to the new continent of America, as virgin soil in which he might plant a society according to his own conception of truth. He had inherited from his father a claim on the government for sixteen thousand pounds. He bartered it for a grant of land in North America. All, however, that he considered purchased was the right of undisturbed colonisation; the actual soil he regarded as belonging to the natives; and any society that might grow up in Pennsylvania he intended should be a free one, and governed by its own laws.

How far in advance of the most liberal ideas of the age was this "enthusiast" may be seen by comparing the constitution which he gave Pennsylvania with that which Locke drew up for the Carolinas. Locke not only perpetuated distinctions of rank, but, to protect the rights of property, placed the legislature in the hands of the great proprietors. Penn, on the other hand, abolished primogeniture, placed the legislative authority in the hands of the people, and provided for annual elections by means of the ballot. The Palatines of South Carolina voted to render

Locke's constitution unalterable; Penn left it free to future generations to subvert or change his plan of government.

In his preface to the Pennsylvanian Constitution, the founder proves the right of government from the New Testament, and shows that its end is not merely the putting down of evil, but that the government of a State is as capable of kindness, goodness, and charity as that of any private society. If the leading provisions of his Constitution are read, it will be found that they embrace nearly all the great reforms, civil and religious, which have since been adopted in England, while the few that remain unrecognised in our laws are felt desirable by many who are not of Penn's persuasion. He was more especially in advance of his age in the wide and liberal toleration in religious matters which distinguished him from all but the most advanced thinkers and statesmen in his day. "All believers in one Almighty God to be permitted to enjoy their own persuasion or practice in matters of faith and worship, and not to be compelled to frequent or maintain any religious worship or ministry whatever." In England only men like William III., John Locke, and a few other latitudinarians, would have dared to advocate such a view; yet in process of time it has come to be a fundamental principle of English law, which no party would wish to see disturbed.

It was, however, in the way William Penn treated the Indians that he obtained his greatest fame. He placed his dealings with them on the only right ground—the common faith in a Great Spirit and a common Father. When he arrived in the country, he determined to form with them a league of amity. The place chosen was a spot on the river Delaware, upon which from time immemorial the tribes had been accustomed to gather, and which they called, "The Meeting-place of Kings."

On one of those fine autumnal days which come in America just before the winter sets in, when the fallen leaves make a brilliant carpeting, around a fire which crackled and flickered in the breeze, a great assembly of unarmed Indians were gathered, waiting the arrival of the white man who had written them such good words. A barge shoots up to the bank, the governor lands—a man not forty years of age, athletic in figure, active in his movements, and graceful in his manner. A sash of blue netted silk fastened round his waist marks him out from those who are with him. As the party approach the elm tree which overshadows the council fire, Tamineud, the great Sachem of the tribe, places in his chaplet a small horn, the emblem of his kingly authority. Penn speaks of the Great Spirit, their common Maker, who knows men's innermost thoughts, assuring them that his object is not to do them injury, and thus provoke the Great Spirit, but to do them good. They have met, he says, on the broad pathway of good faith and goodwill, so that no advantage is to be taken on either side, but all is to be openness, and brotherhood, and love. He then unrolls the treaty, and it is explained article by article. When he has concluded, the Indian orator rises, and, taking Penn by the hand, makes a speech, pledging kindness and good neighbourhood. "The Indians and the English must," he declares, "live in love as long as the sun and the moon shall endure."

This treaty between William Penn and the Indians, Voltaire describes as "the only one between those nations and the Christians which was never sworn to, and never broken." If the despotism of Louis XIV. had its root in Catholic mysticism and the Jesuit principle of passive obedience; if Calvinism is responsible for the polity of the United Provinces, then the constitution upon which Pennsylvania was founded and has developed must be attributed to the religious principles held by William Penn. "By their fruits ye shall know them."

EIGHTEENTH CENTURY.

Section I.

CONTEMPORARY EVENTS IN THE EIGHTEENTH CENTURY.

America.—Franklin experimenting on the lightning.
England.—John Wesley preaching at Gwennap Pitt.
Prussia.—Frederick the Great at Leuthen.
Portugal.—The earthquake at Lisbon.

EIGHTEENTH CENTURY.

SECTION I.

A.D. 1752-1762.

Earthquake at Lisbon—Progress of Science in Europe—Franklin's Discoveries in Electricity—Influence of French Literature—The Philosophy of Enlightened Self-interest—Frederick the Great—The Wesleys—Whitefield—Methodism—The Spirit of Philanthropy.

THERE never was a finer morning in Lisbon than the 1st of November, 1755; the sky shone with perfect lustre, not a breath of wind was stirring. Suddenly the houses began to tremble as when heavily-laden carts pass through the street, then came a noise like the distant rumbling of thunder, followed by a most horrid crash, as if the whole city had tumbled down at once. "The house in which I was living," says one who was living in Lisbon at that terrible time, "shook with such violence that the upper stories immediately fell. The houses continued rocking in the frightfulest manner, the walls opening in many places. The clouds of dust and lime that arose were choking, and rendered the sky as dark as night. When the gloom began to disperse, and the violence of the shock to abate, I put on my coat and shoes, and descended into the street. Making my way through the ruins, I came to the large open space in front of St. Paul's

x 2

Church, which had been thrown down a few minutes before, burying a great part of the congregation. Climbing over the ruins at the west end of the church, in order to get to the river side, I found a prodigious number of people of both sexes, among whom I observed some principal canons of the patriarchal church in their purple robes and rochets, several priests in sacerdotal vestments, ladies half-dressed, some without shoes; all these people were on their knees at prayer, striking their breasts, and crying out incessantly, "*Misereordia mea Dios.*" While they were calling on the Virgin to intercede for them, a second shock, less violent than the first, came on, and completed the ruin of the buildings already shattered. The cry of *Misereordia*, mingled with shrieks, could now be distinctly heard from the top of St. Catherine's Hill, a considerable distance off; and at the same time we could hear the fall of the parish church there, whereby many persons were killed on the spot, and others mortally wounded. On a sudden I heard a general outcry, 'The sea is coming in! we shall all be lost!' Upon this, turning my eyes towards the river, which in this place is nearly four miles broad, I could perceive it heaving and swelling in a most unaccountable manner, as no wind was stirring. In an instant there appeared, at some small distance, a large body of water, rising as it were like a mountain. It came! on foaming and roaring, and rushed towards the shore with such impetuosity that we all immediately ran for our lives as fast as possible; many were actually swept away, and the rest were above the wasting water a good distance from the banks. I should certainly have been lost, had I not grasped a large beam that lay on the ground, till the water returned, which it shortly did, to its channel, with equal rapidity. With my clothes all dripping, I took a sudden resolution to retire back to the area of St. Paul's.

"I had not been long in the area of St. Paul's when I felt a third shock, which, though somewhat less violent than the other two, caused the sea to rush in again. I was up to my knees in water, though I had gotten upon a small eminence at some distance from the river. I now knew not what to do, but resolved to go to the Mint, as it was a very low and strong building. The soldiers who were set there every day to guard the place had fled, and the only person remaining there was the commanding officer, a nobleman's son of about seventeen or eighteen years of age. I entered into conversation with him, and having expressed my admiration that one so young should have the courage to remain at his post, though everyone of his soldiers had deserted theirs, the answer he made was, though he were sure the earth would open and swallow him up, he scorned to think of flying from his post.

"Having attempted to reach the house of a friend without success, I turned back, and tried to get into the square of the palace, twice as large as Lincoln's Inn Fields. The square was full of coaches, chariots, chaises, horses, mules, deserted by their drivers and attendants, as well as their owners. The nobility, gentry, and clergy, who were assisting at Divine service when the earthquake began, fled away with the utmost precipitation.

"From this square the way led to my friend's house, through a long, narrow street; the scenes of horror I met with exceed all description— nothing could be heard but sighs and groans. I could hardly take a single step without treading on the dead or dying; in some places lay coaches with their masters, horses, and riders almost crushed to pieces; here mothers with their infants in their arms; there ladies, richly dressed, priests, friars, gentlemen, mechanics, either in the same condition, or just expiring; some had backs or thighs broken, others vast stones on their breasts; some lay almost buried in the rubbish, and, crying out in vain to the passengers for succour, were left to perish like the rest.

"As soon as it grew dark, the whole city appeared in a blaze, which was so bright that I could easily see to read by it. The city was on fire in almost a hundred places at once; and this continued burning for six days together without intermission, and without the least attempt being made to stop its progress.

"The whole number of persons who perished, including those who were burnt or afterwards crushed to death whilst digging in the ruins, is supposed, on the lowest calculation, to be about sixty thousand; this extensive and opulent city is now a heap of ruins; rich and poor are at present on a level. Thousands of families which but the day before had been easy in circumstances, now want every conveniency in life, and find no one able to relieve them."

This terrifying outburst of the hidden forces of Nature could not fail to have given an impetus to those investigations into the laws of the physical universe for which each successive century now becomes more and more distinguished. The closing years of the seventeenth century had been marked in England by quite a galaxy of men of science. The names of Halley, Flamstead, Hook, Boyle, Wilkins, Ray, Harrison, cluster round that of Sir Isaac Newton, a pioneer in the new fields of discovery as great, if not greater, than Galileo, and born in the very year the Florentine astronomer died. Although the Continent hardly rivalled England at this particular time in scientific research and discovery, there are names such as the Frenchman Papin, the inventor of the steam-engine, and the great Dutch physician, Boerhaave, which would have stood worthily on the roll of the Royal Society, chartered in 1662; and there was one man in Germany, Liebnitz, who even contested the palm with the inventor of the differential calculus and the method of fluxions.

Early in the century comes the Swedish botanist, Linnæus, whose greatest work, the *Species Plantarum*, appeared about the same time that the French zoologist, Buffon, was sending forth his *Natural History;* while a humbler but equally devoted lover of science, the Scotchman, Ferguson, was lecturing with much success on astronomy and science. Nothing, perhaps, can better suggest the universal spread of the new spirit than the biography of this indefatigable student. A shepherd boy, the son of a day-labourer, James Ferguson spent every available moment in reading or investigation; his calling, keeping him out at night on the moors, being made especially profitable in the study of the stars. He lived to become a member of the Royal Society, and by word as well as deed to popularise the study of science.

About the time this Scottish shepherd was reading the stars, and in the very year in which Newton died, a young American had just began business as a printer in Philadelphia. A saving young man, with a great idea of money-getting, he was still more eager after knowledge, and took equal pleasure in diffusing all he had himself obtained. One of his first efforts was to form a literary club of all the young men he could draw together. Although the *Junto* had no special scientific object, there can be little doubt that the necessity it imposed on its members to prepare from time to time for the consideration of the subjects brought under its notice, greatly fostered the spirit of inquisitiveness which henceforth became the distinguishing feature of its founder, Benjamin Franklin. Fifteen years later, a public library was incorporated at Philadelphia, mainly through his exertions; and during his subsequent stay in Europe he acted as its agent, recommending books and forwarding information relative to improvements of every kind. This he did for thirty years; and what made him so indefatigable was, we can hardly doubt, the benefit he had himself derived from news thus conveyed.

In 1745 Peter Collinson, of the Royal Society, sent the Philadelphia Library an account of a number of experiments which had been made in Europe with reference to electricity. The subject had been brought to notice in 1728 by two Englishmen, who demonstrated that electricity might be conveyed from one body to another without their being in contact; and who had found, by suspending rods of iron with silk or hair lines, and then bringing an excited tube under them, that sparks might be drawn. Some Frenchmen, and then a number of German professors, took up the subject; and the result of their researches astonished the European philosophers. They managed to kill small birds and set spirits on fire by electricity. These experiments aroused Franklin's curiosity. He began to make experiments, which resulted in important discoveries, and explanations of phenomena since universally adopted. One, perhaps the greatest, was the discovery of a positive and a negative state of electricity.

But, with that passion to be useful which was so fine a feature of the best minds of this age, Franklin began to think how this new knowledge could be so used as to enable man to control the destructive nature of the electricity which it was evident collected at times in the atmosphere, and discharged itself in the form of lightning. Having observed the power of points in drawing and throwing off the electrical fluid, it occurred to him that buildings, ships, and other objects might be secured from the fatal effects of lightning by the erection of pointed iron rods, the top of which should rise some feet above their most elevated parts, and the base sink some feet into the earth or the water.

How he satisfactorily proved to himself and others the possibility of doing this, affords a most interesting example of the extreme simplicity as well as ingenuity that characterised these early students of science. "Except ye become as a little child, ye shall in no wise enter the kingdom of heaven," is a profound truth, as applicable in the kingdom of Nature as in the kingdom of Grace. In the following letter Franklin informs his friend at the Royal Society in London, Peter Collinson, how he has satisfied himself, and how others may do the same :—

"Philadelphia, October 19, 1752.

"SIR,—As frequent mention is made in public papers from Europe of the success of the Philadelphia experiment for drawing the electric fire from clouds by means of pointed rods of iron erected on high buildings, etc., it may be agreeable to the curious to be informed that the same experiment has succeeded in Philadelphia, though made in a different and more easy manner, which is as follows :—

"Make a small cross of two light strips of cedar, the arms so long as to reach to the four corners of a large thin silk handkerchief when extended. Tie the corners of the handkerchief to the extremities of the cross, so you have the body of a kite; which being properly accommodated with a tail, loop, and string, will rise in the air like those made of paper; but this, being of silk, is fitted to bear the wet and wind of a thunder-gust without tearing. To the top of the upright stick of the cross is to be fixed a very sharp-pointed wire, rising a foot or more above the wood. To the end of the twine next the hand is to be tied a silk ribbon, and where the silk and twine join a key may be fastened. This kite is to be raised when a thunder-gust appears to be coming on, and the person who holds the string must stand within a door or window, or under some cover, so that the silk ribbon may not be wet, and care must be taken that the twine does not touch the frame of the door or window. As soon as any of the thunder-clouds come over the kite, the pointed wire will draw the electric fire from them, and the kite with all the twine will be electrified, and the loose filaments of the twine will stand out every way and be attracted by an approaching finger. And when the rain has wetted the kite and twine, so that it can conduct the electric fire freely, you will find it stream out plentifully from the key on the approach of your knuckle. At this key the phial may be charged, and from electric fire thus obtained spirits may be kindled, and all other electric experiments be performed which are usually done by the help of a rubbed glass globe or tube, and thereby the sameness of the electric matter with that of lightning completely demonstrated.

"B. FRANKLIN."

The interest that Franklin's experiments excited in England may be judged from the following entry in John Wesley's diary:—
"1753. Feb. 17. From Dr. Franklin's letters I learned : 1. That electrical fire is a species of fire, infinitely finer than any yet known ; 2. That it is diffused, and in nearly equal proportions, through most substances ; 3. That as long as it is thus diffused, it has no discernible effect ; 4. That if any quantity of it be collected together, whether by art or nature, it then becomes visible in the form of fire, and inexpressibly powerful ; 5. That it is essentially different from the light of the sun, for it pervades a thousand bodies which light cannot penetrate, and yet it cannot penetrate glass, which light pervades so freely ; 6. That lightning is no other than electrical fire collected by one or more clouds ; 7. That all the effects of lightning may be performed by artificial electric fire ; 8. That anything pointed, as a spire or tree, attracts the lightning just as a needle does the electric fire ; 9. That electrical fire, discharged on a rat or a fowl, will kill it instantly ; but discharged on one dipped in water, it will slide off, and do it no hurt at all. In like manner, the lightning which will kill a man will not hurt him if he be thoroughly wet. What an amazing scene is opened for after ages to improve upon!"

In 1757 Franklin was in London ; and among those who made his acquaintance was a young minister named Joseph Priestley, then preaching to a small Unitarian congregation in Suffolk, at the stipend of thirty pounds a year. Franklin supplied him with books, which enabled him to write his *History and Present State of Electricity*. This was the beginning of Dr. Priestley's scientific career, which he was permitted to crown by the discovery of oxygen in 1774.

The self-taught American must have stood somewhat in the light of a father in science to a number of young men, who were just at the period of life when genius most naturally takes its bent. The letters that so interested John Wesley could not fail to arouse intense interest in young students like Joseph Black, who subsequently gave the world the idea of "latent heat"; Bruce, the traveller; Darwin, the botanist; Cavendish, the founder of pneumatic chemistry; James Watt, for ever associated with the wonders of steam; Galvani, who was to give his name to a branch of electrical science; and Herschel, who was to give his to a new planet. It must have stirred not only these, but many others, whose fame was not to shine among the stars, adding new ardour to the earnest search into the secrets of the universe, which now began to be a passion among men, overmastering in one case the reason, and leading it into a world of vision. Emanuel Swedenborg, who had commenced life as a man of science, published his *Arcana Cælestia* at the very period Franklin was giving the world his observations on electricity.

THE France of Louis XIV. exercised an influence over Europe similar to that which, in a former age, had been exercised by the Italy of Macchiavelli. The European States might rise in arms to escape its political despotism, but they could not deliver themselves from the power of its ideas. Faith in successful force, in glory, in material wealth, soon supplanted every other creed.

Descartes, the great philosopher of the age, had taught that whatever is clearly seen and distinctly thought must be true. Perspicuity of thought and expression became a fundamental test of truth; and all that failed to fit this Procustes' bed was rejected. Religion, poetry, and art began to die down. Nevertheless, a great interval separated the Deism of Collins and Tindal from that of Voltaire; and a similar distance intervened between Voltaire and the atheism of Holbach and Diderot. But such levelling down was the bent of the age; and no influence ever more rapidly spread. What Montesquieu remarked of the England of the early part of this century, was by its middle period true of all Europe: "Everyone laughs, if one talks of religion."

In thus losing faith, Europe lost prudence, for rarely has a more reckless society existed than that of Christendom in the early part of this century. All bonds were rapidly dissolving; and though it tried to look young and active, the philosophers knew that the root was gone and they were casting about for another. Enlightened self-interest they declared a sufficient basis and bond for human society. Every man should pursue his own happiness and pleasure; and if he did this wisely it would be compatible with the happiness and pleasure of every one else. This doctrine looked as wise as one of "Poor Richard's Golden Maxims." What it became in action, was made clear as daylight by one of its most illustrious disciples.

It is not often that a philosopher has a chance of becoming an absolute monarch. Frederick II. of Prussia unites these two characters; and drawing as he did all his philosophical ideas from France and Voltaire, he had a fine opportunity of showing the world what they were in practice. As a prince he had lived a studious life, writing French verse, and talking, like the rest of the philosophers, of humanity, of moderation, peace, liberty, and the happiness that a good mind may derive from the happiness of others. He even undertook to refute that "advocate of crime, that oracle of Satan, the Italian Macchiavelli." He composed a catechism of virtue, in which every maxim of the Florentine was answered by some philosophic axiom. Unfortunately, the Apollo who was to crush the new Python was himself on the side of the enemy; enlightened self-interest being as much the basis of Frederick's philosophy as it was of that of Macchiavelli; he, therefore, who came to curse ended by blessing, and that in a most remarkable manner.

When men beheld this ingenuous young man, so fond of philosophers and versification, they might have expected that a Telemachus was about to rule the little kingdom of Prussia; but Frederick, on the throne, showed that a monarch possessing military talents, a strong will, and a grasping nature must, if he have no other guiding star than his own pleasure, prove a scourge to mankind. Charles IX., Emperor of Germany, having no male issue, had been anxious to secure the peaceable possession of his hereditary dominions to his daughter, Maria Theresa. To this end he had promulgated a solemn ordinance, which, being ratified by all the powers of Europe, Prussia included, was called the Pragmatic Sanction. This arrangement, to which no one had a right to object but the States affected, and which Frederick stood plighted to maintain, he chose to violate, and so to plunge Europe into long and bloody wars. A few months after his accession the Emperor Charles died, and the King of Prussia determined suddenly and secretly to seize the great province of Silesia. In referring subsequently to the transaction, he cynically admitted the extreme selfishness of his motives. "Ambition, interest, the desire of making people talk about me, carried the day, and I decided for war."

Three wars resulted, during which he had ample opportunities of making the world talk about him. The third of these wars continued seven years (1756–1763), and was full of the most extraordinary turns of military fortune.

At first it was very disastrous for Frederick; while he himself was utterly defeated before Prague by the Austrians, his coadjutor, the Duke of Cumberland, had been forced to sign a treaty with the French, which left them free to invade Prussia. Frederick was almost ruined.

The battle of Prague took place on the 18th of June, 1757, and by the end of November things looked still blacker. The Russians had joined his enemies, and were devastating Eastern Prussia; the French were advancing with a great army from the West; Berlin had been taken and plundered by the Croats; suddenly Frederick arose, and, like some giant of romance, not only extricated himself from all these difficulties, but defeated the French and the Austrians, and that in so brilliant and rapid a manner that even Napoleon records his admiration of Frederick's military genius.

The world was at the feet of the conqueror who in such unparalleled difficulties appeared able to command success. England almost exceeded Germany in its enthusiasm. The King of Prussia's birthday was celebrated as if he had been her own king, and London was illuminated. The most varied classes united in his worship. The publicans painted his cocked hat and pigtail on their signboards, as the surest way of attracting customers. The religious world was even more hearty than the publicans, and his praises were declaimed from Dissenting pulpits; at Whitefield's Tabernacle thanksgivings were returned for the great victory of Leuthen. They had concluded that the objects of the Seven Years' War were those of the Thirty, and Frederick appeared to them a new Gustavus Adolphus.

What, then, was the result of this war? Carlyle says that the number of actual fighting men who perished was not less than eight hundred and fifty-three thousand, that Frederick himself lost one hundred and eighty thousand men. The population of Prussia had diminished by half-a-million, nearly every ninth man was missing. Yet, as Frederick was undoubtedly one of the most important among those who have built up the present great power of Prussia, it may very well be maintained that he sacrificed all these hecatombs at the shrine of enlightened self-interest.

So much has been written on the eighteenth century, so many memoirs, sketches, novels, essays given to the world, that we know it even better than we do our own. Debauched and frivolous in France, debauched and brutal in Germany; debauched, frivolous, brutal, and money-getting in England, a wise man might have said, as Lord Chesterfield did of France, that it presented everywhere the signs of a coming revolution.

That the revolution took in Great Britain a course so different to the rest of Christendom was, in the first place, due to the fact that the British Constitution was already established on the principles of civil and religious liberty. The Bill of Rights and the Act of Settlement were declarations of popular sovereignty, while the Toleration Act affirmed the rights of the individual conscience. These principles, it is true, were not put forth with the uncompromising distinctness of the decrees of the French Convention, but they contained the germs of a revolution even more thorough than the one which that famous assembly inaugurated.

Thus it was that the Spirit which was convincing the worn-out feudal society of Europe of sin, of righteousness, and of judgment to come, did a work still more profound in Great Britain. Its people, made to feel, not merely their secular, but their eternal wretchedness, were led once again to that River which had so many times refreshed the earth, and the national life was purified in its cleansing waters. Britain was thus fitted to become the source of the influence which was to be the basis and the bond of the new society.

About the year 1730 a few young men in the University of Oxford met to encourage one another in a holy life. The eldest amongst them was not more than twenty-seven, but very sincere and gifted, with a strong will. John Wesley had been much affected by reading William Law's *Serious Call to the Unconverted*, and with several other friends had determined upon leading a religious life. Their ideas were not greatly in advance of those which, in old times, had influenced earnest men to form monasteries; they considered it necessary to submit their lives to a certain rule, a course of conduct which earned them the title of Methodists.

They soon, however, began to make great progress. John Wesley went to America, to preach to the Colonists and to the Indians. Among his fellow-passengers were some Moravians, members of a very ancient religious society, which had its seat in Bohemia, and which, under the influence of Count Zinzendorf, had experienced a great revival. The Moravians were full of zeal and devotion, and went unhesitatingly wherever they felt called in the service of their Divine Master. Wesley felt much drawn to them, and after his return from America attended one of their meetings in London, where he heard read Luther's *Preface to the Epistle to the Romans*. This powerful work had such an influence upon him that he always regarded the time in which he listened to it as the period of his conversion. "I felt my heart strangely warmed," he said; "I felt I did trust in Christ, Christ alone for salvation; and an assurance was given me that He had taken away MY sins, even *mine*, and saved me from the law of sin and death." This henceforth became John Wesley's Gospel—the word which stirred the heart of the millions who listened to him and to his preachers.

During the next year he visited the Moravian settlement at Herrnhut, and entered into friendly relations with Zinzendorf, who was a few years his elder by age, and many years by grace. While in Germany he was introduced to Frederick II., then Prince Royal of Prussia.

One of the most beautiful testimonials to the personal character of Wesley is the affection in which he was held by his brother. Charles Wesley would never have entered alone on this great movement; but, as it is, his work will be one of the most enduring results of Methodism. He expressed the soul of the movement in song, and made it sound through the country like a sacred melody. Many others caught his gift, and the English language was enriched by a number of spirit-stirring hymns, such as had made religion so popular in Germany. Thus the epic of popular conversion sung forth its deliverance, its irrepressible joy, as the people of Israel did on the shores of the Red Sea.

The greatest of all the new evangelists was one who had been one of the youngest among the members of the "Holy Club." George Whitefield was a youth compared to John Wesley, but he no sooner began to preach than it was clear that a great power had arisen in England. It was reported that his first sermon, delivered in Gloucester Cathedral, had driven five persons mad with fear and excitement. His mind was less methodical and under control than Wesley's; and he would have suffered from this defect more than he did, had he not found a powerful friend in the Countess of Huntingdon. This noble woman devoted her life to the movement; she introduced it at its earliest stage to the English aristocracy, and it was through her fostering care that the fruit of Whitefield's labours was preserved. It was a real revolution in society when she invited such persons as the old Duchess of Marlborough, Lord Bolingbroke, and Lord Chesterfield to hear the young evangelist preach in her drawing-room. The Duchess of Buckingham, a natural daughter of James II., expressed, no doubt, the thoughts of many of the company when she told the countess in a letter: "The doctrines are most repulsive, and strongly tinctured with impertinence: it is monstrous to be told that you have a heart as sinful as the common wretches that crawl the earth; this is highly offensive and insulting; and I cannot but wonder that your ladyship should relish any sentiments so much at variance with high rank and good breeding."

But Whitefield soon turned from the upper to the lower strata of society, and, instead of holding forth to select audiences in drawing-rooms, he began to preach the Gospel in the open air. Manners were exceptionally brutal in the days when Whitefield thus dared to place himself against public opinion. Bear-baiting, bull-baiting, and cock-fighting were the sports of the day—the last-mentioned amusement, as well as boxing-matches, being as popular among the nobility as among the lower orders. At night young "bloods" coursed the streets of London, wrenching knockers, felling watchmen, and assaulting passengers. London mobs were notoriously brutal. It was a hazardous thing to provoke their attention at any time; only a man smitten with a "Divine madness" could have dared to argue with them concerning righteousness and judgment to come. Whitefield had the courage not only to go into the streets, but actually to stand up for hours preaching amidst the capers of merry-andrews, the jests of clowns, the noise of drums and bassoons, and the roar of twenty to thirty thousand people in Bartholomew Fair. And, stranger still, his effort was successful, for the next day he received a thousand notes from persons who spoke of convictions through which they had passed while he was thus preaching.

Wesley hesitated to follow Whitefield's example, but when he did he more than equalled him in his indefatigable energy, and in the length of time he was able to sustain the labour. For years Wesley travelled on an average forty miles a day, constantly preaching. Some of his sermons were delivered, like those of Whitefield, under circumstances of unusual sublimity. Methodism was especially successful among the Cornish miners. A famous gathering-place was Gwennap Pit, a natural amphitheatre capable of containing thirty thousand people. When it was known that Wesley was to preach there, the miners and fishermen, their wives and families, poured into this great temple; and when the hymn arose from its vast congregation, no human heart could have maintained itself untouched. Whitefield was the sapper and miner of the movement, and soon wore himself out with his exhausting labours. He went seven times to America, on the last occasion visiting Lisbon. It was the year before the earthquake, and he saw a miracle play. The scene was the crucifixion. The Virgin appeared in ruffles and widows' weeds, and the Apostle John in a bob wig and a green silk dress. What a sight for George Whitefield! In 1741 he made a missionary tour in Scotland. At Cambuslang, in Lanarkshire, extraordinary scenes broke out among the colliers; thousands were seized with religious convictions, and their mental anguish exhibited itself in physical manifestations: foaming at the mouth, bleeding of the nose, and convulsions.

This "revival" in Scotland synchronised with a similar one in America, in which the great theologian, Jonathan Edwards, played an important part. Thus in the land of learning, the land of "the Kirk," the movement was conducted by an Anglican clergyman of little learning, whilst in America, among the rough, uncultured colonists, its leader was one who, according to general admission, is to be numbered among the most eminent Christian divines of any age or country.

The effect of the movement is to be seen in the way it helped to raise the working classes, to give an impetus to philanthropy, and to elevate the moral tone of the world. When a man begins to feel that God not only cares for him, but has made him care for others, he must rise in self-respect and true virtue. And this was exactly the truth that the Methodists induced people to believe. The elevation these Methodists effected would not have been great, and the human conscience under their teaching would have made but little advance, had not the Divine ideal they set forth been a real progress in Christian theology. Men may have held the doctrine that God loved the world, but no one ever got the world to believe it like these eighteenth-century Methodists.

The philanthropic spirit of the new movement is seen in such affecting histories as that of Silas Told. Never before had any man spent night after night in the condemned cell, ridden again and again, with those about to suffer, in the cart to Tyburn, stood with them under the gallows, felt their quivering lips close to his face, and pressed their cold trembling hands in his. But all this, and more than this, did Silas Told, for he breathed into these outcasts a manly courage, a trust in God, almost a joy, such was his intense faith, his intense humanity.

It would be misleading to represent the Methodist movement as the source of the philanthropy of the eighteenth century. The spirit was everywhere, exhibiting itself in all kinds of forms, and in men of the most opposite parties and the most diverse sentiments. One might almost say the eighteenth century gave birth to the philanthropist, seeing that its own peculiar children made good will to men the leading thought of their existence. John Howard, Jean Frederic Oberlin, and Johann Heinrich Pestalozzi, are much more really the representative men of the eighteenth century than Frederick II. or John Wesley.

It would seem as if the earthquake at Lisbon was the event that aroused Howard's sympathy for his suffering fellow-creatures. His first wife died in the very month in which it took place, and he determined to visit the scene. However, he never reached Lisbon, the packet in which he sailed being taken by a French privateer. The sufferings he endured made him acquainted with the barbarous system by which many hundreds of prisoners perished miserably, and he was thus led to devote himself to prison reform.

It was time, for with regard to cruelty, men's consciences seemed seared with a hot iron. During the decade of which we are writing, in the year 1757, a man who tried to kill Louis XV. was put to death in the following manner. The hand by which he attempted the murder was burned at a slow fire; the fleshy parts of his body were then torn off by pincers; and finally he was dragged about for an hour by four strong horses, while into his numerous wounds were poured molten lead, resin, oil, and boiling wax.

Atrociously cruel as the law was in France, the actual administration of the prisons was much more humane than in England. To rot in gaol Howard found to be no mere figure of speech. Prisoners, especially those for debt, were starved, sometimes they had hardly any water, they lay on rags, almost worn to dust, or even on the bare floors; all classes were huddled together, men and women, old offenders and young boys; the air was so malignant that it rendered intolerably offensive the very vinegar

Howard carried as an antidote. Gaol fever was continual, sometimes carrying off the judge and other officials who conducted the assizes. The prisons in England were virulent centres of disease and crime.

And this is only one aspect of the hard-heartedness that generally prevailed. When we read of a king pulling his son's hair out by the roots, and striking him in the face with the knob of his stick; or of a mad king lashed by his keepers; or of a Christian man taking an active share in the slave-trade; or of the cruelties perpetrated by the masters and elder boys in the great public schools; when we look at Hogarth's pictures, and see the atrocities which amused London boys; when, indeed, we read any history of the time, we must admit that of the leaves of the Tree of Life none have seemed to possess more healing power than those which Howard and so many like him began to apply at this time to the many wounds of poor humanity.

If the sixteenth and seventeenth centuries spoke the language of Paul, of Augustine, of Calvin, the eighteenth spoke that of the Master. If in the strength of sovereign, predestinating grace the former had fought and won the battle of human liberty, the latter declared the right of every man to be good, the right of every man to love and serve God. "The Spirit and the bride say, Come, and whosoever will, let him take the water of life freely." "If any man thirst, let him come unto Me, and drink."

GRAVE OF JOHN HOWARD.

EIGHTEENTH CENTURY.

Section II.

CONTEMPORARY EVENTS IN THE EIGHTEENTH CENTURY.

America.—Washington inaugurated as first President of the United States.
Australia.—The founding of Sydney.
France.—Taking of the Bastille.
England.—William Carey meditating missions to the heathen.

EIGHTEENTH CENTURY.

SECTION II.

A.D. 1781-1792.

Causes of the French Revolution—American Revolution—Taking of the Bastille—Inauguration of Washington—German Poets and Philosophers—England's Colonial Progress—Australia—India—William Carey—Mission of the Anglo-Saxon Race.

HE magnificent despotism of Louis XIV. ended in an empty exchequer, ruined industries, and a starving population. The royal egoism spread downwards; every seigneur in France reflected the "Grand Monarque," and absorbed for the benefit of his own individual self the labour, the wealth, and the talents of all who came beneath his control. No one could lift hand or foot, no one could buy or sell, could grind his corn or eat a meal, could till his fields, or glean in those of another, without paying a due to the lord. Everything was taxed; the little tithes went to the Church, but the great ones were eaten up by the omnivorous giant—the great seigneur. Nor were the taxes all: there was the duty-service, ploughing, sowing, weeding, haymaking, reaping, carting, and, in vinelands, the vintage, to be done for the lord, before the poor labourer could look to his own concerns. No wonder his cottage was little more than a hut, his clothes patched, his cheeks

haggard; no wonder men wore " a panic-stricken look, as if the oppression of the great were like the hail and the thunder, a thing irremediable, the ordinance of nature "; no wonder women looked sixty when they were not yet thirty; no wonder children became brutal and thievish; no wonder humanity in France was dying out quietly, and the land gradually returning to the silence of the desert.

As everyone who could left the country, the great cities became congested. Paris spread far beyond the walls, and in the outskirts was a huge encampment of canvas and planks, filthy and overcrowded. Inside, the houses rose to six, to seven, or even to eight stories high, with roofs and garrets open to wind and rain. From one gutter to another the water dripped, making long green stains down the gaunt walls, until the courtyards below were as dank as the bottom of a well. Horrible were the garrets in which the apprentices slept, and still more unhealthy the dark shops where the women sat the livelong day, leaning against the humid walls. All was foul and malarious, symbolising the moral life which crawled in the gloomier quarters, or careered madly in the saloons of fashion.

The court had sunk into the grossest licentiousness. Humanity shudders to think of the "Parc aux cerfs," and the example set by the *bien-aimé*. Surely there were signs enough that the old society was near its end. The ruin was precipitated by the wretched management of the public revenues. Clever controllers of the finances had not been wanting during the era of magnificence; Colbert was a great genius; but the officials he could best rely on were driven away because they were Protestants, and his efforts proved in the end little better than filling a cask pierced with holes. Those who followed him went from bad to worse, until French finance fell into the hands of scheming gamblers or of ignoramuses. A number of horse-leeches, called receivers and farmers-general, duped the Government and robbed the people. To the latter alone the law was terrible, defaulters being sent to the galleys.

There might have been some hope, had the clergy been as those in the Middle Ages—able and willing to stand between the oppressor and the oppressed; but nothing could well exceed the degradation of the Gallican Church. In the previous age it had been distinguished for genius; its high-priests were now notorious rather than noted; the Cardinals Dubois and De Rohan were among its most prominent members. In digging the grave of Protestantism, the Church of Bossuet made one for herself. Infidelity threw in a few shovels of earth, and danced upon the corpse.

Devotion and dragonnades, a Christian people driven mad by Catholic cruelty, a Church impossible without apostolical succession and sacramental grace—who can wonder if men educated by the Jesuits, as was Voltaire, confounded Catholicism and Christianity; and, knowing the former to have been the curse of France, rushed blindly to tear up what they thought its root? Thus the first part of this century was spent in destroying the base of society—the very principle of its life. And this in a country which, for fifteen centuries, had been under Catholic education—an education which, in each successive age, led men more and more to rely on authority rather than upon their own consciences, to believe that the test of truth was its universal acceptance, to detest, abhor, and utterly to extirpate the unfortunate dissident who, unable or unwilling to be of the opinion of the majority, had the honesty to say so, to consider death the proper punishment of the heretic, and suspicion, espionage, and persecution noble work for the Christian.

As Roman Catholic prelates, Bossuet and Fénelon could not think freely; their influence in France passed to one who not only did, but expressed himself in a manner so venomous as to make *libre-penseur* a name of almost as evil repute as Catholic. Sinister omen for Catholic Europe, to owe liberty of conscience to Voltaire!

None knew better than the historian of the age of Louis XIV. all it had to bestow; yet he turned away from it, and looked to Protestant England as the real source of intellectual and political light. "Voltaire," says Victor Cousin, "was the scholar of England. Before Voltaire knew England by his travels and his friendships, he was not Voltaire, and the eighteenth century had yet to discover him." He was the first in France to study Shakespeare, to popularise Newton, and to recommend Locke. He was enthusiastic with reference to English political life. "How I love," he exclaims, "the boldness of the English; how I love men who say what they think!" And what Voltaire thought, all the mind of France in the eighteenth century thought.

Thus the philosophers and statesmen of the English Revolution were the schoolmasters of the fathers of the French Revolution, and the institutions of England their school-books. If we ask who created the atmosphere of free thought in which these philosophers were reared, and whose faith and works won the battle that made free institutions possible in England, there can be but one answer: the children of Calvin, the English Puritans, and the Scotch Covenanters.

This influence from England played a great part in bringing about the Revolution in France; there is another like it, though it traces its root rather to Augustine than to Calvin. In the reign of Louis XIV., a very powerful religious party arose in the Gallican Church—the Jansenists. Their doctrine was drawn from Augustine, and they might very well be called Catholic Calvinists, since their theology was essentially that of the Genevan Reformers. They were for a time overpowered by the Jesuits, of whom they were the bitter opponents, and their famous convent of Port Royal suppressed. In 1713 the Jansenist doctrines were condemned by Clement XI. in the famous Bull Unigenitus. The author of this bull was Le Tellier, the Jesuit confessor of Louis XIV.; he did it in opposition to De Noailles, Archbishop of Paris, who was inclined to Jansenism. Rome thus unreservedly took the side of the Jesuits. The learned, who adhered to Augustine, the orders, who followed Thomas Aquinas, and the parliaments, who always stood up for Gallican rights, joined in opposition. Jansenist doctrine spread again through all the Catholic kingdoms, in Austria, Flanders, Spain, Portugal, and even in Italy. In 1715 it was believed half the serious people in Naples were Jansenists.

In France, after a short struggle, they were again suppressed, and were thrown into prisons, where some lay so long that they were quite forgotten, and nobody could tell for what crime they were immured. Those who were bishops were hurried out of existence. However, their influence went on increasing; and an illustration of this is seen in the popular belief in the miracles performed in the church of St. Médard in Paris, at the tomb of a Jansenist saint, the deacon Paris, who died in 1727.

But what most of all promoted and preserved the influence of Jansenism in France during the later portion of the eighteenth century, was the existence of a mysterious publication called *Nouvelles Ecclésiastiques*, which the Jansenist party was able to maintain from about the time of these miracles until the era of the Revolution, a space of sixty-two years, without stoppage by the police. It is supposed that it was printed in a boat; it was certainly distributed by an ingenious system, which afterwards became the model for many secret societies. The method portrayed on a card was the only ornament in the library of the Jacobin Club, founded in 1791, the year after the *Nouvelles Ecclésiastiques* ceased to exist—a striking proof of the connection of Jansenism and the Revolution.

As the century moved on the Jansenists had many friends in the Parliament and the court. Some of the king's ministers inclined to their opinions. Turgot, one of the greatest French statesmen during the century, is said to have been of the number. What still further helped the Jansenists was the decay and ruin of their old rivals the Jesuits. Statesmen arose in France, Spain, Portugal and Naples, who made it the leading thought of their policy to diminish the ecclesiastical power; and since the Jesuits were its soul, it became an object with these statesmen to bring about their suppression. The Portuguese Government succeeded in inducing Benedict XIV. to appoint Cardinal Saldanha to make a report of the state of the order. In 1759 they were expelled from Portugal. In 1762 a similar fate befel them in France. Being involved in certain mercantile reverses, they were dragged into the courts. The Parliament took occasion to order their statutes to be brought up for review; after a few preliminary severities, they were condemned without being heard, their property sold, their order secularised, and they themselves declared unfit to be admitted into a well-governed country. The example of Portugal and France was soon followed in Spain, Naples, and Parma; and if Austria did not go so far as to drive the Jesuits out of its dominions, the policy of Joseph II. broke them down, and destroyed all their influence. At last, in 1773, Clement XIV., one of the purest and best of the whole papal line, a Franciscan, inclined himself, it is said, to Jansenist views, abolished the whole Jesuit order, its offices, houses, and institutions. As the main work of the Jesuits was education, their suppression throughout Catholic Europe at this particular time, and especially in France for the twenty-seven years preceding the Revolution, is a fact of the highest importance. It was during this period that all the actors in that Revolution were at school; their teachers were the disciples of Augustine or the Encyclopædists, who drew all their inspiration from England.

But the philosophers and Jansenists combined had less to do with the education of revolutionary France than a poor hypochondriac, a man with heart half-broken, penniless, hopeless, and tortured by remorse. Napoleon said that there would have been no Revolution had it not been for Jean Jacques Rousseau. Born in the capital of French Protestantism, the son of a Geneveso artisan, Rousseau became a wanderer on the face of the earth when Voltaire was the petted guest of the great and rich. As poor drudge or spoilt plaything, as the creature of circumstance, Rousseau tasted all the sin and all the bitterness of life. His heart was gangrened, its sweetness became unutterably soured, and all the force that was in him turned against a world which had brought him to such a pass. Society, as it appeared in the refined and civilised eighteenth century, with its powdered wigs, its cosmetics, and its beauty-spots, its heavy learning, its profound philosophies, its atheism, its moral looseness, its incredible baseness and tyranny, he utterly and totally condemned. Every evil, in his view, had come from civilisation. The simple untutored savage leading the life of nature, little removed from the beast that roared in the forest; this was the golden age: the only true life. Yet Rousseau had a mind capable of following the profoundest philosophy, a heart capable of feeling the appeals of evangelic love, a soul capable of the highest worship, a spirit independent, loving justice, beauty, and truth. He formed for himself no career, could do nothing well, yet by the force of his very misery he spoke so fully the welling thoughts of the oppressed, sin-stricken souls who in thousands sent up sighs and groans to heaven, that Europe welcomed him as its true teacher, and, following out his thoughts, because they were so truly its own, gave them the force of forty million minds in place of one. Nothing has ever equalled the enthusiasm with which his later works were received. When his *Nouvelle Héloïse* appeared, the demand was so great that copies were lent by the libraries at twelve sous the volume, only one hour being allowed for the perusal.

ROUSSEAU, in some of his ideas, may perhaps give signs of a half-crazed intellect ; but the real force of his thoughts was to re-establish the dominion of the individual conscience, and to make men feel that a sound education must be in accordance with the laws of nature. Moreover, he differed from the Encyclopædists in that he recognised the transcendent importance of the religious sentiment. A right heart, with Rousseau, was of more importance than a right head. Thus, though he gave an impetus and an intensity, and even a fanaticism to the Revolution, he gave it some constructive principles, so that after its fury had subsided it was plain that the foundations of society had been relaid, and that in the midst of the fires a new phœnix had arisen.

To the influence of the philosophers, of the Jansenists, and of Rousseau, in bringing about the Revolution, must be added that of the War of Independence in America. The struggle between England and the colonists awoke in France the liveliest interest. This interest was, no doubt, chiefly due to the ill-feeling entertained against England, as the successful rival of France both in America and in India; but it was fed by the growing desire for political liberty. The general sympathy was shown by the extraordinary reception given to Benjamin Franklin on his arrival in Paris, as the representative of the colonists.

After two years' fighting, the English were so decidedly worsted that they had to sign the Convention of Saratoga, whereby their army laid down its arms, and marched as prisoners of war into Massachusetts. Lord North determined on a compromise; he was ready to recognise virtually though not verbally the Independence of the United States. But when it was known that France had entered into a treaty with the Americans, not merely of amity and commerce, but with the avowed object of securing the absolute and unlimited independence of the new republic, the pride of England was aroused, and Lord Chatham, who had always defended the colonists, declared in the House of Lords that he would never consent to the surrender of the rights of the empire. "Shall we now," he said, "fall prostrate before the House of Bourbon?"

So the war recommenced, the French aiding the Americans by a loan of six million livres and a military and a naval force. The former was commanded by Lafayette; and in 1781 he and Washington combined their forces, and shut the English general up in York Town, the French fleet blockading the York river. Cornwallis surrendered, Lord North resigned, and George III. was in such dejection that he thought of retiring to Hanover. In the end, however, he made the best of the position, and, in opening Parliament on the 5th of November, 1782, announced his intention of recognising the Independence of the United States.

Doubtless King George thought himself the most unfortunate of monarchs; but the American Republic was far less injurious to him than to King Louis, who, in assisting at its birth, signed his own death-warrant.

The descendant of the founder of despotism in France, of the defender of the unity of the Church, of the extirpator of the Protestants, the King of France leagued himself with the descendants of the Pilgrim Fathers, the Calvinistic emigrants who came over in the *Mayflower*, and thereby endorsed their famous Declaration of Independence, in which it was affirmed that "all men are created equal; that they are endowed by their Creator with certain inalienable rights, among which are life, liberty, and the pursuit of happiness; that to secure these rights governments are instituted among men, deriving their just powers from the consent of the governed; that whenever any form of government becomes destructive of these ends, it is the right of the people to alter and abolish it, and to institute a new government."

The door being thus opened in France to Republican sentiments, their greatest professor, Thomas Jefferson, stepped in, and being settled in Paris as the American Minister, he became the adviser of the *Tiers Etat*, indeed, it is surmised that it was by his advice that they took the title *l'Assemblée Nationale*. His pupil, Lafayette, brought with him from America the doctrine of the "Rights of Man," and it was by his instigation that it was adopted by the National Assembly.

The new Constitution of the United States was signed September 17, 1787, and it was to come into effect March 4, 1789, between any nine States by whom it should then have been adopted. When that date came ten States entered the Union, and unanimously chose George Washington as the President of the New Republic. On the 16th of April, Washington left Mount Vernon for New York, then the seat of government. His progress was a continual ovation. He was escorted through each State by its most eminent citizens, and at one place the enthusiasm displayed itself in triumphal arches, floral decorations, and young girls chanting his praises. He crossed the Hudson river with a procession of thirteen boats, symbolising the thirteen States. His reception in New York was marked by unusual enthusiasm, and when he appeared on the balcony of the Federal Hall, and in the sight of all the people took the oath to preserve, protect, and defend the Constitution of the United States, the people broke out into cries: "Long live Washington, President of the United States!"

This event took place on the 30th of April, 1789. Four days after the States General was formally opened by Louis XVI. at Versailles, and very shortly developed into the National Assembly. In less than three months the populace in Paris had risen and had taken the Bastille. The inauguration of Washington was the coronation of the American Republic; the fall of the Bastille, the knell of the French Monarchy.

Thus the new society was born in the New World at the very moment that the old society had commenced its death-throes in the Old World. In New York men rejoiced with the simple joy of childhood; in Paris humanity raged in the last delirium of mortal disease.

WE turn away with horror from the details of the Revolution; why it was so envenomed is clear enough, and ought not to be forgotten. The old society divided itself into two classes—those who enjoyed, and those who drudged. All natural kindness had departed from the hearts of those who drudged, and a hard, inhuman loathing had taken its place. But this was not all; bad food, bad dwellings, unrequited labour, terrible ignorance, a religion full of lies, of oppression and hatred, vile examples of life in the king, the higher clergy and the nobility, had rendered the French people physically, morally, and mentally diseased. The Revolution was accompanied by the signs of lunacy, suspicion, moral blindness, frenzy, wild outburst of homicidal rage. The taking of the Bastille is an example of all this. That one of the strongest fortresses in Europe should fall in a single day before a mob is only to be explained by the strength of frenzy.

This event—the inauguration of the Revolution—took place on the 14th of July, 1789. Necker, the Genevese Calvinist, who had been hailed as the saviour of France: Necker, the People's Minister, had been dismissed. The news is announced to Paris by Camille Desmoulins, the prophet of the hour. " To arms ! " is the general cry; and after spending a day in working themselves up to a pitch of frenzy, the populace proceed to the Invalides, where they seize (no guards attempting to prevent) twenty-eight thousand muskets, with which they sally forth in streaming hosts towards the Bastille. All Paris has been crying, " To the Bastille ! " Strange, since none were ever lodged there save noblemen, literary men, priests, or publishers. During the whole of that day the Faubourg St. Antoine is a boiling crater, from whose sides pour forth streams of human lava, which, all incandescent, surge round the nine-towered fortress. Delaunay, the governor, looks down on the multitude, doubtful what to do. He has a garrison of two companies of Invalides, and some fifty Swiss. Parley after parley is held, but he will hear of no surrender; he takes his stand on military duty. A great gun is fired, and the withering grapeshot sweeps over the mob of human beings. It would have made but little difference had it swept through it, for the crowd in its madness knows nothing of fear. Blindly it rushes on like a swarm of ants or locusts; human beings are covering every accessible and inaccessible spot, have mounted high walls, have filled the great ditch, have seized upon the huge drawbridge, have broken its chain, so that it falls with an awful crash. But still the tall fortress, with its grim nine towers, bids defiance to the roaring tumult below. Four hours has the storm been raging, and Delaunay is beginning to lose heart. He runs to and fro; he declares that he will blow up the fortress rather than surrender. But why talk of surrender? Whoever heard of a great fortress being surrendered in four hours? True, he has only one day's provisions; but it is not that, it is the terror that strikes the heart of the most courageous when the million is all of one mind and one heart. Delaunay capitulates; a brave man runs along the heads of the mob, and receives the terms. The Bastille is taken!

The people masters, they show themselves truce-breakers and murderers. Delaunay is dragged to the Hotel de Ville, slain on the way, and his head placed on a pike; some of his soldiers share his fate. St. Just, afterwards himself a Terrorist, writes:—

"Weakness gives birth to cruelty. I do not know that even among savages a people has ever been seen carrying at the ends of their lances the heads of those they most detested, drinking their blood, tearing out their hearts and eating them. I have seen this in Paris. I have heard the cries of joy of an ungovernable people amusing itself with shreds of human flesh as it cried, 'Vive la Liberté.'"

COMPARED with the political whirlpool in France, Germany presented the appearance of some peaceful inland lake, whose waters are only ruffled by soft summer breezes. During the French Revolution the greatest minds in Germany were living in so exalted a world, that they took little or no heed of what, to the rest of Europe, seemed the most stupendous events that had happened since the fall of the Roman Empire. Duke Karl-August of Saxe-Weimar surrounded himself with a court the like of which had not been seen in Europe since the days of Charlemagne. Goethe, Wieland, Herder, and Schiller rendered his little capital the most brilliant intellectual centre in Europe—a Teutonic Athens. To pass from Paris to Weimar during the years 1789–1793 must have been like turning from the incantations of the witches in *Macbeth* to the enchantments of *A Midsummer Night's Dream*.

Yet these poet-philosophers in Germany were doing a work as revolutionary and more profound than their contemporaries in France. The magnificent literature they produced, the ripe fruit of the poetic genius which had its spring-time in the days of Hans Sachs, Ulrich von Hutten, and Martin Luther, gave the German peoples a real consciousness of that national unity which has since become their one dominant idea, and has made Germany such a powerful factor in European politics. Not that the sages at Weimar had any such object: they lived only for philosophy and art. Goethe's nature was truly cosmopolitan; he was as really a citizen of the world as Anarcharsis Clootz himself; Wieland lived in ancient Greece rather than in Germany; and as to Herder, he has been well described as "a Christian Brahmin." He lived in the unhistoric ages, his speculations extending to the utmost limits of the universe. In the realms of thought these Germans were doing just what their neighbours were doing in the realms of action—changing, deepening, widening. For good or evil, they had commenced a revolution which men would recognise to be terrible and searching as that in the political sphere—a revolution which, like that in France, would run over the whole gamut, and have its Robespierre as well as its Mirabeau. As the French Revolution claimed for every individual the rights of a man and a brother, so these Germans have compelled men to recognise a value in all the productions of human thought. Through them the world's literary treasures have been studied afresh; and the result has been to draw together mind in all quarters of the globe; they have especially united the East and the West—ancient India and modern Europe.

IN this work, so fraught with great consequences to the future of the world, England played a part as important as that of Germany. Her warriors, her statesmen, her explorers, her men of science, and her missionaries, were drawing all the quarters of the globe into closer union, and the various tribes of the human race into a stronger sympathy.

Captain Cook is another example of the thirst for scientific discovery so characteristic of this century. The son of an agricultural labourer in Yorkshire, he took to a seafaring life. His talents as a marine surveyor introduced him to the notice of the Royal Society, who, in 1768, sent him out on an expedition to the Pacific Ocean, to make an observation of the transit of Venus over the face of the sun. In the course of this voyage he arrived at New Holland, now Australia; he called the land New South Wales, and took possession of it in the name of Great Britain (April 19th, 1770). He was accompanied by Joseph Banks, afterwards President of the Royal Society, in the capacity of naturalist. As the expedition sailed along the eastern coast of Australia, a commodious inlet was observed, and, from the profusion of wild flowers which bloomed near the water's edge, was called Botany Bay.

When, some years later, it became a question where to send criminals sentenced to transportation for life, Australia was thought of, and it was determined to send them to Botany Bay. In 1787, a small fleet, carrying, besides their crews, seven hundred and fifty-seven convicts, five hundred and sixty-five men, and one hundred and ninety-two women, set sail for this unknown land of flowers. Stores and provisions for two years were taken, and live stock and seeds obtained at the Cape of Good Hope. On January 20, 1788, the fleet arrived at Botany Bay; but, finding water scarce, and a general appearance of aridity, Governor Philip decided to go farther, and seven miles to the north they found a creek. A sailor named Jackson declared that a great haven lay between the rocks, and, the fleet entering, soon reached a vast sheet, twenty miles in extent, and ramifying in every direction. This fine harbour, capable of containing vessels of the largest size, was surrounded by rocky shores, presenting a succession of picturesque views, the cliffs often rising to the height of two hundred or three hundred feet. The place chosen to land was a stream of fresh water flowing under some trees; and here, in a small clearing made in the virgin forest, the foundations of the great city of Sydney were laid. Its beginnings were feeble and unfortunate, owing to the unhappy nature of the community sent to make the settlement; but after a time these difficulties were overcome, and now there are few more flourishing cities than the capital of New South Wales. Placed opposite to the great States which the future will probably bring into being on the western shores of the Americas, standing as it does in the centre of a vast coal-field, and possessing so magnificent a harbour, Sydney has, it can scarcely be doubted, a great destiny in the world that is to be.

But it was not only on the newest land in the globe that Great Britain planted her race and her language; it was during the later half of this century that she laid a firm grasp on the most ancient of all lands—the great and wonderful Indian Empire. In becoming the masters of India, the methods used were often reprehensible, and sometimes disgraceful; but since the British people have awoke to their responsibility, no foreign rule through all history has ever been more founded on a sense of duty than that of the English in India.

THAT it is so, is to be attributed to the spirit which arose in the great age now under consideration—the age that declared the rights of man, and that governments exist only for the benefit of the governed.

It was in no such spirit that England had governed her dependencies up to that time. America, Ireland, and India could all rise up one after the other and denounce her selfishness. Edmund Burke, the most philosophic, and one of the most disinterested statesmen England ever produced, did a great work for humanity when, in the name of the people of India, he impeached Warren Hastings.

About a year before the inauguration of Washington, and the meeting of the States General at Versailles, that memorable scene took place when, before the highest court of English justice, in the great hall of Rufus, the noblest orator of the day thrilled even those most opposed to him with a denunciation of the administration of the great Indian pro-consul. "I impeach Warren Hastings," he concluded, "of high crimes and misdemeanours. I impeach him in the name of the Commons House of Parliament, whose trust he has betrayed. I impeach him in the name of the English nation, whose ancient honour he has sullied. I impeach him in the name of the people of India, whose rights he has trodden under foot, and whose country he has turned into a desert. Lastly, in the name of human nature itself, in the name of both sexes, in the name of every age, in the name of every rank, I impeach the common enemy and oppressor of all!"

Burke was almost vindictive in his resentment of wrong-doing; but it was a great lesson administered to all who should hereafter rule India. The severity shown the first Governor-General rendered tyranny well nigh impossible where tyranny was almost invited, and where in the long run it would have done infinitely more harm to the rulers than the ruled.

As Burke was moved to plead the wrongs of the Hindoos, and Grattan those of the Irish, Wilberforce became the advocate of a race who had suffered more cruelty than either—the African slaves. Up to this period no one seems to have had his conscience aroused to the cruelty of the slave-trade. Can we suppose the great and good men of old times had not hearts as tender and sensitive as our own? yet were they blind to the iniquity of holding their fellow men in slavery, and even to the horrors of the middle passage. Christian men, sincere and pious, took a share in the traffic, and thought it no sin.

Nothing explains such blindness, except the doctrine that God is educating the human race as a whole; and that in each age the Spirit of Christ, which is in the world convincing it of sin, of righteousness, and of judgment to come, bestows on it a new enlightenment, compelling it to feel the duty of a nearer approach to the Divine ideal of morality—the Sermon on the Mount.

It is difficult to say in such matters what individual conscience is aroused first. Wilberforce was only a boy at school when he wrote a letter to a York paper in condemnation of the odious traffic in human flesh. Clarkson while a student at Cambridge wrote a Latin prize essay in 1785 on the question, "Is it right to make slaves of others against their wills?" A translation that he published had an extensive circulation, and he determined to devote his life to the cause. In 1787 a society was formed in London for the suppression of the slave-trade, and Wilberforce became the leader of the movement. He introduced a Bill into the House of Commons; but it was not until early in the next century that Great Britain gave up the iniquitous traffic.

Speaking one day in the House of Commons, Wilberforce said: "A sublimer thought cannot be conceived than when a poor cobbler formed the resolution to give to the millions of India the Bible in their own language." The cobbler referred to was Dr. Carey, and no injustice was done him in the description, as the learned translator of the Scriptures into Hindustani had never attained a higher grade in his original trade. Being on some occasion at the house of the Governor-General, he overheard an officer ask if Dr. Carey had not once been a shoemaker. "No, sir," Carey exclaimed, "only a cobbler!"

Ne sutor ultra crepidam was never more out of place than here, for Carey was altogether a failure until he got beyond his last; nay, he failed in everything he undertook until he began his translation of the Bible into the languages of India. Shoemaker, gardener, schoolmaster, preacher—he did not shine in any calling until he attained the dream of his existence, and began to disseminate the Gospel among the heathen.

It was reading the account of Captain Cook's voyages and studying geography that gave direction to the earnest soul of this poor young cobbler. He made for himself a map composed of several sheets pasted together, into which he had entered every particular relative to the natural characteristics, the population, and the religion of every country then known to England. It was his delight, while making and mending shoes, to look at this map, and while traversing the world in thought to devise means for evangelising its various tribes.

But he had not only to meet the indifference of the world, but also of his religious friends. Attending one day a meeting of ministers at Northampton—for while still engaged in shoemaking he became pastor of a small congregation—he proposed as a subject for discussion: "The duty of Christians to attempt to spread the Gospel among the heathen." The chairman frowning, cried in a loud, hard voice, "Young man, sit down. When God pleases to convert the heathen, He will do it without your aid or mine."

A friend gave him ten pounds to publish a pamphlet on the subject; but while it was being written he and his family were nearly starved. At last his brethren, wearied out with his importunities, agreed to form a little society to send missionaries to the heathen (Oct. 2, 1792). Carey at once offered to go wherever the society chose to send him. But one hindrance after another arose, just of a nature to have deterred any ordinary man. But Carey's faith and enthusiasm were not to be shaken. He persevered, and at last found himself in India with his wife and family.

But now a new series of difficulties began. He was reduced to the utmost poverty. A benevolent native lent him a wretched, ill-ventilated house in the suburbs of Calcutta; and in this poor home he had not the happiness of domestic peace, for his wife, unsustained by his enthusiasm, was unable to bear the trials of her lot. Having been offered a bungalow in the Soonderbuns, he borrowed five hundred rupees, and went. He found himself in the midst of a vast tract of jungle, infested by tigers. Nothing could seem more hopeless. But at this juncture a ray of light appeared. He was offered the situation of assistant manager in an indigo factory. Carey had now a comfortable home, but one of his children died, and the event so preyed on the mother that she went out of her mind. Her husband worked on, studying, translating the New Testament, preaching, and managing the factory. His co-manager was his fellow-missionary, Thomas, who, though apparently the more powerful preacher of the two, was of so excitable a temperament that the baptism of the first convert sent him frantic with joy.

It seemed the climax of Carey's troubles when he had to proceed to the baptism of Krishnu and of his own son amidst the ravings of his wife and those of his companion. Moreover, the factory did not succeed, and the proprietor gave it up. However, the interest in missions had so advanced in England that the Baptist Missionary Society determined to send out six more missionaries. The little company arrived, and included two men of some culture—William Ward and Marshman. Not daring to enter British India at once, they proceeded to the Danish settlement of Serampore, where they placed themselves under the protection of the Governor, a brave and excellent man. Very soon an order arrived for their immediate withdrawal; but, after an explanation, the Governor-General, Lord Wellesley, gave way. The missionaries now requested Carey to come and join them at Serampore, and to bring his printing-press. This he did, and they formed a little society on the principles of Christian communism. Henceforth his existence passed smoothly in the pursuit of the great object of his life—the translation of the Bible into the languages of India. In this work he was so indefatigable that, before his death, the Serampore Mission had issued above two hundred thousand Bibles, or portions of Bibles, in about forty oriental languages or dialects.

William Carey was the first man in England to feel that Christians had a duty to perform towards the heathen world. His example and the record of his labours stirred up others; and before this century had run its course there was scarcely a Christian denomination in England without its missionary society.

Like the mighty angel in the Apocalypse, with the little book open in his right hand, the Anglo-Saxon race with its two wings—the British Empire and the American Republic—spread over the whole world, offers mankind an open Bible. It is this which makes William Carey not only the first, but the typical Anglo-Saxon missionary. He determined to give India the Bible. To him it contained the Word of Life, the Saving Truth, and he discerned before anyone else that the greatest gift England could offer India was to make her acquainted with the secret power that can renew the life of a people and perpetually reform its institutions.

For what is the lesson which this rapid flight through the Christian centuries teaches, if not that there dwells in the faith that Christendom has ever had in a kingdom of heaven, a regenerative power elsewhere unknown?

Brahminism, Buddhism, Mohammedanism have each produced one form of society, and then remained torpid and sterile for a thousand years. But where this faith in a kingdom of heaven exists, change is and must be the law. No Christian century thinks as its predecessor, but is ever pressing on to a new horizon.

By whatever name the progressive movement is known, however false its method or mistaken its arguments, it will be found that at bottom it seeks a new realisation of the kingdom of heaven; the revolution takes place, and Christendom rises a step higher in its pursuit of "better manners, purer laws." Until the doctrine of the Sermon on the Mount has found full expression in the institutions of Christendom, the Tree of Life will not have yielded its final harvest.

In the midst, then, of the revolution which seems so rapidly dissolving old forms, the least real study of the Christian centuries makes us more certain than ever of the truth of our Lord's declaration, "Heaven and earth may pass away, but my words shall not pass away." As every cycle of the seasons ends in decay and death, so every human institution has its spring and winter. The fashion of this world passeth away, but "Christ shall reign unto the ages of the ages," and "of His kingdom there shall be no end."

TAKING OF THE BASTILLE.

INDEX.

Abbassides, 119
Abdallah, Cruelty of the Caliph, 119
Abder Rahman, Reign of, 120
Abelard, Peter, Career of, 168; at Sens, 170
Adrian IV., 172
Ætius, Plots of, 59; Joins the Huns, 60
Agricola, Julius, 6
Aidan made King of Scotland, 83
Akbar, Emperor of India, 263
Albigenses, Crusade against, 185
Alboin, King of the Lombards, 76
Alexander II. of Scotland and Dominic, 191
Alexandria, Hadrian at, 23; Levity of, 14
Alexius, Emperor of the East, 188
Ali, Story of, vizier of Mohammed, 97
Alva, Cruelty of, 257
Alypius of Antioch, 50
American Independence, War of, 331
Anabaptists, Outbreak of, 241
Anacletus, 171
Anselm of Aosta, 151
Antioch, Description of, 10
Antony, Legacy of, 92
Arbrissel, Robert d', 169
Arius, Opinions of, 43
Arnold of Brescia, Character of, 171; Enters Rome, 172; Death of, 172
Asceticism, 91
Athanasius, at Nicæa, 44; Character of, 45; Struggles of, 45; Persecuted by Julian, 47
Athens, Hadrian at, 21, 23
Attila, Wars of, 59; Death of, 62
Augustine, Career of, 56
Aurelian, Wars of, 31; Triumph of, 33; Largess of, 33; Character of, 34

Bacon, Francis, Philosophy of, 277
Bagdad, The Ommiades at, 120
Baliol, John, of Scotland, 208
Bannockburn, Battle of, 210
Barbarossa, Frederick, 172
Barmecides, 121
Barnabas and Paul go to Antioch, 11; Return to Jerusalem, 13
Bartholomew, St., Massacre of, 253
Bastille, Taking of the, 333
Bec, Story of Abbey of, 150
Bernard of Clairvaux, Character of, 167; at Sens, 170
Béziers, Fall of, 185
Blood Council in Antwerp, 256
Boniface, Missionary journeys of, 107; Cuts down Thor's Oak, 108; Martyrdom of, 109
Boniface VIII., Inauguration of, 199; Disputes with King of France, 199; Death of, 202
Borgia, Alexander, 220
Botany Bay discovered, 336
Brescia, Massacre at, 217
Britain, Second invasion of, 4
Bruce, Robert, Daring of, 209
Brunehilda, Second marriage of, 74; Murder of, 76
Buckingham, Duchess of, quoted, 319
Buckingham, Duke of, Career of, 280; Death of, 281
Buddhism in China, 8
Burke impeaches Warren Hastings, 337

Cædmon, 107
Calvin, Doctrines of, 250
Canossa, Henry IV. at, 154
Canti Carnascialeschi, 215
Cape of Good Hope doubled, 226
Caractacus, Defeat of, 5

314   INDEX.

Carey, Dr., Career of, 339
Carlyle on Wars of Frederick the Great, 316
Caxton, William, 214
Celestine II., 172
Charlemagne, Wars of, 125; Puts down idolatry, 125; Assists the pope, 126; Defeat of, in Spain, 127; Crowned at Rome, 128; Policy of, 130; Laws of, 131; Character of, 132
Charles Martel defeats the Saracens, 112
Charles I. and the Commons, 281; Tries to arrest the five members, 285
Charles IX. of France, Crimes of, 252
China, Introduction of Buddhism into, 8; Nestorian missionaries in, 89
Chrysostom, Troubles of, 58
Cid, Career of the, 157
Clairvaux, Abbey of, 166
Clarkson and Negro Slavery, 338
Clement VII. wars against the Spaniards, 218
Clermont, Council at, 160
Clothcr, King of the Franks, 72
Coligny, Death of, 253
Colonna and Boniface VIII., 201
Columba, Apostle of Scotland, 80
Columbus, Christopher, Schemes of, 227; Discovers America, 229; Return of, to Spain, 229; Death of, 230
Conrad Von Hohenstauffen, 174
Constantine, Recognition of Christianity by, 41
Constantine Copronymus, 115
Constantius, Edicts of, 43; Character of, 45
Constantinople, Council at, 115; Taken by the Venetians and French, 189; Taken by the Turks, 214
Cook, Captain, Voyages of, 336
Copernicus, 271
Cordova, Mosque of, 120
Coroticus, 66
Cortes, Hernan, 242
Cosmas Indicopleustes, Statements of, 89
Covenant, Signing of the, 283
Crowland Abbey founded, 105
Crusades, The, 160
Cyprian, Genius of, 37; Martyrdom of, 38

Dandolo, Enrico, Career of, 187
Dante, Poetry of, 197

Declaration of Independence quoted, 332
Descartes, Philosophy of, 277
Diaz, Bartholomew, doubles Cape of Good Hope, 225
Domesday Book, 152
Dominic, Career of, 184
Dominicans, Order of, founded, 191
Dragonnades, The, 291
Drake, Francis, Career of, 262
Dunstan, Story of, 138

Eadward, King, Murder of, 138
Eadwine, Conversion of, 99
Eegberht, first King of the English, 130
Education, Roman, 6
Edward I., Wars of, against the Scotch, 209
Einsidlen, Abbey of, attacked, 206
Electricity, Experiments by Franklin in, 311
England, Condition of, under Stephen, 163
Eudoxia, Quarrels of, 58; Capture of, 63

Falkirk, Battle of, 209
Famines, Awful, in Tenth Century, 139
Ferguson, James, 310
Feudalism, 177
Florence under the Medici, 219
Fontevrault, Abbey of, 169
France before the Revolution, 325
Francis of Assisi, Character of, 192; Legends of, 192; Faith of, 193
Franciscans, Order of, founded, 191
Franklin, Benjamin, Experiments of, 311
Franks, The, in Gaul, 30
Fredegonda, Teaching of, 73; Death of, 76
Frederick II. of Prussia, Character of, 315; Victories of, 316
Frederick, Elector, Defeat of, 273
Friars, their work in England, 203
Friars, Black, 191
Friars, Grey, 192
Fulk, of Neuilly, preaches a new crusade, 187

Galeswintha, 73
Galileo, Career of, 274
Gama, Vasco de, Voyages of, 226
Geissler, Tyranny of, 204

INDEX.

Geneva, Calvin at, 250
George of Cappadocia, 47
Gerbert, Pope (Sylvester II.), 138
German free cities, 173
Gilbert, William, Discovery of, 277
Goths in Dacia, 30; Conquests of, 57
Greek fire, 109
Gregory I., Character of, 78; At the slave-market, 79
Gregory II., Insolence of, 114
Gregory VII. *See* Hildebrand
Guelph and Ghibelin, origin of, 174
Guiscard, Robert, 155
Gustavus Adolphus, Career of, 278; Death of, 279
Gustavus Vasa, Work of, 249
Guthlac founds Abbey of Crowland, 105

Hadrian, Character of, 18; Travels of, 19; Entrenchments of, in Britain, 21; At Athens, 21; At Alexandria, 23; In Syria, 24; Conquers the Jews, 25
Hampden, John, Case of, 283
Haroun al Raschid, Character of, 121; Cruelties of, 122; Death of, 124
Harvey, William, Discovery by, 277
Hastings, Warren, Trial of, 337
Henry of Portugal, Prince, Expedition of, 224
Henry the Fowler, 173
Henry the Proud, 174
Henry IV. of Germany at Canossa, 154; At Rome, 155; Coronation of, 155
Herlouin, founder of Abbey of Bec, 150
Highlanders, Scottish, Origin of, 207
Hilarion, 92
Hildebrand, Character of, 153; Made pope, 153; Opposes Henry IV., 154; Death of, 156
Hilperick, Story of, 73; Trial of, 74
Hobbes, Arguments of, 296
Holy Club, The, 317
Howard, John, 321
Huguenots, Troubles of, 290
Huns, Incursions of, 59
Huntingdon, Countess of, 318

Image Worship, 93
India, Missions in, 340
Indulgences, Sale of, 239

Innocent II., 171
Innocent III., Pretensions of, 178; Lays England under an interdict, 180
Interdict in England, The, 180
Irene, Empress, 115

Jaafar, Murder of, 122
Jansen, inventor of the microscope, 277
Jansenists, Doctrines of, 328
James I., Character of, 280
James II., Policy of, 296
Japan, Catholic converts in, 273
Jerusalem destroyed by Hadrian, 25
Jesuits, Society of, founded, 246; The character of, 272; Successes of, 273; Expelled from France, &c., 327
Jews, Condition of, 25
John, King, of England, Character of, 179; Submits to the pope, 181; Signs Magna Charta, 182
John of Leyden, Outbreak of, 244
John XII., Crimes of, 137
Julian, Earlier years of, 46; Accession of, 47; Treatment of Athanasius, 47; Earnestness of, 48; Character of, 49; at Antioch, 50; Fails to rebuild the Temple, 50; Marches against Persia, 51; Retreat of 52; Death of, 52

Kepler, Discoveries of, 276
Knox, John, Character of, 254; Death of, 255

Lanfranc at Bec, 150; Anecdotes of, 151
Langton, Cardinal, Views of, 180; Opposes King John, 182
Las Casas, Benevolent efforts of, 244
Lateran Council, 186
Latin Christianity, Rise of, 35; Character of, 37
Laud, Archbishop, Tyranny of, 281
Leo, Pope, before Attila, 61; Before Genseric, 62
Leo the Isaurian, 109; Puts down idolatry, 113
Leo X. and Luther, 239
Leyden, Siege of, 258
Linnæus, 310
Lisbon, Earthquake at, 307
Locke, Doctrines of, 296
Lombardy, Condition of, 154
Louis XIV., Policy of, 290
Lowlanders, Scottish, Origin of, 207

INDEX.

Loyola, Ignatius, Early years of, 242; Travels of, 246; Founds the Society of Jesus, 246
Lucius II., 172
Lugdunum, Description of, 10
Luther, Conversion of, 237; Goes to Rome, 238; Defies the Papacy, 240; at Worms, 241
Lützen, Battle of, 279

Magdeburg, Sack of, 278
Magna Charta Signed, 182
Magyars, Incursions of, 136
Mahmoud of Ghuznee, 141
Martin of Tours, 65
Maximilian of Bavaria, Victory of, 273
Medici, Catharine de, Policy of, 251
Medici, Lorenzo de, Ballads of, 215; Death of, 218
Merovig, 74; Death of, 75
Mésur, Executioner to Haroun al Raschid, 122
Methodist Revival, The, 319
Mexico, Cortes in, 243
Ming-ti, Emperor of China, 9
Mohammed, Marriage of, 95; Sincerity of, 96; Pretensions of, 96; Flight of, 97; Preaching of, 97
Mortgarten, Battle of, 206
Munster, Outbreak of fanaticism at, 244

Nail from the Cross, Story of a, 92
Neoplatonists, Failure of, 50
Nestorians in China, 89
Nestorius, Teaching of, 88
Netherlands, Struggles in the, 256
New South Wales, Discovery of, 336
Nicæa, Council of, 44
Nogaret opposes the pope, 201
Normandy, Condition of labourers in, 138
Normans, Character of, 148
Northmen, Incursions of, 135; in Russia, 142
Novatus, 36

Odenatus, 32
Ogané, King, 225
Ommiades, The, 119
Ostorius Scapula, Conquests of, 4
Oswald, 104
Otto II., 147

Packington buys Tyndal's Testaments, 235
Palmyra taken by Romans, 33; Destruction of, 34
Papacy, Degradation of, 137; Tyranny of, 178; Persecutes heretics, 184; Infamy of, 215
Paris in the Eighteenth Century, 326
Parliament, The Establishment of, at Paris, 200
Parma, Battle of, 247
Patrick, Call of, 65; at Tara, 66; Escapes of, 66
Paul and Barnabas visit Antioch, 11; Return to Jerusalem, 13
Paulinus, 99
Pedanius Secundus, Murder of, 7
Penn, William, Career of, 302; Treaty with Indians, 303
Pennsylvania founded, 302
Perim, God of Thunder, Whipping of, 143
Peter of Wakefield, Prophecy of, 181
Peter the Hermit, Pilgrimage of, 159; Before the pope, 159; Preaching of, 160
Philip II., Policy of, 256
Philippe le Bel quarrels with the pope, 200
Phocas, Cruelty of, 94
Pizarro, Conquests of, 244
Placidia, 59
Prætextus, 74
Pragmatic Sanction, The, 315
Prester John, Legend of, 225
Priestley, Joseph, 313
Prince of Orange, Career of, 296; Lands at Brixham, 298
Printing, Invention of, 214
Ptolemy of Alexandria, 24
Pulcheria, Quarrels of, 58

Raoul, Count of Normandy, 139
Relics, Idolatry of, 92
Revocation of the Edict of Nantes, 294
Richelieu, Intrigues of, 278
Robert of France, King, Character of, 140
Roman Empire, Power of, 17
Roman neglect of children, 6
Roman Wall in Britain, 21
Rome, Description of, 23; Sacked by Attila and Genseric, 62; Taken by the French, 248
Roncesvalles, Charlemagne's defeat at, 127
Rosamund, Queen of Alboin, 77
Rousseau J. J., Opinions of, 330

Saracens, Conquests of, 109
Savonarola, Early life of, 215; Preaching of, 216; Visit of, to Lorenzo de Medici, 218; Tries to reform the Florentines, 220; Excommunication of, 220; Imprisonment of, 222; Death of, 223
Saxon Chronicle quoted, 164
Saxon Invasion of Britain, 63
Scipio Æmilianus, Sarcasm of, 3
Sea Dogs, The, 262
Senatus, Character of, 7
Sens, Council of, 170
Ship Money, Attempts to levy, 283
Sigebert, Murder of, 74
Simon Stylites, 67
Slave-trade abolished, 338
Slaves, Invasions of, 136
Sobieski, Victory of, 301
Spain, conquered by Saracens, 110; Condition of, under the Moors, 141
Stephen of Blois, Condition of England under, 163
Strafford, Earl of. *See* Wentworth
Succat. *See* Patrick
Sweden, Rise of, 249
Switzerland, Tyranny of Geissler in, 204
Sydney founded, 336

Tell, William. *See* William of Burglen
Temple, Julian fails to rebuild, 50
Tetzel sells Indulgences, 239
Teutons, Character of, 77; Condition of, 128
Thebaid, The, 45
Theodore of Tarsus, 129
Theodosius of Cappadocia, 91
Thorough, The policy of, 282
Tilly, Death of, 279
Tonstall, Bishop of London, buys Tyndale's Testaments, 235; Burns them, 236
Turcomans, Conquests of, 156

Turks, Defeat of, before Vienna, 301
Tyndale, Version of the Bible by, 235; Death of, 236

United States of America, Independence of, 331
Urban VIII., Vanity of, 274

Venetians conquer Constantinople, 189; Further conquests, 190
Victoria, Success of, 31
Vienna, Siege of, by the Turks, 300
Vladimir, Conversion of, 112
Voltaire, 327

Waiblinger and Welf, 174
Wallace, William, Exploits of, 208; Death of, 209
Wallenstein, Battles of, 279
Washington, George, Inauguration of, 332
Weimar, Court at, 335
Weinsberg, Siege of, 174
Wentworth, Sir Thomas, Character of, 282; Death of, 284
Wesley, Charles, 318
Wesley, John, Diary of, quoted, 313; Career of, 317
Whitefield, George, Labours of, 318
Wilberforce opposes the Slave-trade, 338
William of Burglen, or Tell, Story of, 205
William the Conqueror, Character of, 151; Orders the making of Domesday Book, 152
William III., Prince of Orange, 297
William the Silent, Struggles of, 257
Wittikind, 126

Ximenes, Cardinal, 211
Ximena, wife of the Cid, 157

Zara, Siege of, 188
Zenobia, Career of, 32
Zinzendorf, Count, 317

www.ingramcontent.com/pod-product-compliance
Lightning Source LLC
Chambersburg PA
CBHW020246240426
43672CB00006B/650